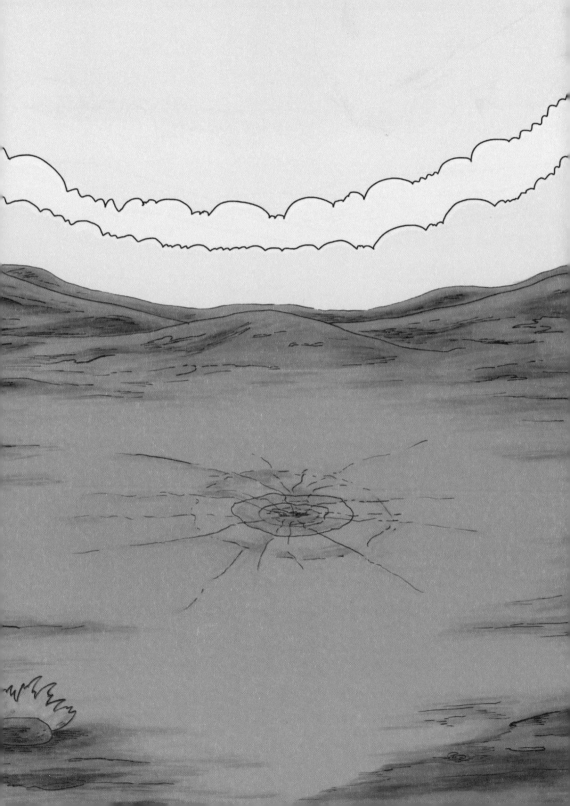

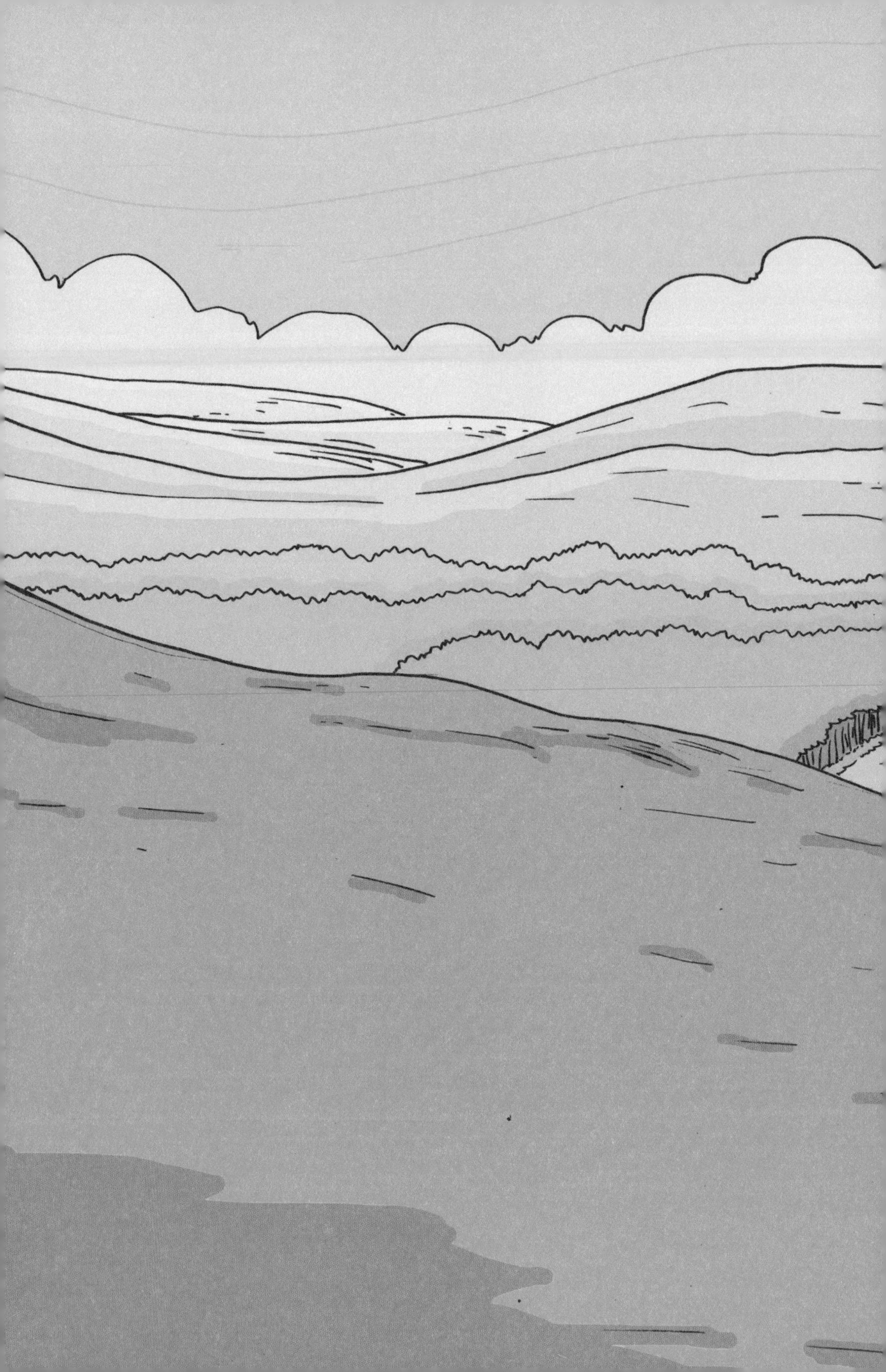

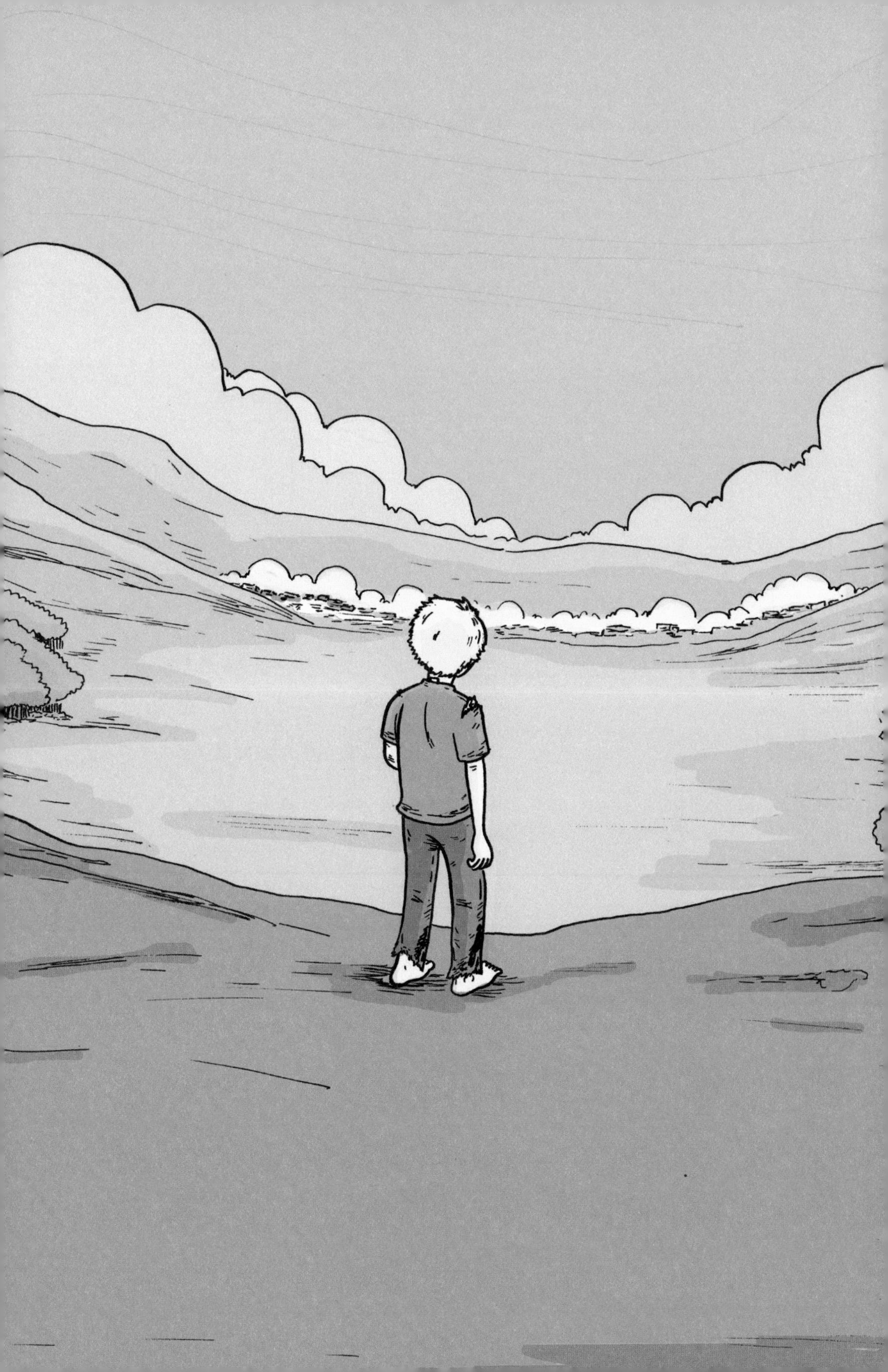

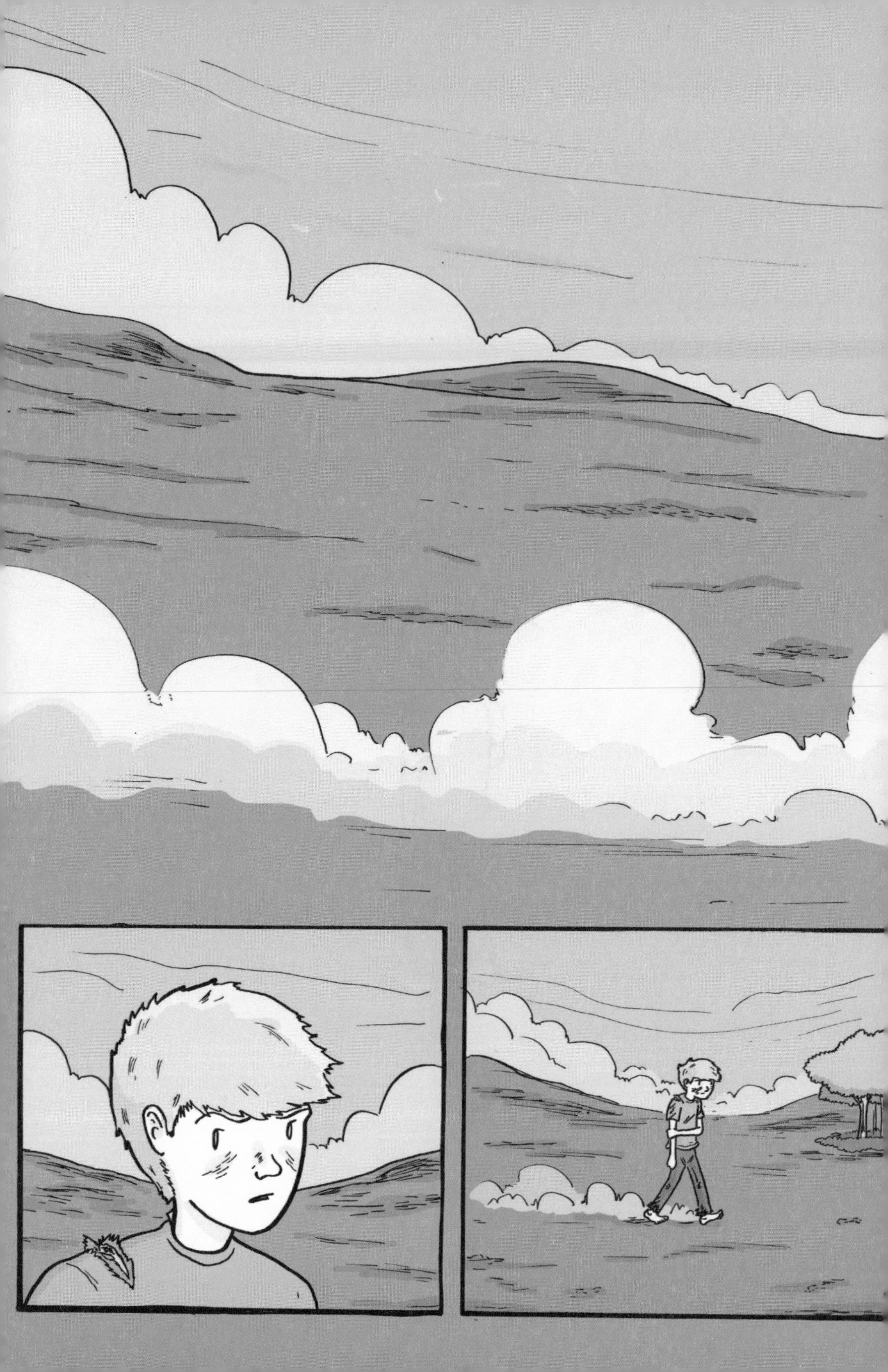

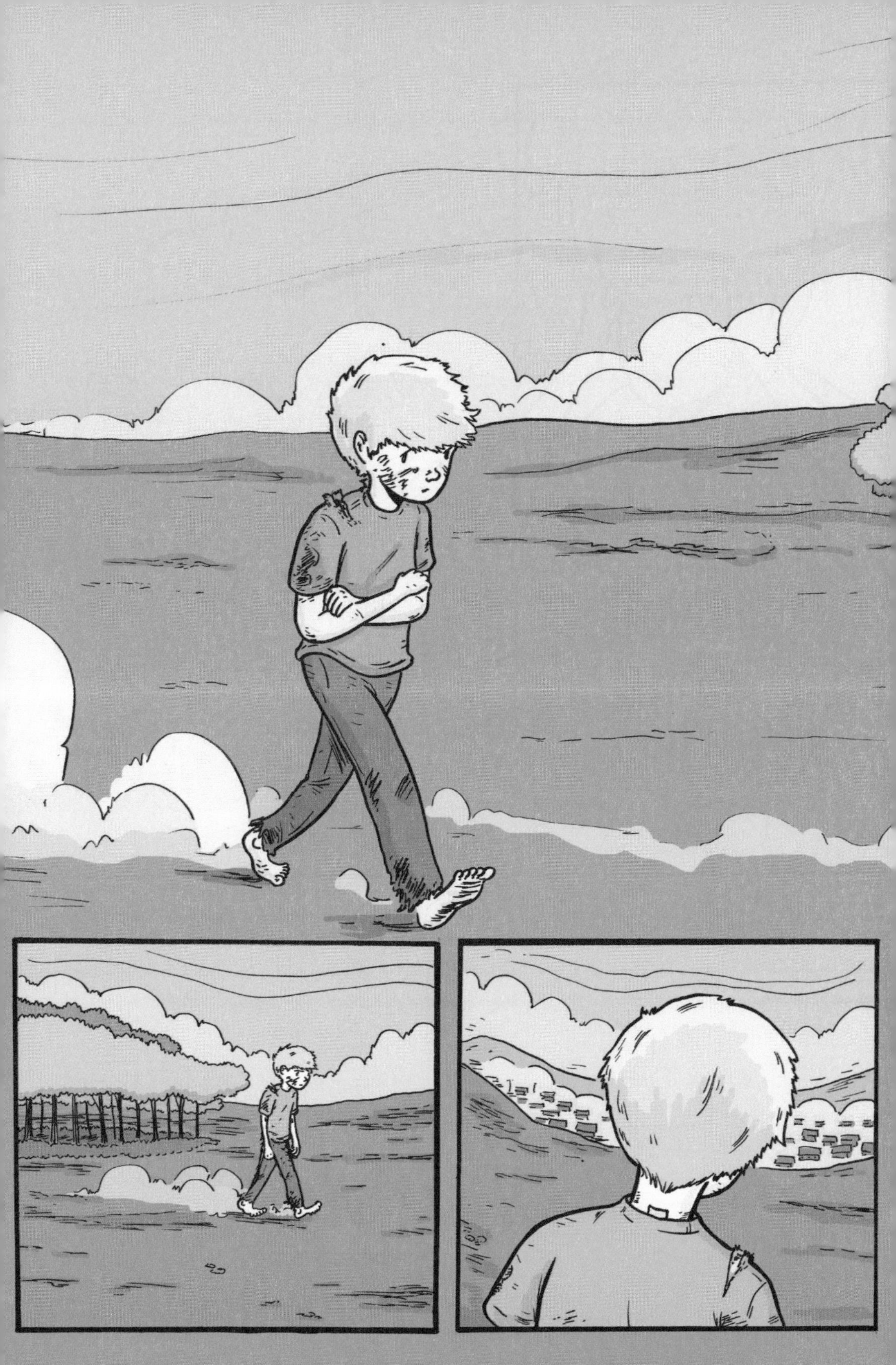

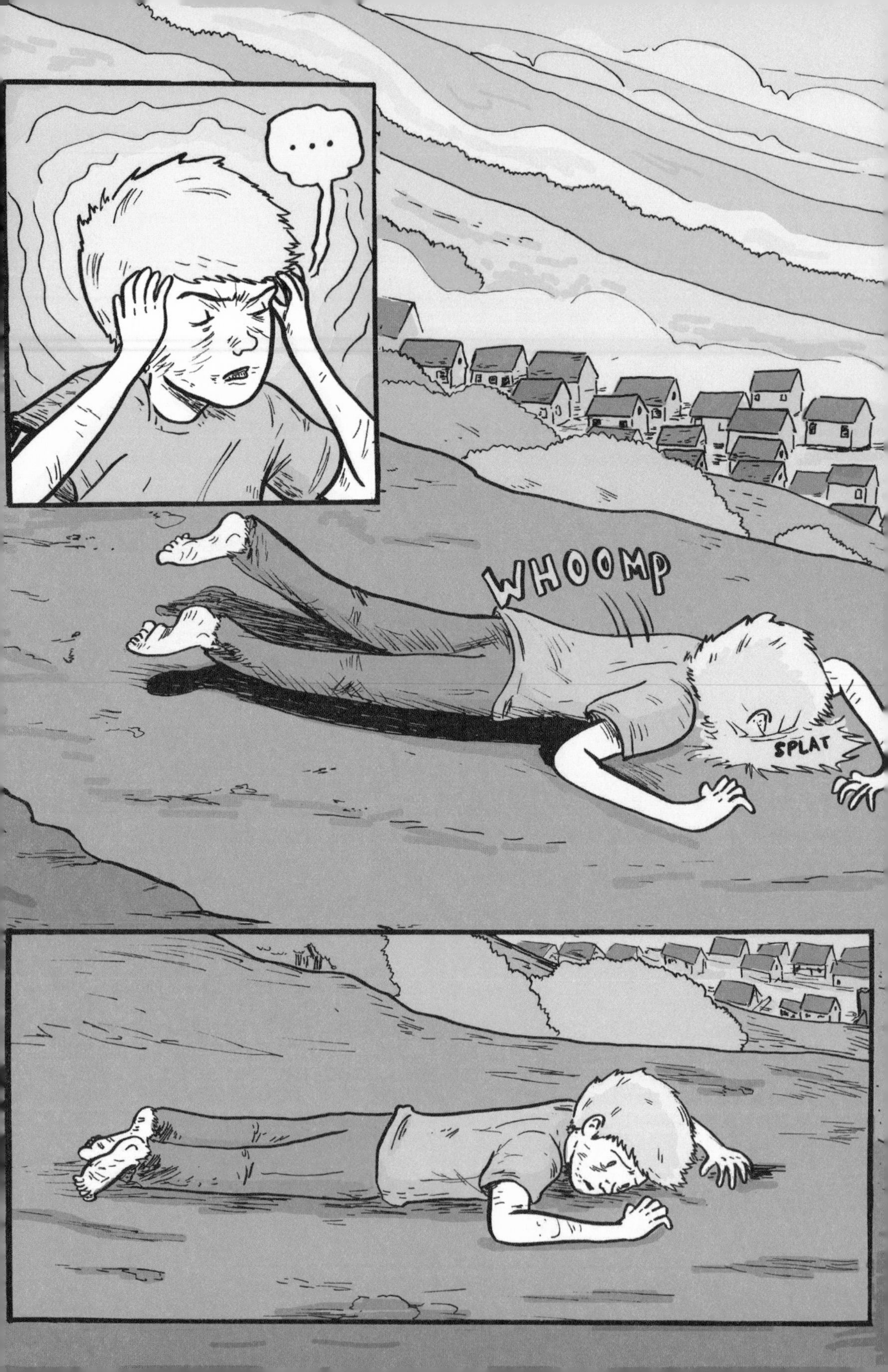
...
WHOOMP
SPLAT

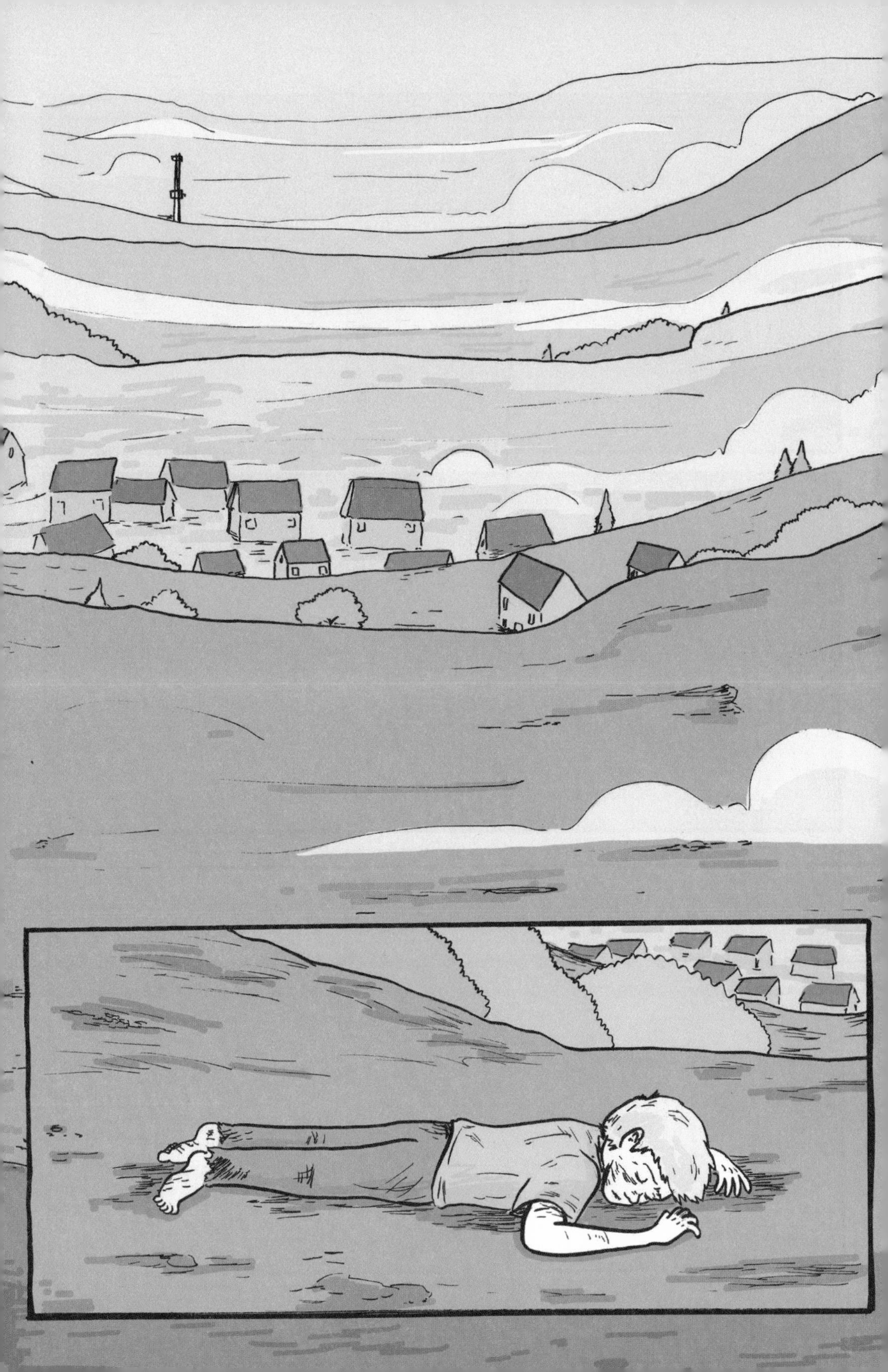

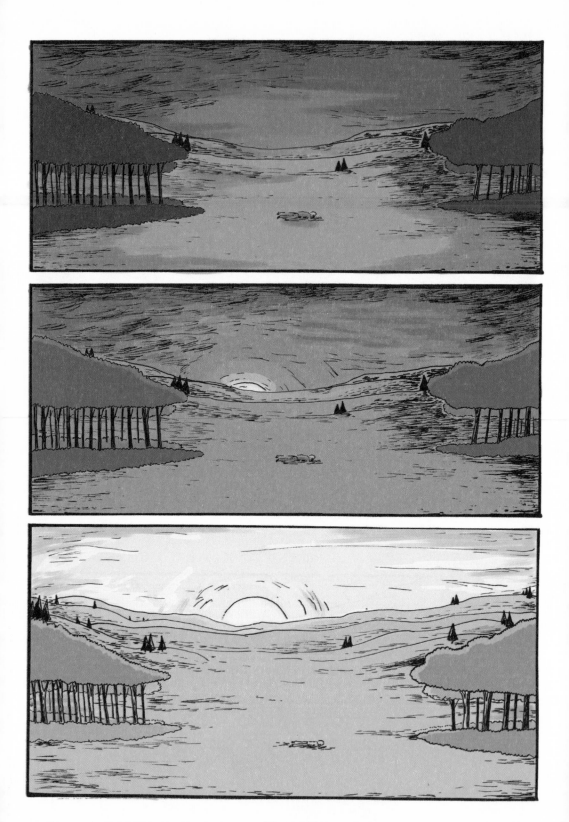

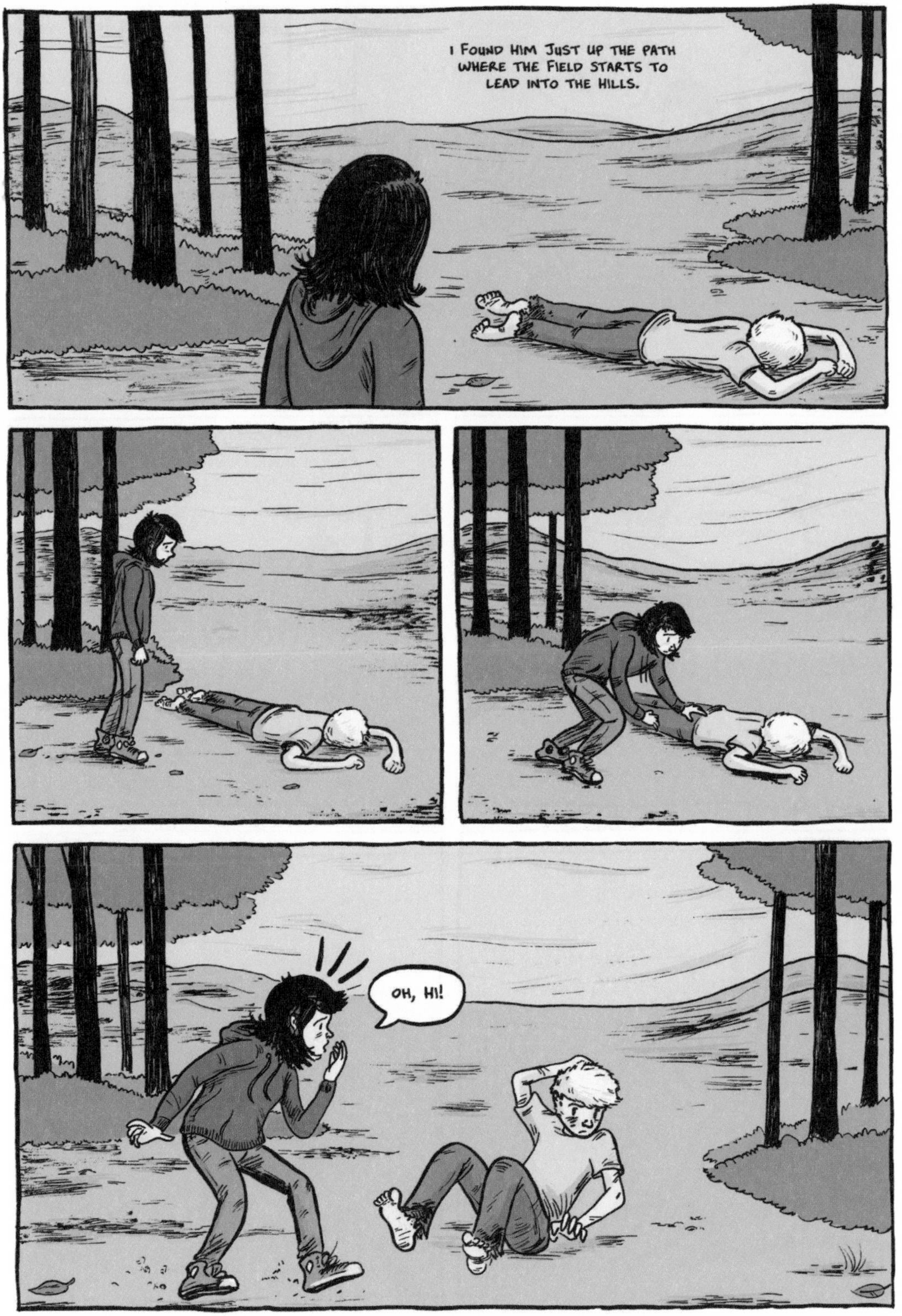
I FOUND HIM JUST UP THE PATH WHERE THE FIELD STARTS TO LEAD INTO THE HILLS.
OH, HI!

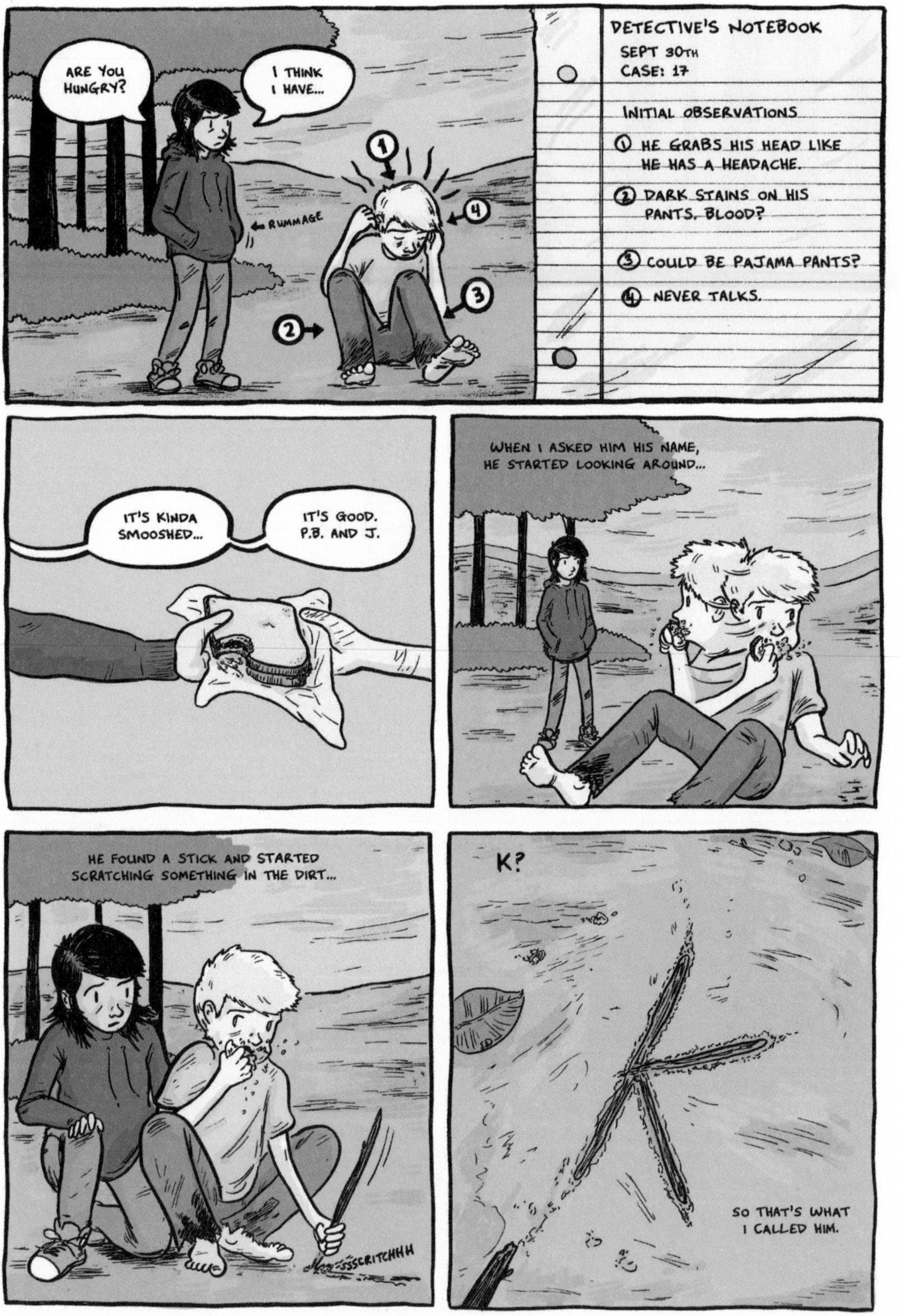
ARE YOU HUNGRY?
I THINK I HAVE...
RUMMAGE
DETECTIVE'S NOTEBOOK
SEPT 30TH
CASE: 17
INITIAL OBSERVATIONS
1 HE GRABS HIS HEAD LIKE HE HAS A HEADACHE.
2 DARK STAINS ON HIS PANTS. BLOOD?
3 COULD BE PAJAMA PANTS?
4 NEVER TALKS.
IT'S KINDA SMOOSHED...
IT'S GOOD. P.B. AND J.
WHEN I ASKED HIM HIS NAME, HE STARTED LOOKING AROUND...
HE FOUND A STICK AND STARTED SCRATCHING SOMETHING IN THE DIRT...
SSSCRITCHHH
K?
SO THAT'S WHAT I CALLED HIM.

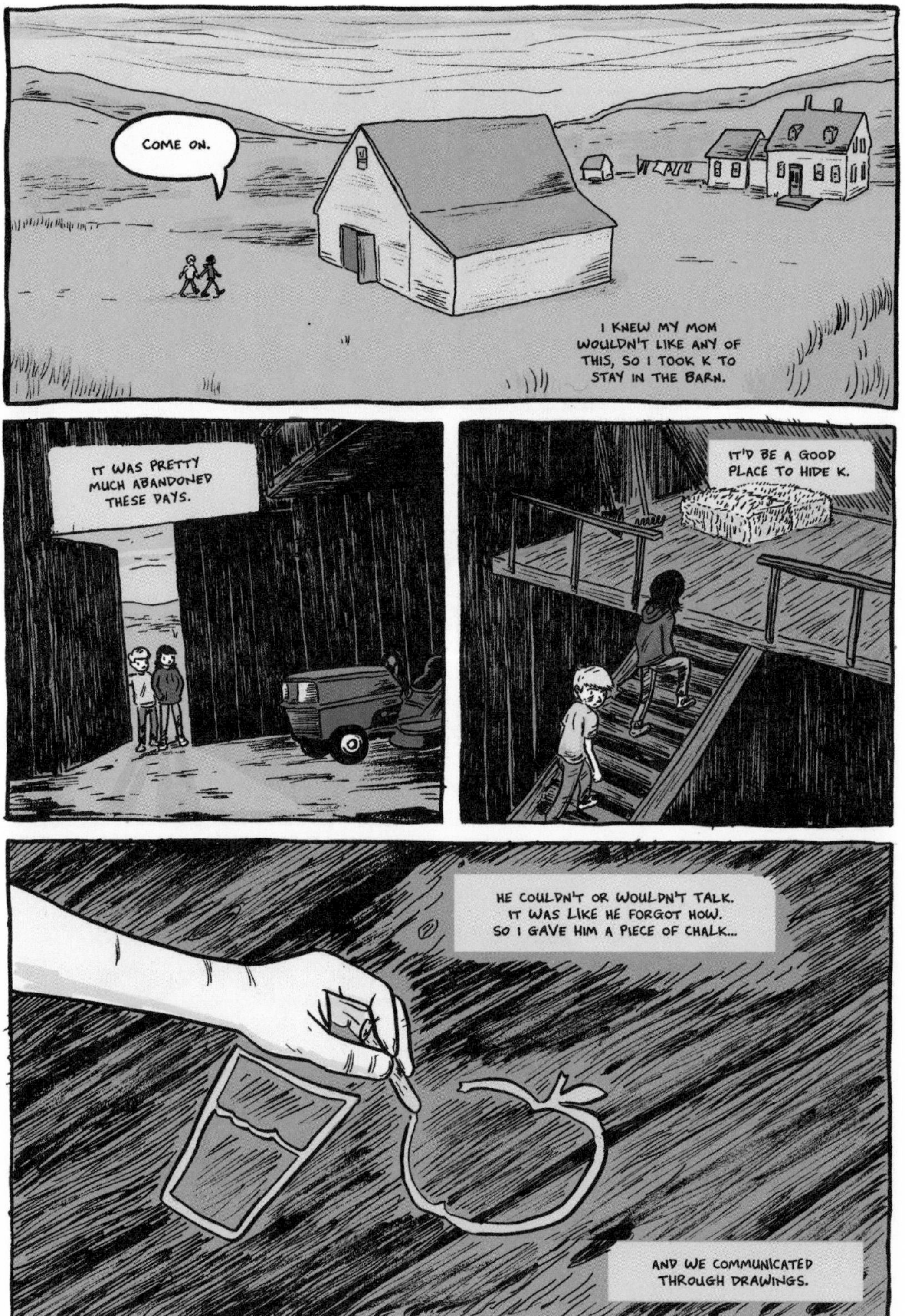
COME ON.
I KNEW MY MOM WOULDN'T LIKE ANY OF THIS, SO I TOOK K TO STAY IN THE BARN.
IT WAS PRETTY MUCH ABANDONED THESE DAYS.
IT'D BE A GOOD PLACE TO HIDE K.
HE COULDN'T OR WOULDN'T TALK. IT WAS LIKE HE FORGOT HOW. SO I GAVE HIM A PIECE OF CHALK...
AND WE COMMUNICATED THROUGH DRAWINGS.

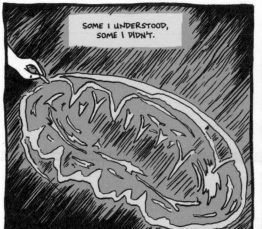

SOME I UNDERSTOOD, SOME I DIDN'T.

I WANTED TO FIGURE OUT HOW TO HELP HIM.

UM...

I SHOWED HIM MAPS TO SEE IF HE COULD REMEMBER WHERE HE CAME FROM...

SHADOW HILLS

...HE COULDN'T.

I'LL BE BACK IN THE MORNING. GOOD NIGHT.

ONCE HE RESTED UP A BIT, I PLANNED TO HELP HIM FIND HIS HOME.

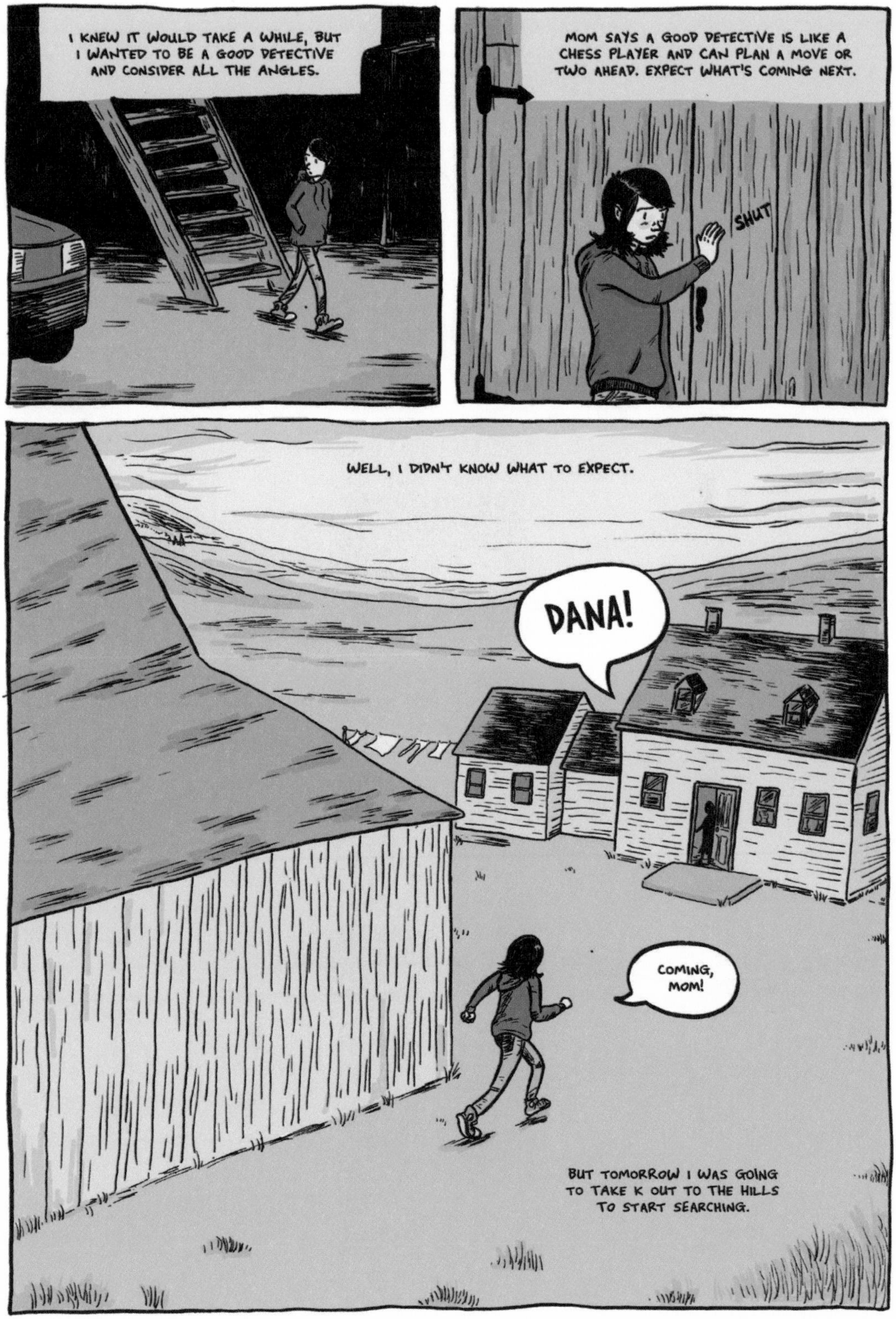
I KNEW IT WOULD TAKE A WHILE, BUT I WANTED TO BE A GOOD DETECTIVE AND CONSIDER ALL THE ANGLES.
MOM SAYS A GOOD DETECTIVE IS LIKE A CHESS PLAYER AND CAN PLAN A MOVE OR TWO AHEAD. EXPECT WHAT'S COMING NEXT.
SHUT
WELL, I DIDN'T KNOW WHAT TO EXPECT.
DANA!
COMING, MOM!
BUT TOMORROW I WAS GOING TO TAKE K OUT TO THE HILLS TO START SEARCHING.

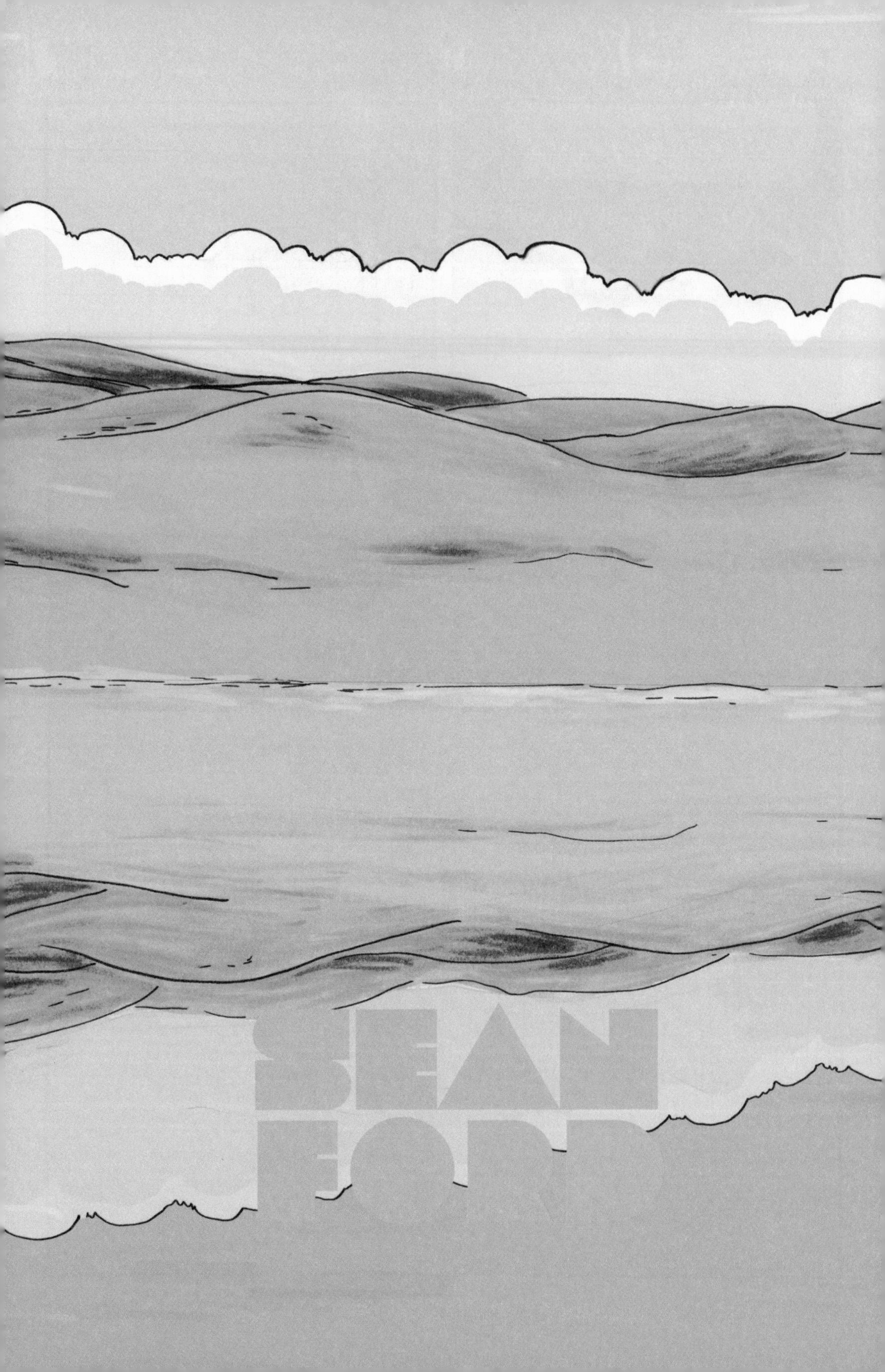
SEAN

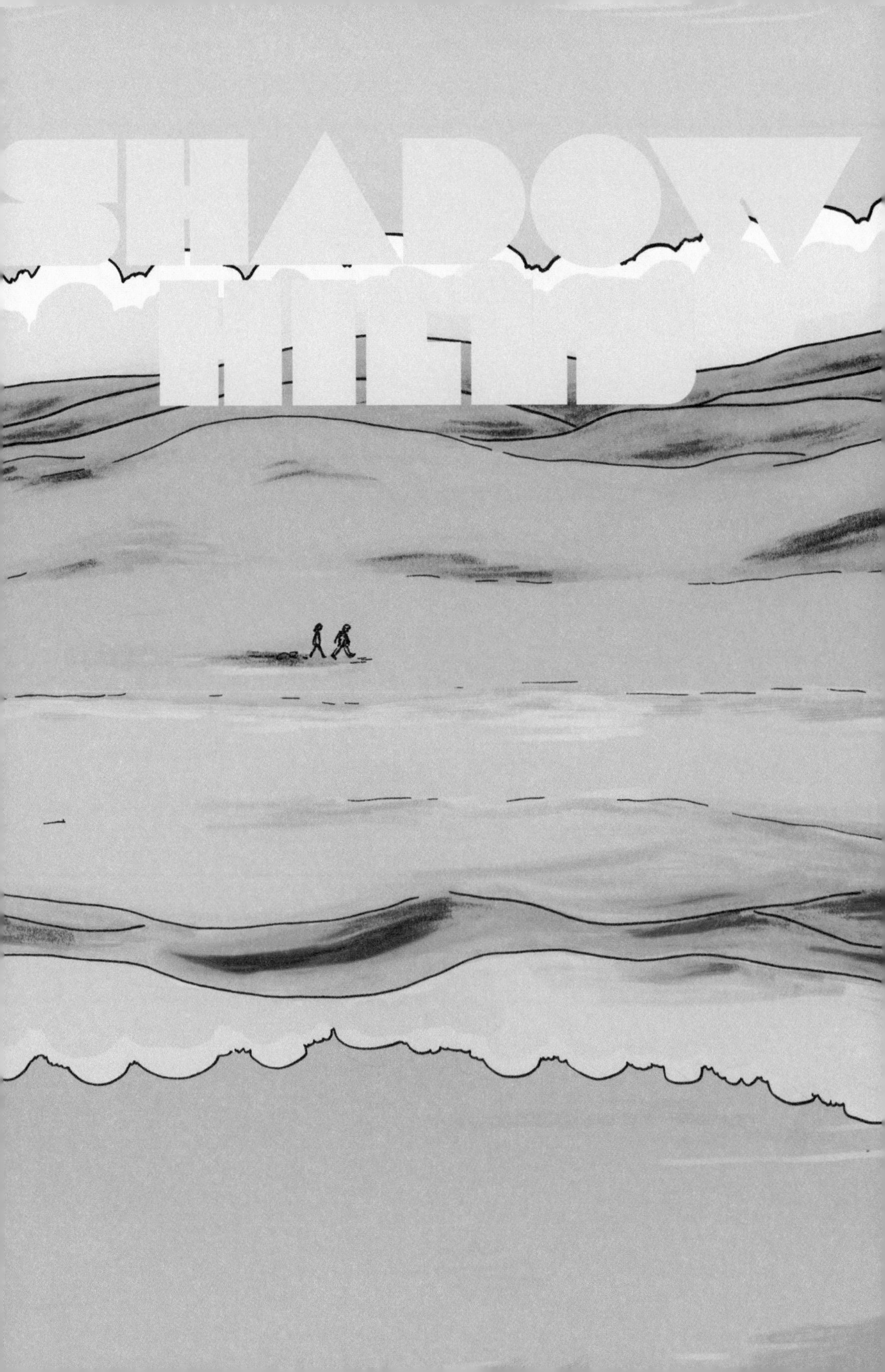
SHADOW
HILLS

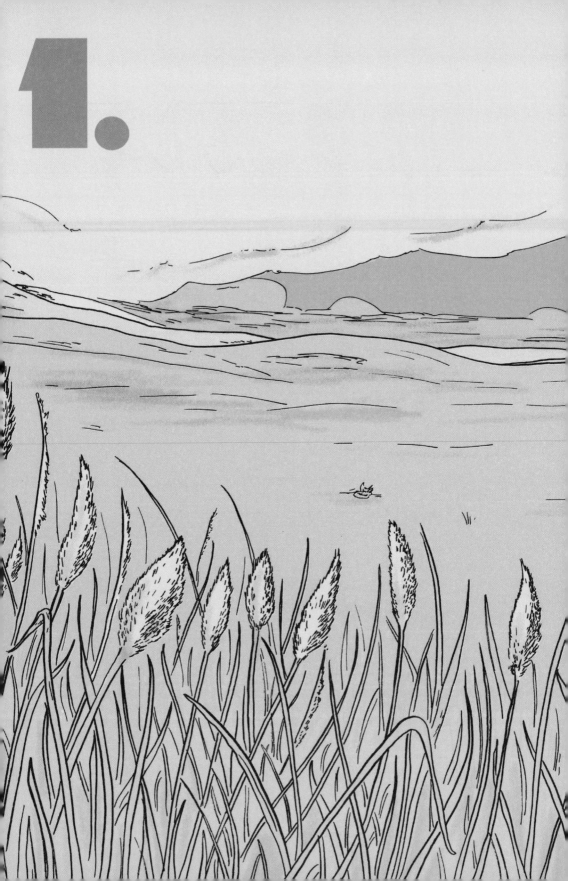

1.

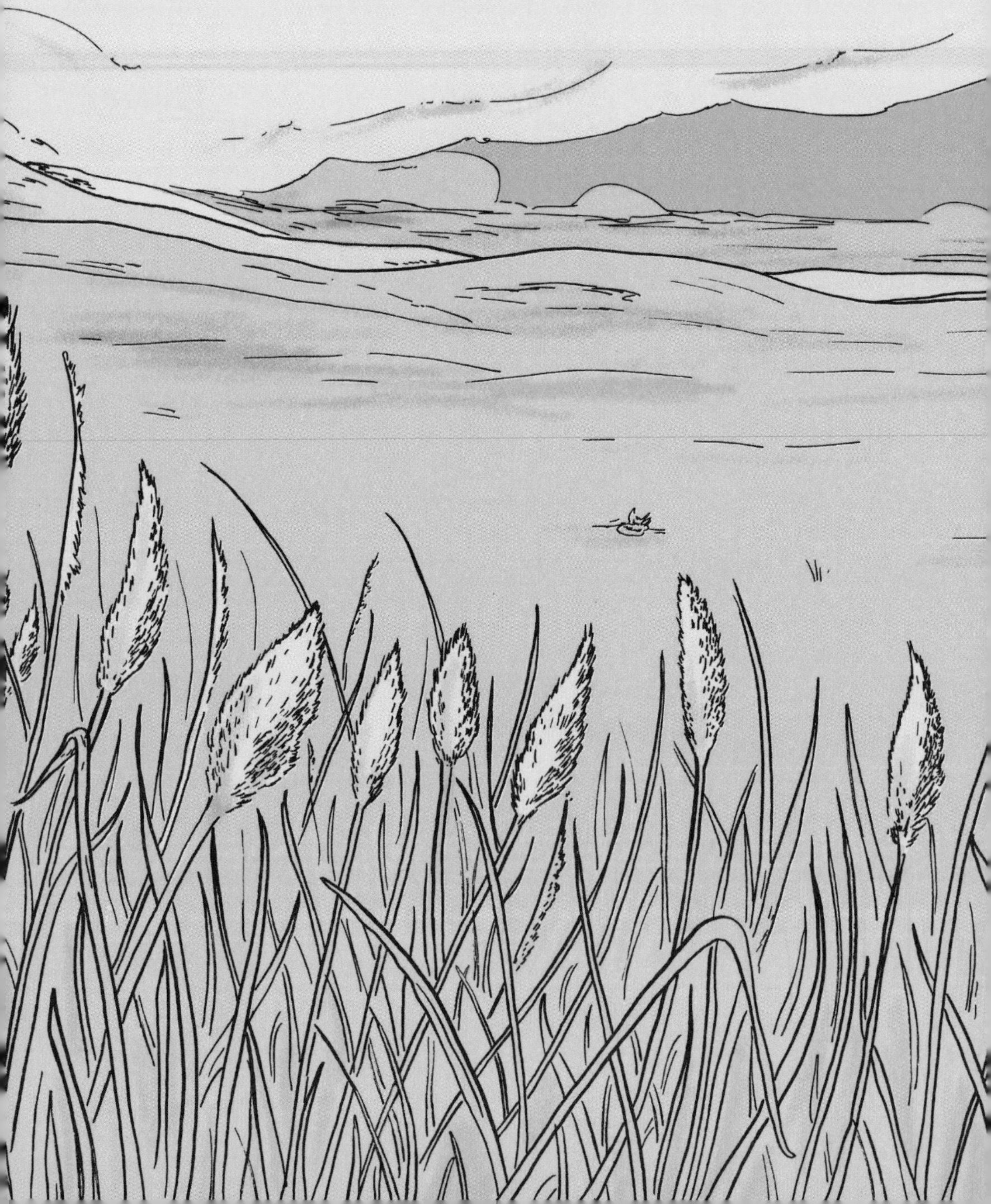

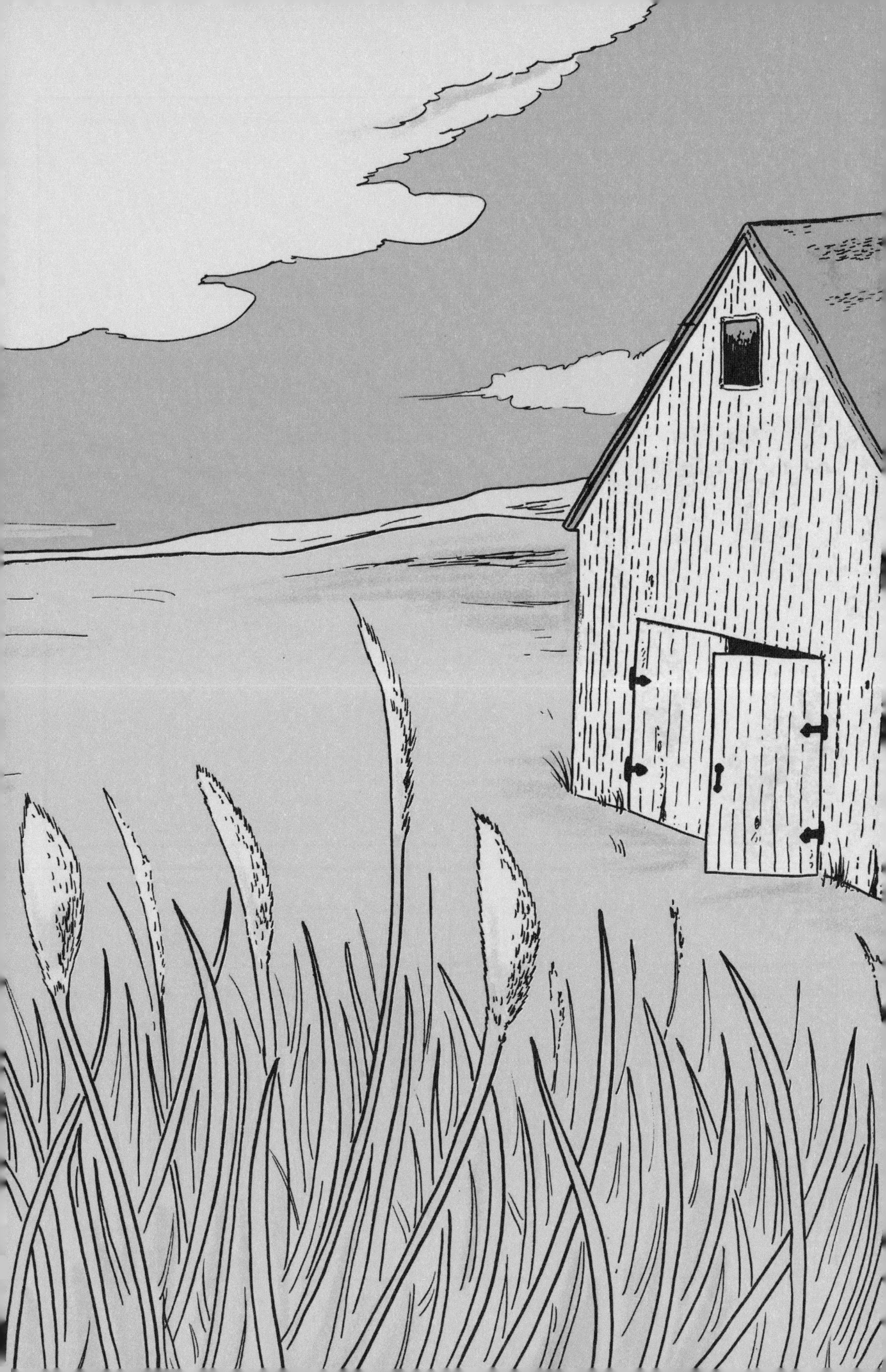

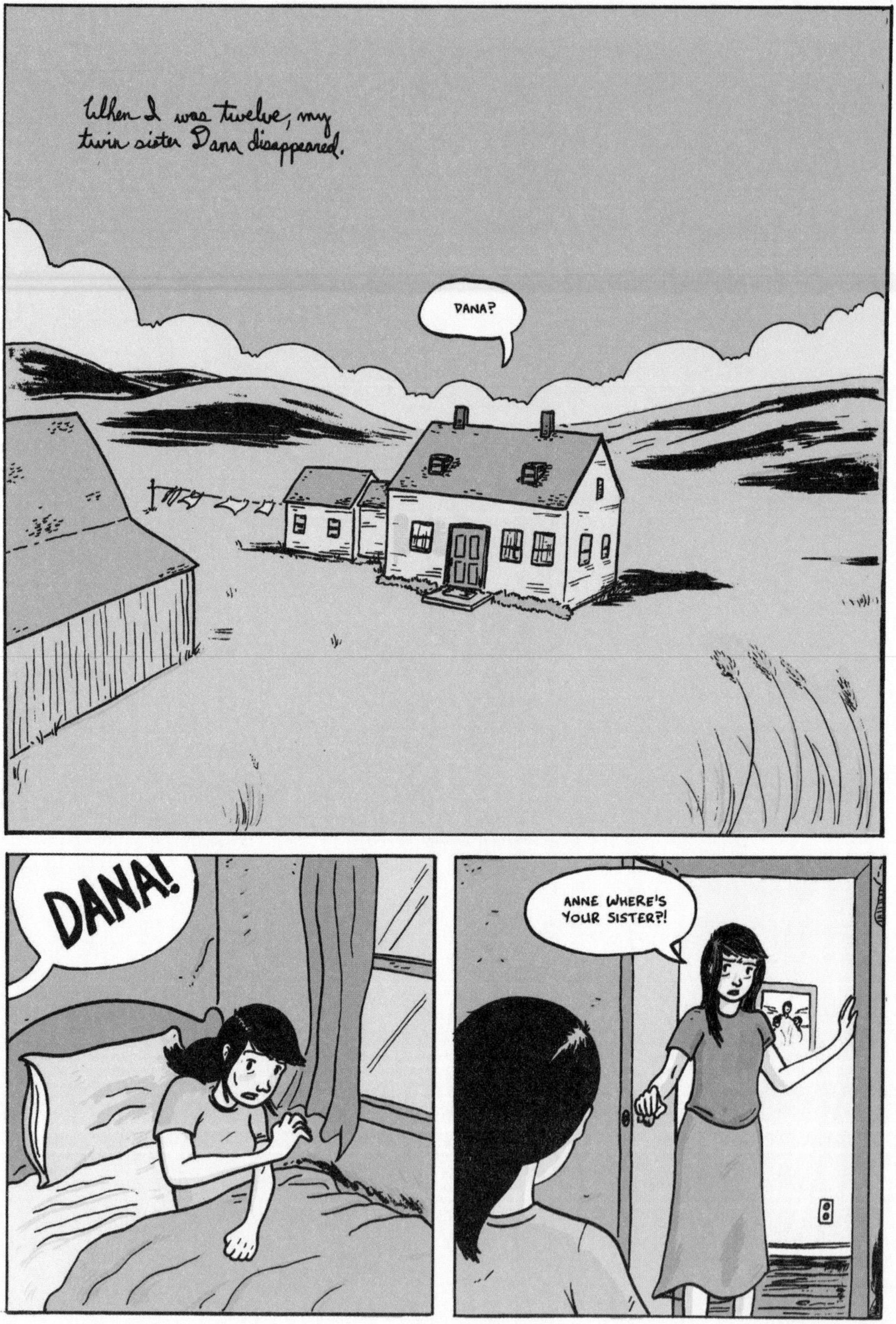
When I was twelve, my twin sister Dana disappeared.
DANA?
DANA!
ANNE WHERE'S YOUR SISTER?!

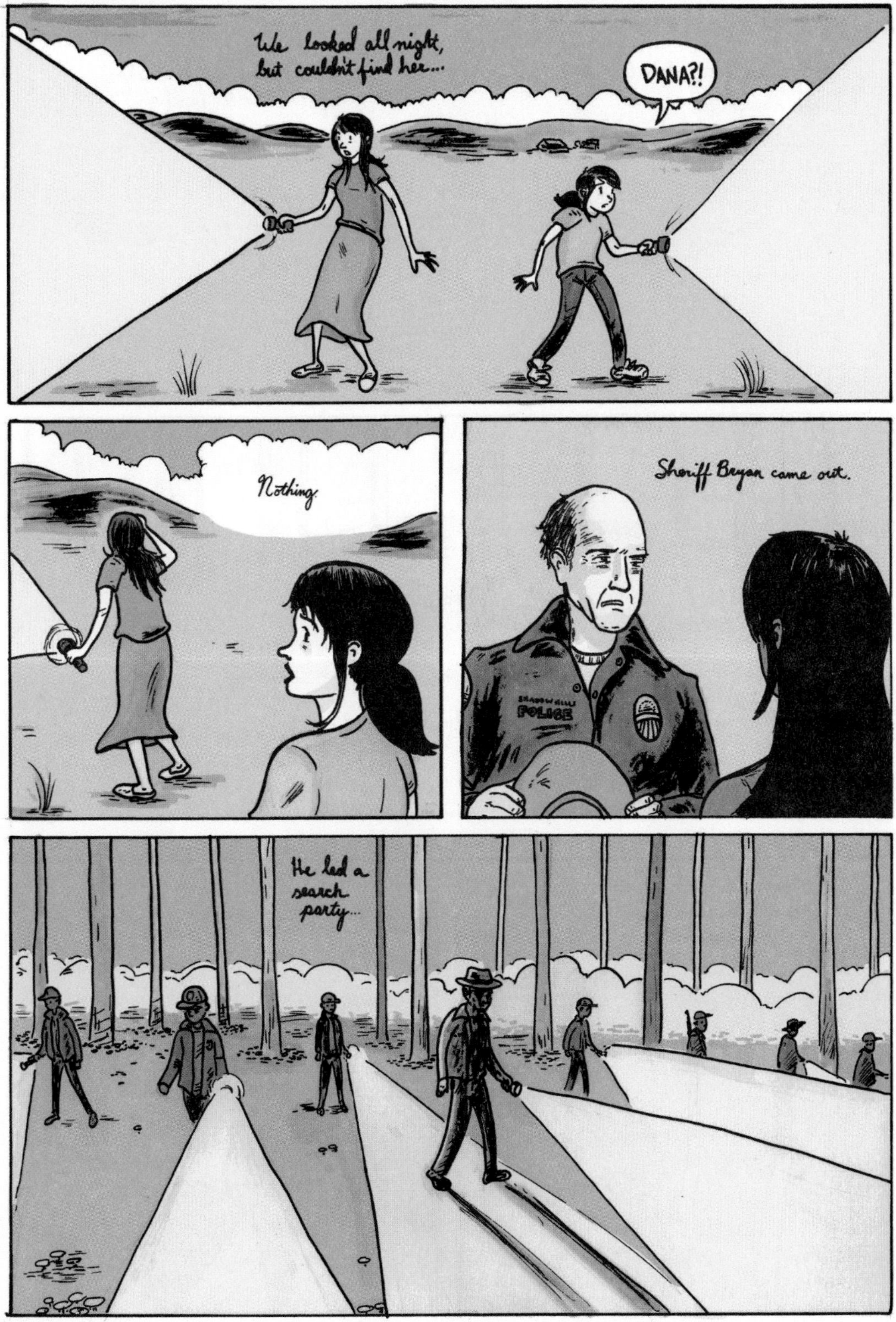
We looked all night, but couldn't find her...
DANA?!
Nothing.
Sheriff Bryan came out.
SHADOW HILLS POLICE
He led a search party...

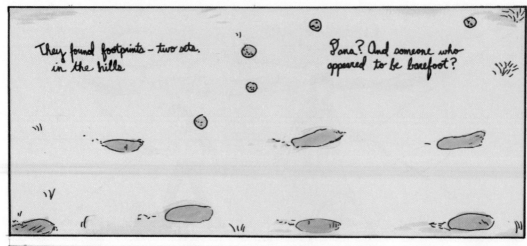

They found footprints – two sets in the hills

Pana? And someone who appeared to be barefoot?

The footprints led into a cave on the Fuller property.

The Fuller boys were questioned, but they seemed so shocked most assumed they were innocent.

So a search team went into the caves...

The system was revealed to be massive, stretching under the town and through out the valley.

They searched for weeks and never found Dana.... but they did find something

WAIT...
IS THIS...?

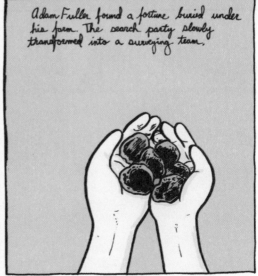

Adam Fuller found a fortune buried under his farm. The search party slowly transformed into a surveying team.

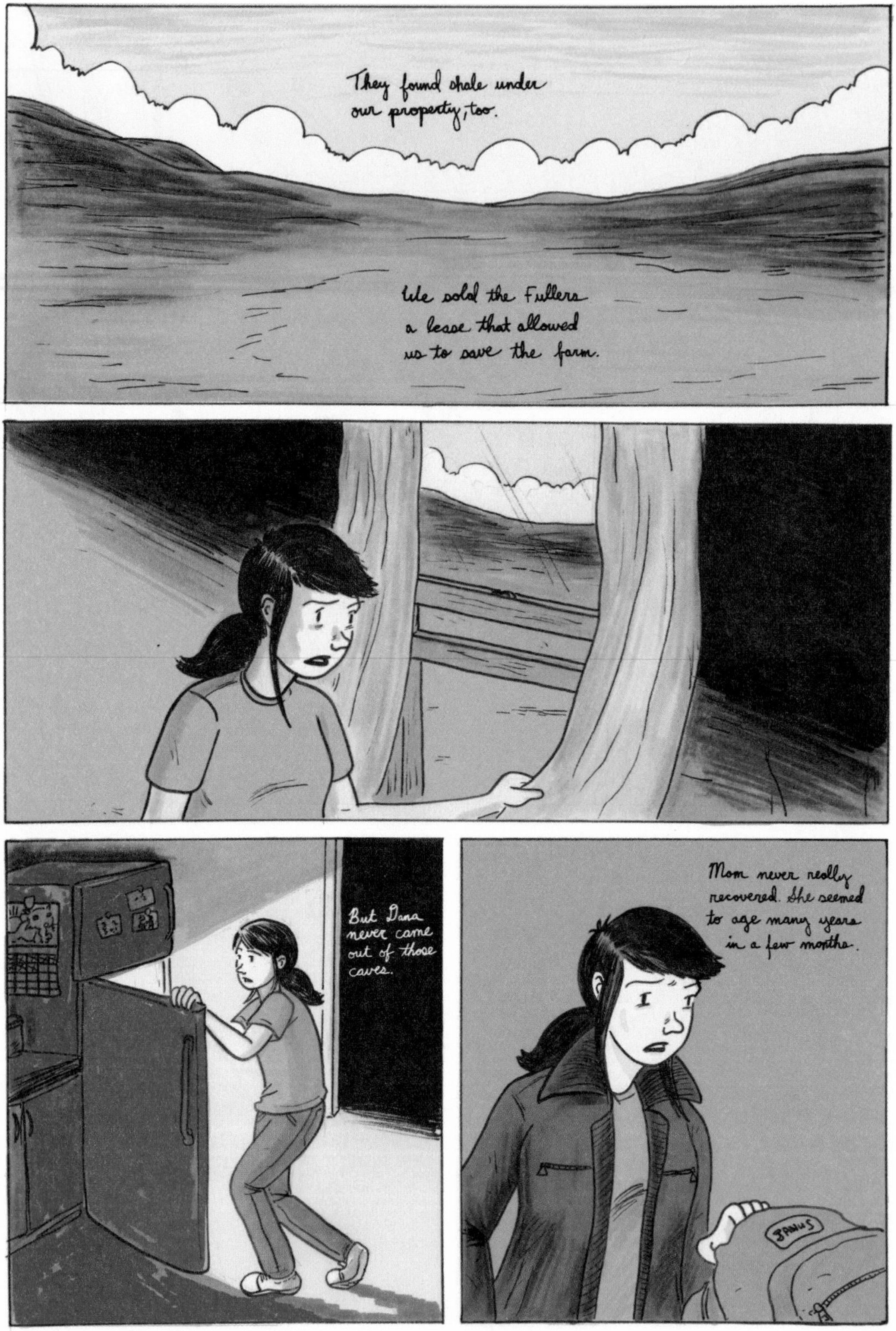
They found shale under our property, too.
We sold the Fullers a lease that allowed us to save the farm.
But Dana never came out of those caves.
Mom never really recovered. She seemed to age many years in a few months.
JANUS

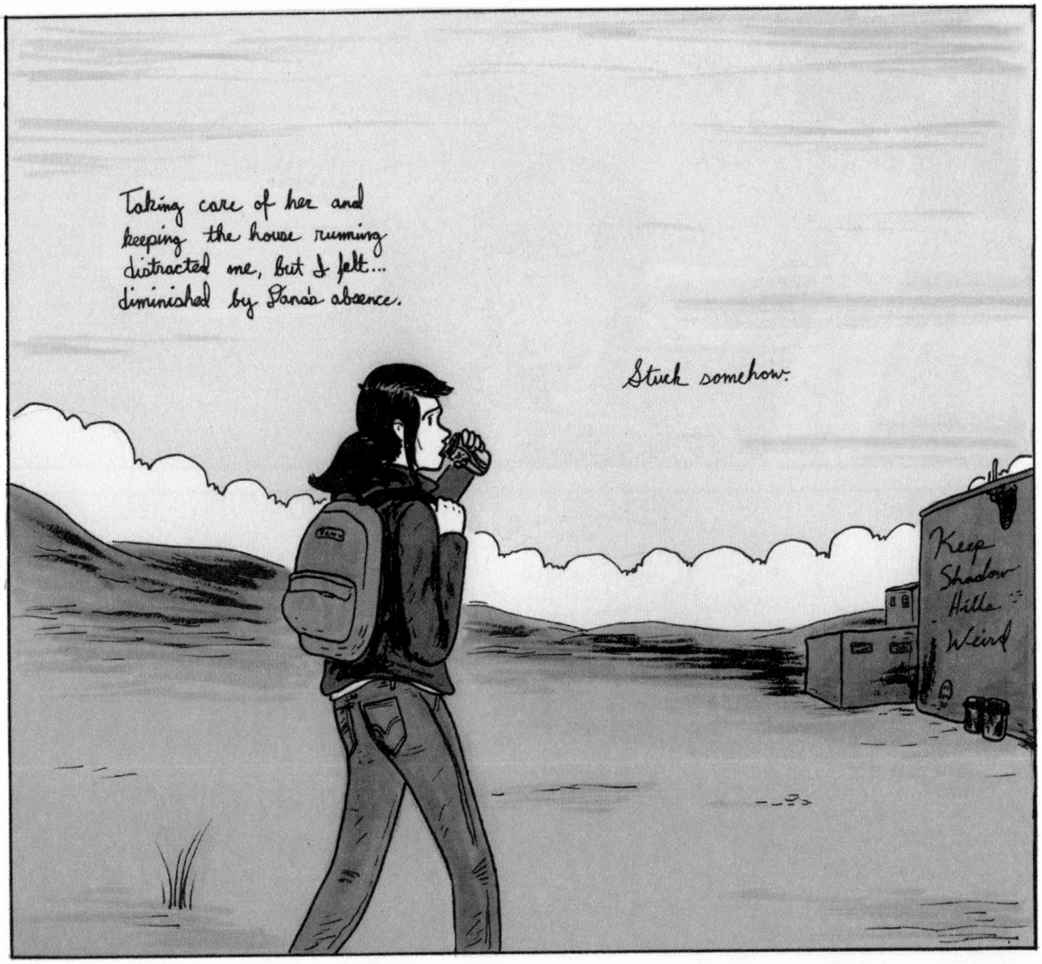
Taking care of her and keeping the house running distracted me, but I felt... diminished by Dana's absence.
Stuck somehow.
Keep Shadow Hills Weird

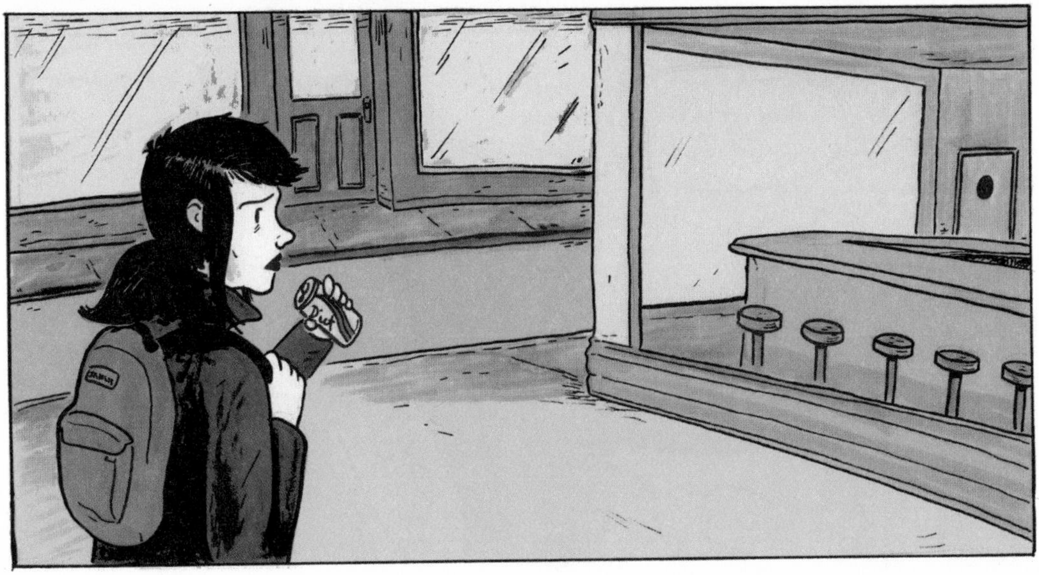
Diet

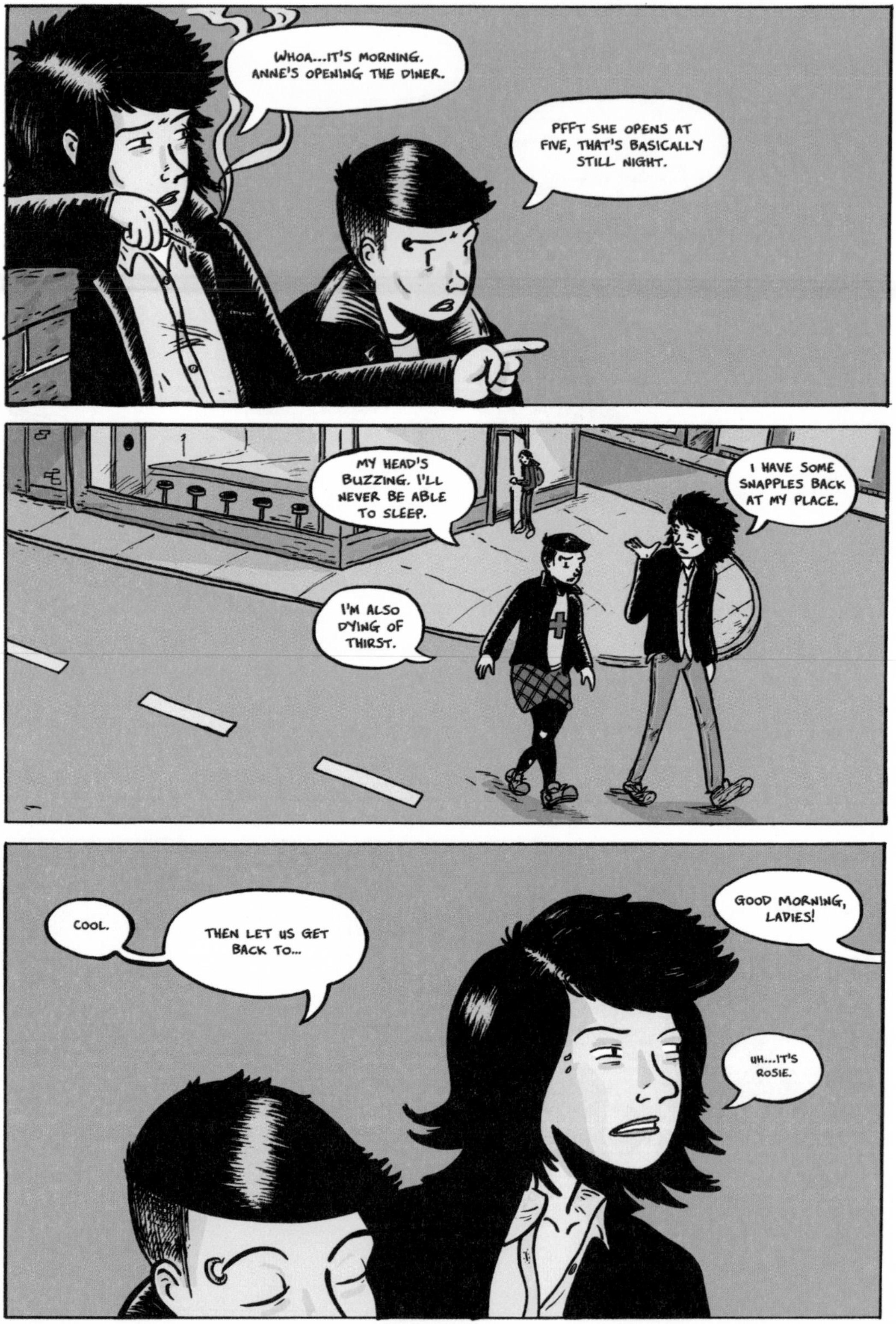
WHOA...IT'S MORNING. ANNE'S OPENING THE DINER.
PFFT SHE OPENS AT FIVE, THAT'S BASICALLY STILL NIGHT.
MY HEAD'S BUZZING. I'LL NEVER BE ABLE TO SLEEP.
I'M ALSO DYING OF THIRST.
I HAVE SOME SNAPPLES BACK AT MY PLACE.
COOL.
THEN LET US GET BACK TO...
GOOD MORNING, LADIES!
UH...IT'S ROSIE.

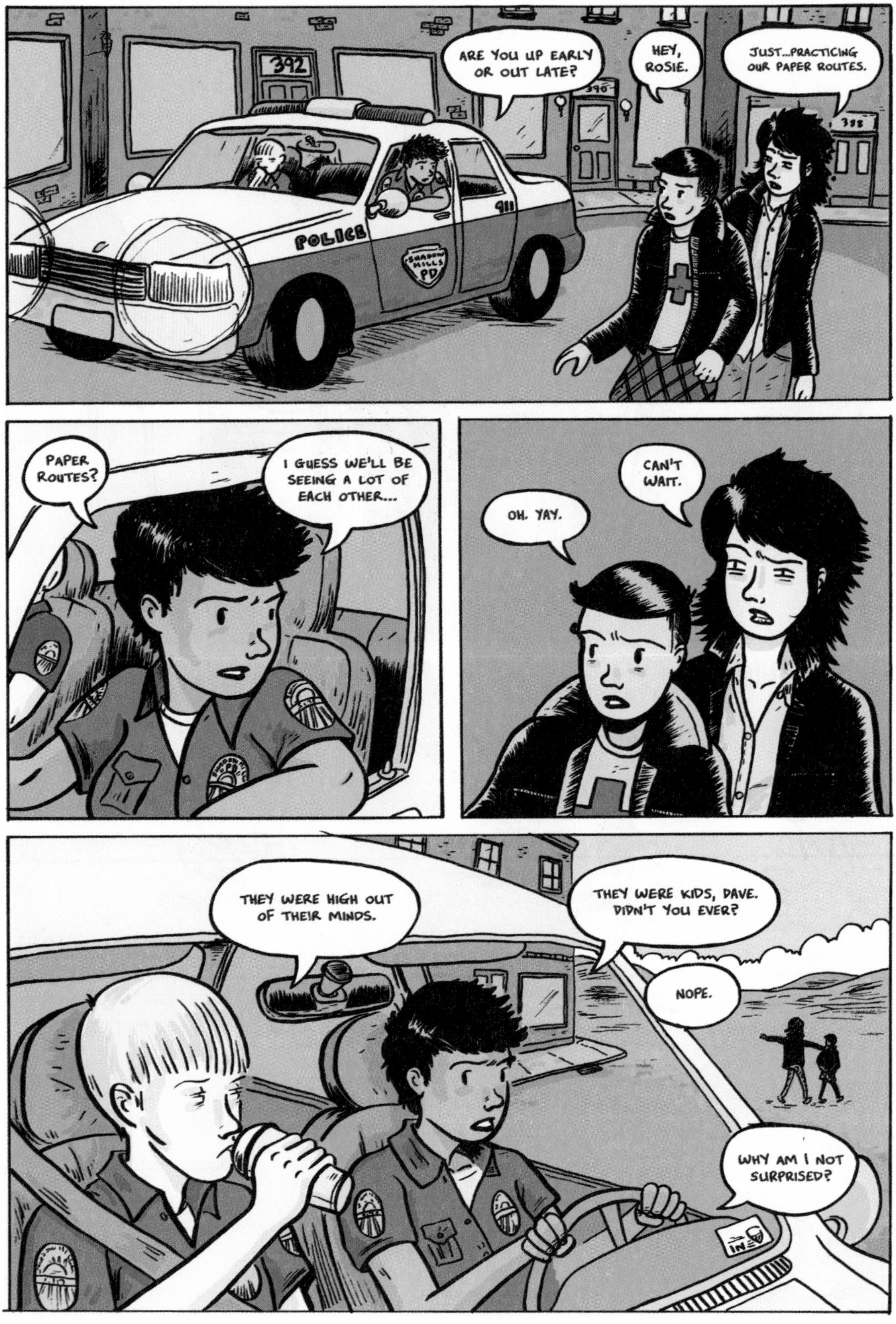
ARE YOU UP EARLY OR OUT LATE?
HEY, ROSIE.
JUST...PRACTICING OUR PAPER ROUTES.
PAPER ROUTES?
I GUESS WE'LL BE SEEING A LOT OF EACH OTHER...
CAN'T WAIT.
OH. YAY.
THEY WERE HIGH OUT OF THEIR MINDS.
THEY WERE KIDS, DAVE. DIDN'T YOU EVER?
NOPE.
WHY AM I NOT SURPRISED?

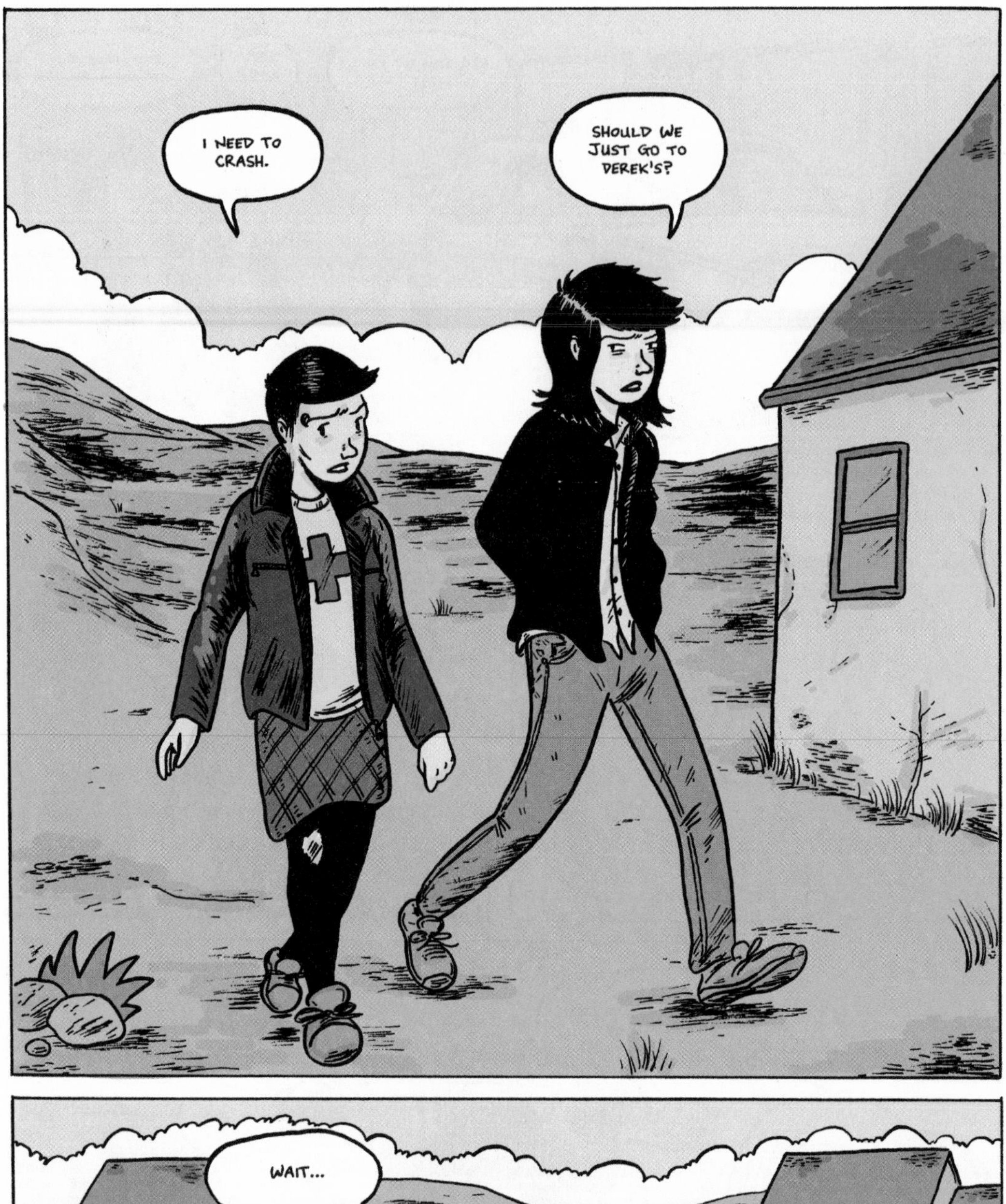
I NEED TO CRASH.
SHOULD WE JUST GO TO DEREK'S?

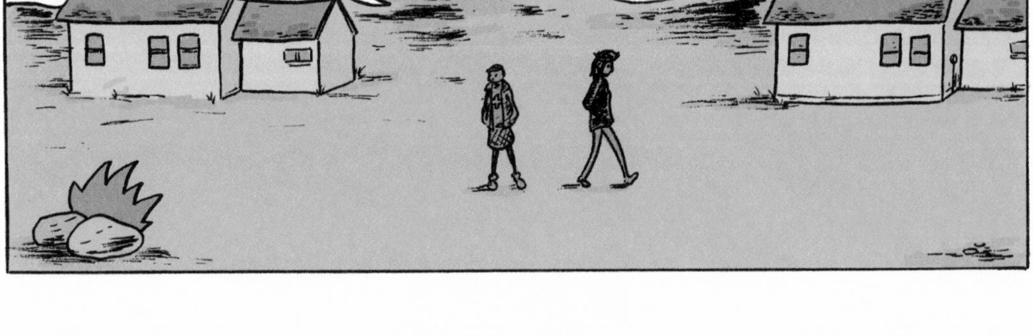
WAIT...

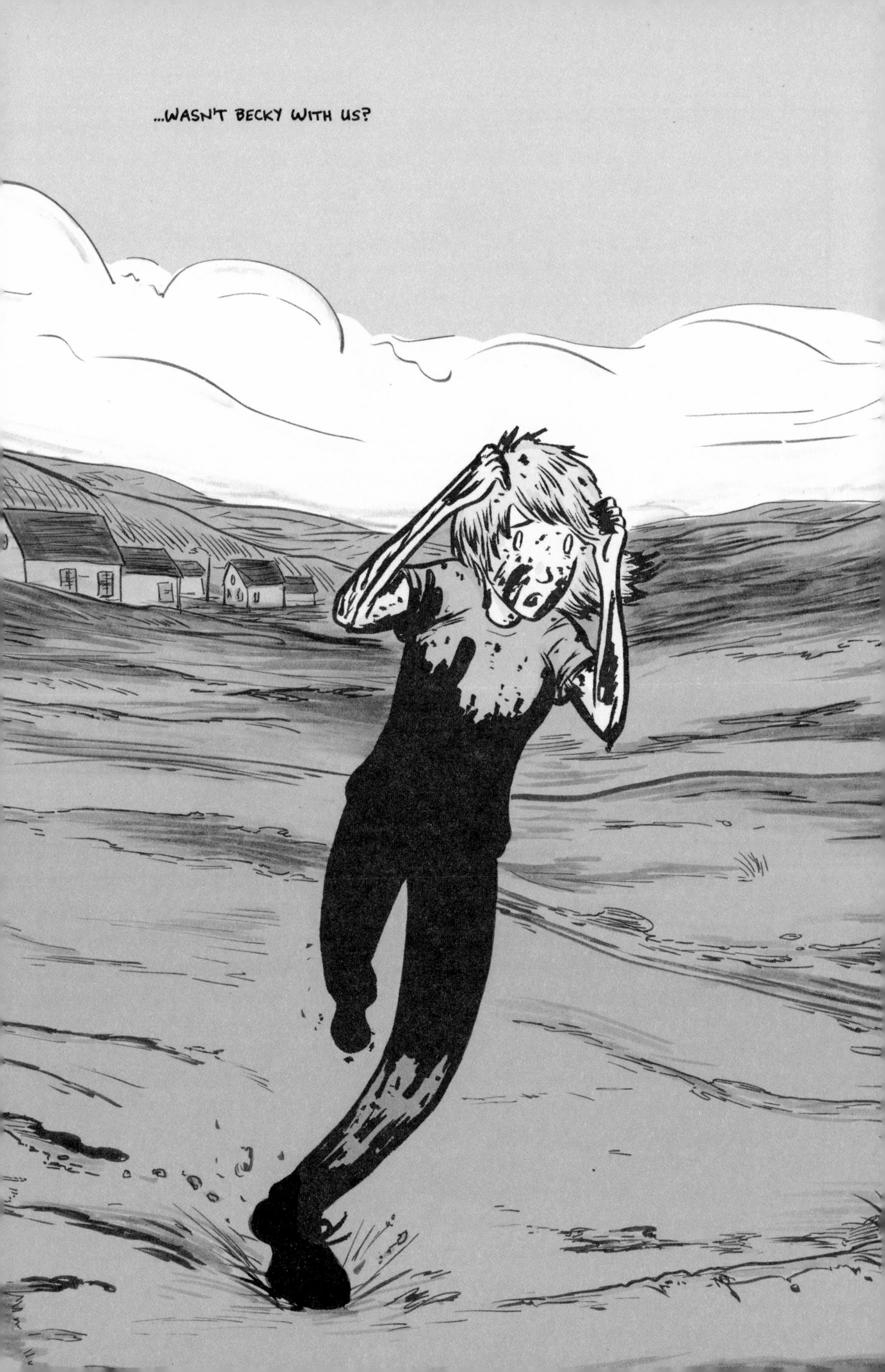
...WASN'T BECKY WITH US?

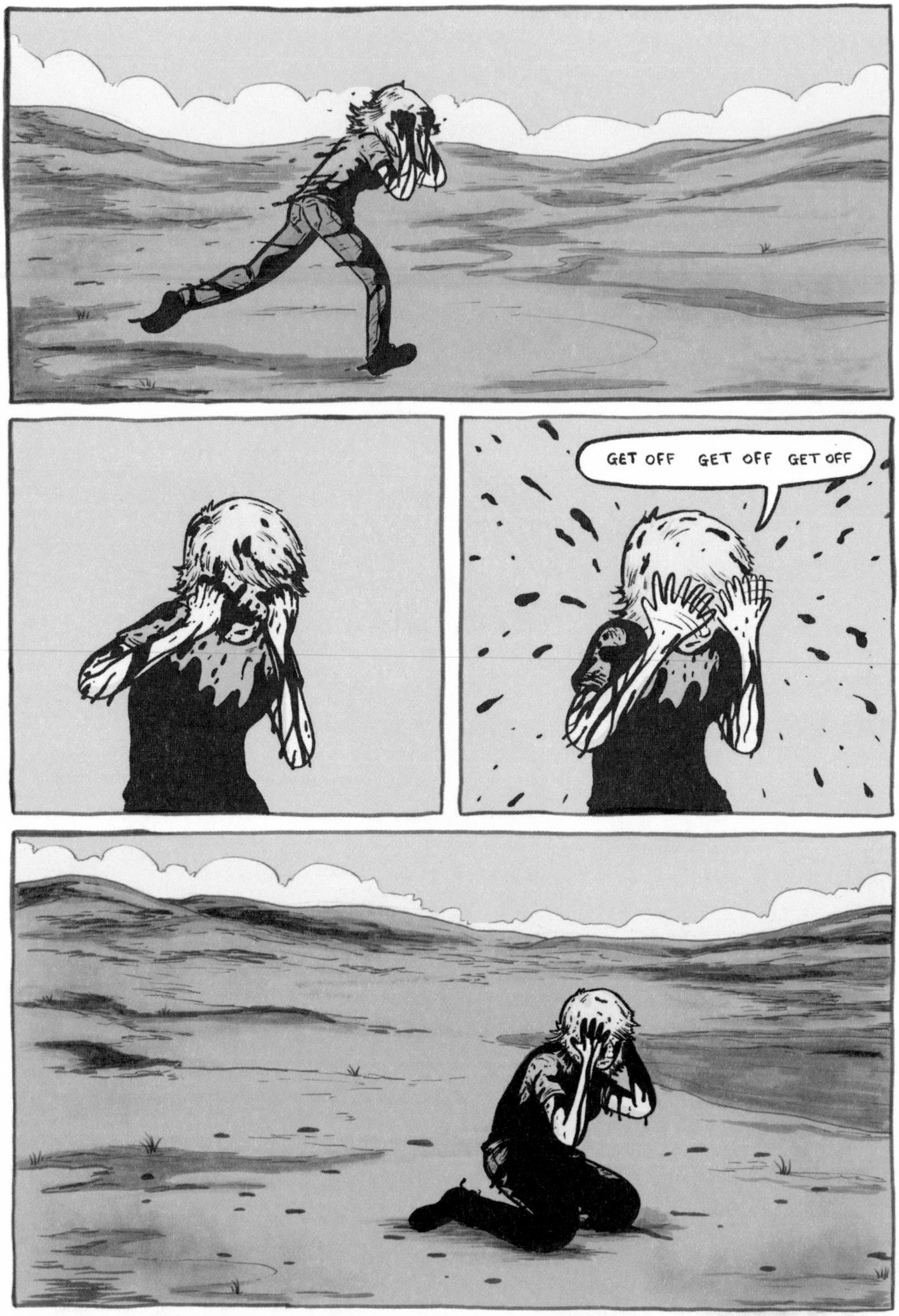
GET OFF GET OFF GET OFF

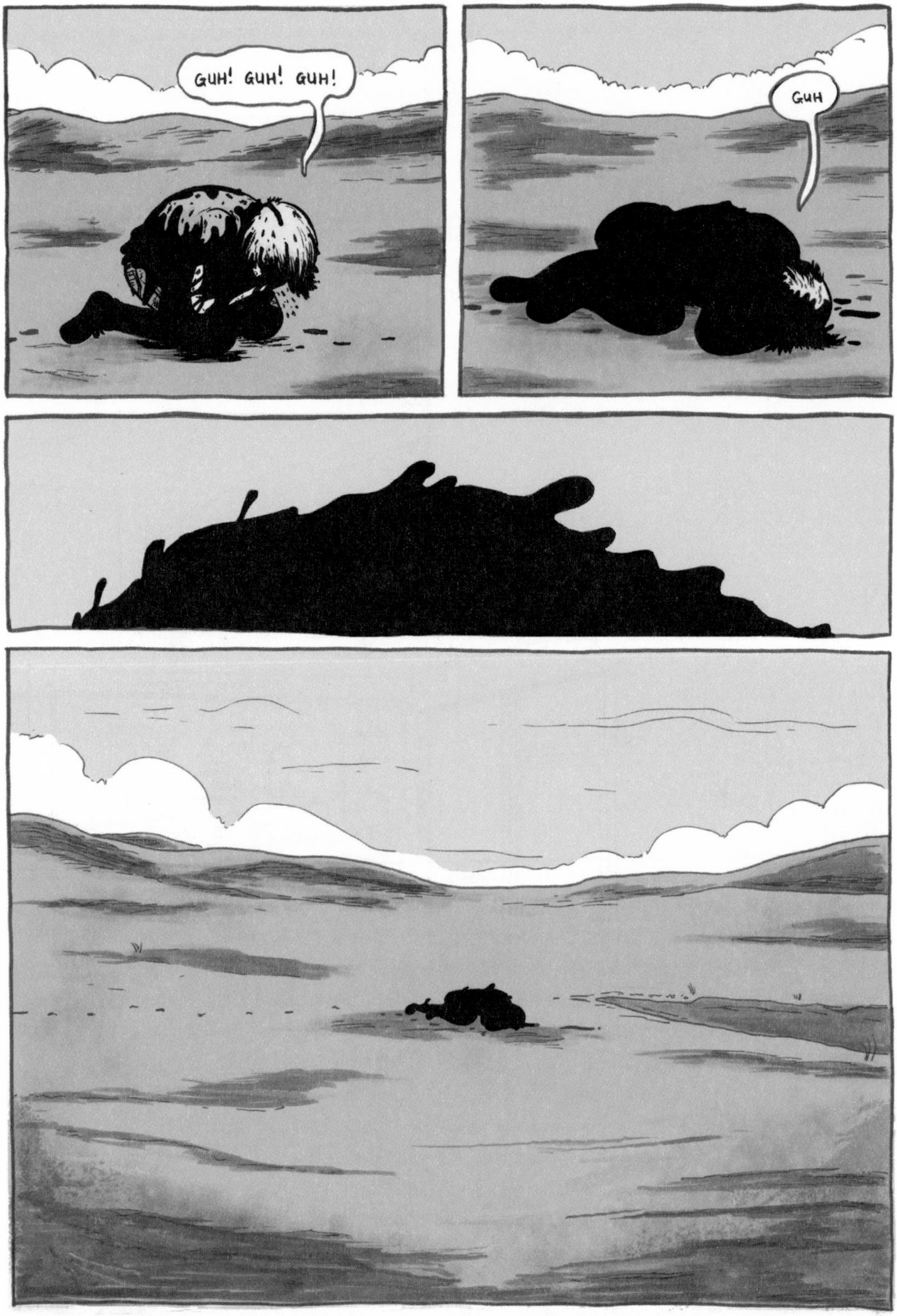
GUH! GUH! GUH!
GUH

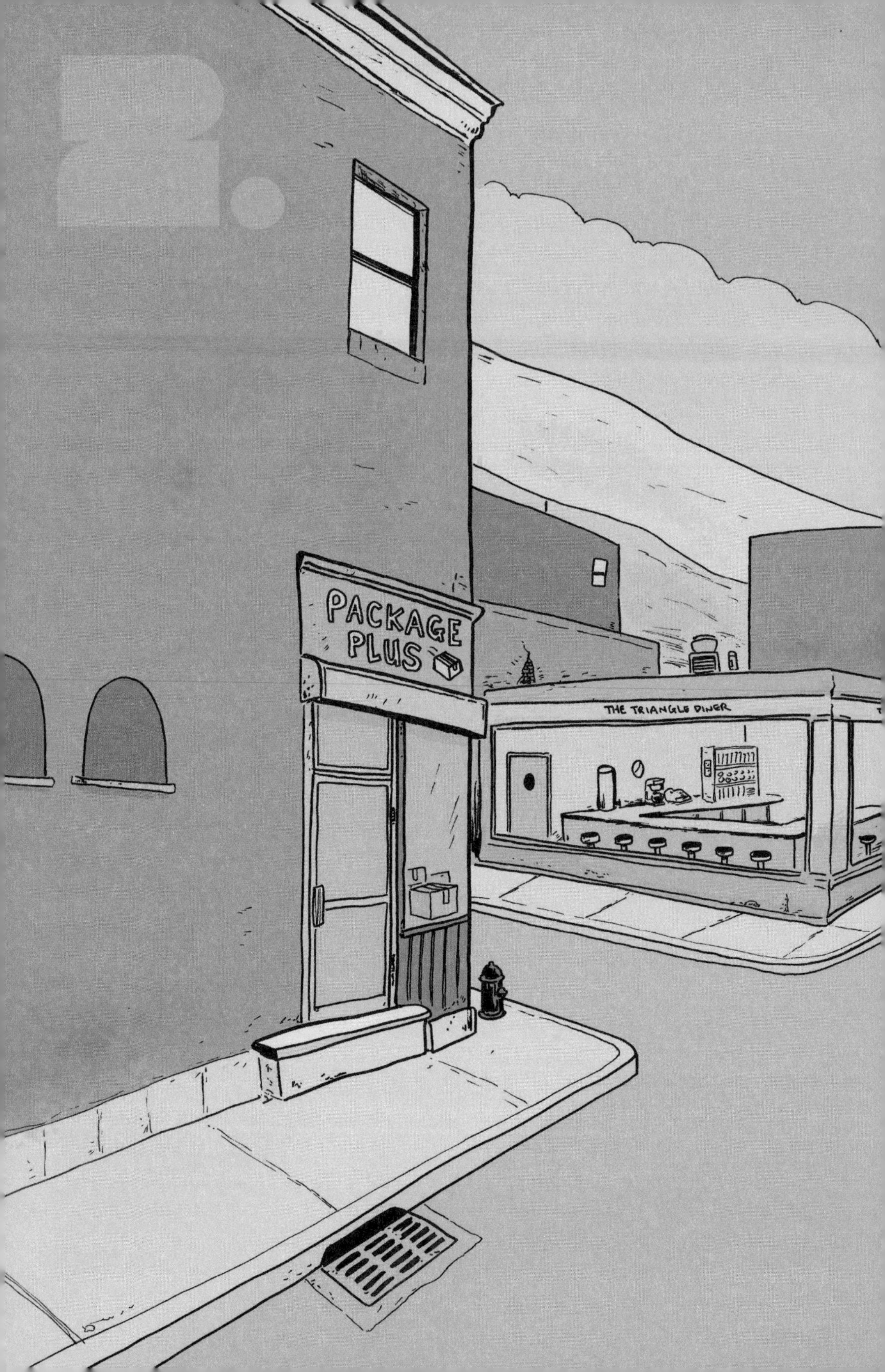
PACKAGE PLUS
THE TRIANGLE DINER

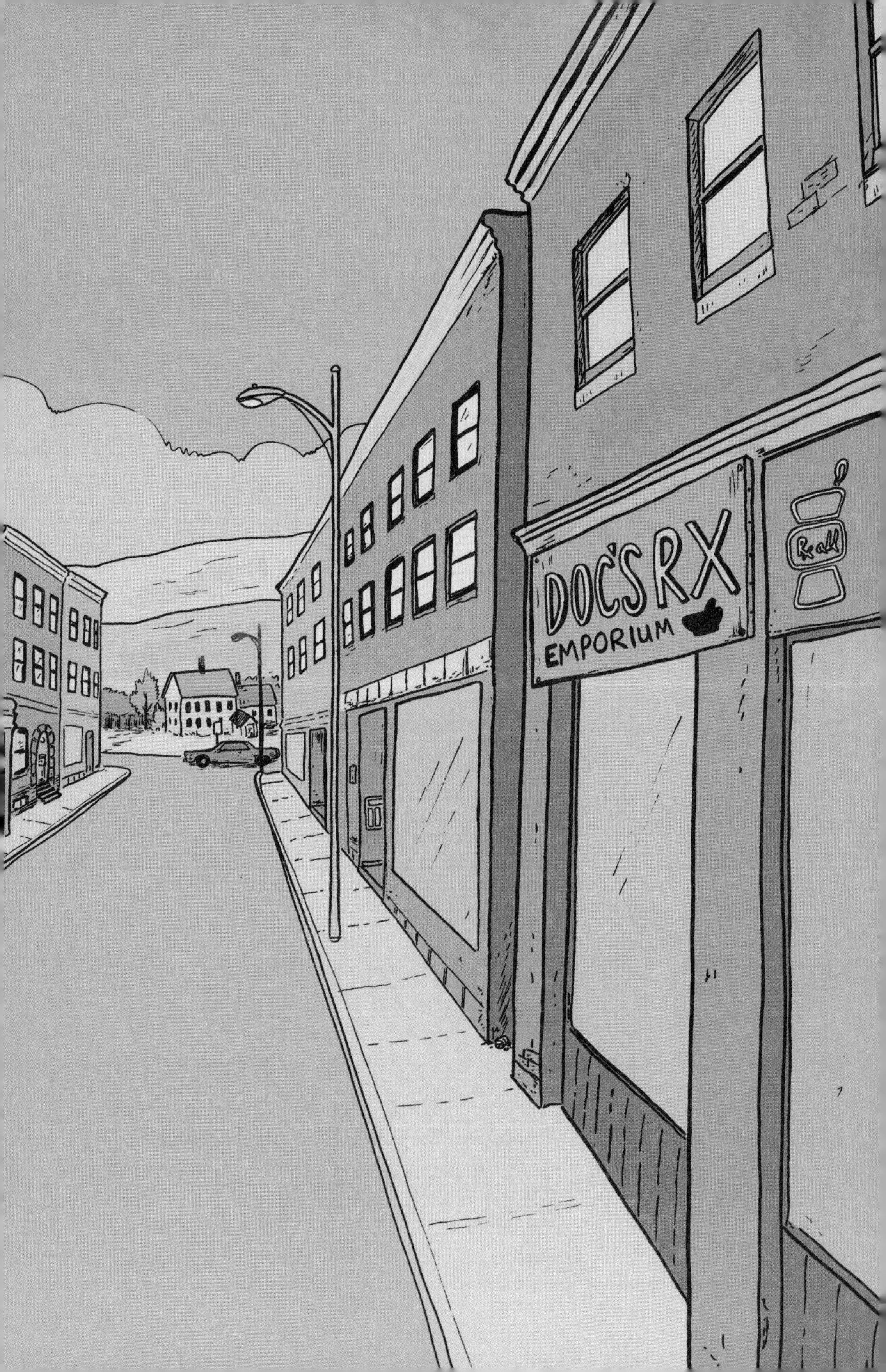
DOC'S RX
EMPORIUM
Rexall

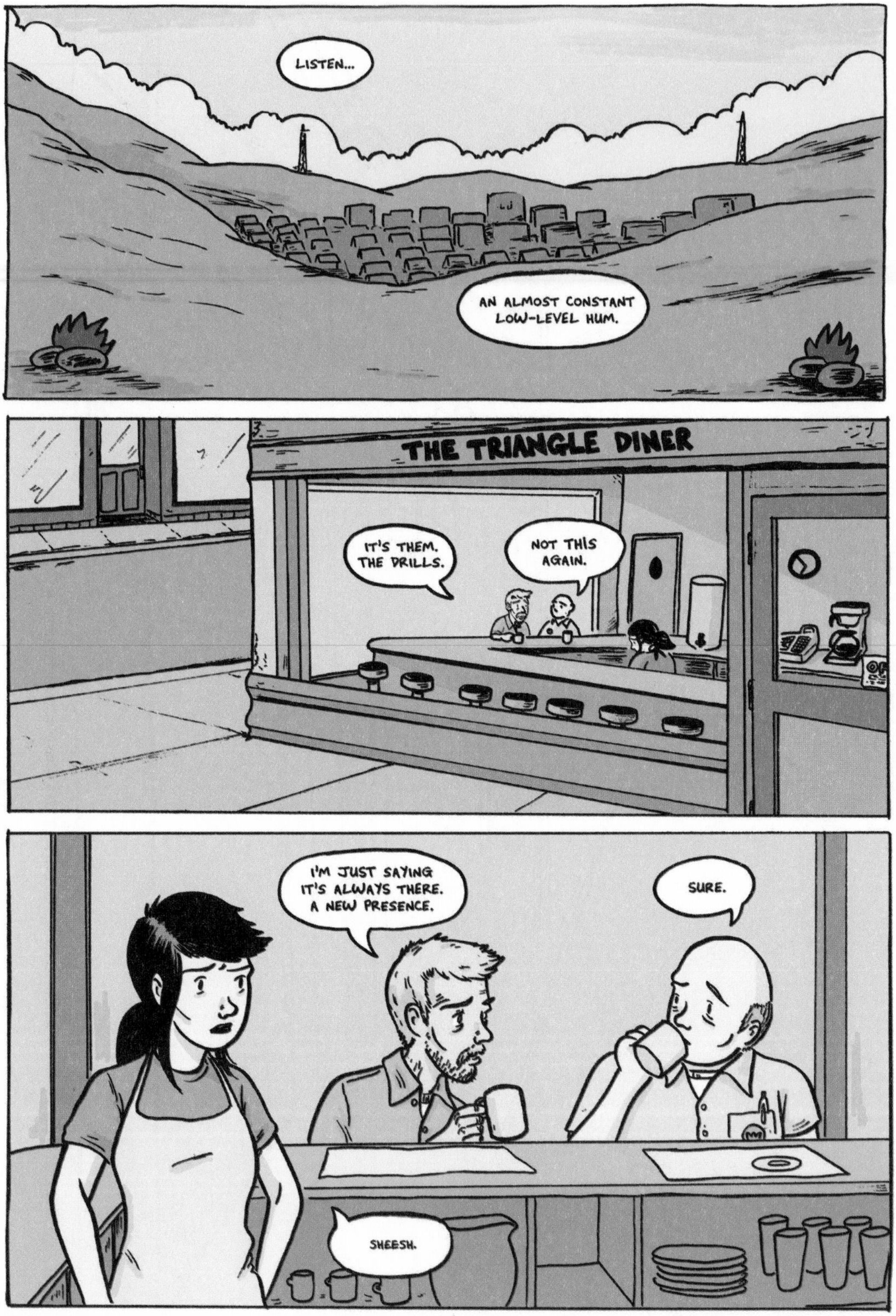
LISTEN...
AN ALMOST CONSTANT LOW-LEVEL HUM.
THE TRIANGLE DINER
IT'S THEM. THE DRILLS.
NOT THIS AGAIN.
I'M JUST SAYING IT'S ALWAYS THERE. A NEW PRESENCE.
SURE.
SHEESH.

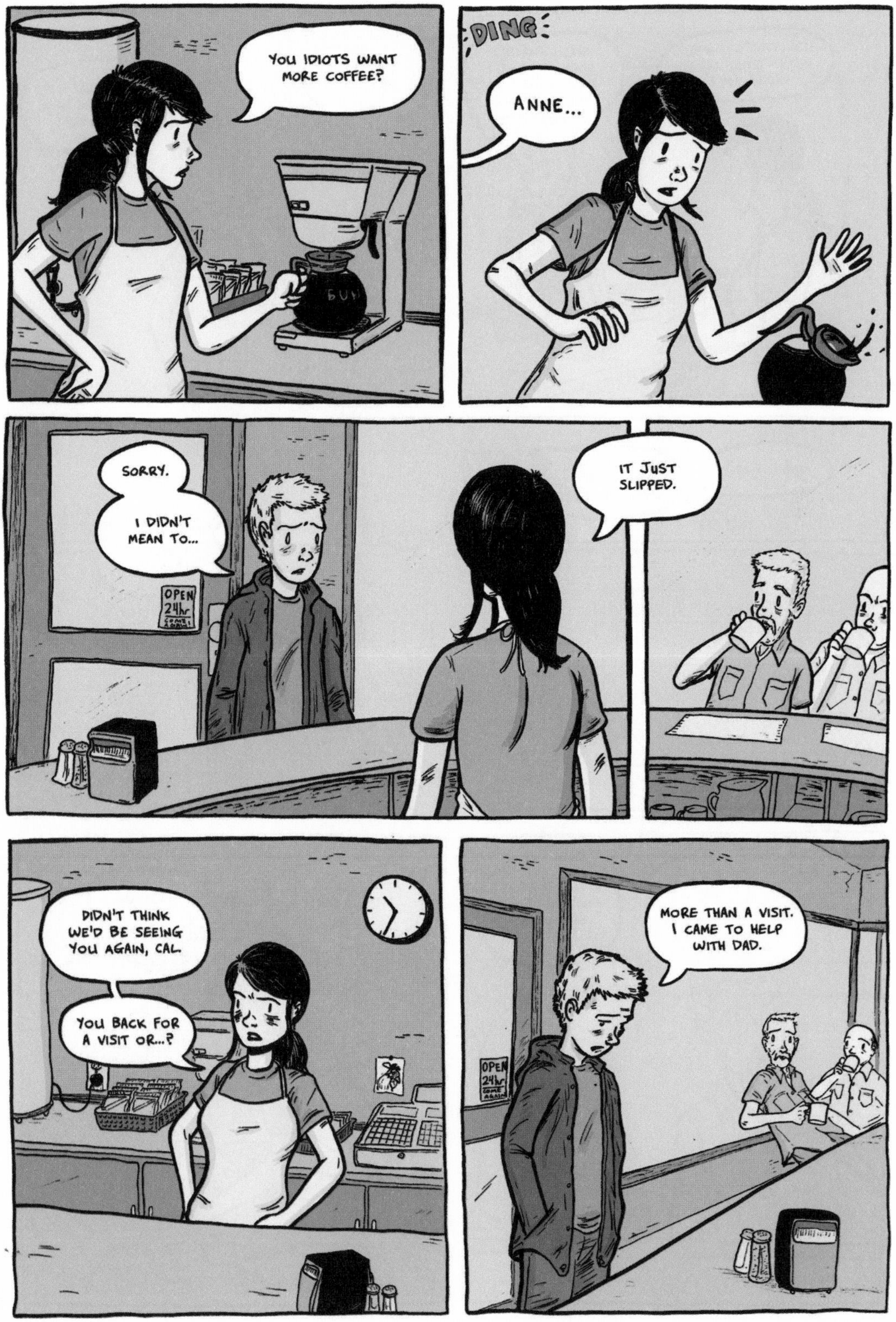
YOU IDIOTS WANT MORE COFFEE?
DING
ANNE...
SORRY.
I DIDN'T MEAN TO...
IT JUST SLIPPED.
OPEN 24hr
DIDN'T THINK WE'D BE SEEING YOU AGAIN, CAL.
YOU BACK FOR A VISIT OR...?
MORE THAN A VISIT. I CAME TO HELP WITH DAD.
OPEN 24hr

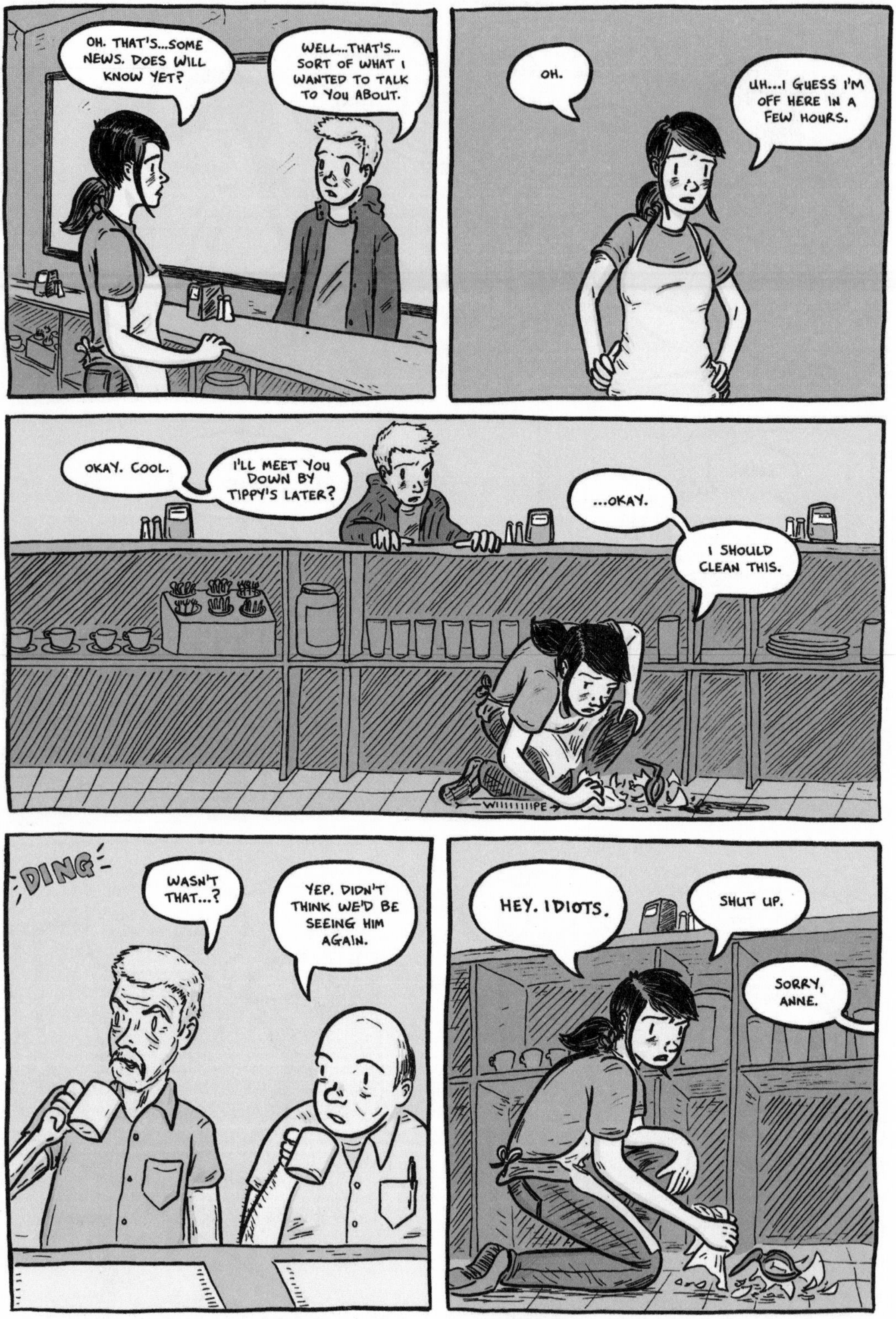
OH. THAT'S...SOME NEWS. DOES WILL KNOW YET?
WELL...THAT'S... SORT OF WHAT I WANTED TO TALK TO YOU ABOUT.
OH.
UH...I GUESS I'M OFF HERE IN A FEW HOURS.
OKAY. COOL.
I'LL MEET YOU DOWN BY TIPPY'S LATER?
...OKAY.
I SHOULD CLEAN THIS.
WIIIIIIIPE
DING
WASN'T THAT...?
YEP. DIDN'T THINK WE'D BE SEEING HIM AGAIN.
HEY. IDIOTS.
SHUT UP.
SORRY, ANNE.

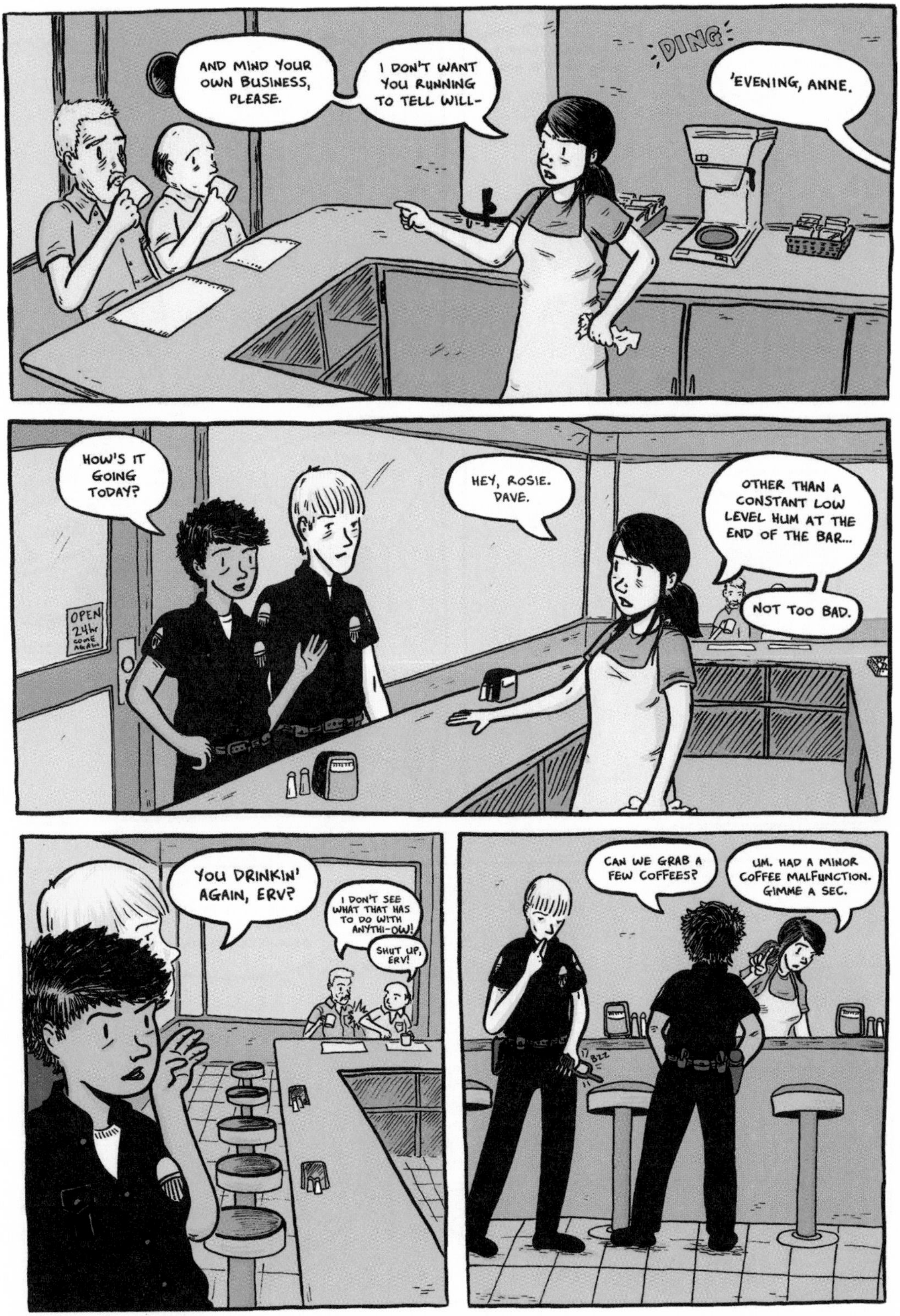
I DON'T WANT YOU RUNNING TO TELL WILL-
AND MIND YOUR OWN BUSINESS, PLEASE.
DING
'EVENING, ANNE.
HOW'S IT GOING TODAY?
HEY, ROSIE. DAVE.
OTHER THAN A CONSTANT LOW LEVEL HUM AT THE END OF THE BAR...
NOT TOO BAD.
OPEN 24hr COME AGAIN
YOU DRINKIN' AGAIN, ERV?
I DON'T SEE WHAT THAT HAS TO DO WITH ANYTHI-OW!
SHUT UP, ERV!
CAN WE GRAB A FEW COFFEES?
UM. HAD A MINOR COFFEE MALFUNCTION. GIMME A SEC.
BZZ

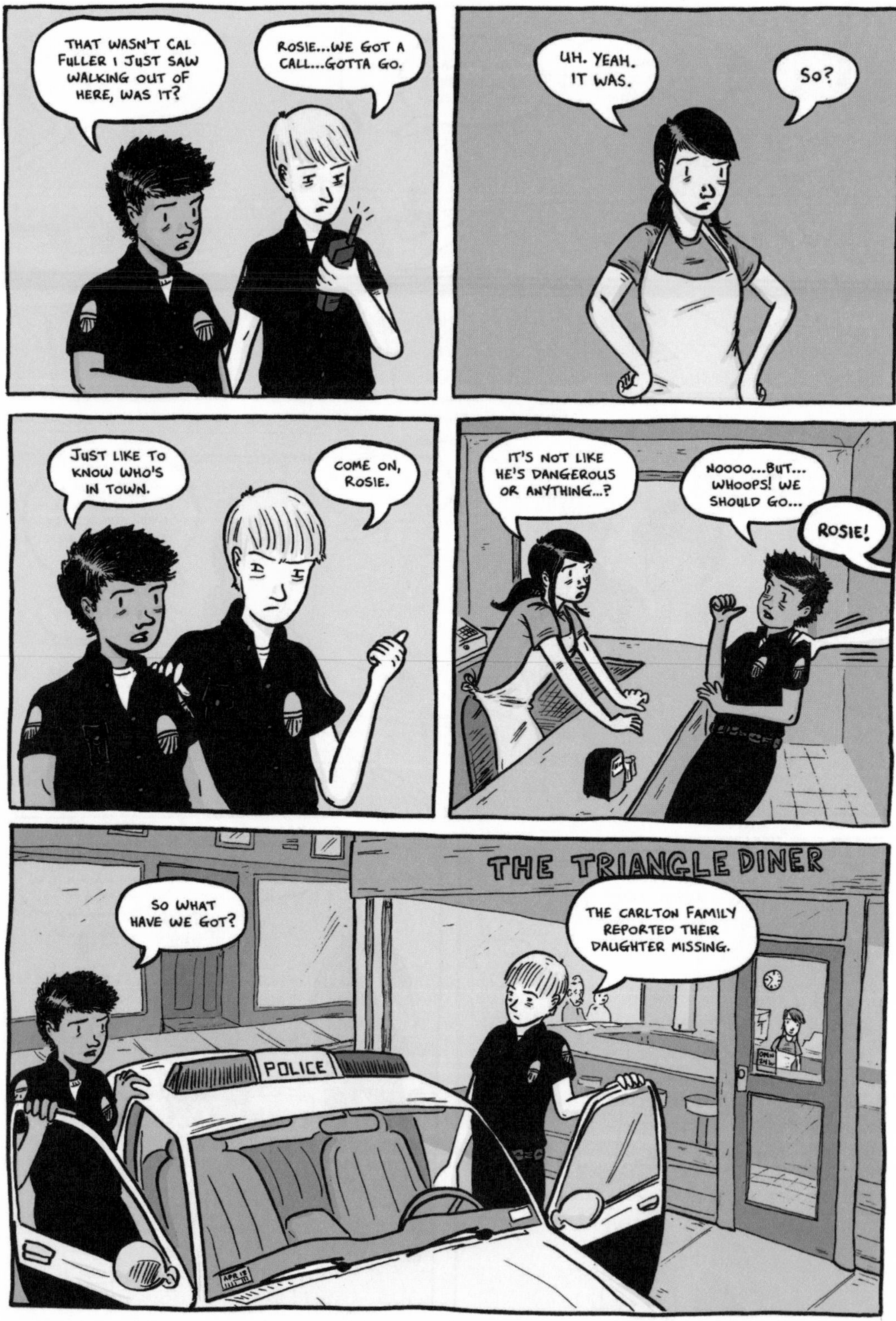
THAT WASN'T CAL FULLER I JUST SAW WALKING OUT OF HERE, WAS IT?
ROSIE...WE GOT A CALL...GOTTA GO.
UH. YEAH. IT WAS.
SO?
JUST LIKE TO KNOW WHO'S IN TOWN.
COME ON, ROSIE.
IT'S NOT LIKE HE'S DANGEROUS OR ANYTHING...?
NOOOO...BUT... WHOOPS! WE SHOULD GO...
ROSIE!
THE TRIANGLE DINER
SO WHAT HAVE WE GOT?
THE CARLTON FAMILY REPORTED THEIR DAUGHTER MISSING.
POLICE

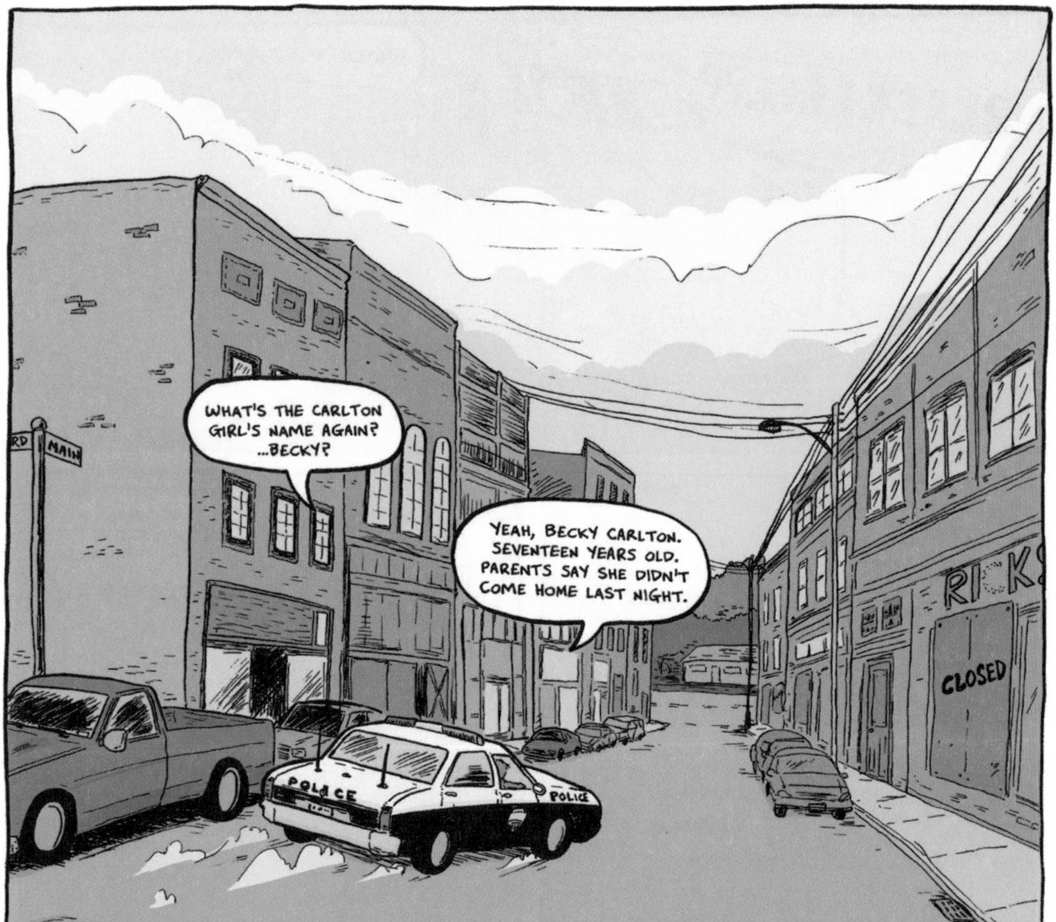
RD
MAIN
WHAT'S THE CARLTON GIRL'S NAME AGAIN? ...BECKY?
YEAH, BECKY CARLTON. SEVENTEEN YEARS OLD. PARENTS SAY SHE DIDN'T COME HOME LAST NIGHT.
RICKS
CLOSED
POLICE
POLICE

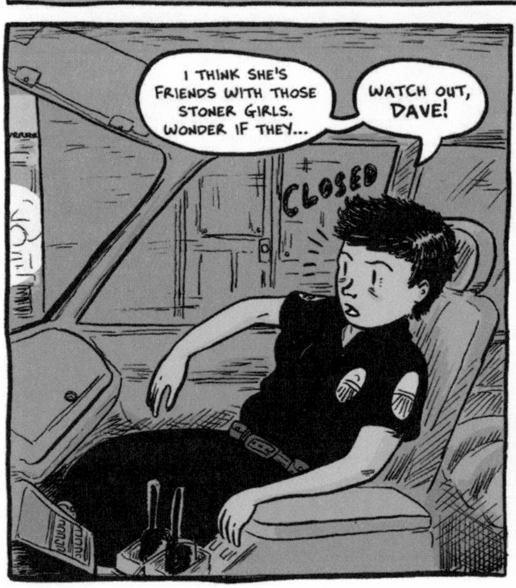
I THINK SHE'S FRIENDS WITH THOSE STONER GIRLS. WONDER IF THEY...
WATCH OUT, DAVE!
CLOSED

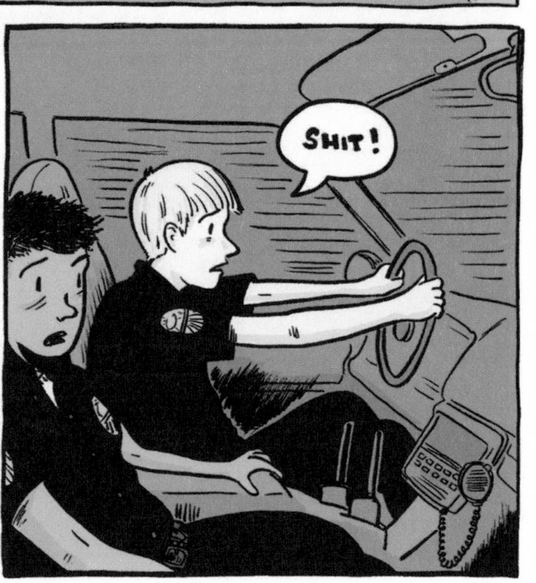
SHIT!

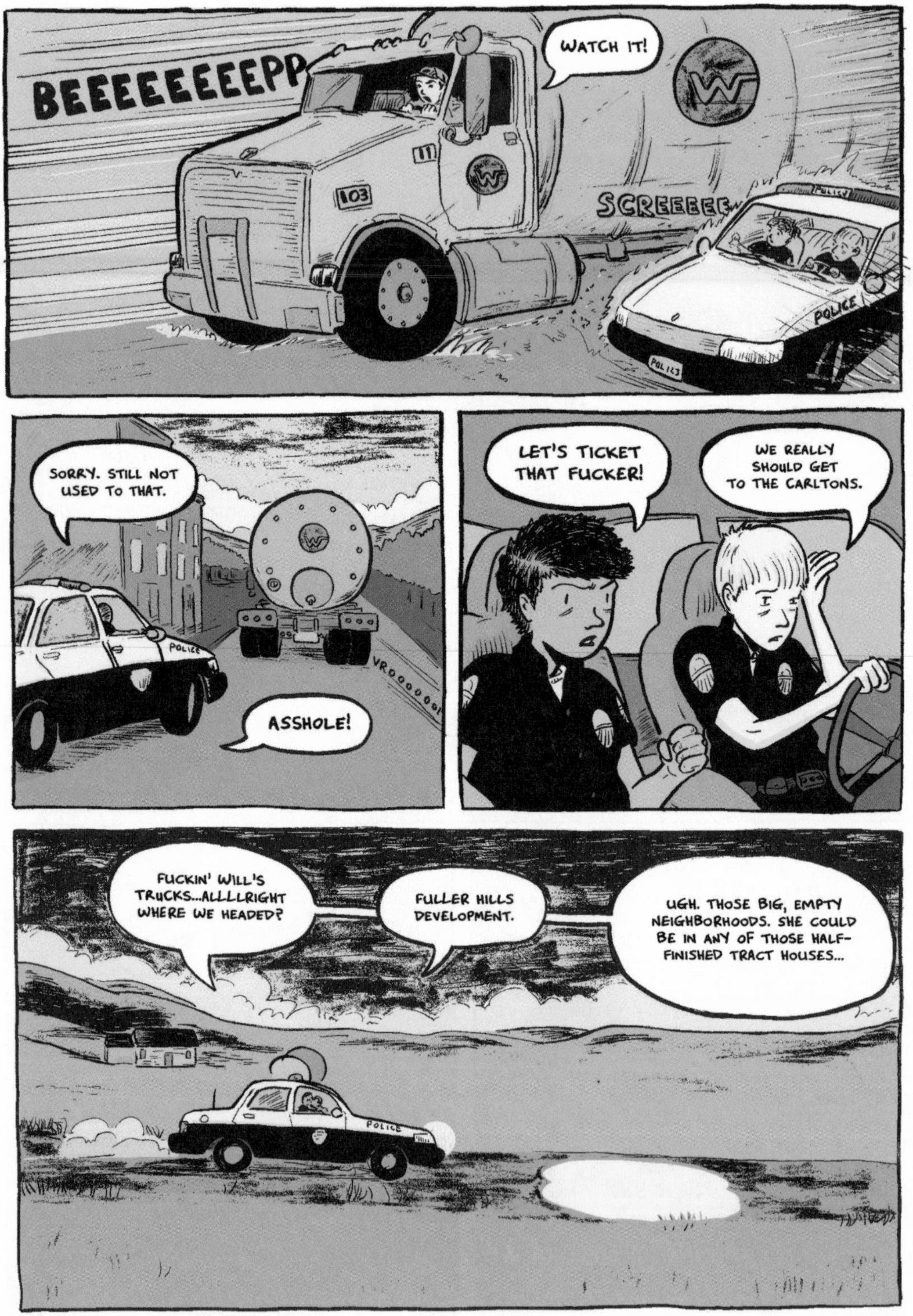
BEEEEEEEEEPP
WATCH IT!
SCREEEEEE
SORRY. STILL NOT USED TO THAT.
ASSHOLE!
VROOOOOO
LET'S TICKET THAT FUCKER!
WE REALLY SHOULD GET TO THE CARLTONS.
FUCKIN' WILL'S TRUCKS...ALLLLRIGHT WHERE WE HEADED?
FULLER HILLS DEVELOPMENT.
UGH. THOSE BIG, EMPTY NEIGHBORHOODS. SHE COULD BE IN ANY OF THOSE HALF-FINISHED TRACT HOUSES...

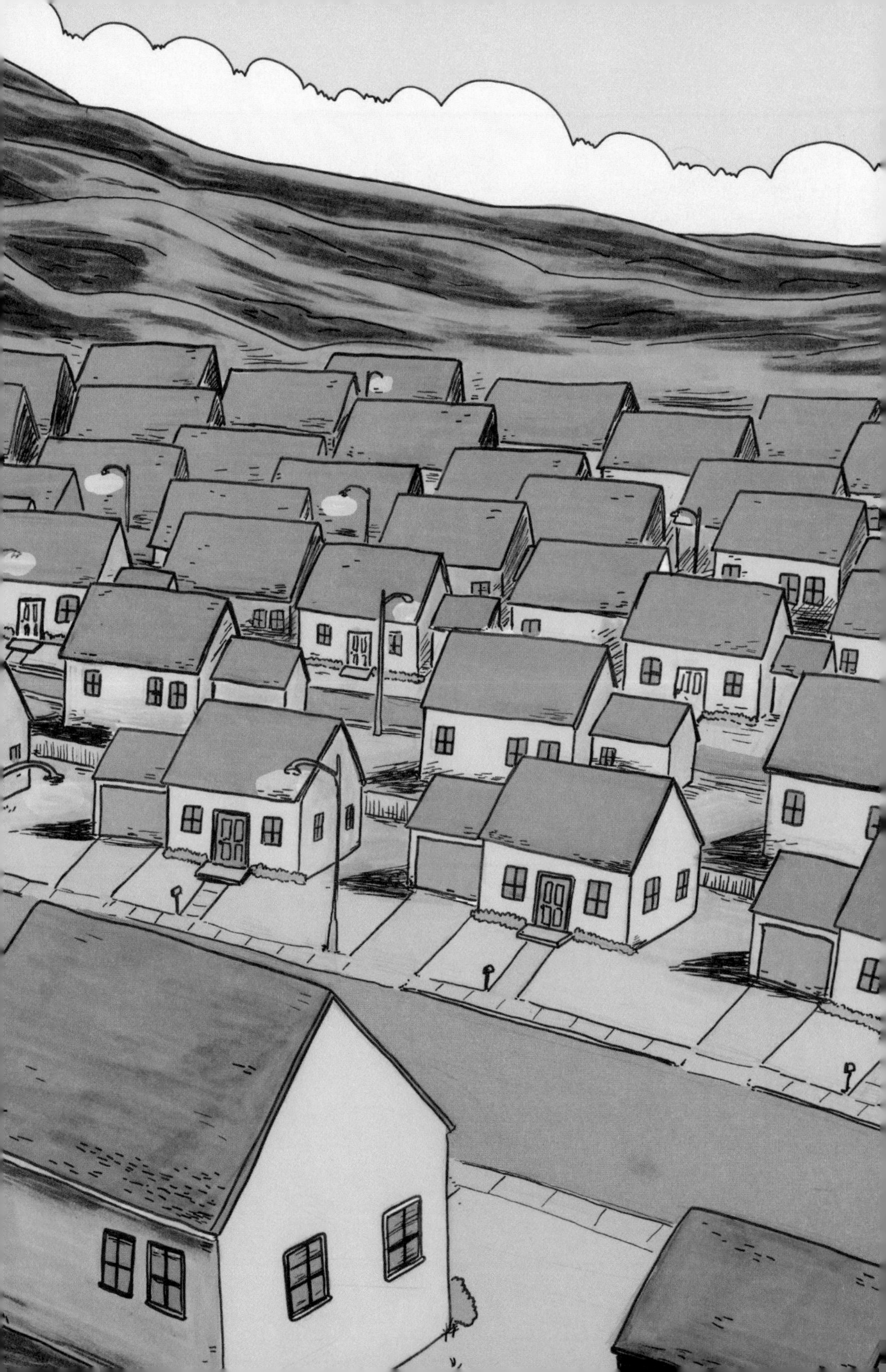

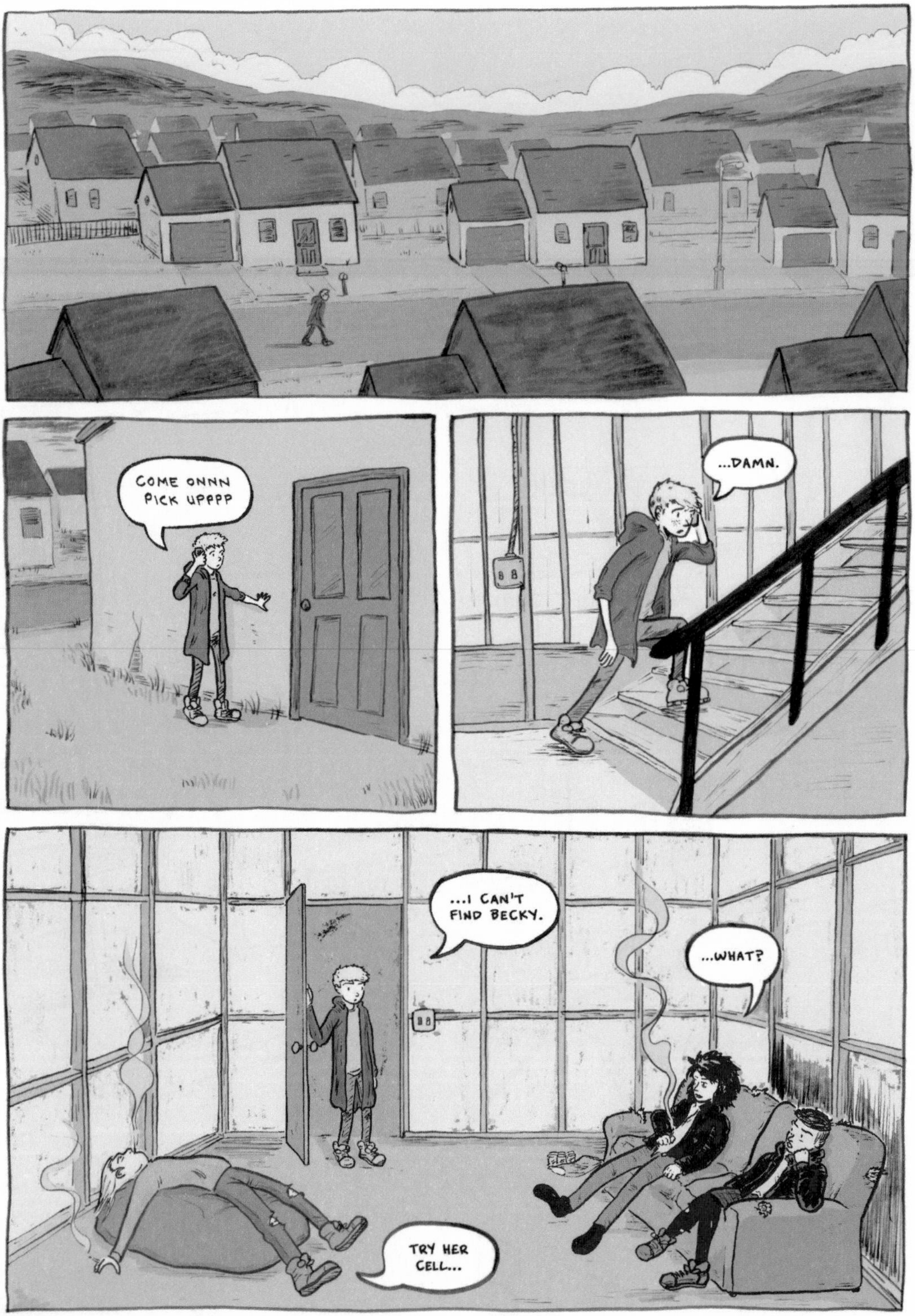
COME ONNN PICK UPPPP
...DAMN.
...I CAN'T FIND BECKY.
...WHAT?
TRY HER CELL...

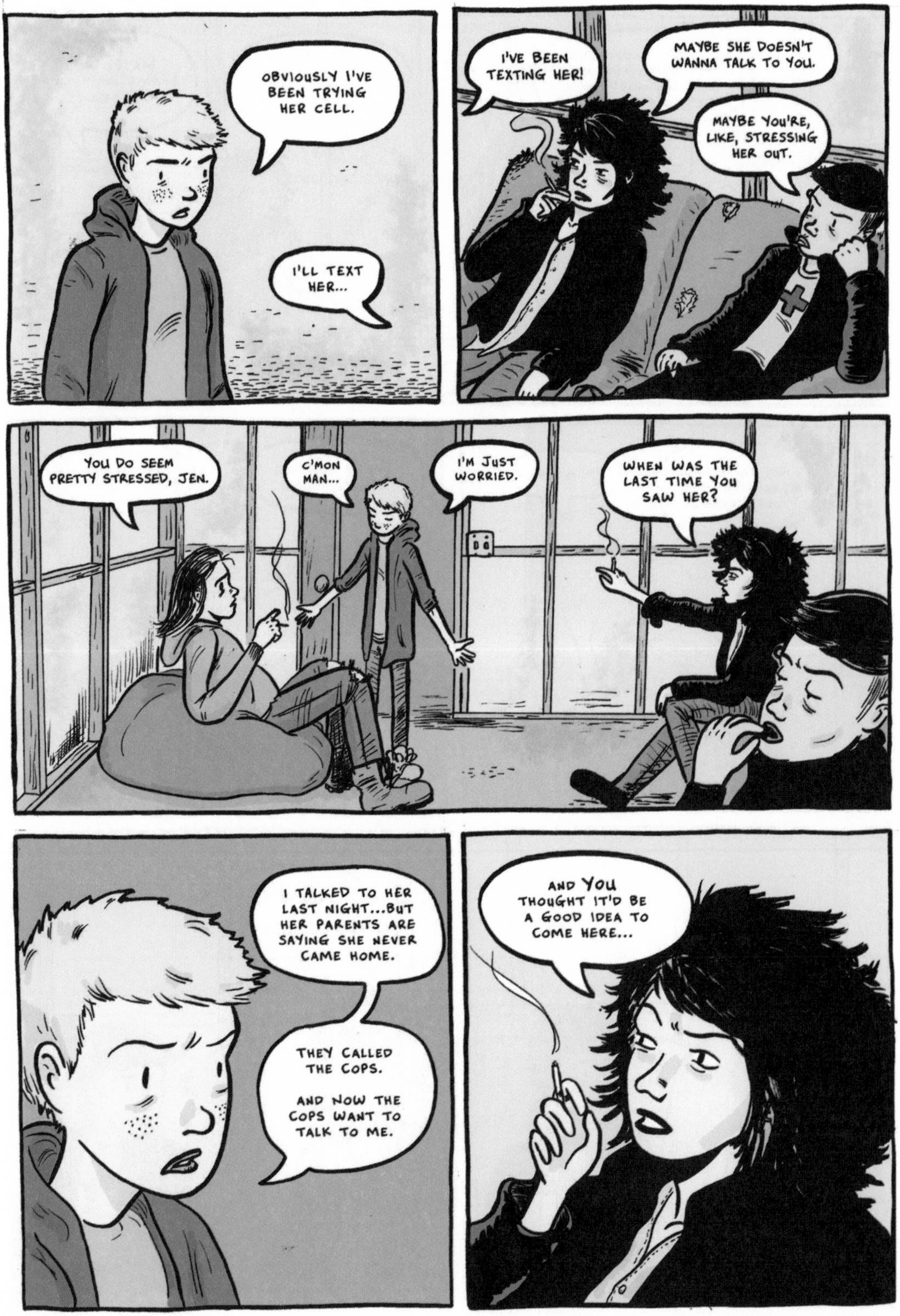
OBVIOUSLY I'VE BEEN TRYING HER CELL.
I'LL TEXT HER...
I'VE BEEN TEXTING HER!
MAYBE SHE DOESN'T WANNA TALK TO YOU.
MAYBE YOU'RE, LIKE, STRESSING HER OUT.
YOU DO SEEM PRETTY STRESSED, JEN.
C'MON MAN...
I'M JUST WORRIED.
WHEN WAS THE LAST TIME YOU SAW HER?
I TALKED TO HER LAST NIGHT...BUT HER PARENTS ARE SAYING SHE NEVER CAME HOME.
THEY CALLED THE COPS.
AND NOW THE COPS WANT TO TALK TO ME.
AND YOU THOUGHT IT'D BE A GOOD IDEA TO COME HERE...

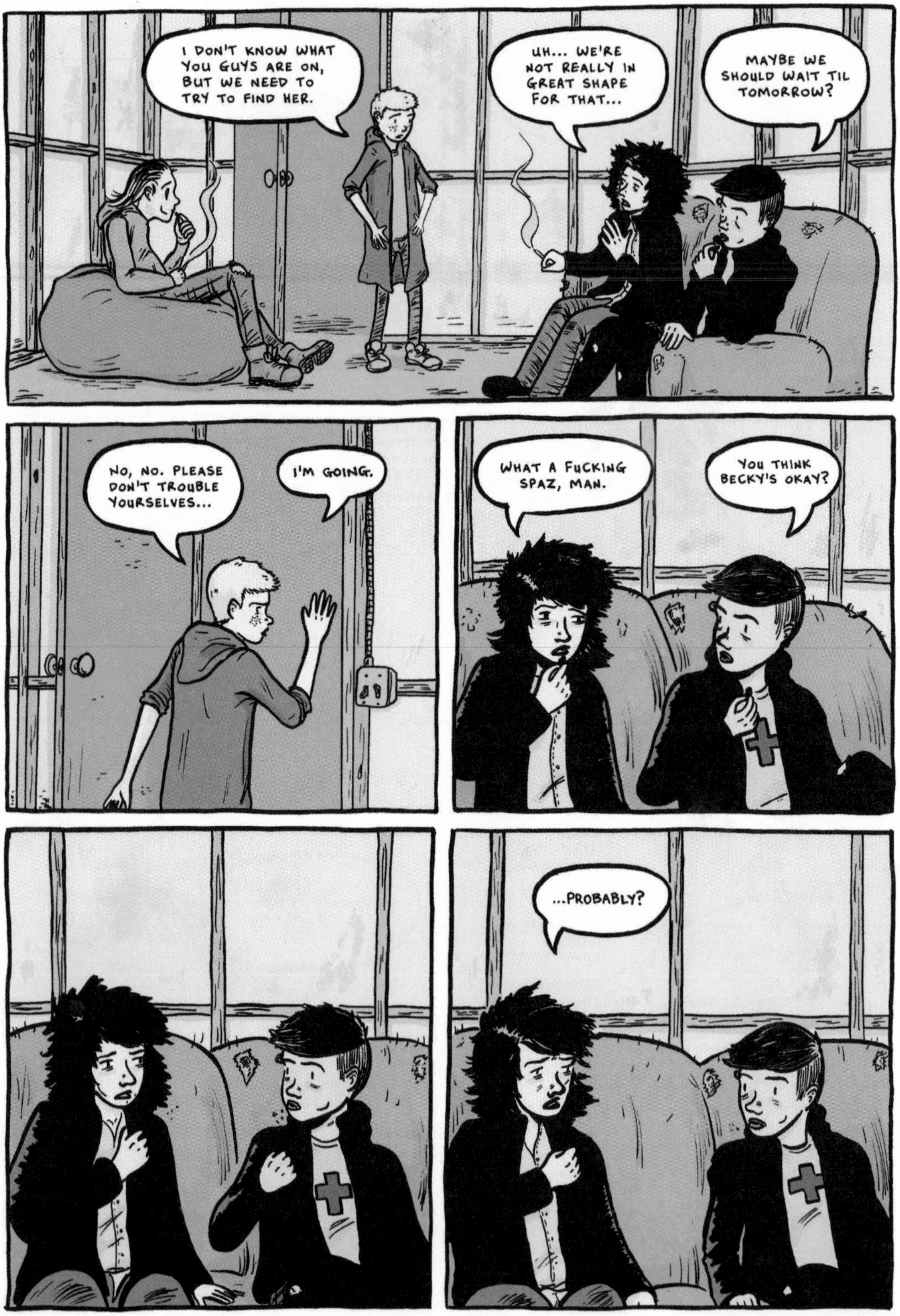
I DON'T KNOW WHAT YOU GUYS ARE ON, BUT WE NEED TO TRY TO FIND HER.
UH... WE'RE NOT REALLY IN GREAT SHAPE FOR THAT...
MAYBE WE SHOULD WAIT TIL TOMORROW?
NO, NO. PLEASE DON'T TROUBLE YOURSELVES...
I'M GOING.
WHAT A FUCKING SPAZ, MAN.
YOU THINK BECKY'S OKAY?
...PROBABLY?

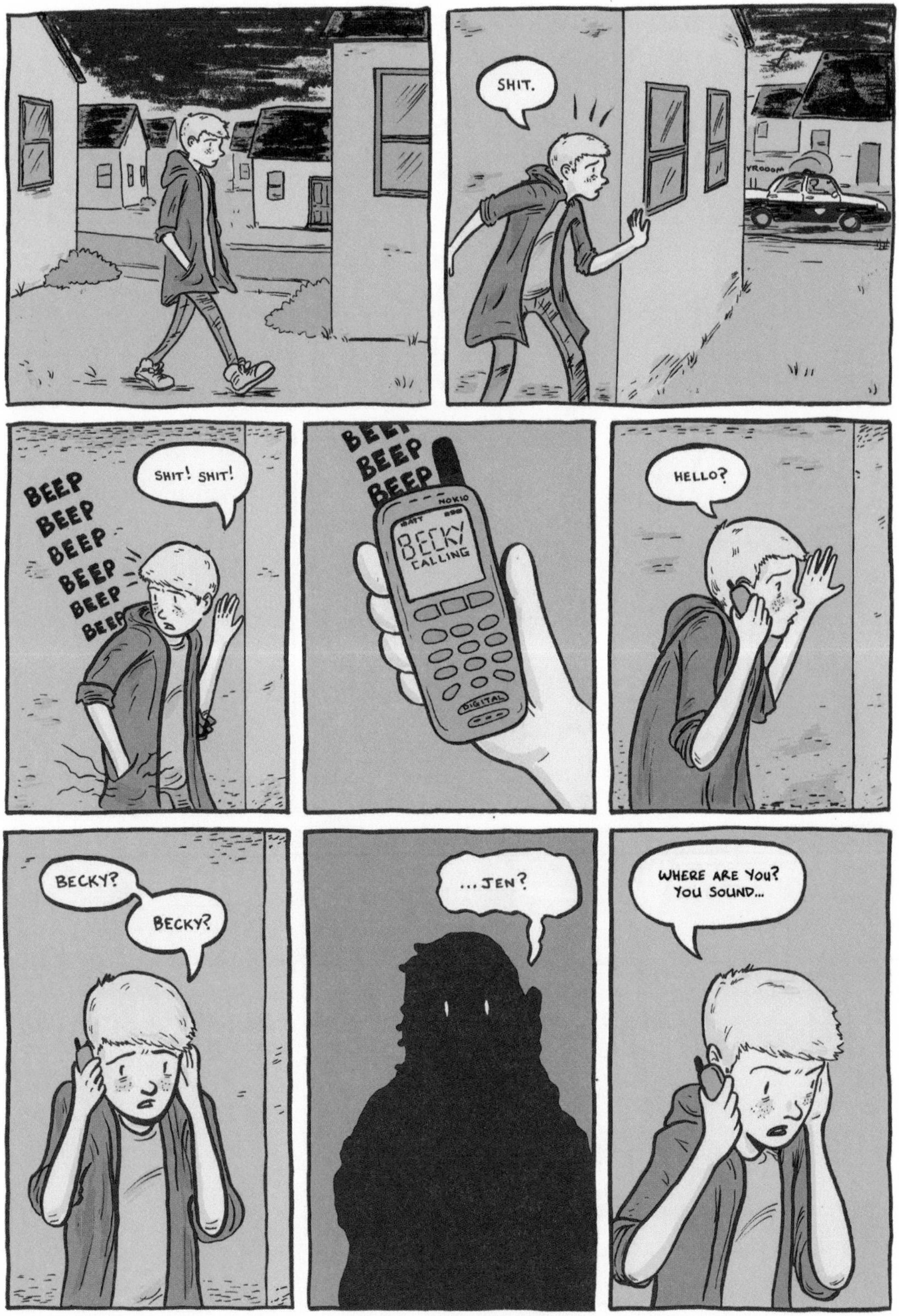

SHIT.
VROOOM
SHIT! SHIT!
BEEP BEEP BEEP BEEP BEEP BEEP
BEEP BEEP BEEP
NOKIO
BECKY CALLING
DIGITAL
HELLO?
BECKY?
BECKY?
...JEN?
WHERE ARE YOU? YOU SOUND...

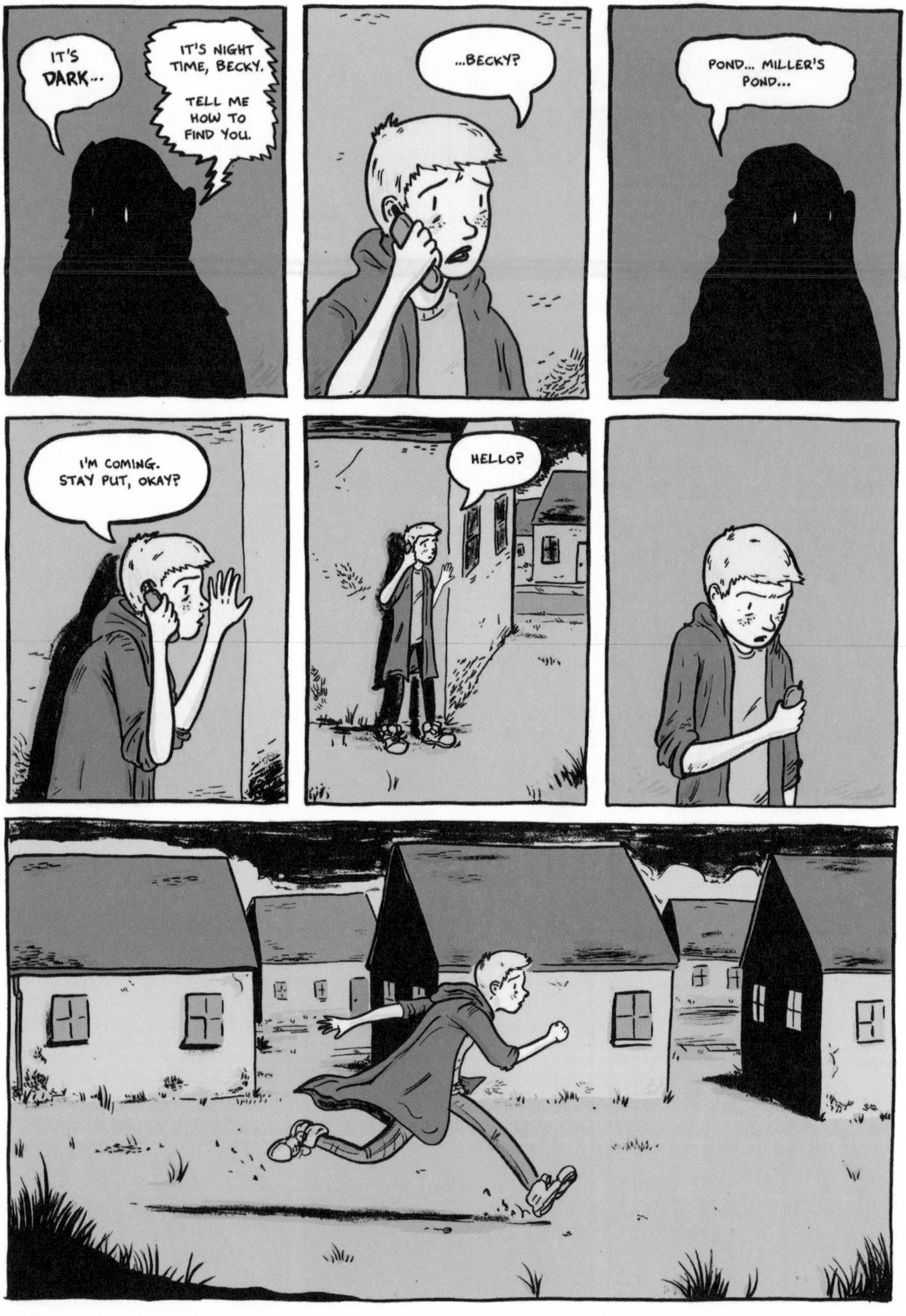
IT'S DARK...
IT'S NIGHT TIME, BECKY.
TELL ME HOW TO FIND YOU.
...BECKY?
POND... MILLER'S POND...
I'M COMING. STAY PUT, OKAY?
HELLO?

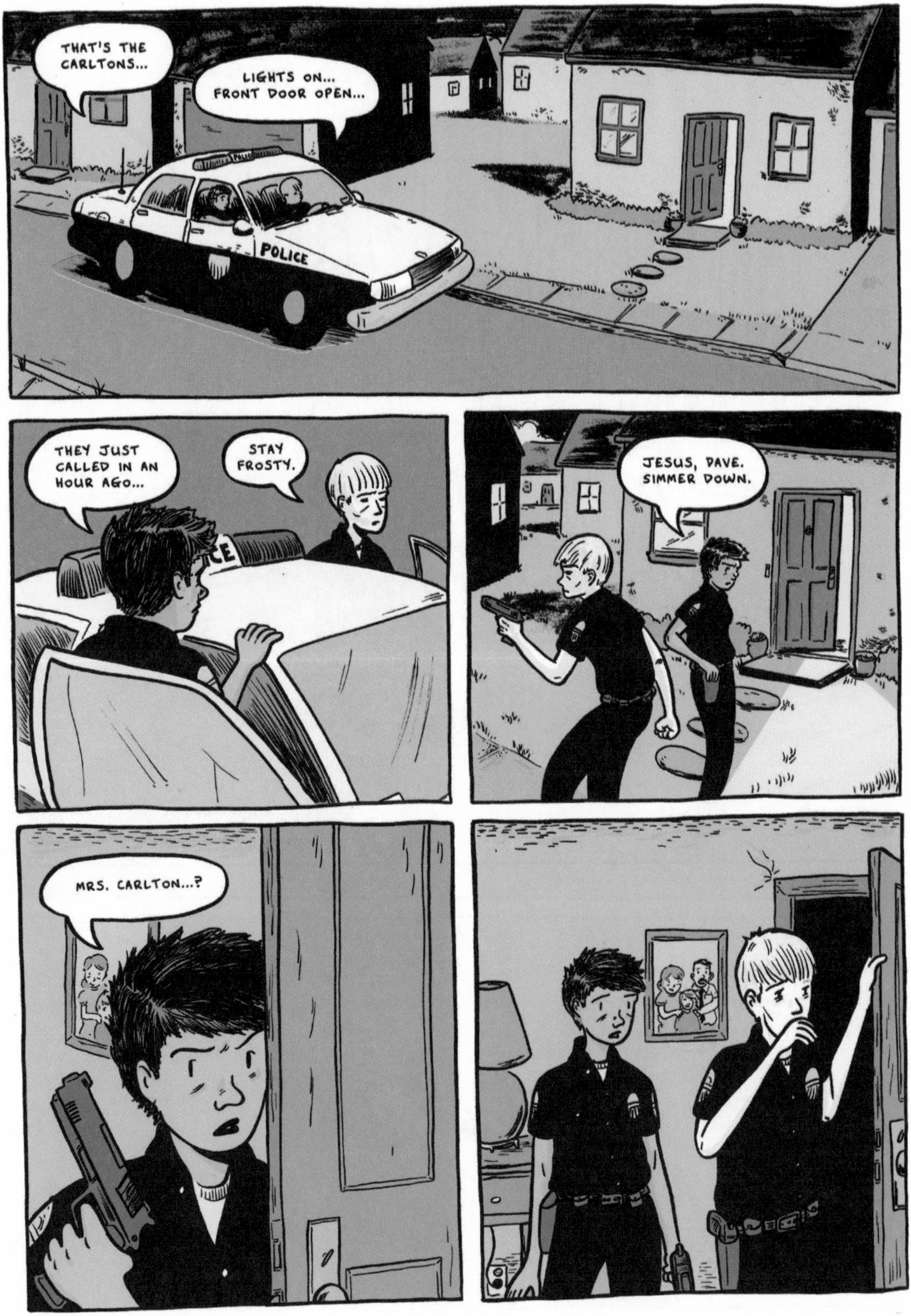

THAT'S THE CARLTONS...
LIGHTS ON... FRONT DOOR OPEN...
THEY JUST CALLED IN AN HOUR AGO...
STAY FROSTY.
POLICE
JESUS, DAVE. SIMMER DOWN.
MRS. CARLTON...?

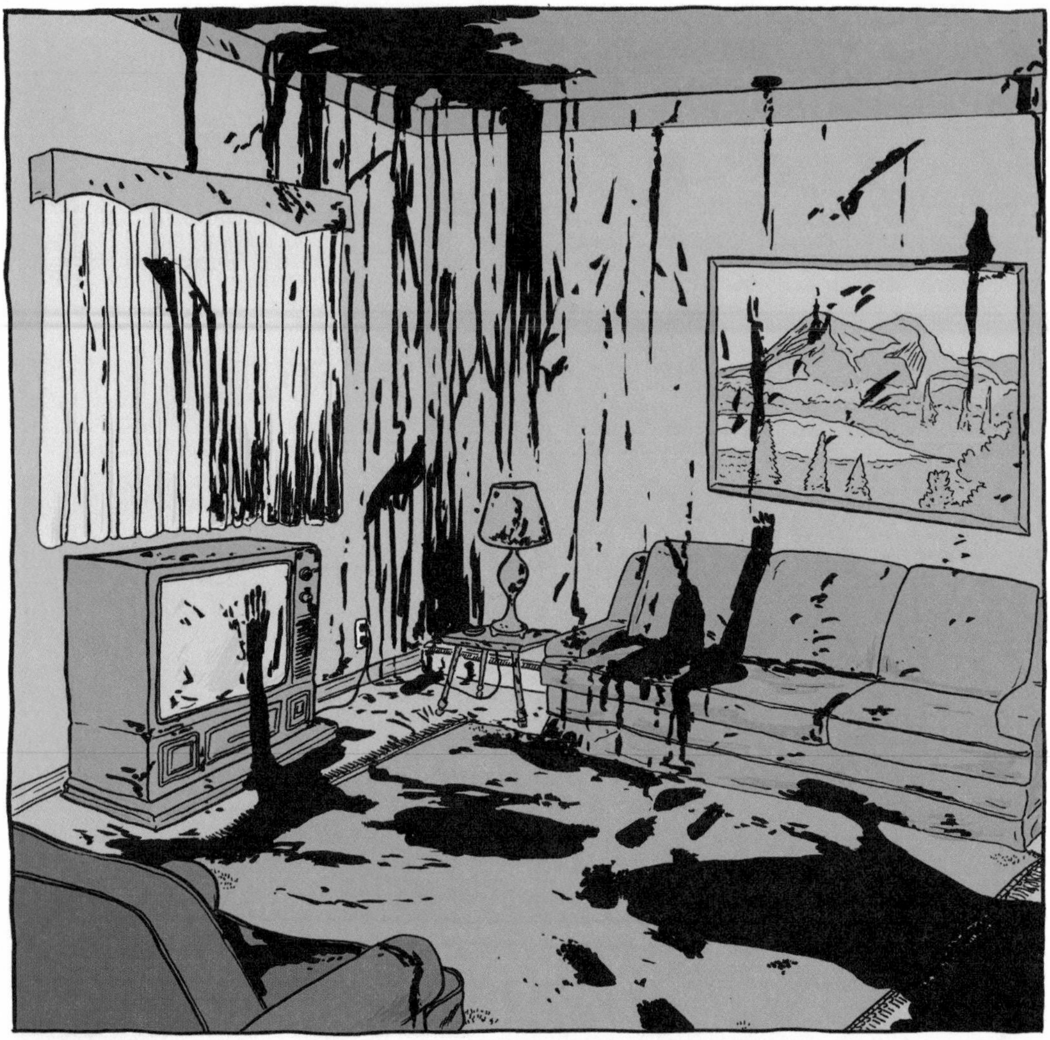

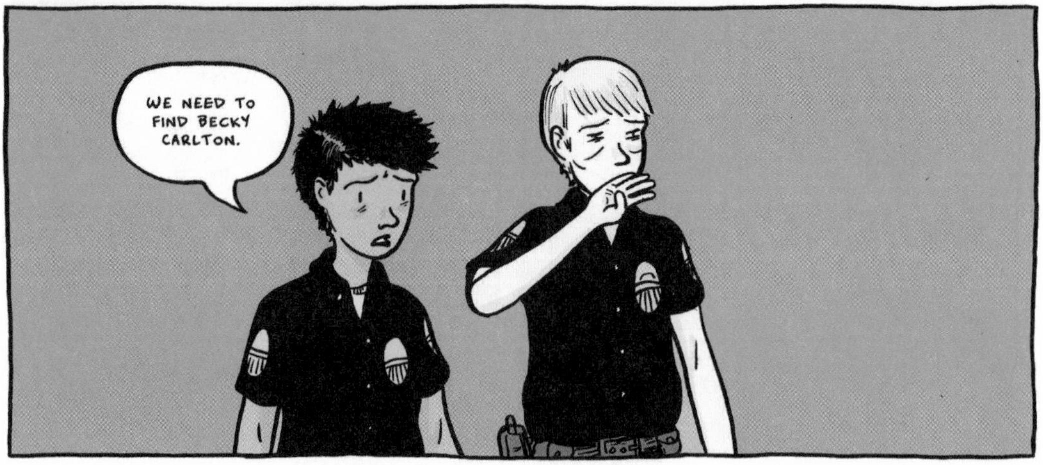
WE NEED TO FIND BECKY CARLTON.

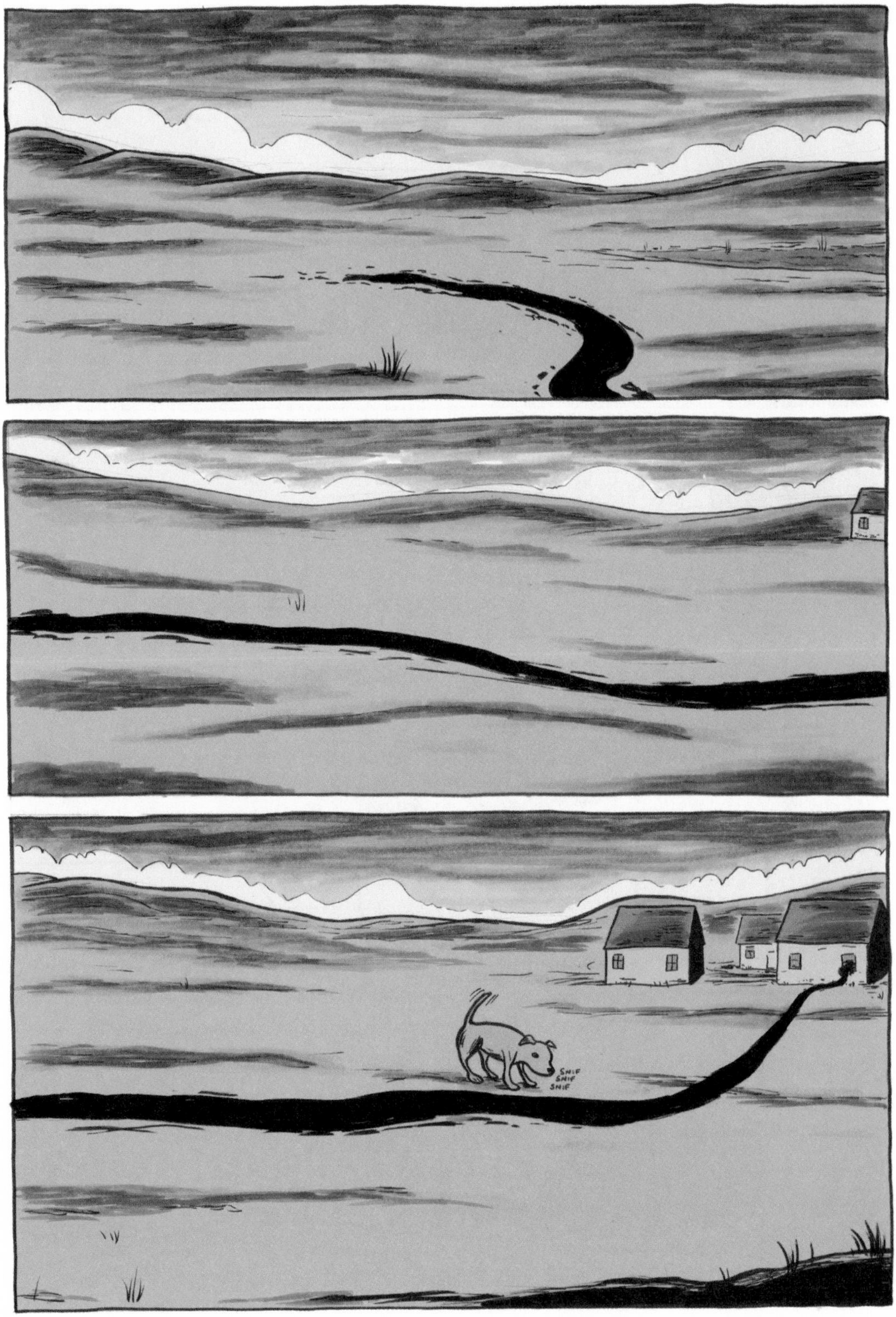
SNIF
SNIF
SNIF

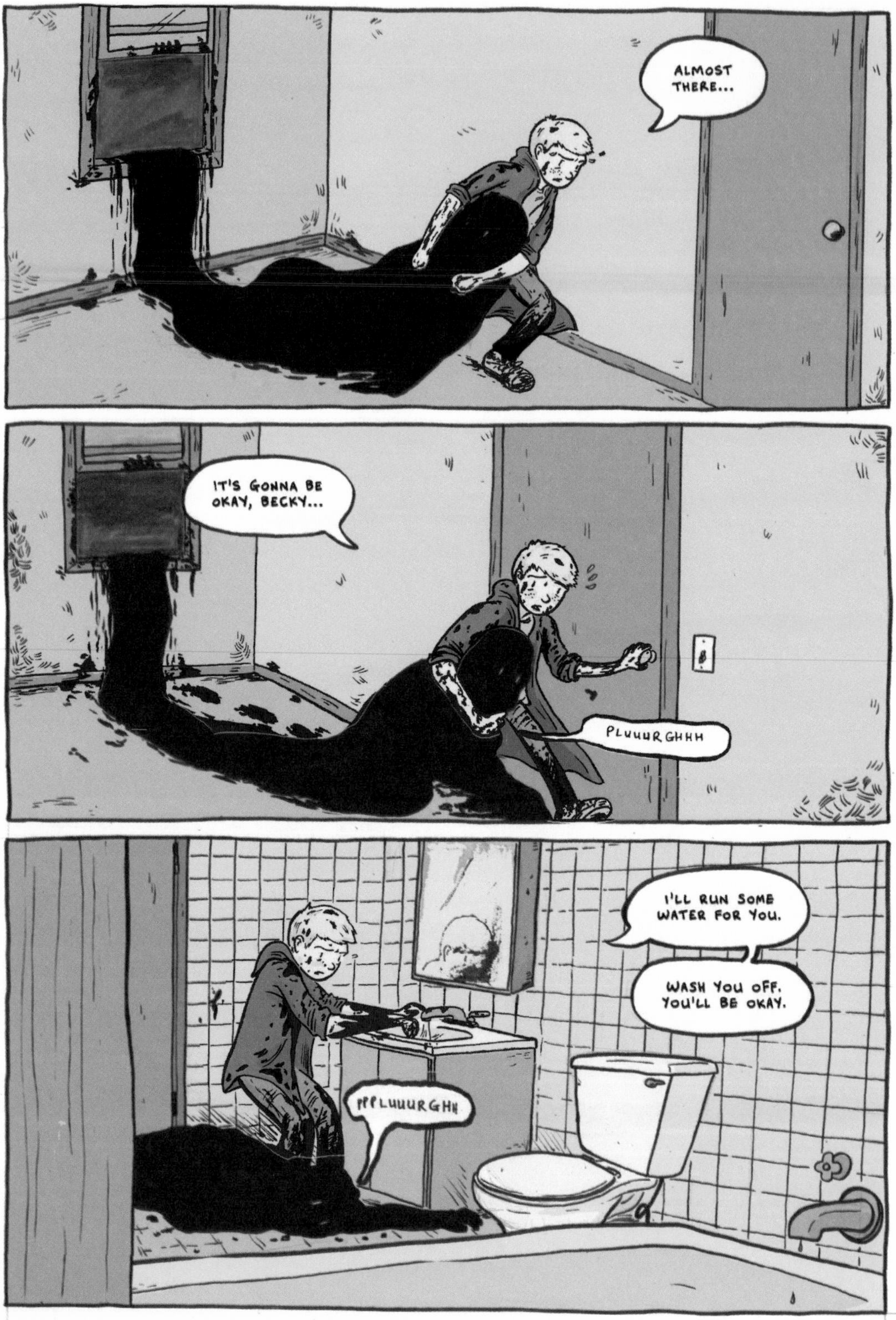
ALMOST THERE...
IT'S GONNA BE OKAY, BECKY...
PLUUURGHHH
I'LL RUN SOME WATER FOR YOU.
WASH YOU OFF. YOU'LL BE OKAY.
PPPLUUURGHH

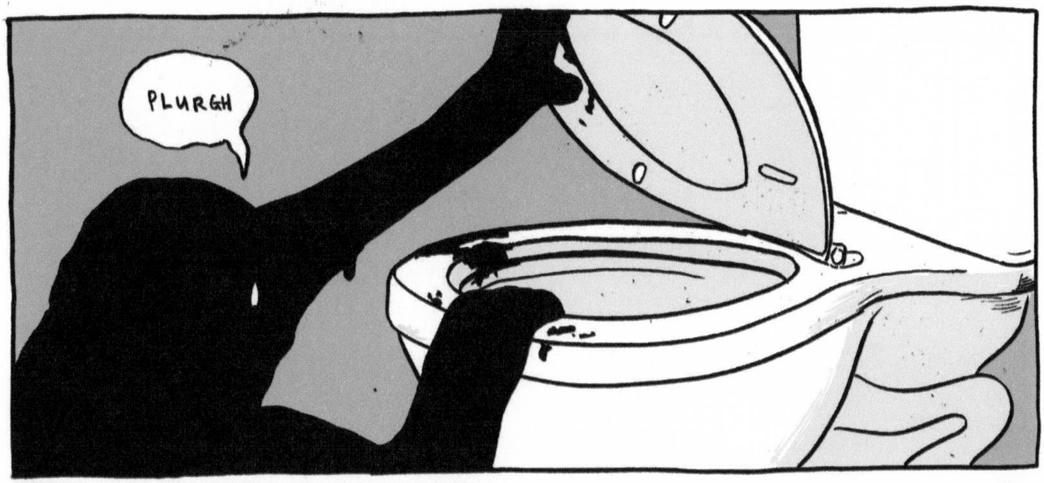
PLURGH

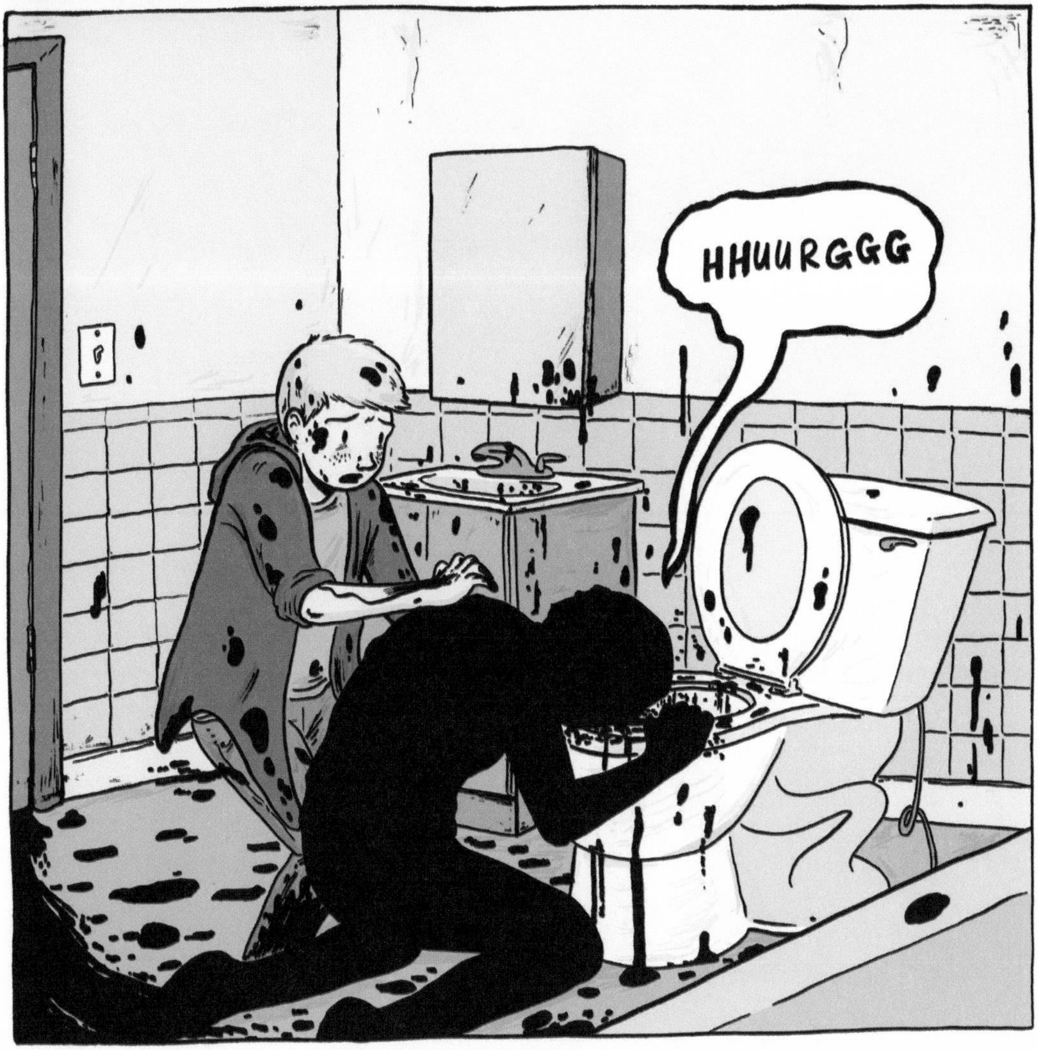
HHUURGGG

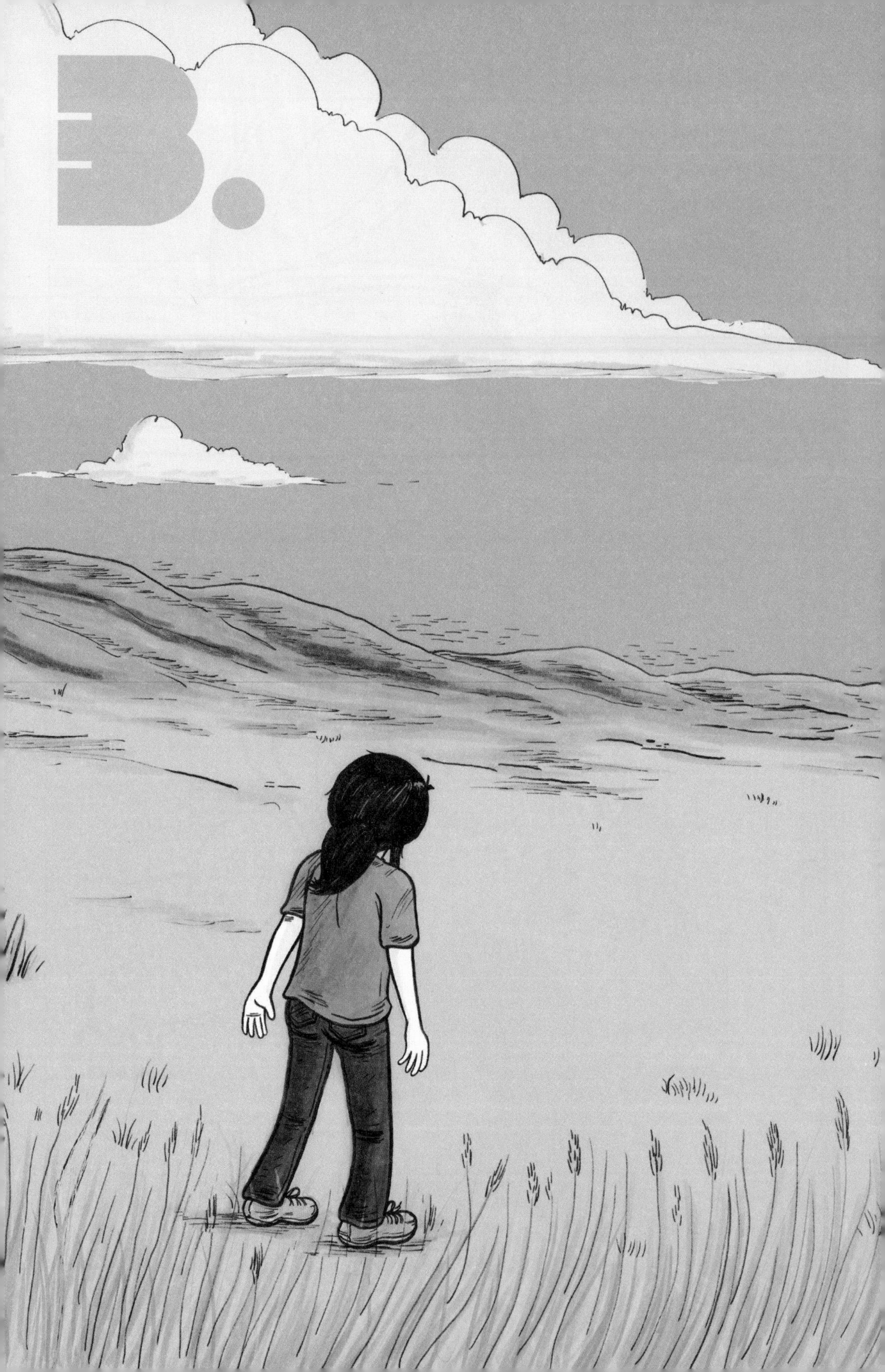
B.

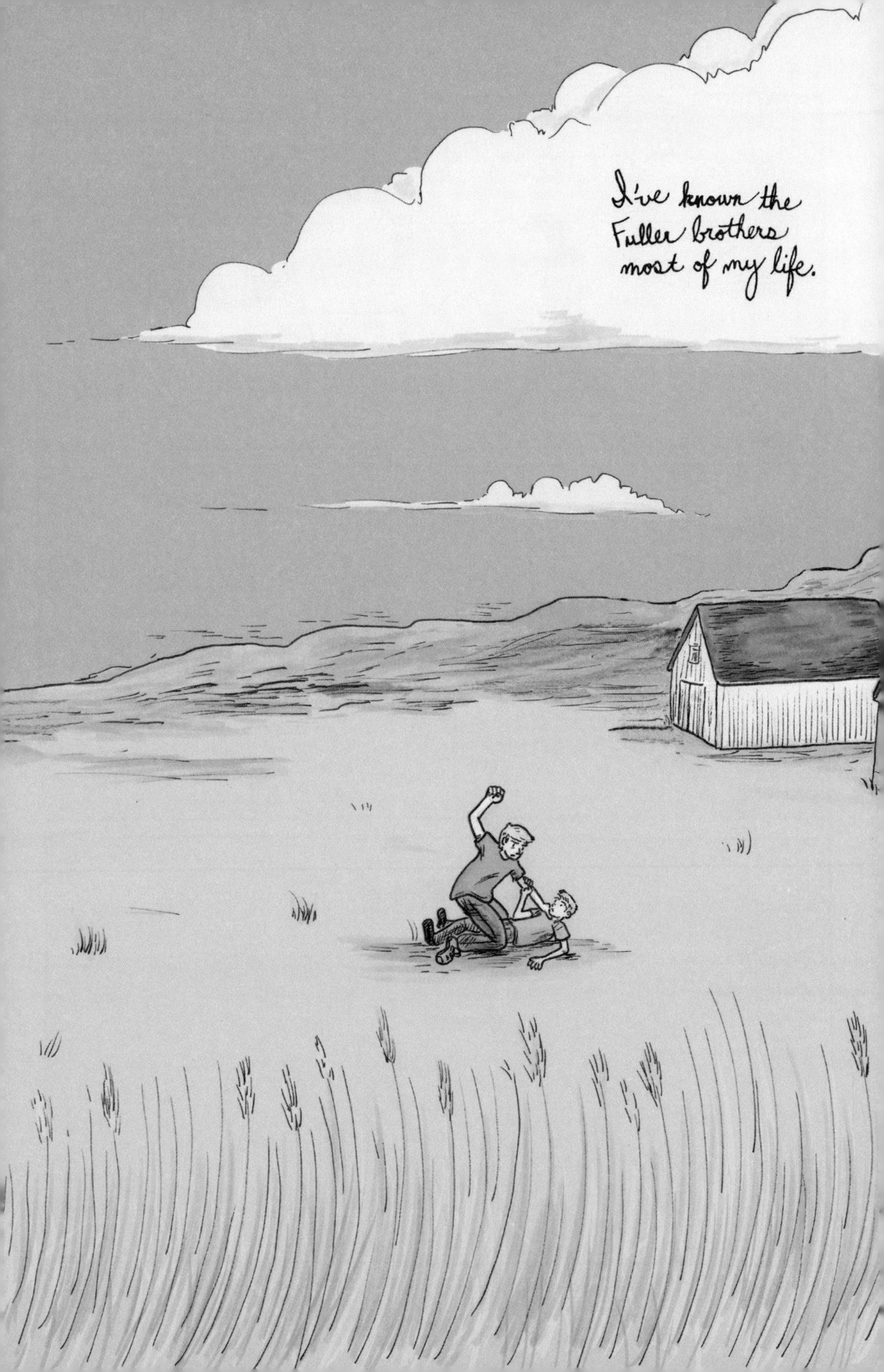
I've known the Fuller brothers most of my life.

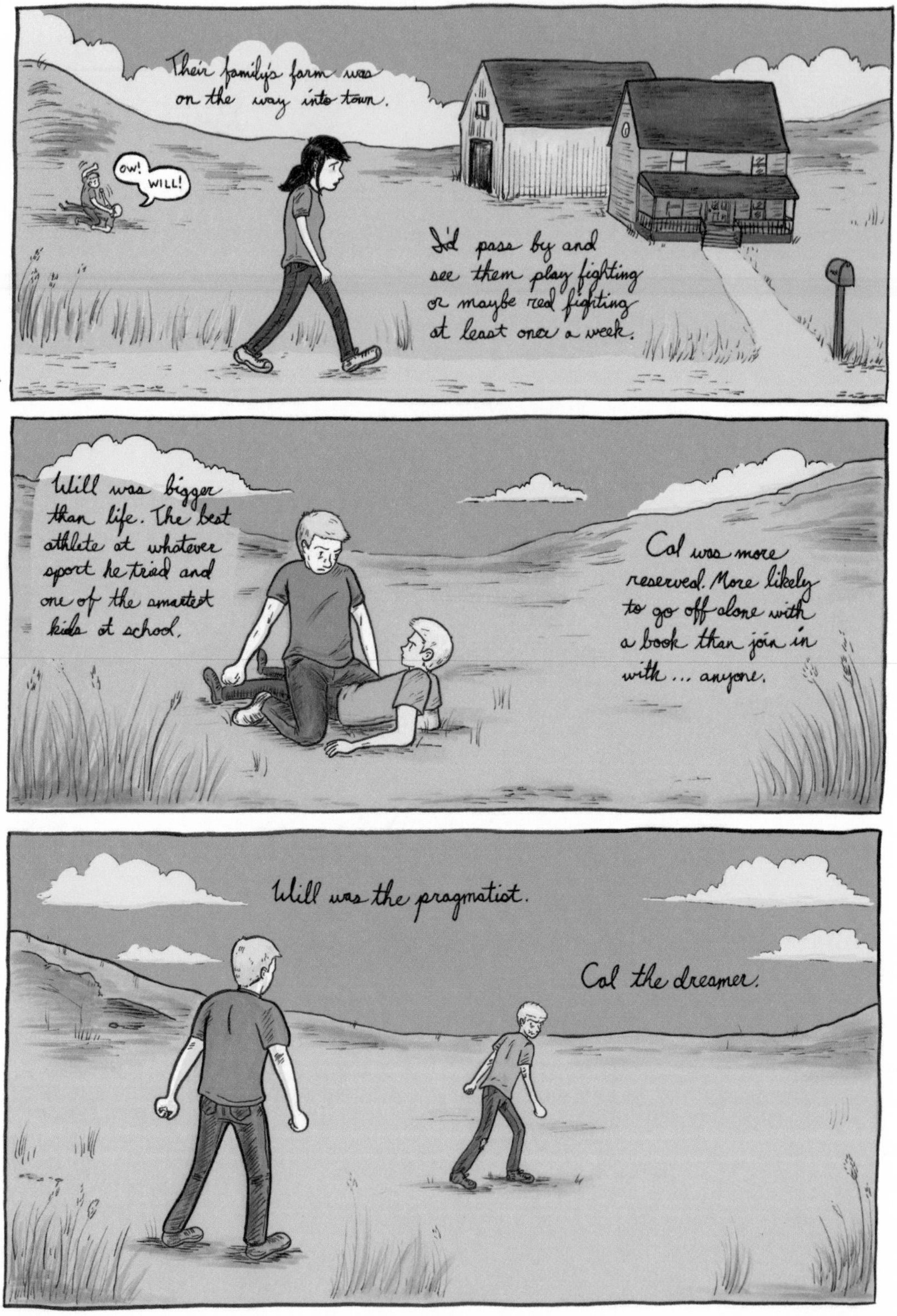
Their family's farm was on the way into town.
OW! WILL!
I'd pass by and see them play fighting or maybe real fighting at least once a week.
Will was bigger than life. The best athlete at whatever sport he tried and one of the smartest kids at school.
Cal was more reserved. More likely to go off alone with a book than join in with ... anyone.
Will was the pragmatist.
Cal the dreamer.

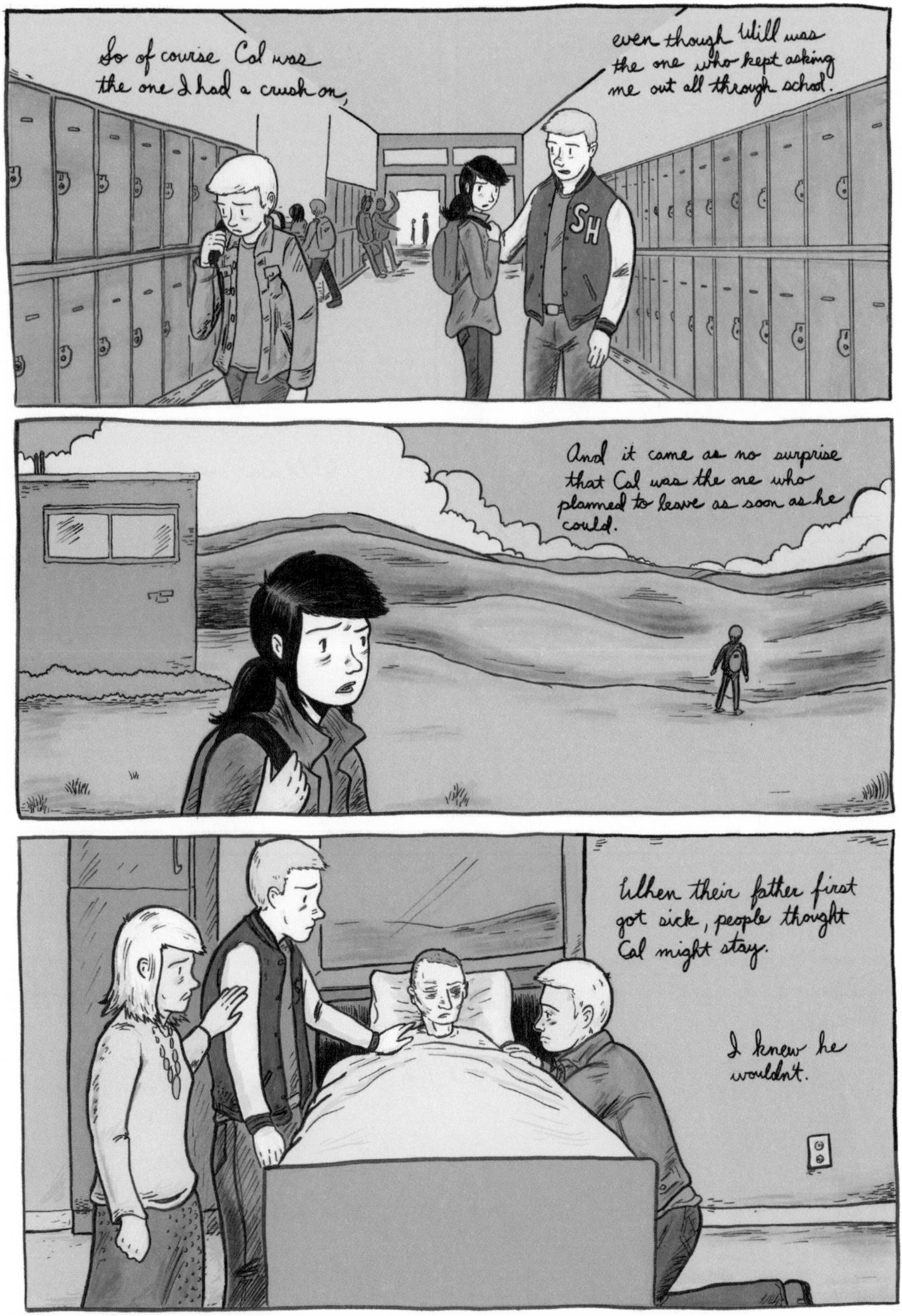
So of course Cal was the one I had a crush on,
even though Will was the one who kept asking me out all through school.
SH
And it came as no surprise that Cal was the one who planned to leave as soon as he could.
When their father first got sick, people thought Cal might stay.
I knew he wouldn't.

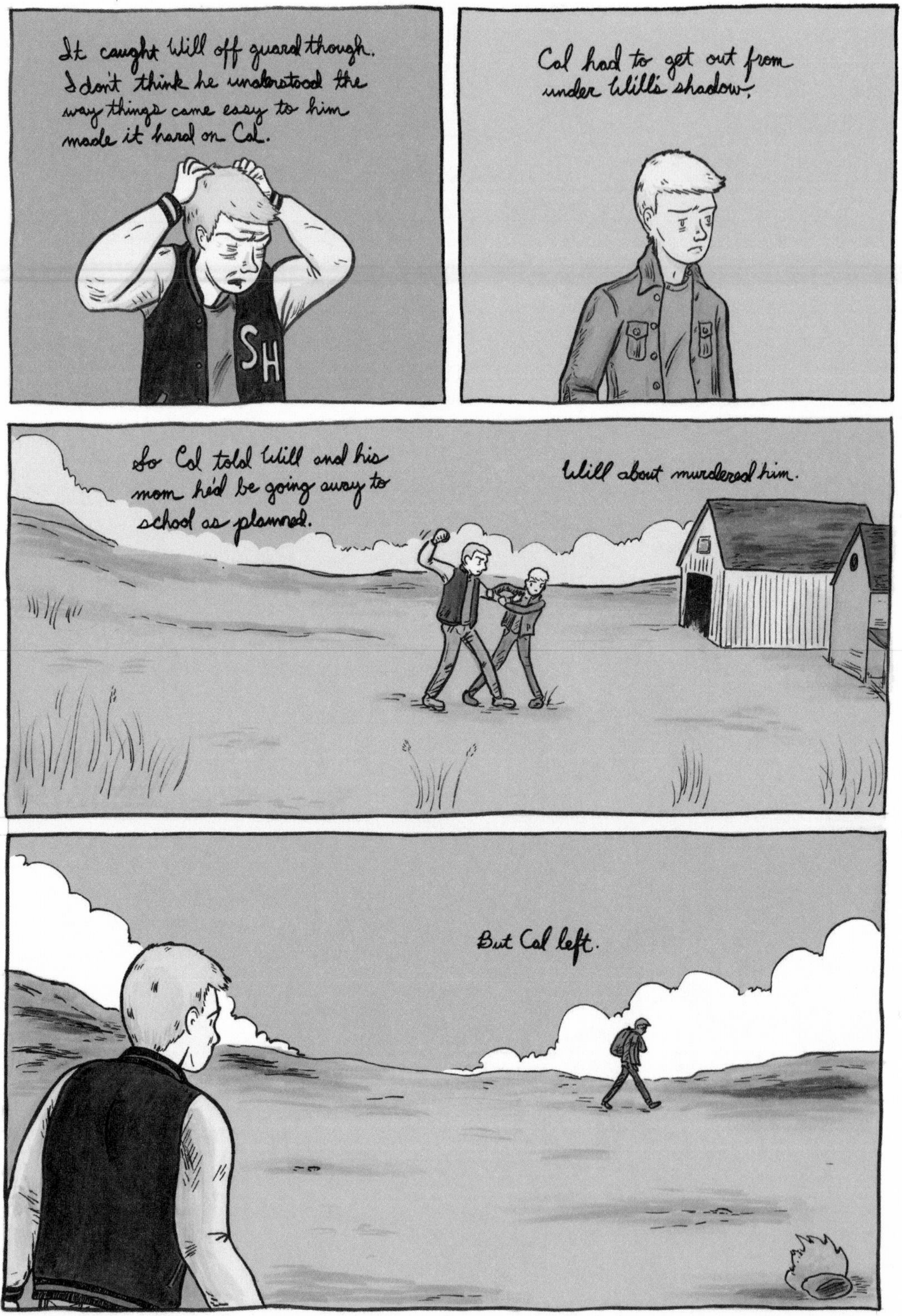
It caught Will off guard though. I don't think he understood the way things came easy to him made it hard on Cal.
Cal had to get out from under Will's shadow.
So Cal told Will and his mom he'd be going away to school as planned.
Will about murdered him.
But Cal left.

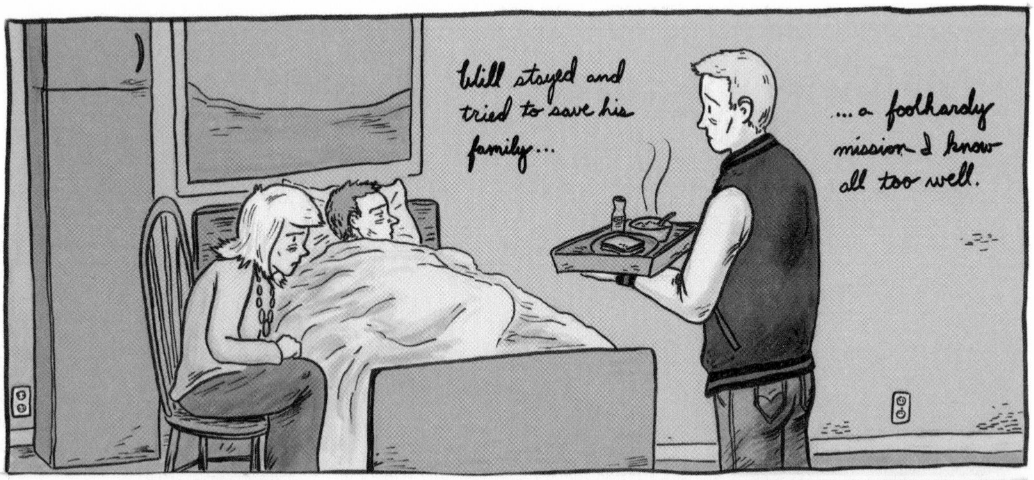
Will stayed and tried to save his family...
...a foolhardy mission I know all too well.

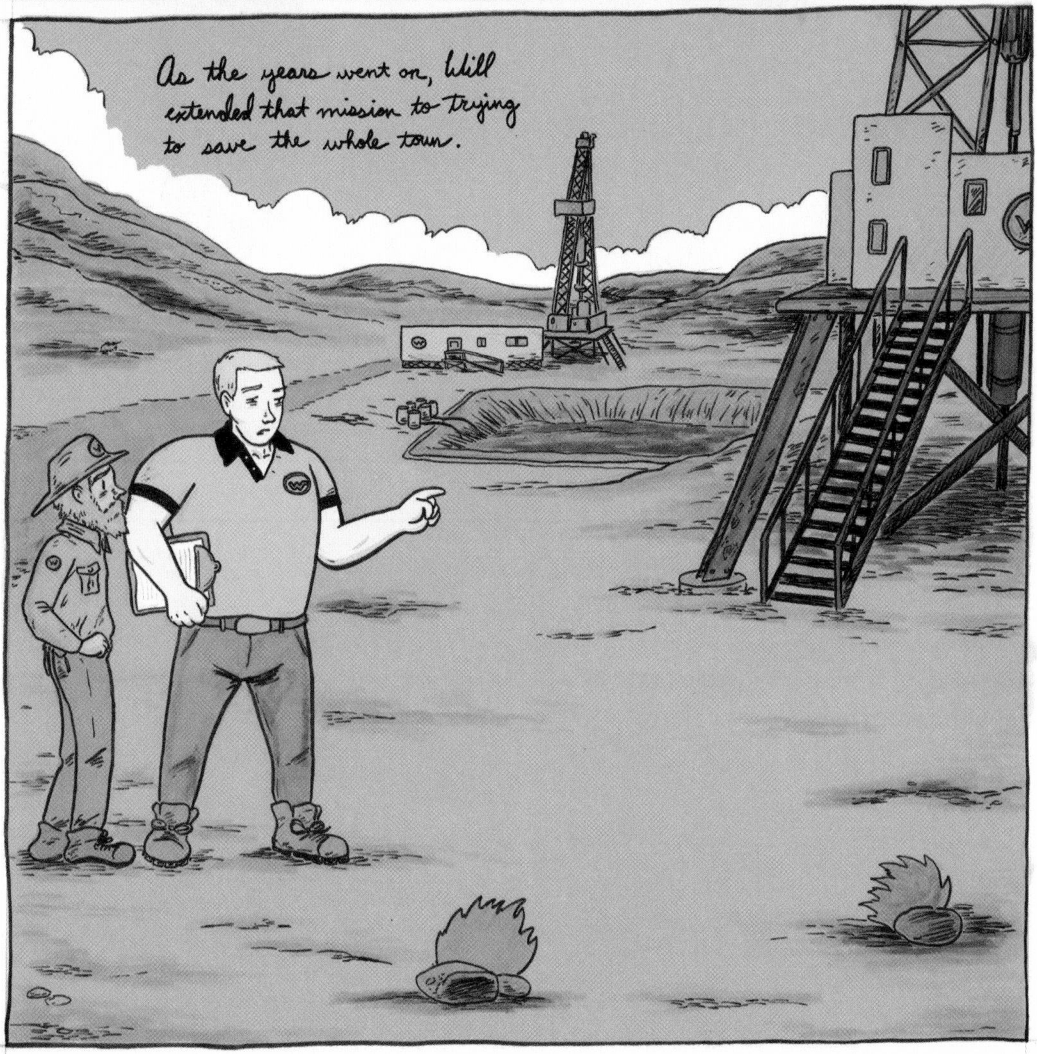
As the years went on, Will extended that mission to trying to save the whole town.

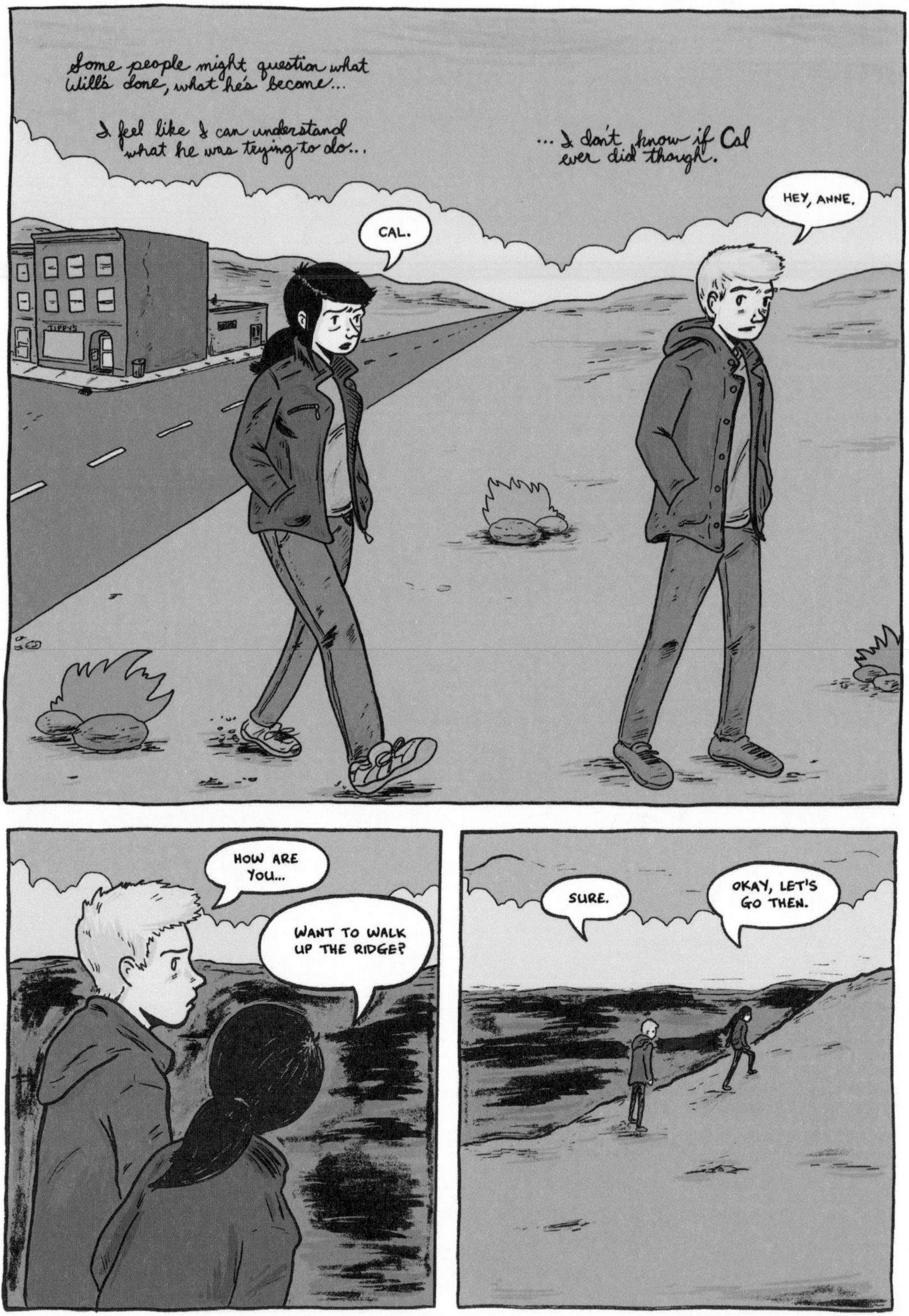
Some people might question what Will's done, what he's become...
I feel like I can understand what he was trying to do...
... I don't know if Cal ever did though.
CAL.
HEY, ANNE.
HOW ARE YOU...
WANT TO WALK UP THE RIDGE?
SURE.
OKAY, LET'S GO THEN.

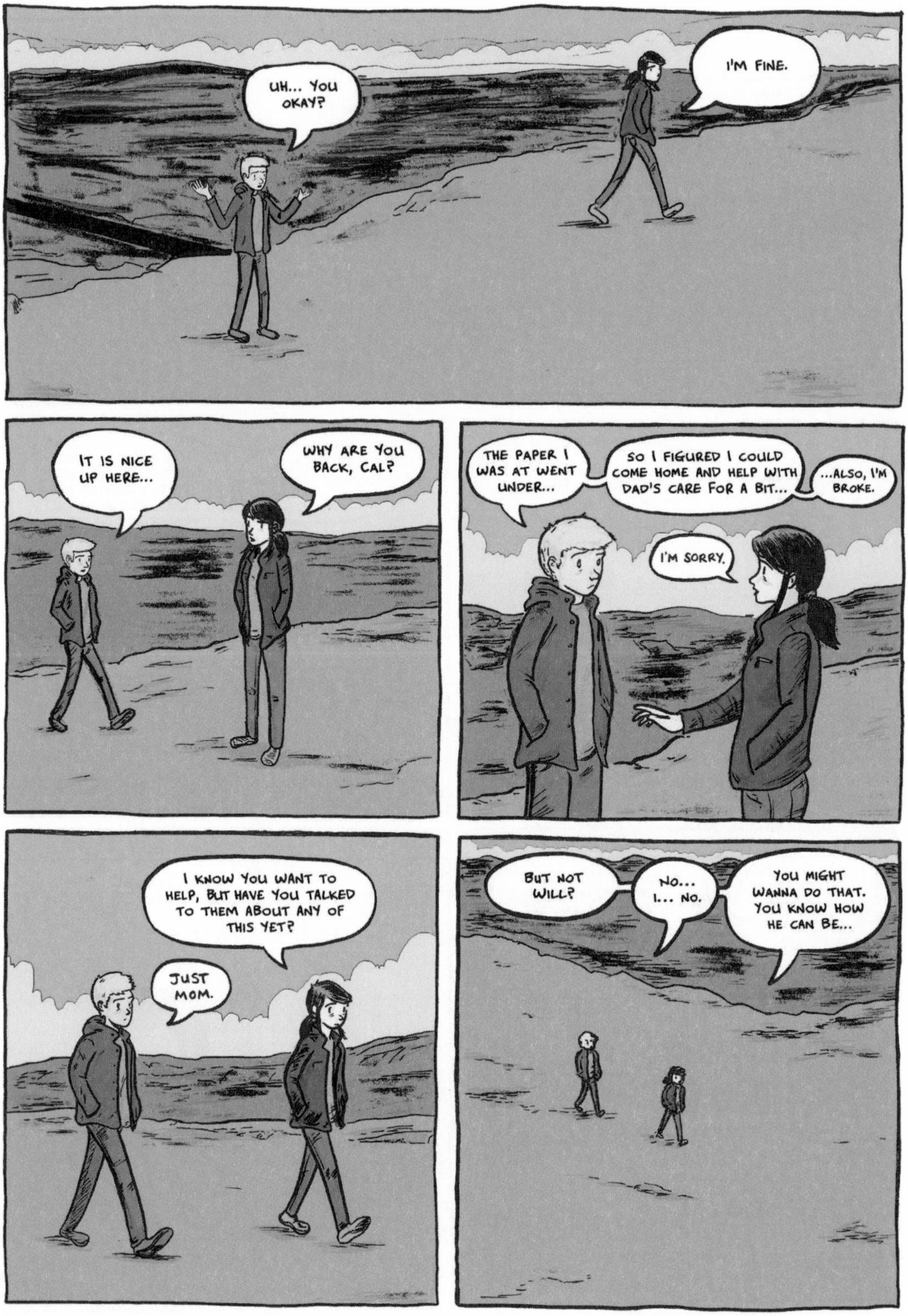
UH... YOU OKAY?
I'M FINE.
IT IS NICE UP HERE...
WHY ARE YOU BACK, CAL?
THE PAPER I WAS AT WENT UNDER...
SO I FIGURED I COULD COME HOME AND HELP WITH DAD'S CARE FOR A BIT...
...ALSO, I'M BROKE.
I'M SORRY.
I KNOW YOU WANT TO HELP, BUT HAVE YOU TALKED TO THEM ABOUT ANY OF THIS YET?
JUST MOM.
BUT NOT WILL?
NO... I... NO.
YOU MIGHT WANNA DO THAT. YOU KNOW HOW HE CAN BE...

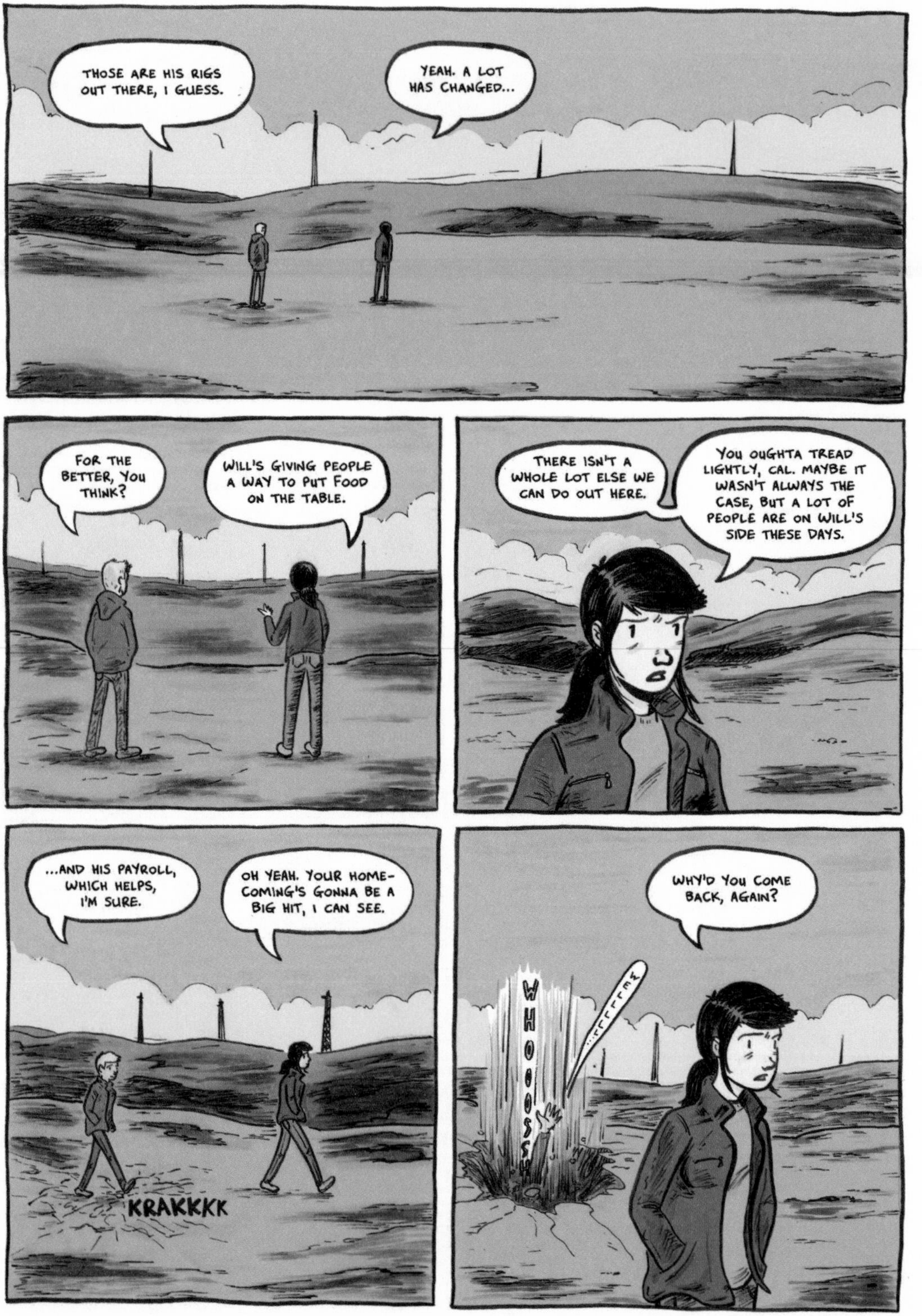
THOSE ARE HIS RIGS OUT THERE, I GUESS.
YEAH. A LOT HAS CHANGED...
FOR THE BETTER, YOU THINK?
WILL'S GIVING PEOPLE A WAY TO PUT FOOD ON THE TABLE.
THERE ISN'T A WHOLE LOT ELSE WE CAN DO OUT HERE.
YOU OUGHTA TREAD LIGHTLY, CAL. MAYBE IT WASN'T ALWAYS THE CASE, BUT A LOT OF PEOPLE ARE ON WILL'S SIDE THESE DAYS.
...AND HIS PAYROLL, WHICH HELPS, I'M SURE.
OH YEAH. YOUR HOME-COMING'S GONNA BE A BIG HIT, I CAN SEE.
KRAKKKK
WHOOOOSH
WHY'D YOU COME BACK, AGAIN?

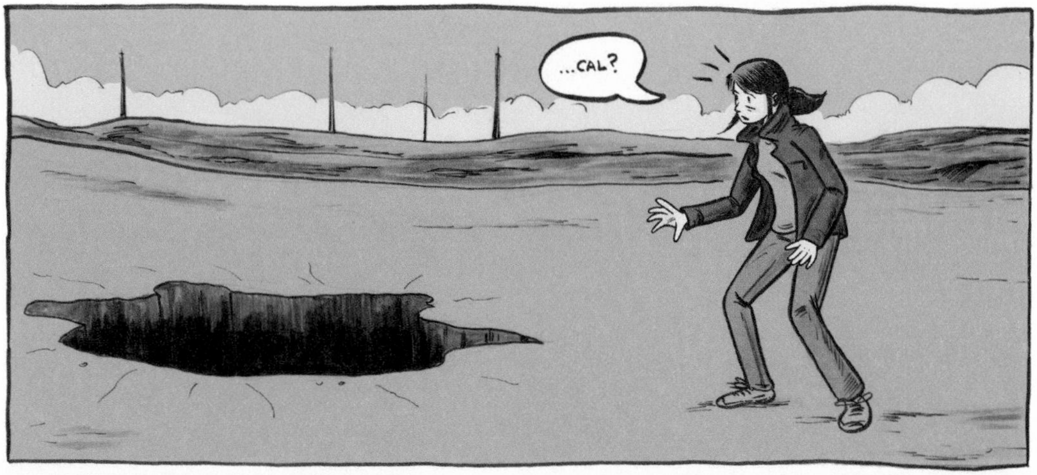
...CAL?

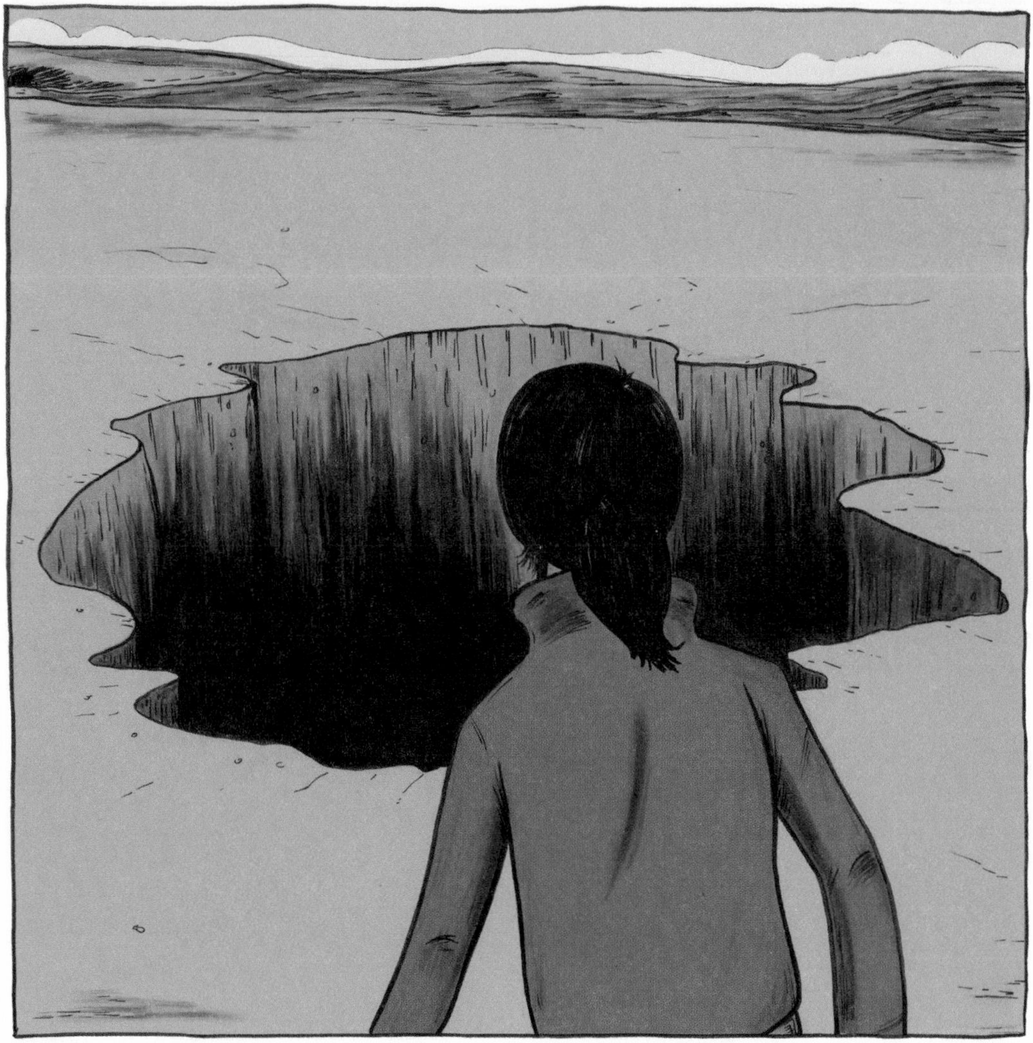

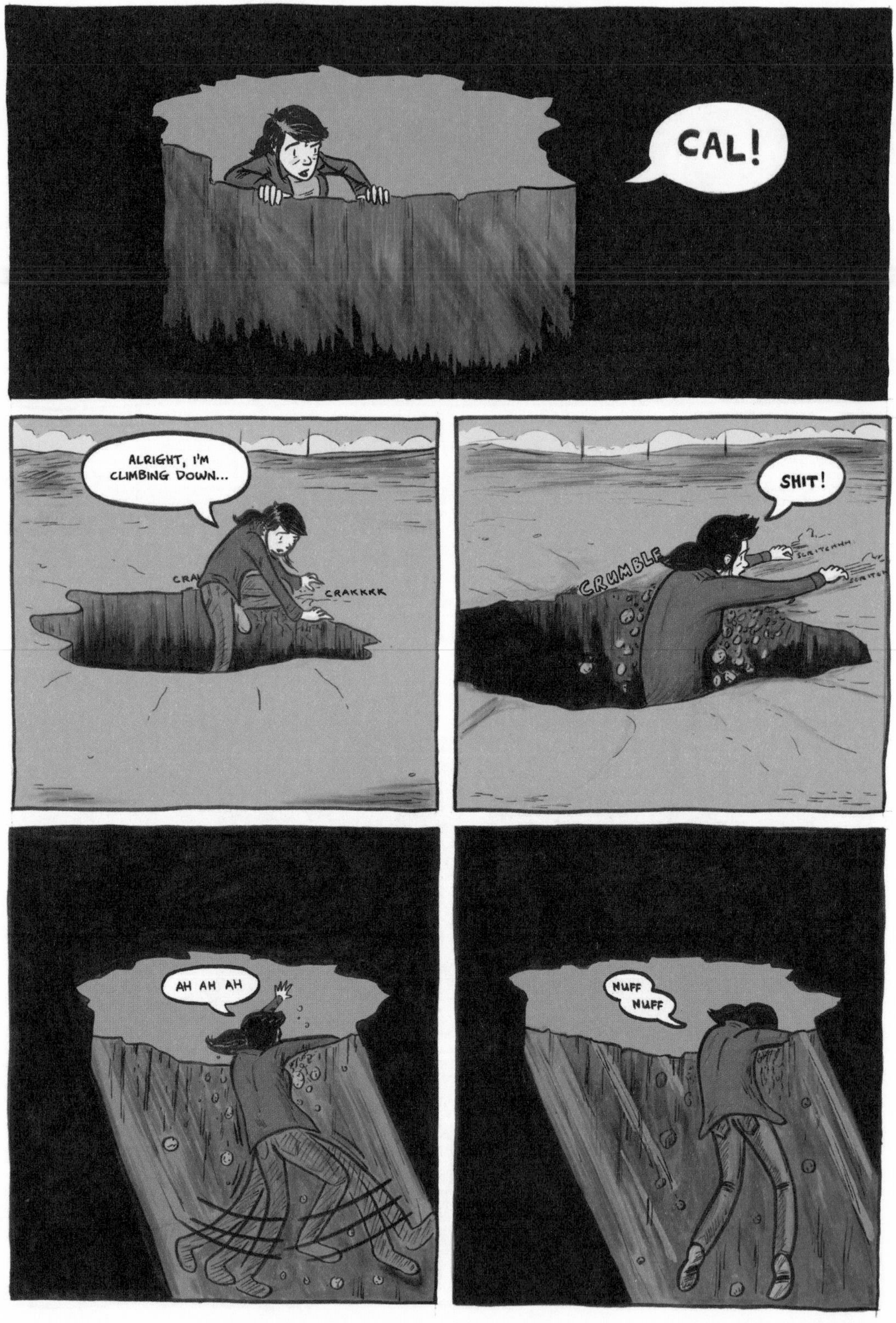
CAL!
ALRIGHT, I'M CLIMBING DOWN...
CRAKKKK
SHIT!
CRUMBLE
SCRITCHHH
AH AH AH
NUFF NUFF

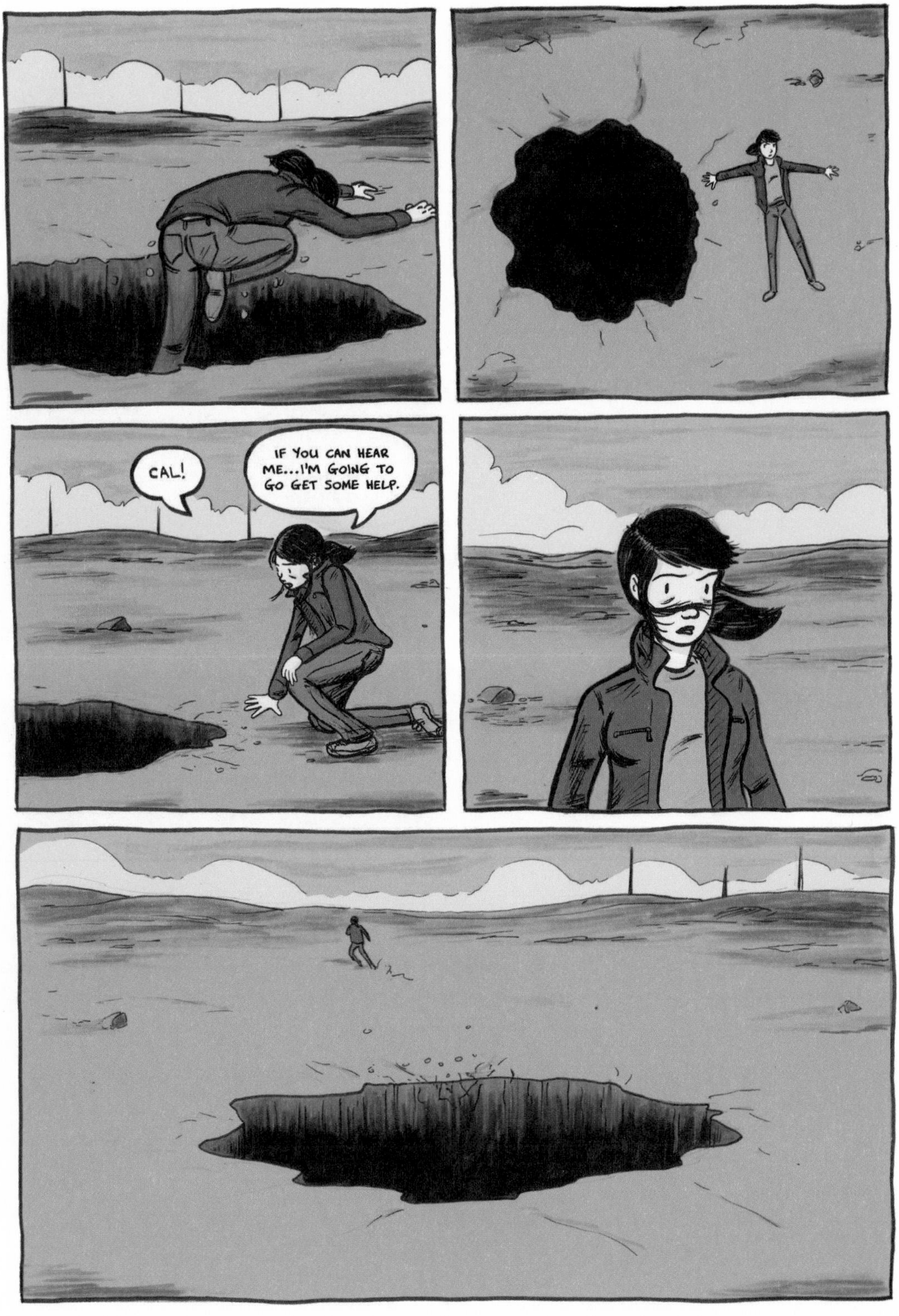
CAL!
IF YOU CAN HEAR ME...I'M GOING TO GO GET SOME HELP.

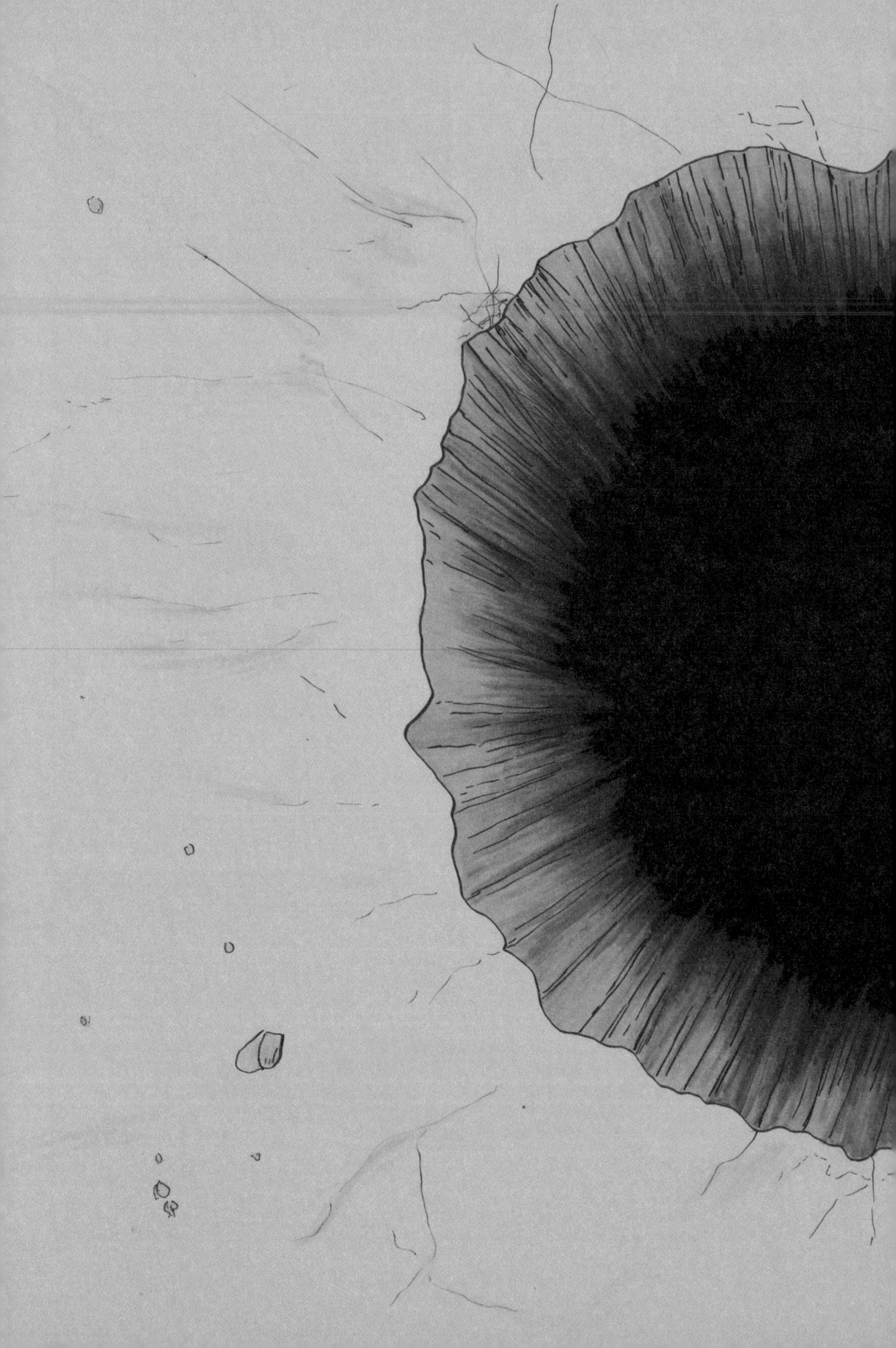

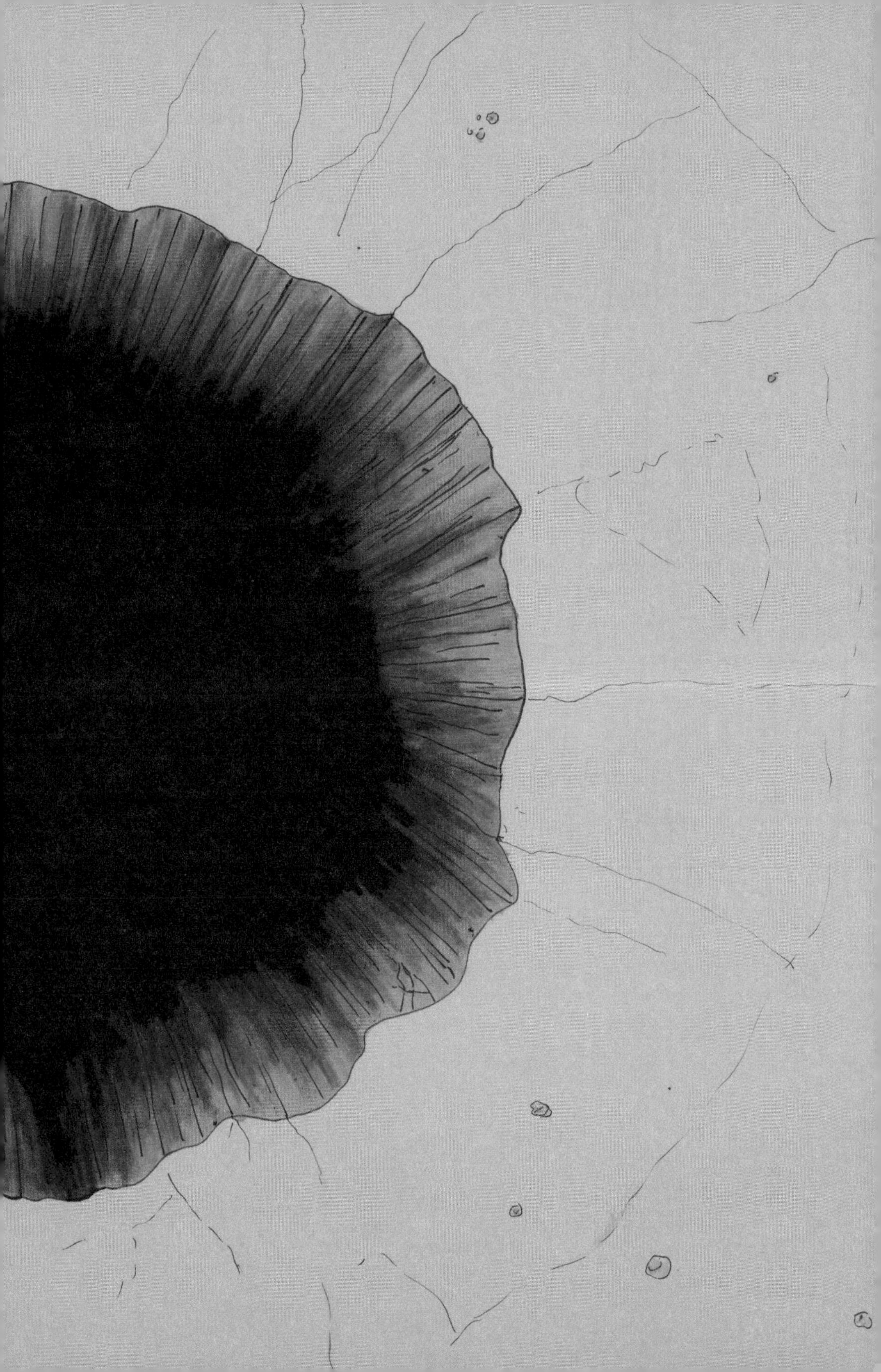

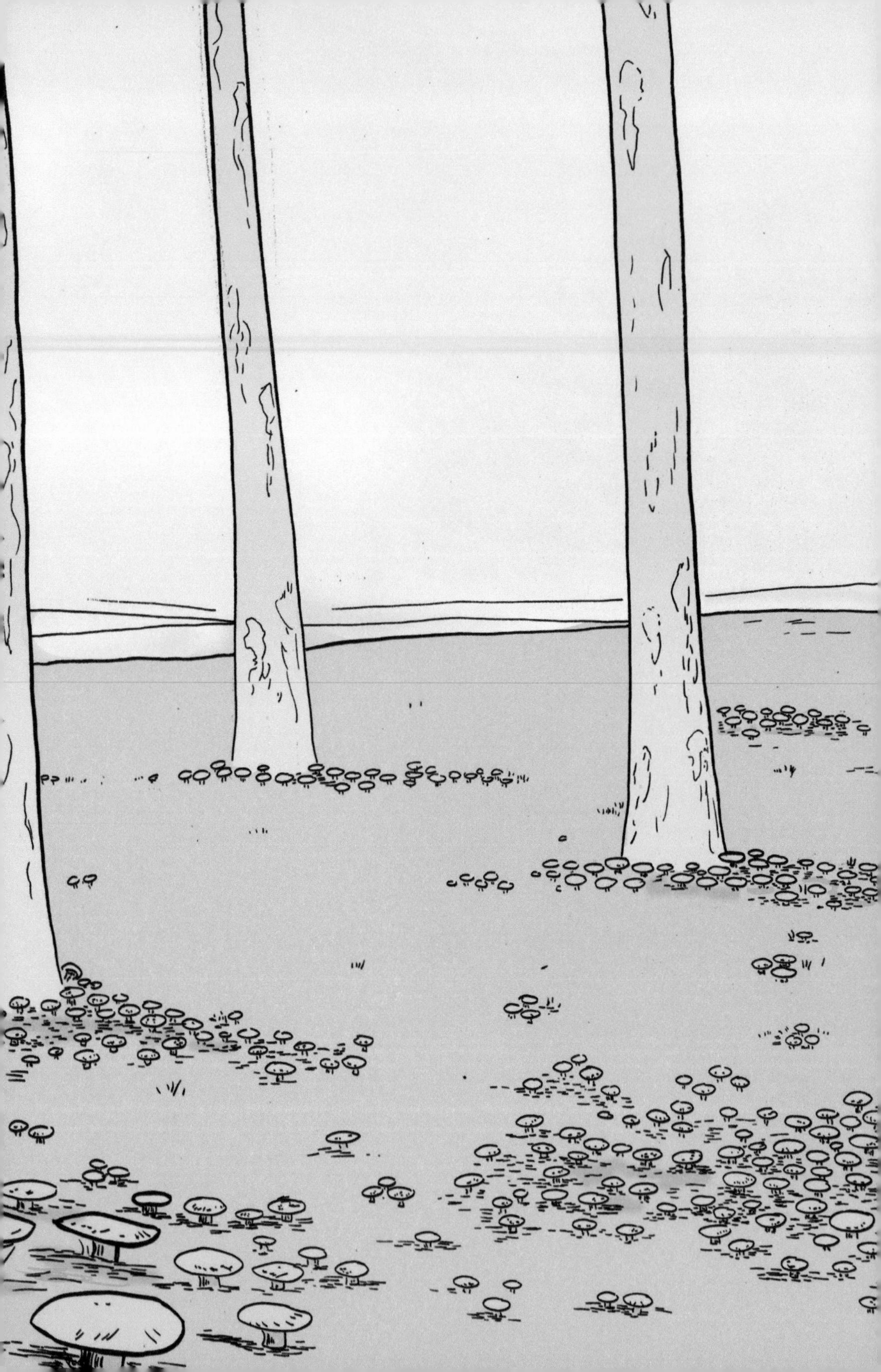

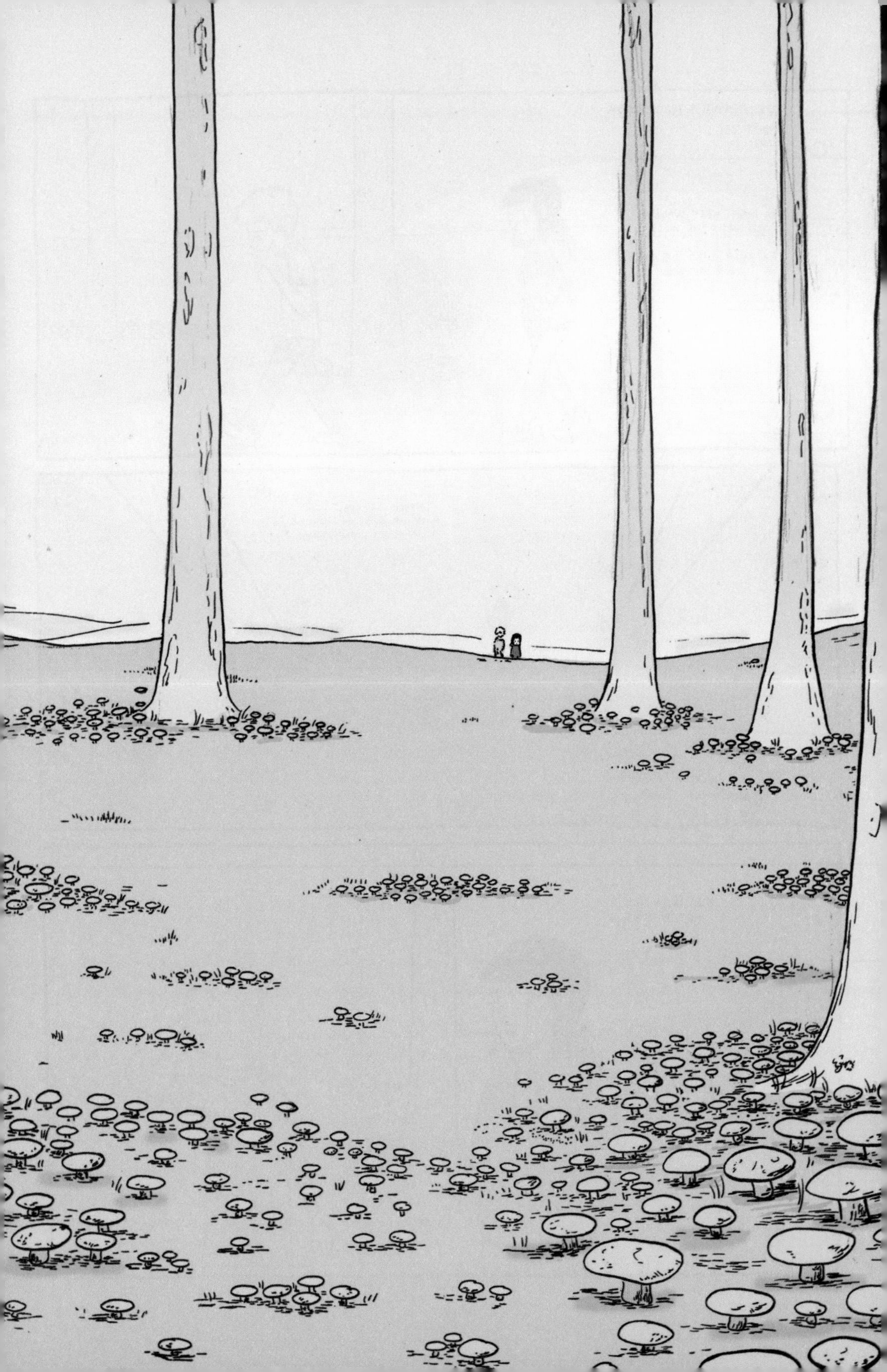

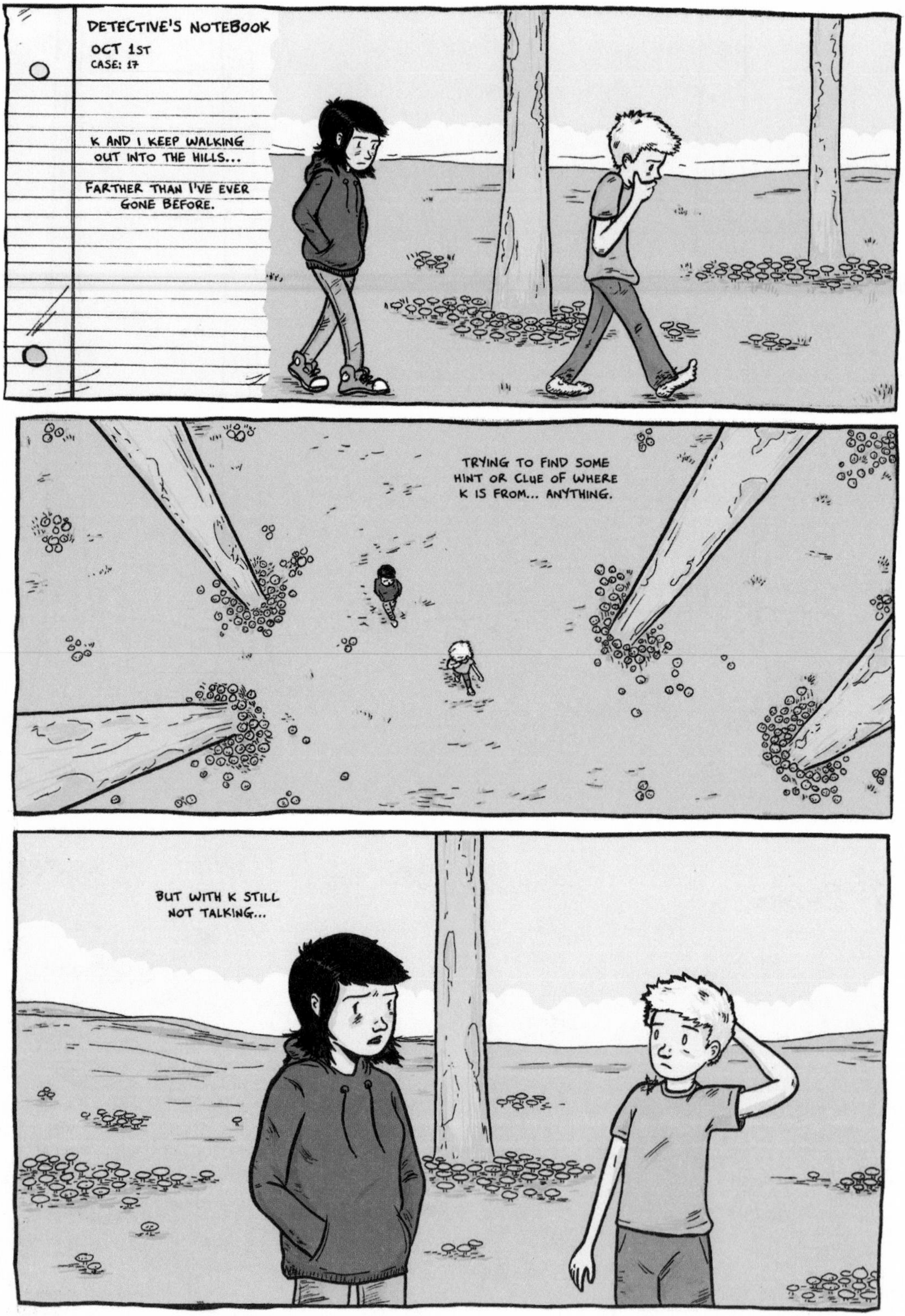
DETECTIVE'S NOTEBOOK
OCT 1ST
CASE: 17
K AND I KEEP WALKING OUT INTO THE HILLS...
FARTHER THAN I'VE EVER GONE BEFORE.
TRYING TO FIND SOME HINT OR CLUE OF WHERE K IS FROM... ANYTHING.
BUT WITH K STILL NOT TALKING...

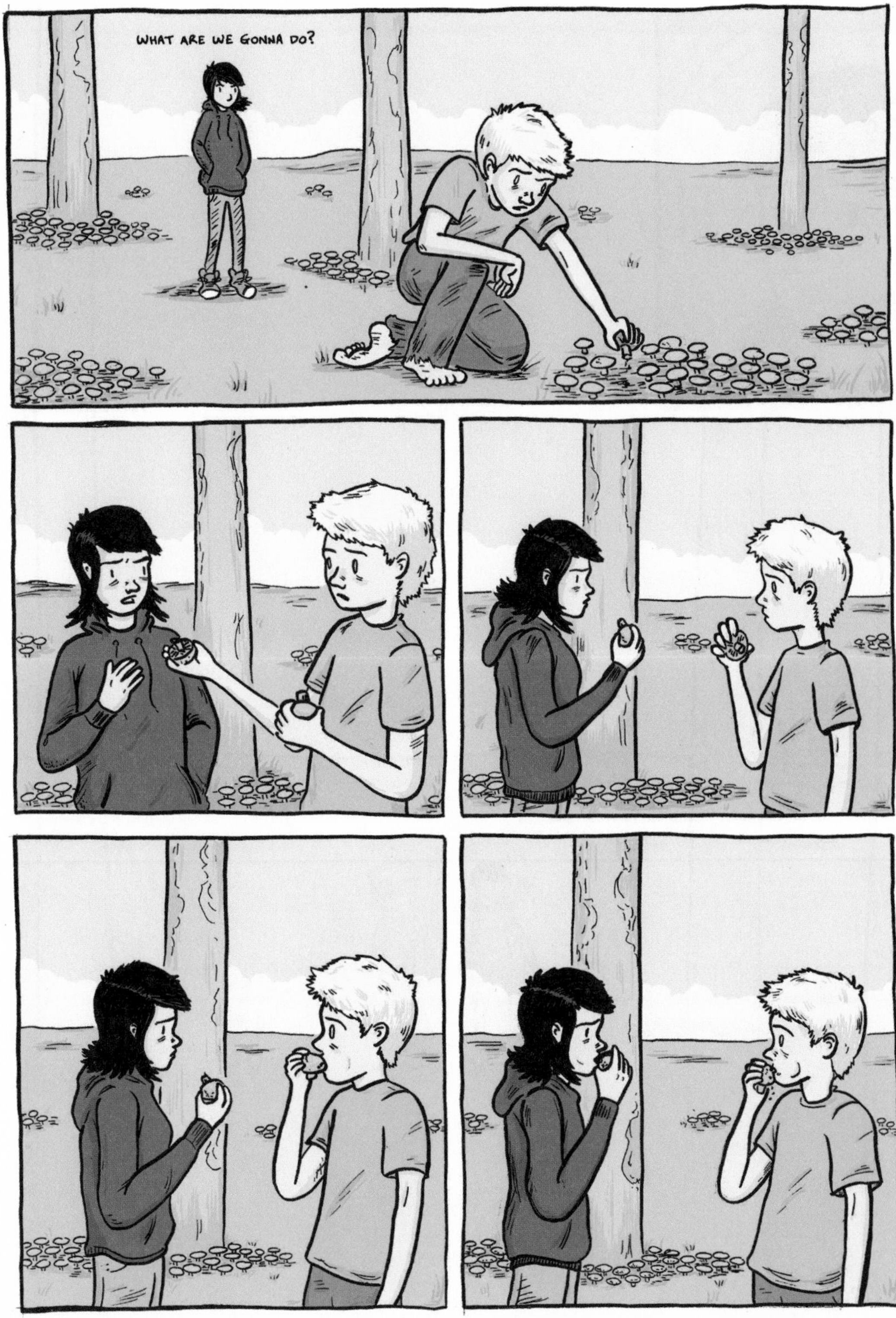
WHAT ARE WE GONNA DO?

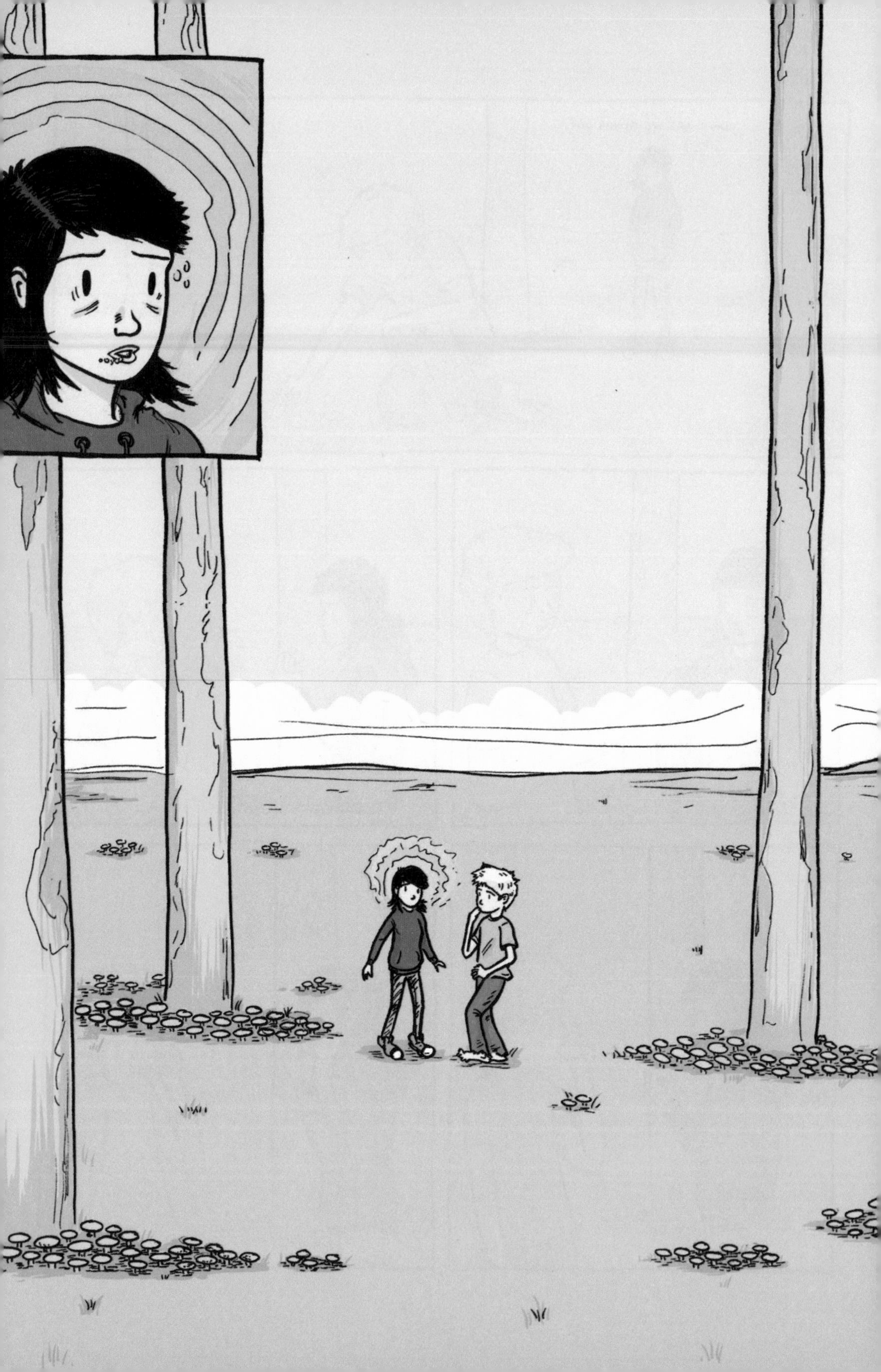

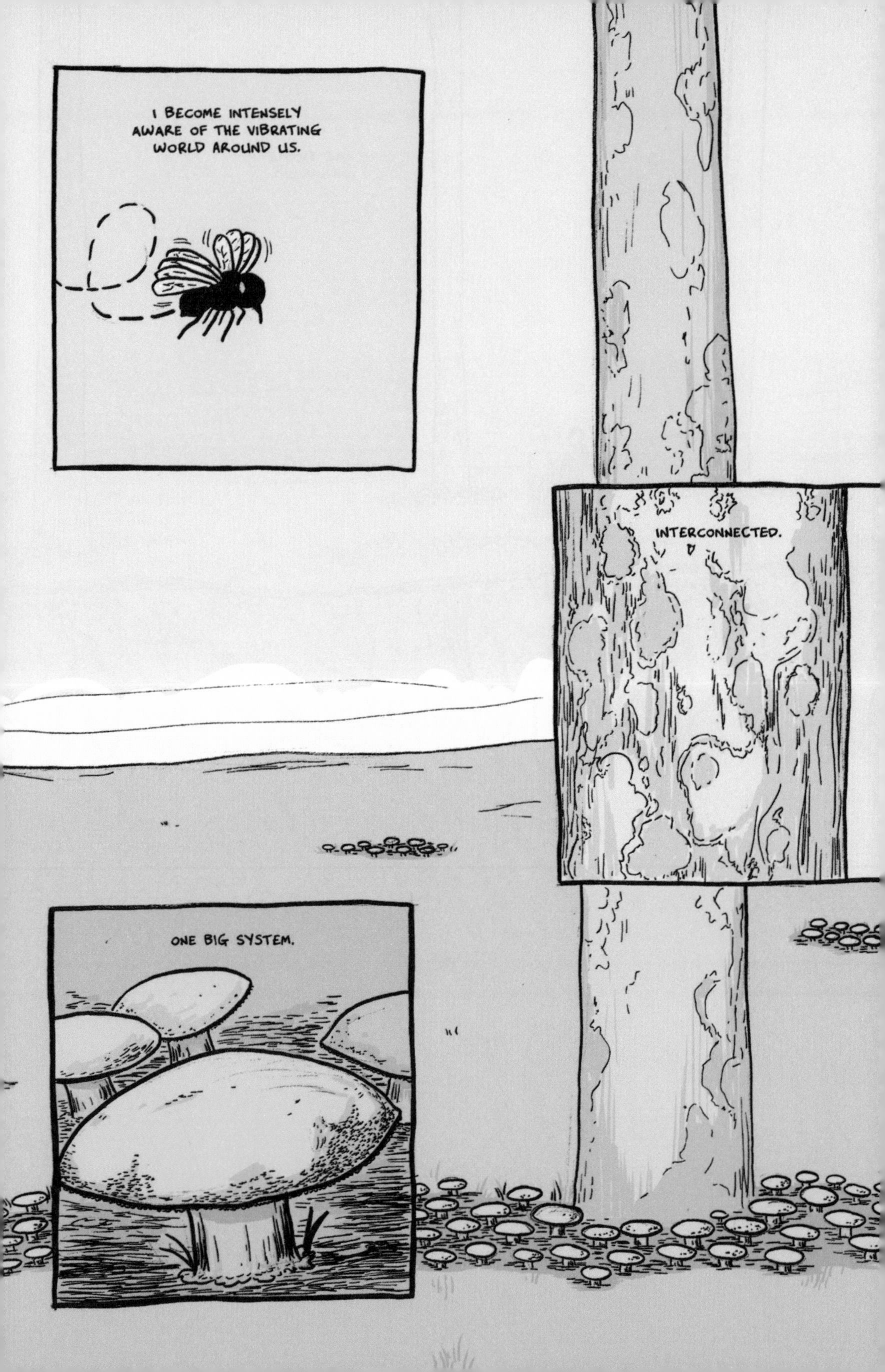
I BECOME INTENSELY AWARE OF THE VIBRATING WORLD AROUND US.
INTERCONNECTED.
ONE BIG SYSTEM.

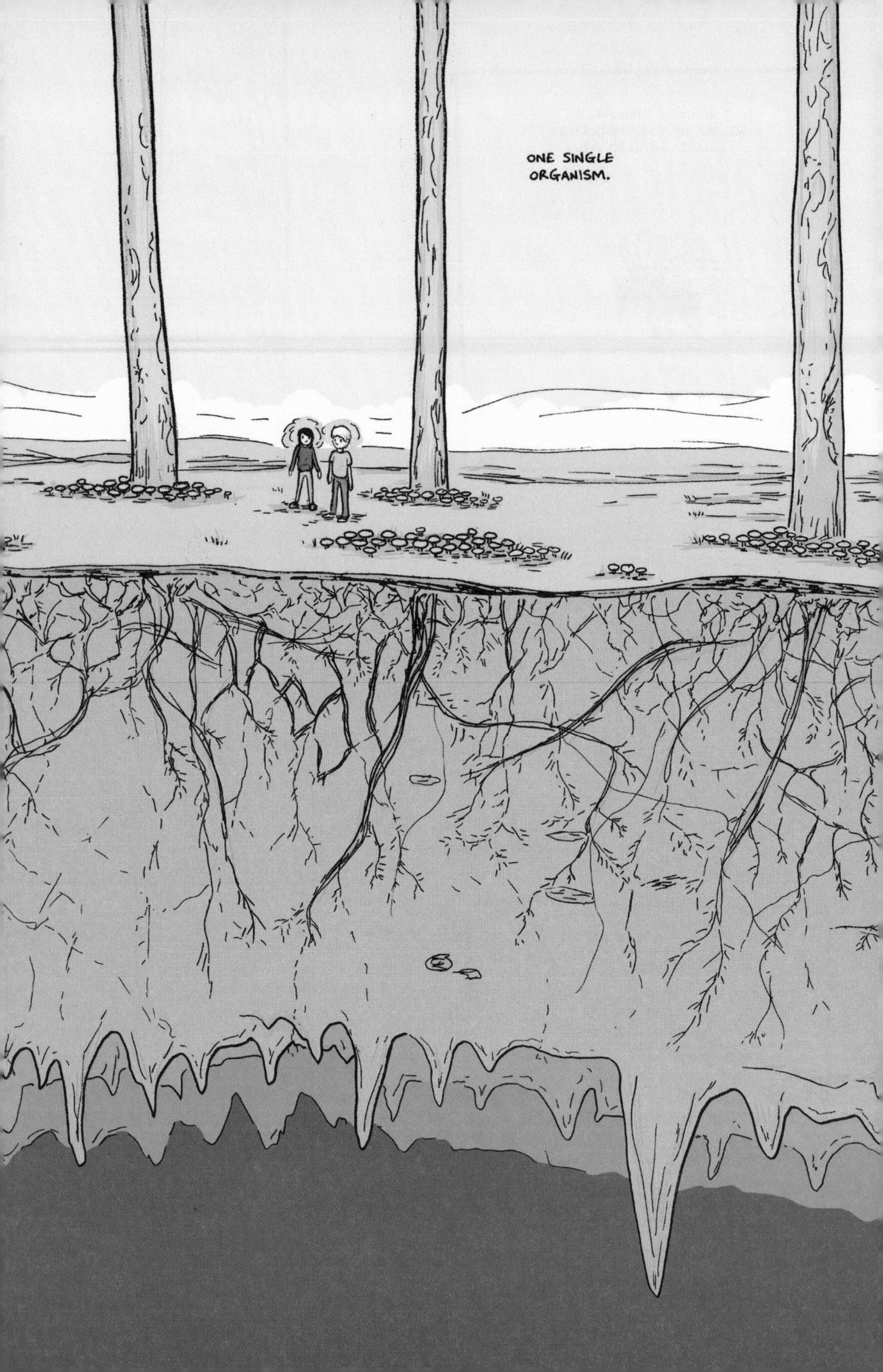
ONE SINGLE ORGANISM.

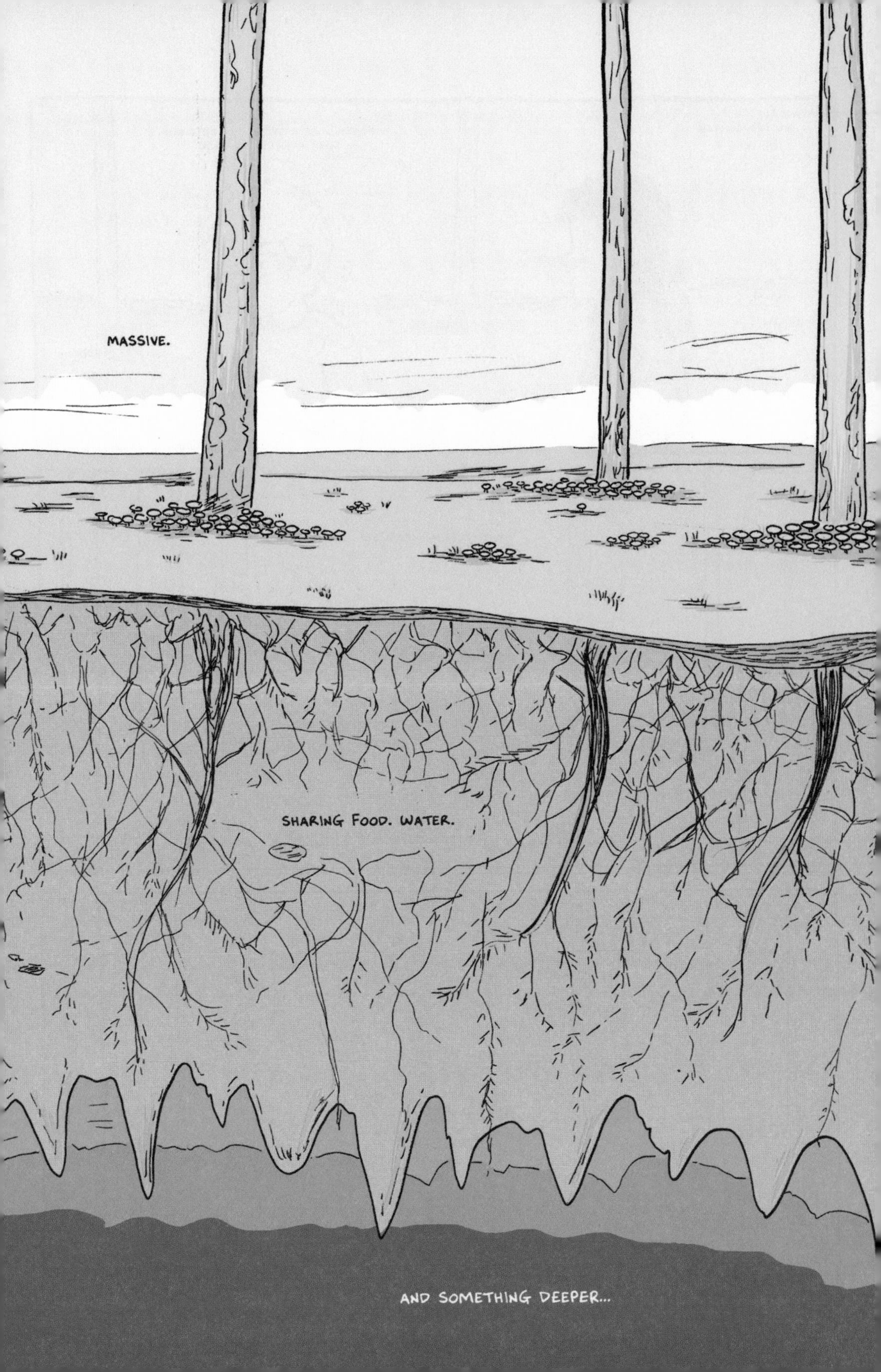
MASSIVE.
SHARING FOOD. WATER.
AND SOMETHING DEEPER...

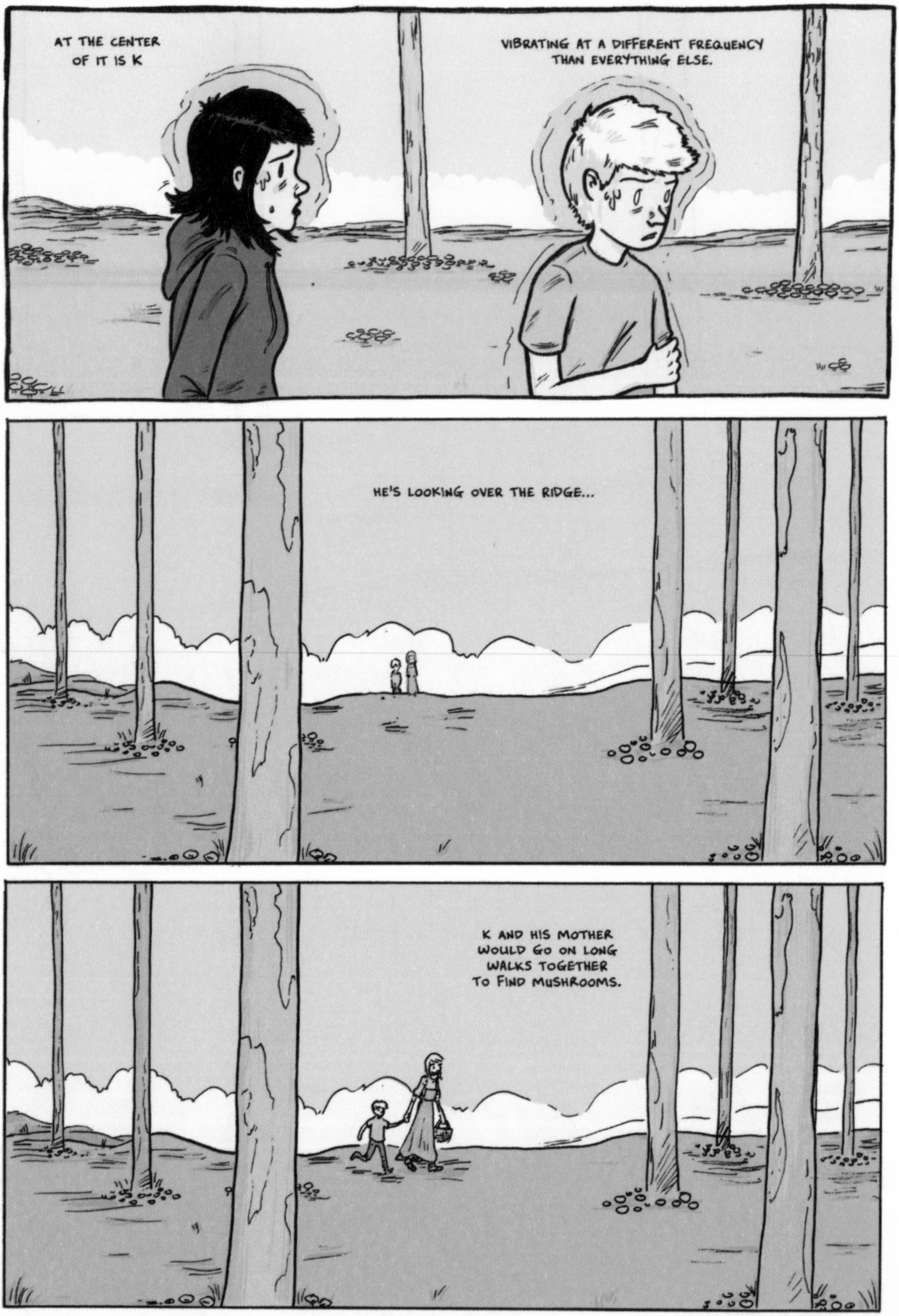
AT THE CENTER
OF IT IS K
VIBRATING AT A DIFFERENT FREQUENCY
THAN EVERYTHING ELSE.
HE'S LOOKING OVER THE RIDGE...
K AND HIS MOTHER
WOULD GO ON LONG
WALKS TOGETHER
TO FIND MUSHROOMS.

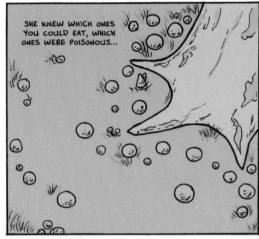

SHE KNEW WHICH ONES YOU COULD EAT, WHICH ONES WERE POISONOUS...

...AND WHICH ONES LET YOU SEE THINGS AND TALK WITHOUT USING YOUR VOICE...

WHAT WAS THAT? AM I SEEING WHAT HE WANTS ME TO SEE?

K STARTS WALKING AGAIN...

I FOLLOW.

9.

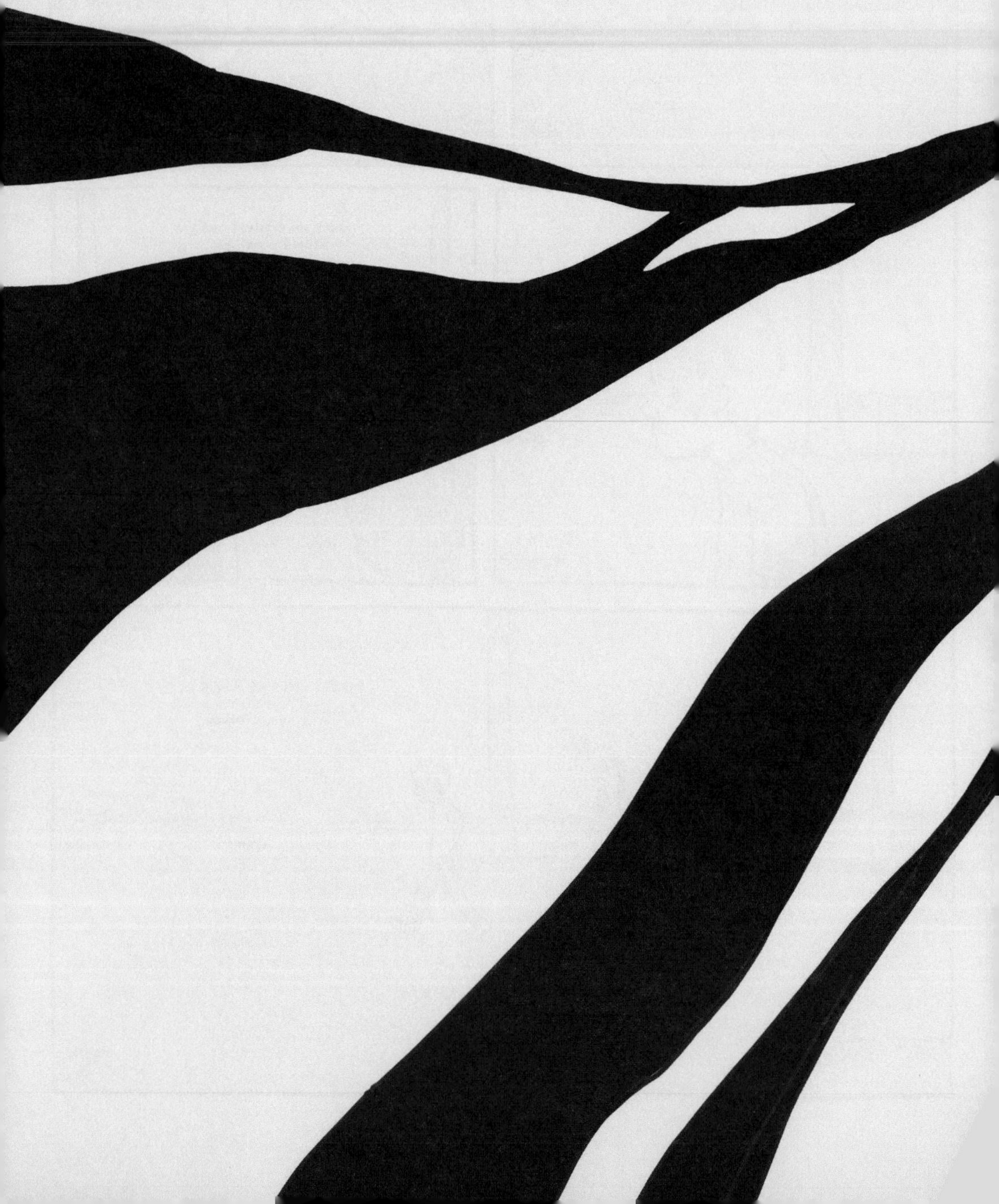

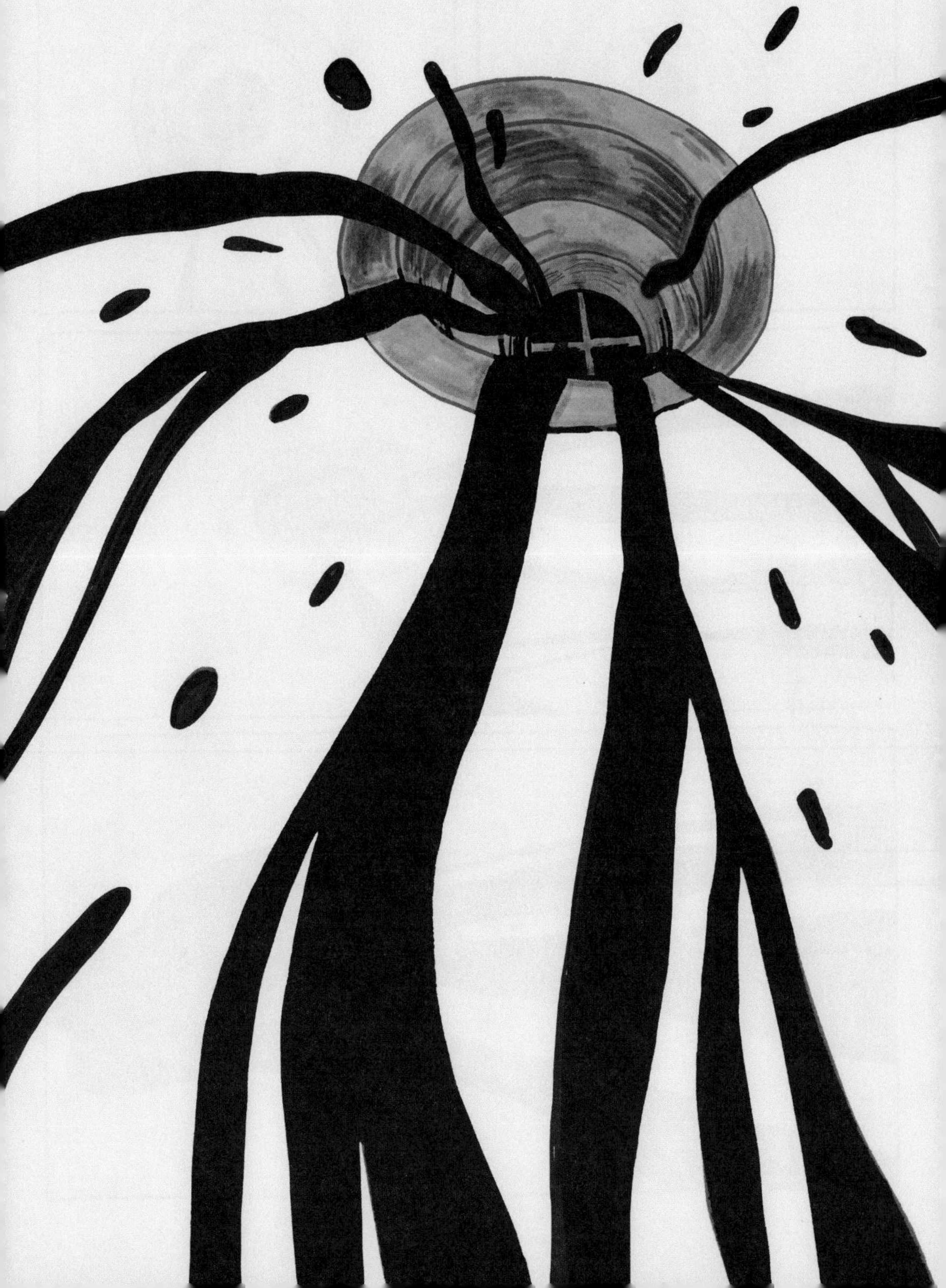

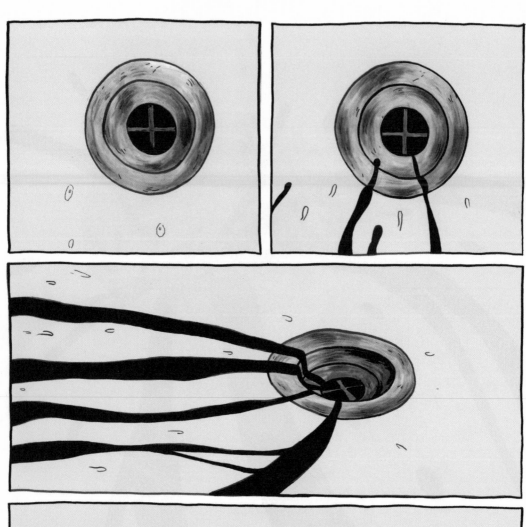

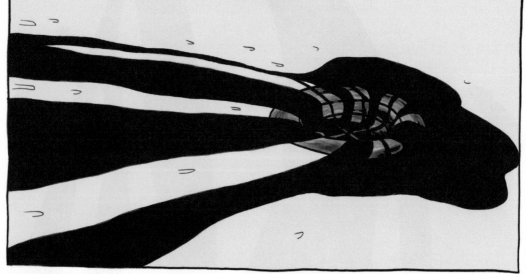

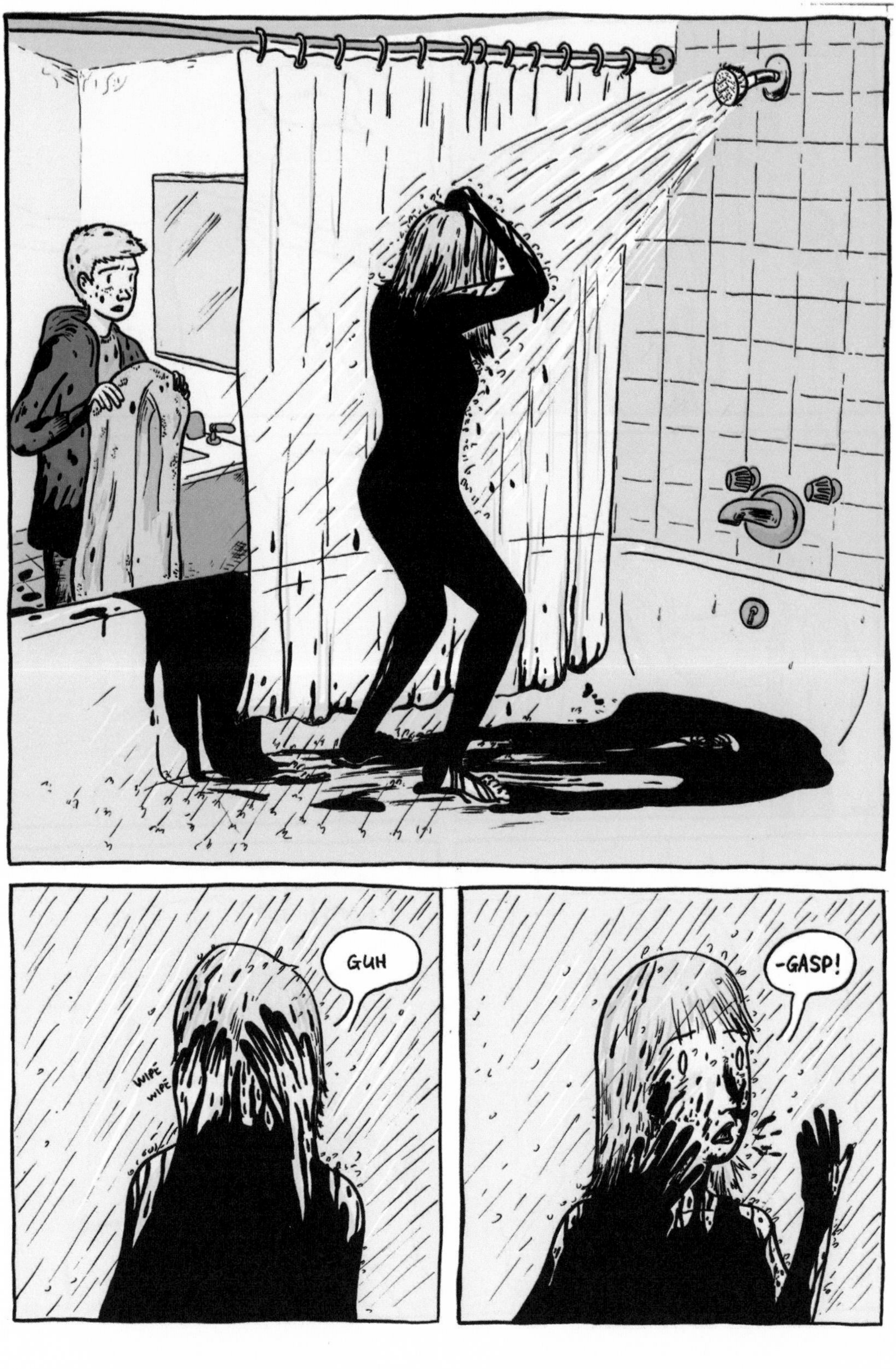
GUH
WIPE WIPE
-GASP!

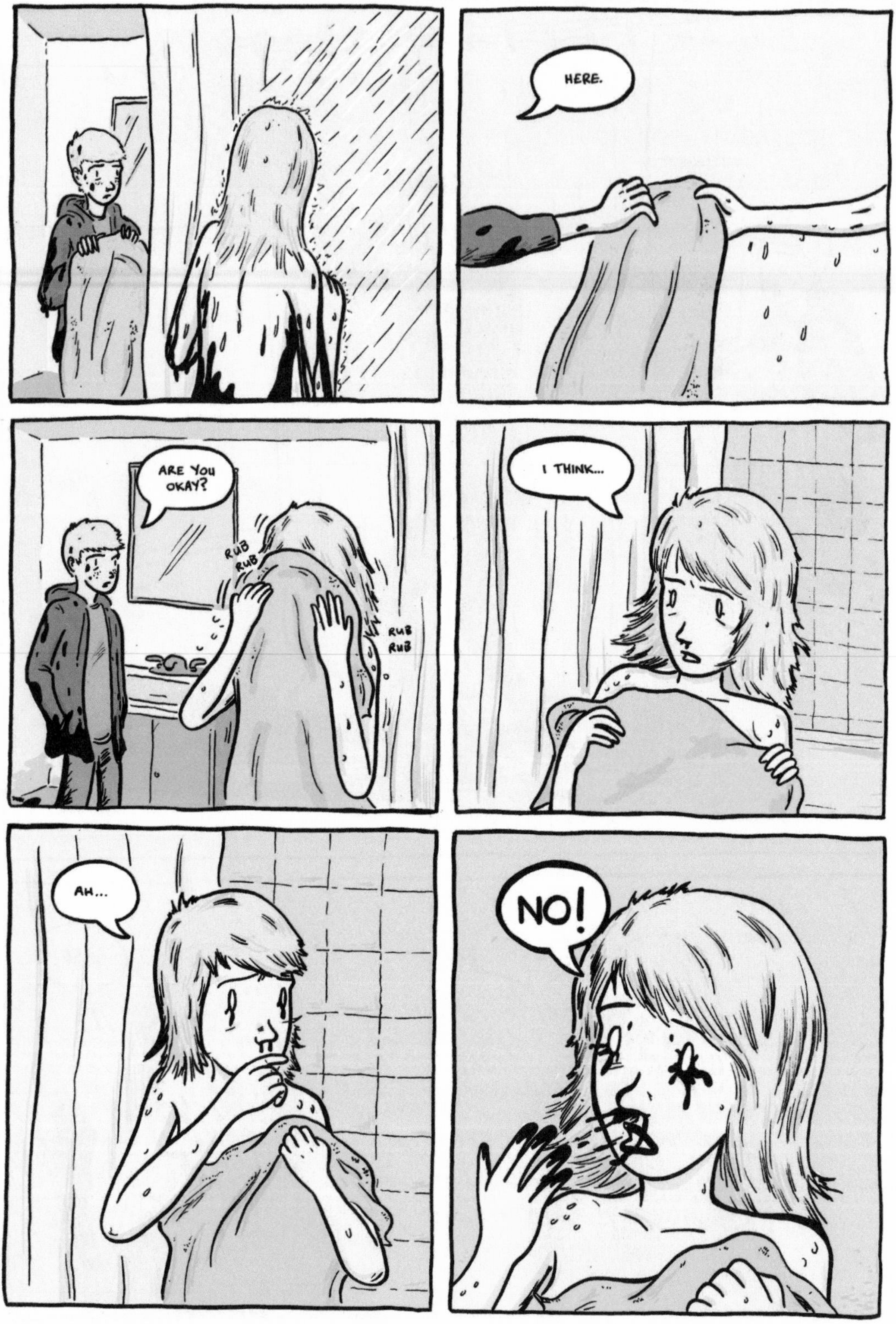
HERE.
ARE YOU OKAY?
RUB RUB
RUB RUB
I THINK...
AH...
NO!

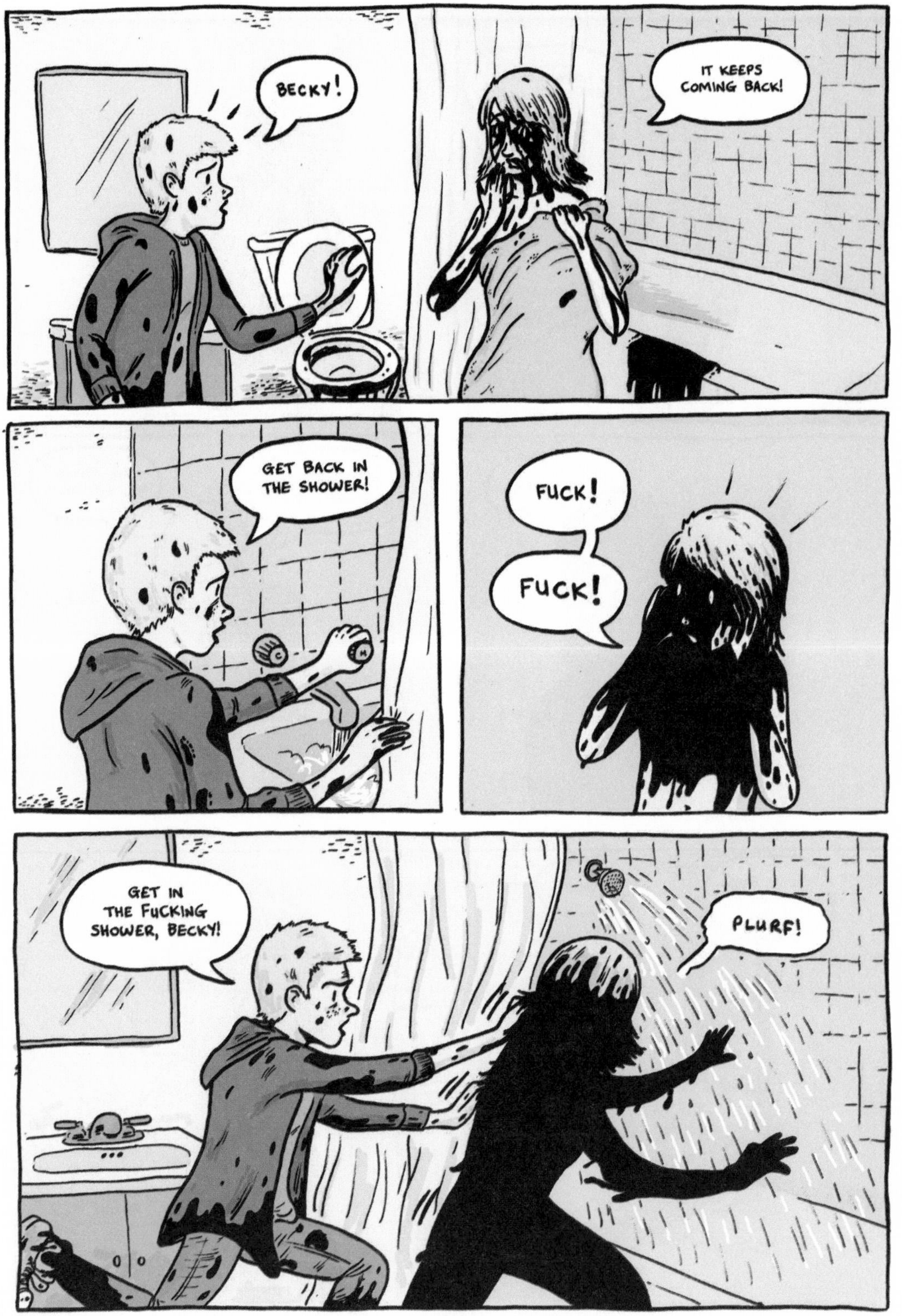
BECKY!
IT KEEPS COMING BACK!
GET BACK IN THE SHOWER!
FUCK!
FUCK!
GET IN THE FUCKING SHOWER, BECKY!
PLURF!

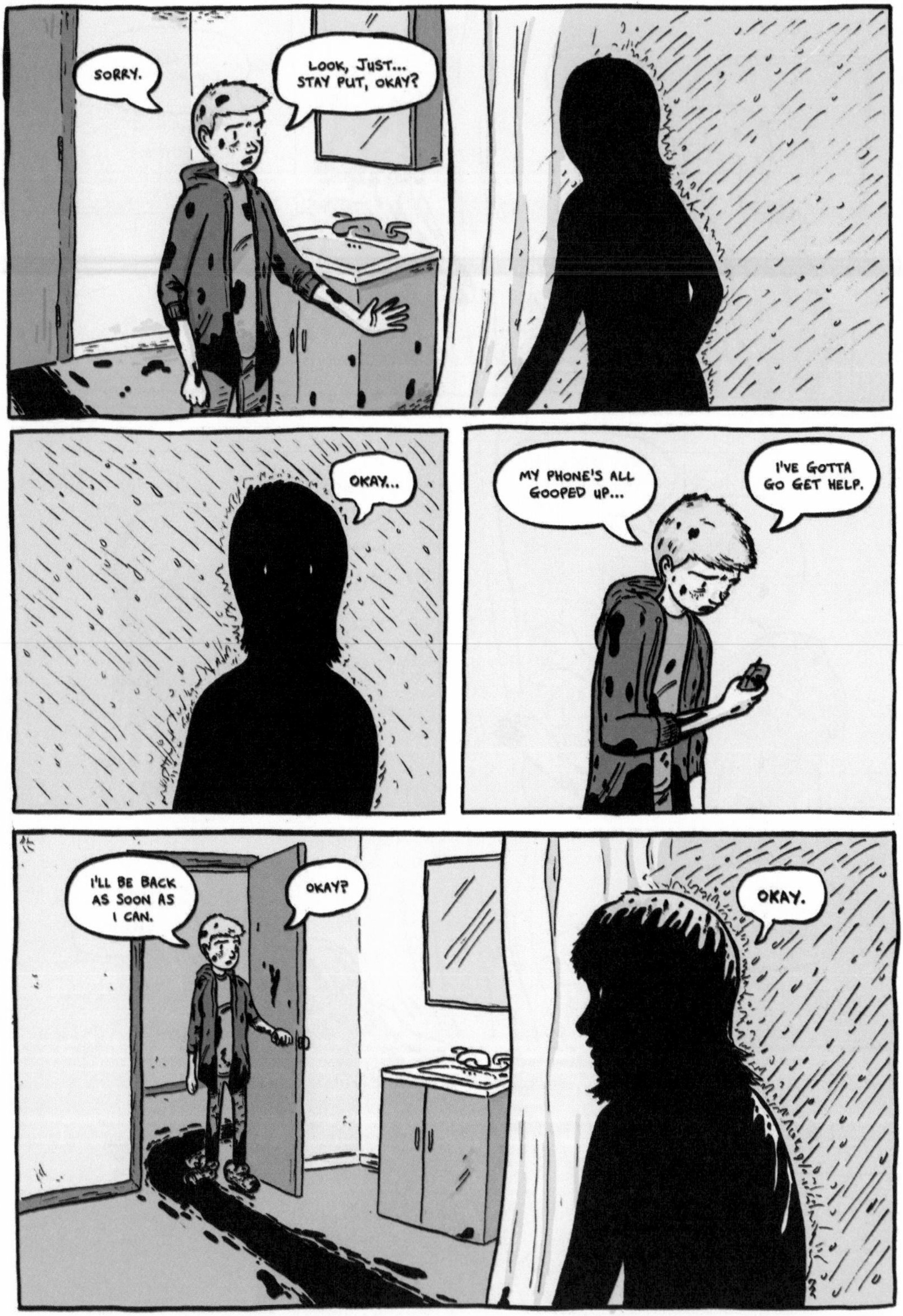
SORRY.
LOOK, JUST... STAY PUT, OKAY?
OKAY...
MY PHONE'S ALL GOOPED UP...
I'VE GOTTA GO GET HELP.
I'LL BE BACK AS SOON AS I CAN.
OKAY?
OKAY.

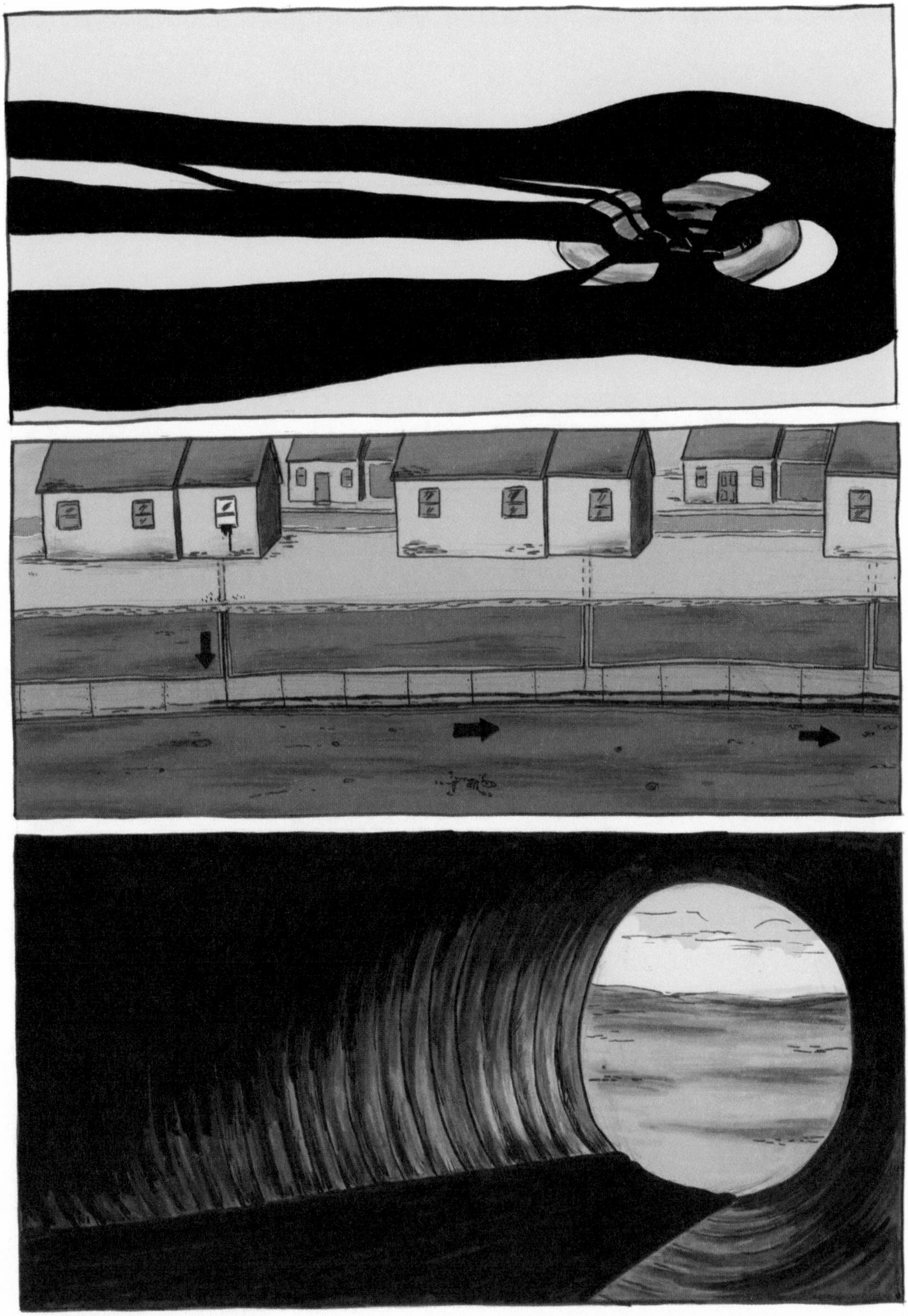

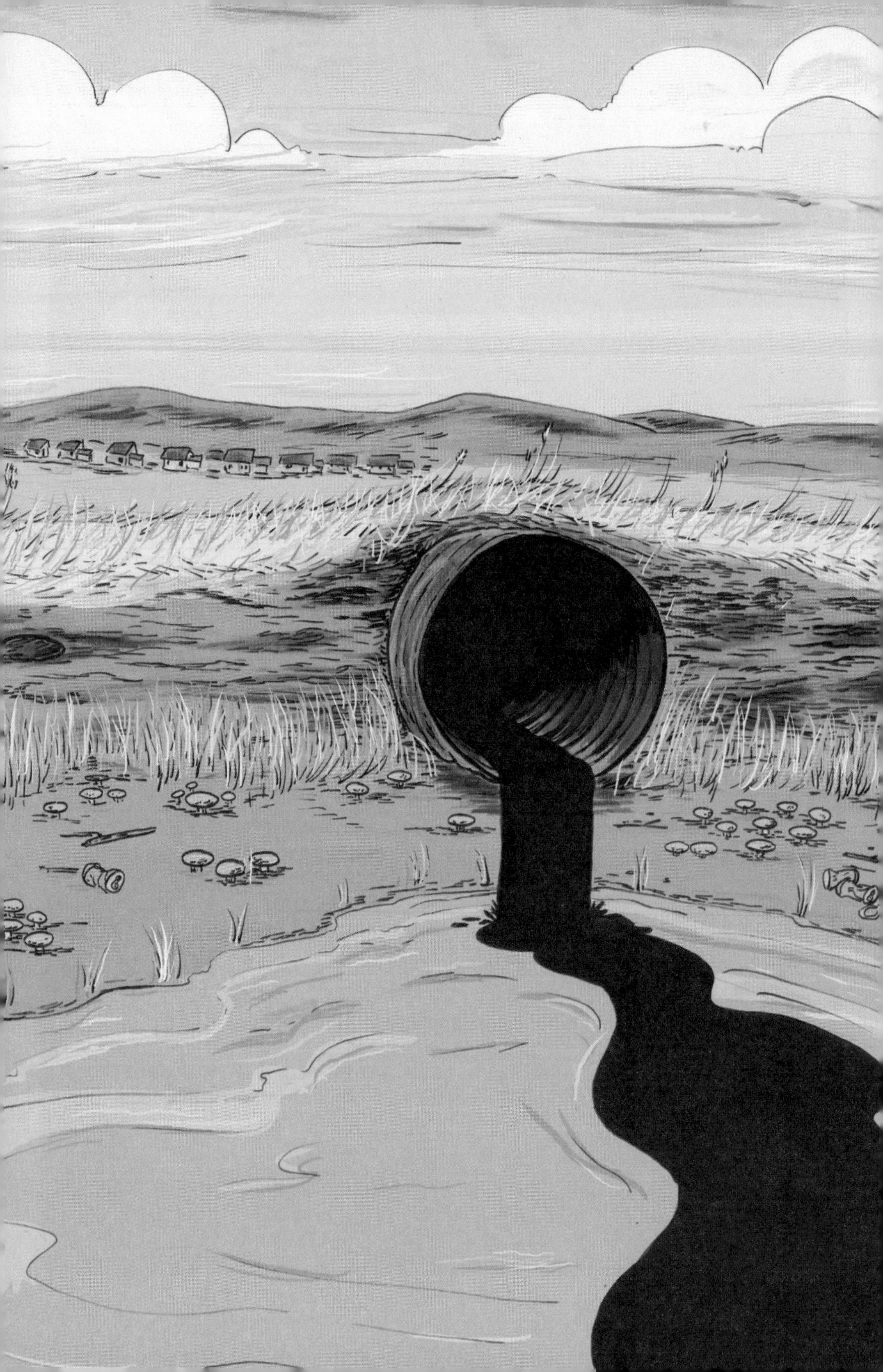

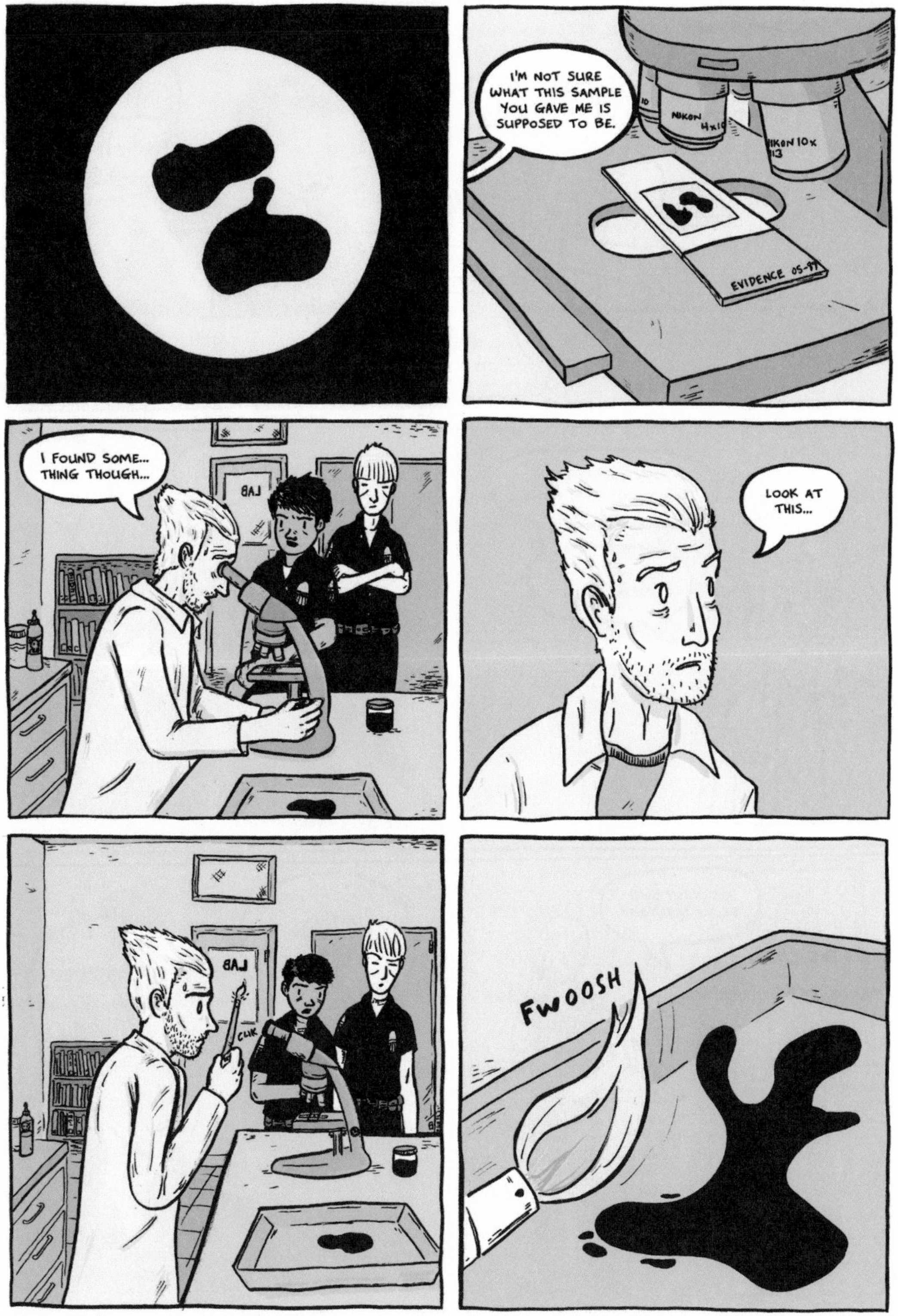
I'M NOT SURE WHAT THIS SAMPLE YOU GAVE ME IS SUPPOSED TO BE.
NIKON
NIKON 10x
EVIDENCE 05-99
I FOUND SOME... THING THOUGH...
LAB
LOOK AT THIS...
LAB
CLIK
FWOOSH

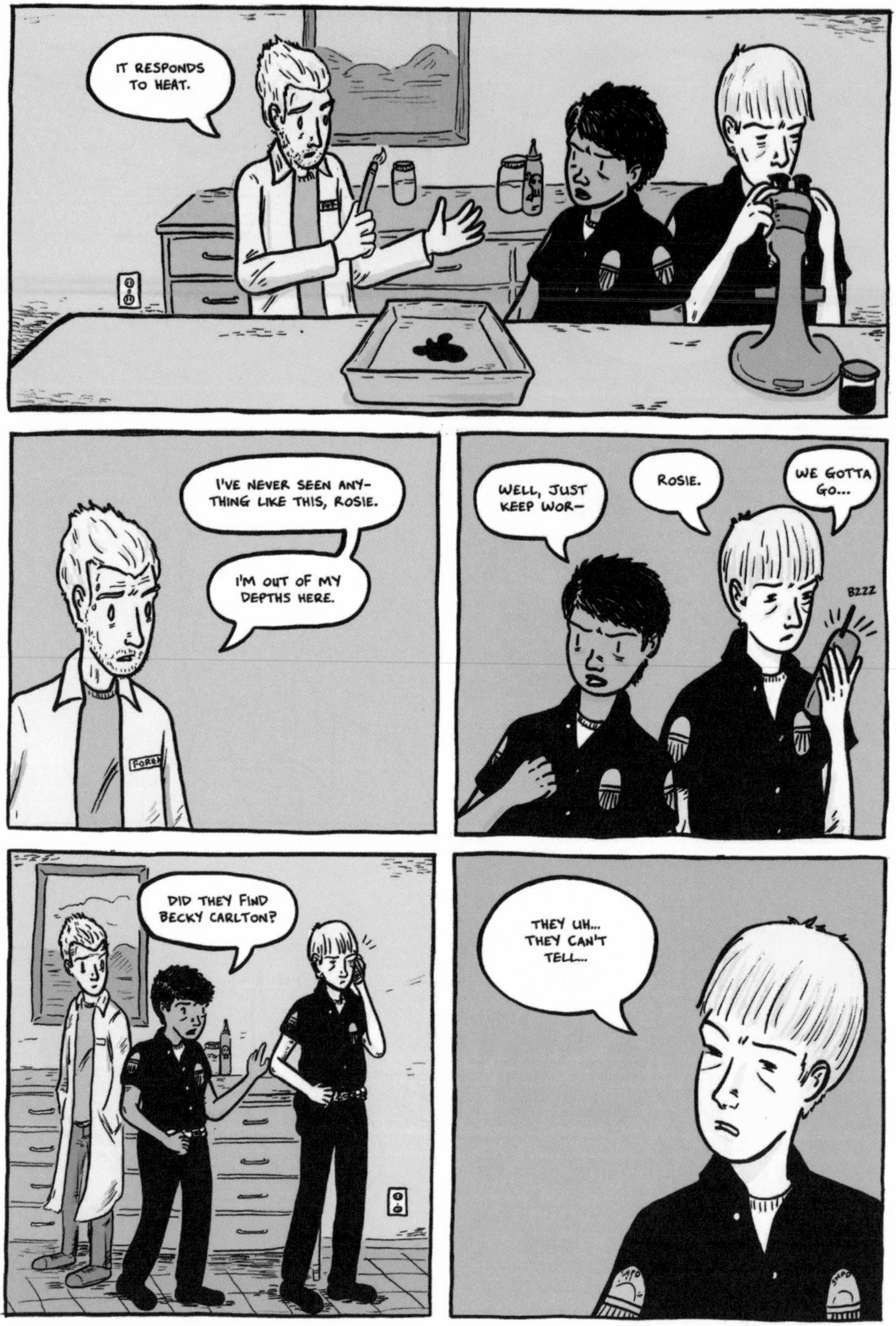
IT RESPONDS TO HEAT.
I'VE NEVER SEEN ANY-THING LIKE THIS, ROSIE.
I'M OUT OF MY DEPTHS HERE.
WELL, JUST KEEP WOR—
ROSIE.
WE GOTTA GO...
BZZZ
DID THEY FIND BECKY CARLTON?
THEY UH... THEY CAN'T TELL...

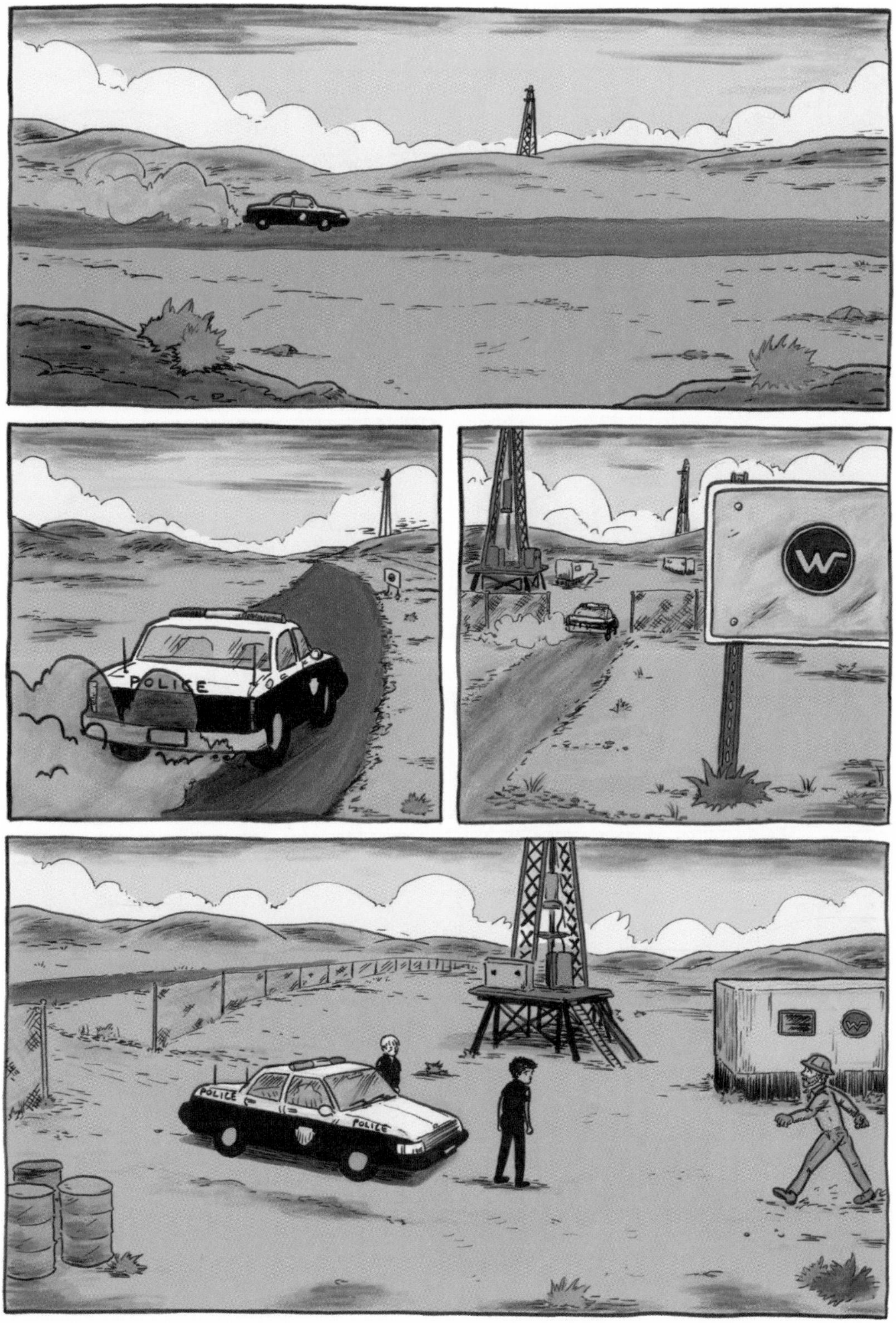
POLICE
POLICE
POLICE

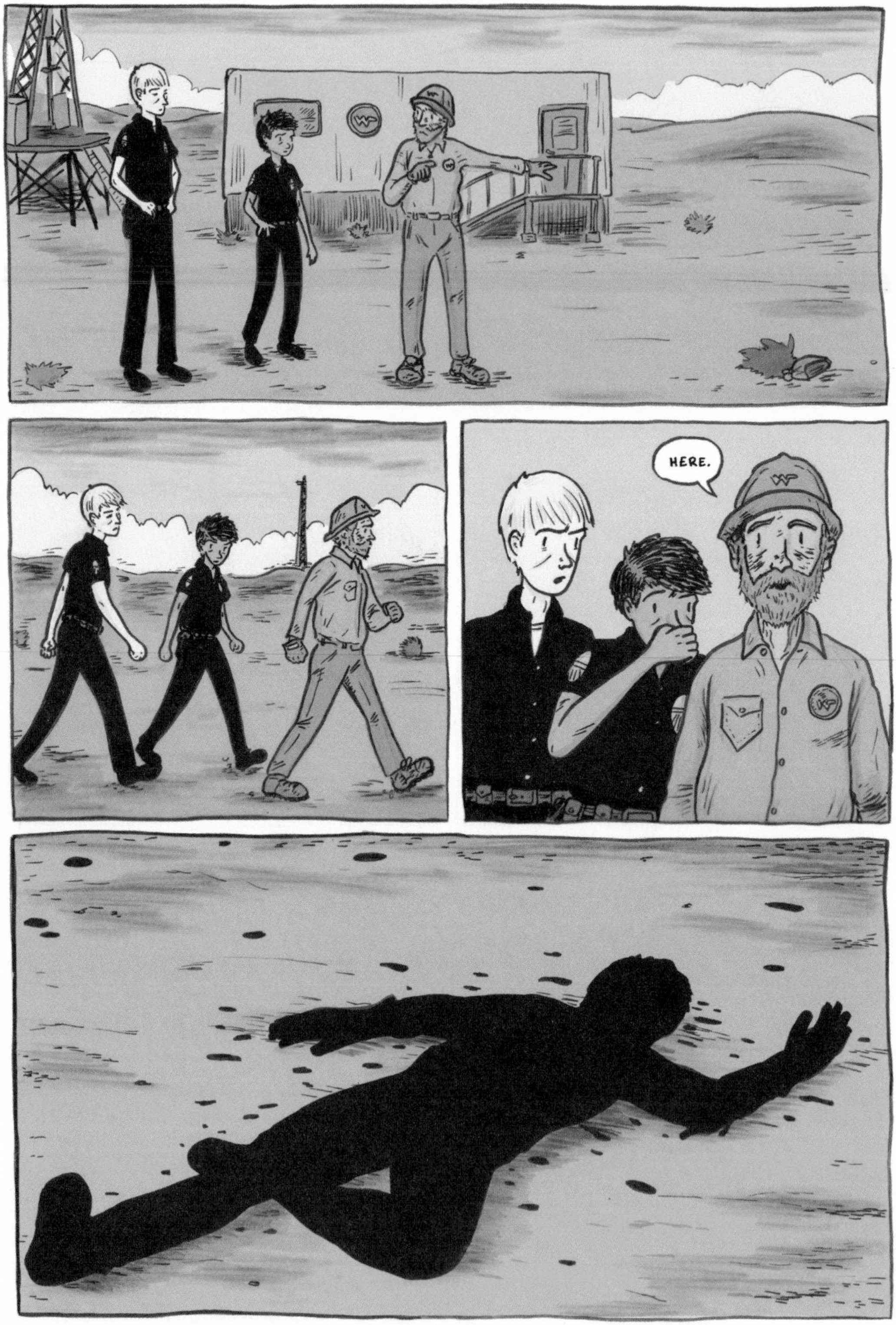
HERE.

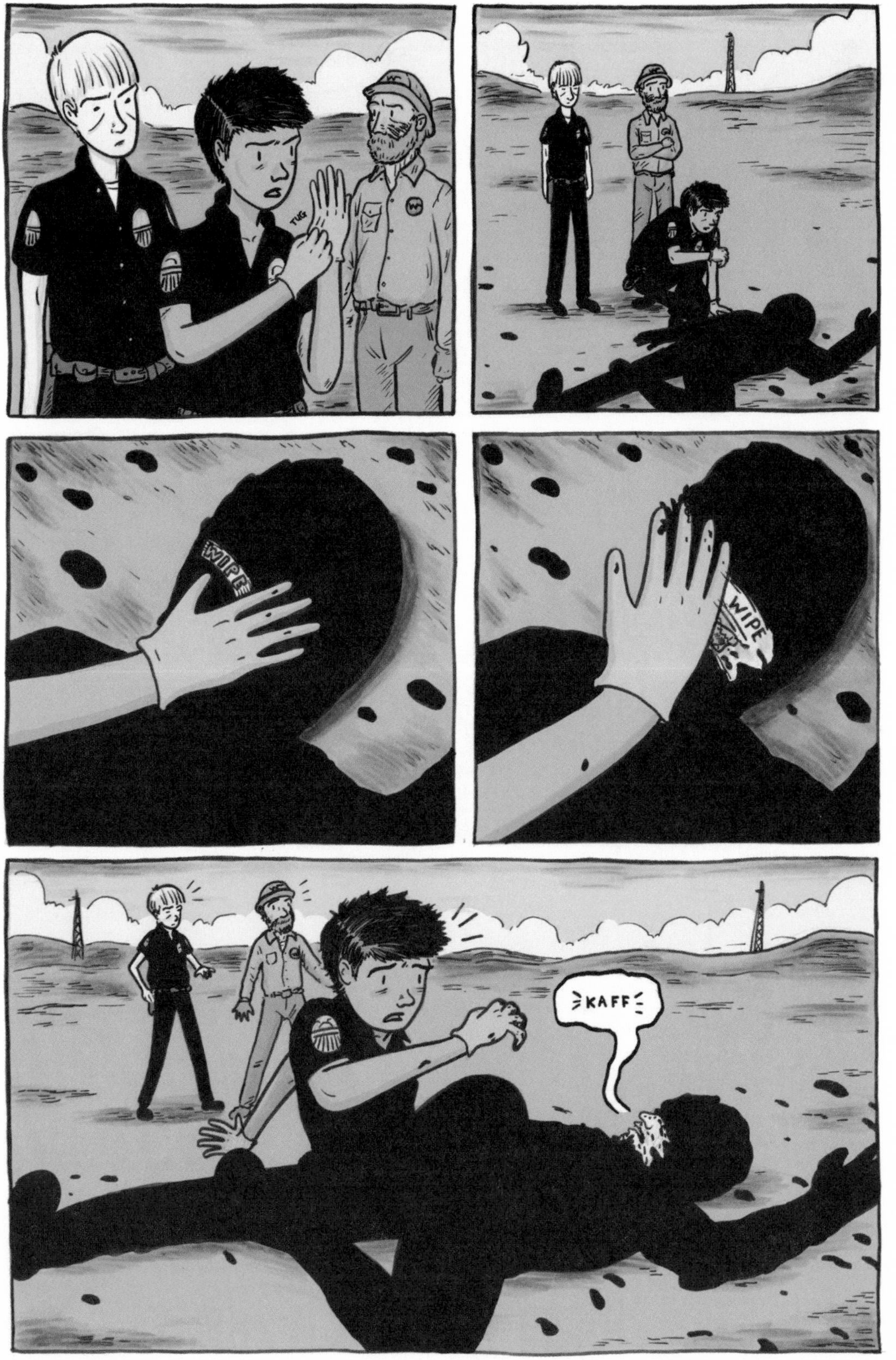
TUG
WIPE
WIPE
KAFF

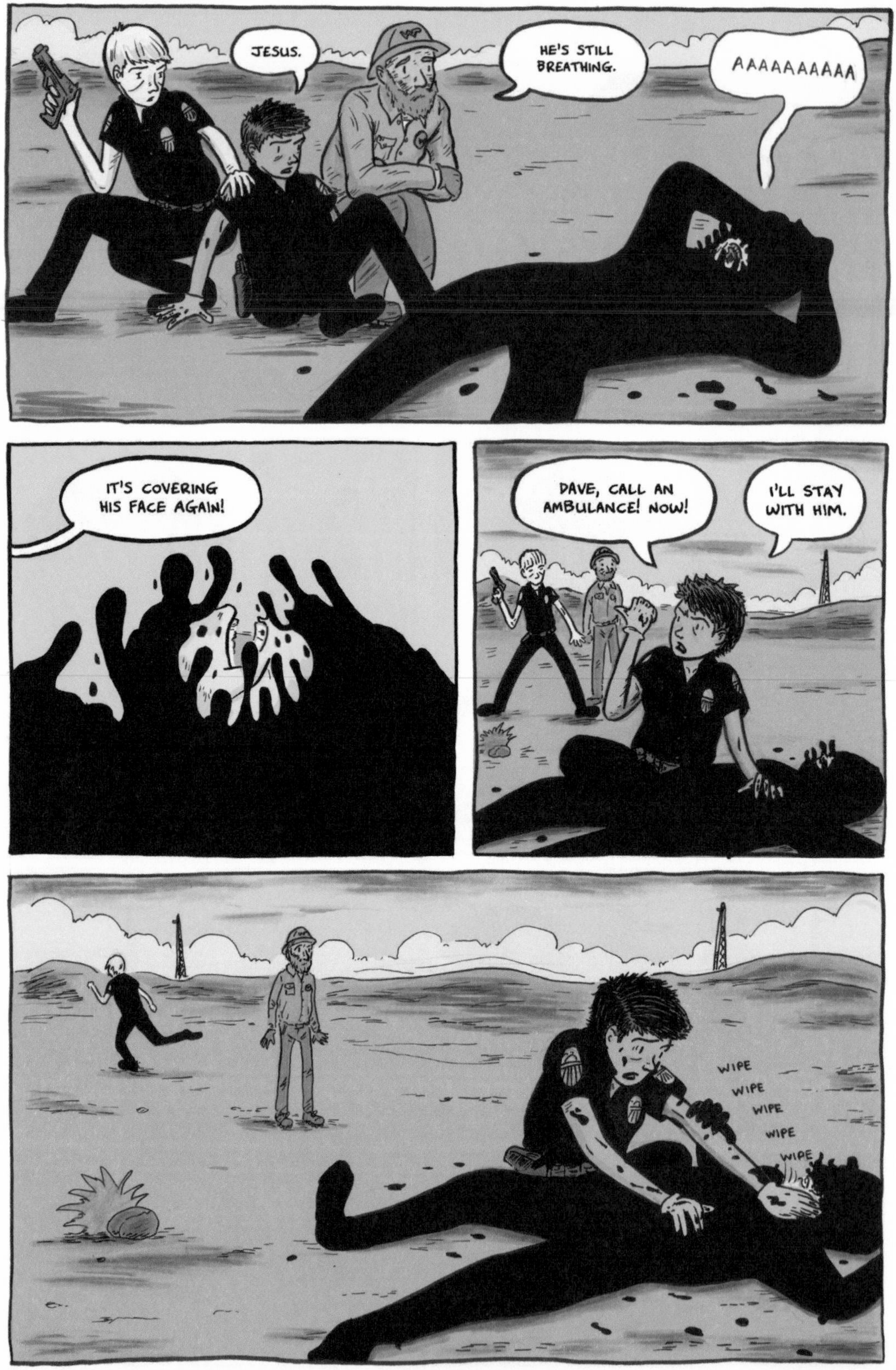
JESUS.
HE'S STILL BREATHING.
AAAAAAAAAA
IT'S COVERING HIS FACE AGAIN!
DAVE, CALL AN AMBULANCE! NOW!
I'LL STAY WITH HIM.
WIPE
WIPE
WIPE
WIPE
WIPE

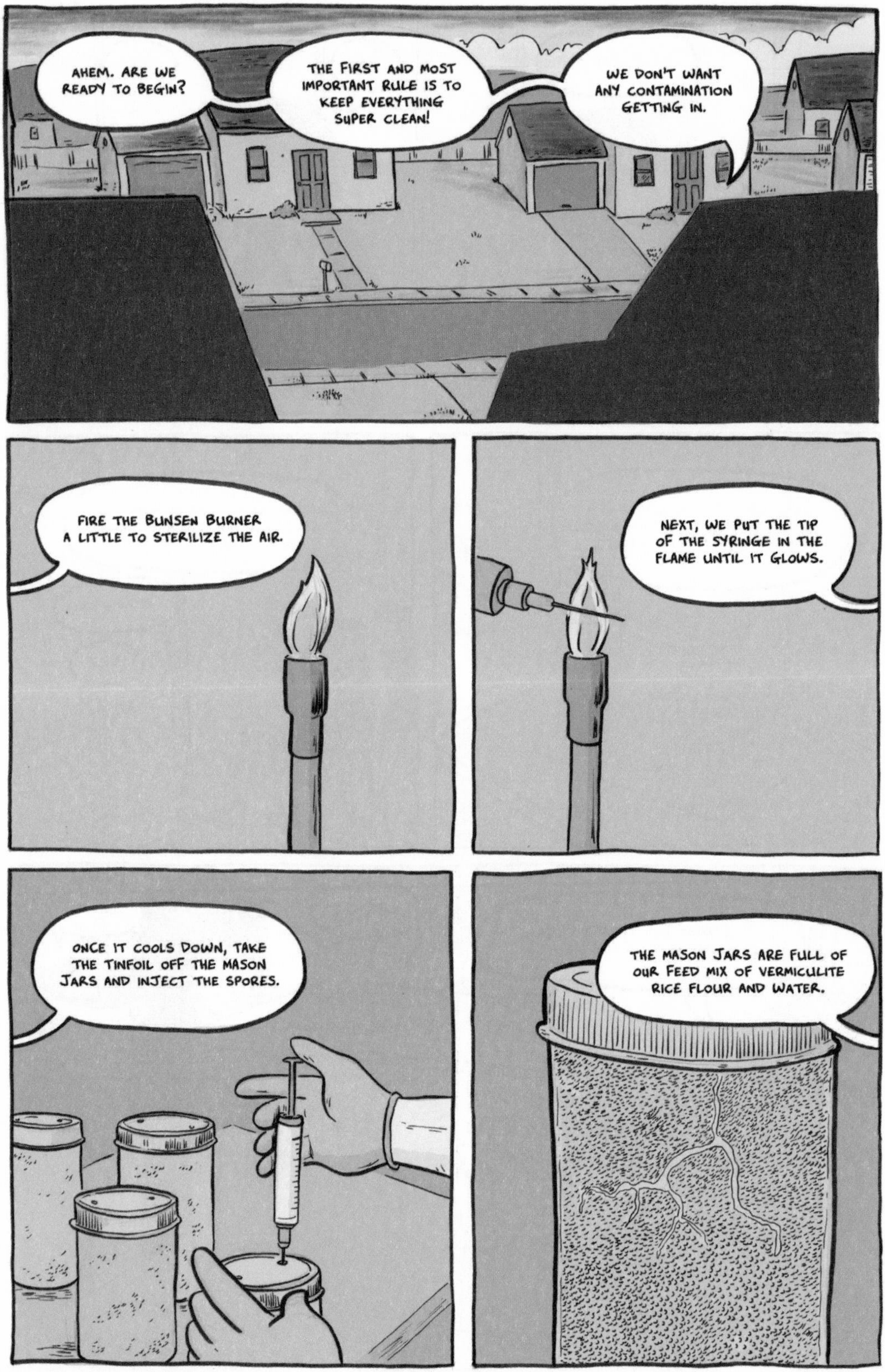
AHEM. ARE WE READY TO BEGIN?
THE FIRST AND MOST IMPORTANT RULE IS TO KEEP EVERYTHING SUPER CLEAN!
WE DON'T WANT ANY CONTAMINATION GETTING IN.
FIRE THE BUNSEN BURNER A LITTLE TO STERILIZE THE AIR.
NEXT, WE PUT THE TIP OF THE SYRINGE IN THE FLAME UNTIL IT GLOWS.
ONCE IT COOLS DOWN, TAKE THE TINFOIL OFF THE MASON JARS AND INJECT THE SPORES.
THE MASON JARS ARE FULL OF OUR FEED MIX OF VERMICULITE RICE FLOUR AND WATER.

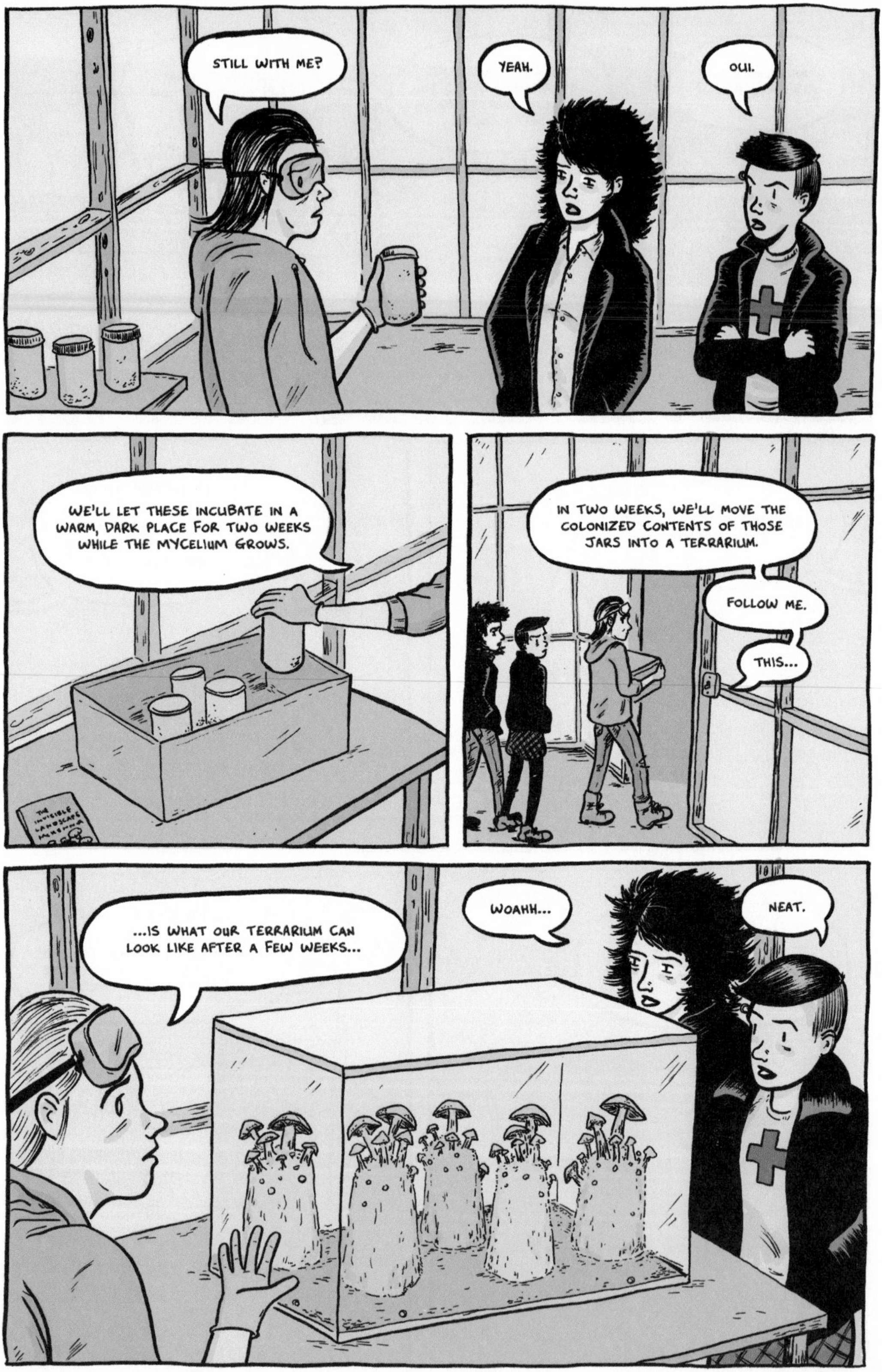
STILL WITH ME?
YEAH.
OUI.
WE'LL LET THESE INCUBATE IN A WARM, DARK PLACE FOR TWO WEEKS WHILE THE MYCELIUM GROWS.
IN TWO WEEKS, WE'LL MOVE THE COLONIZED CONTENTS OF THOSE JARS INTO A TERRARIUM.
FOLLOW ME.
THIS...
...IS WHAT OUR TERRARIUM CAN LOOK LIKE AFTER A FEW WEEKS...
WOAHH...
NEAT.

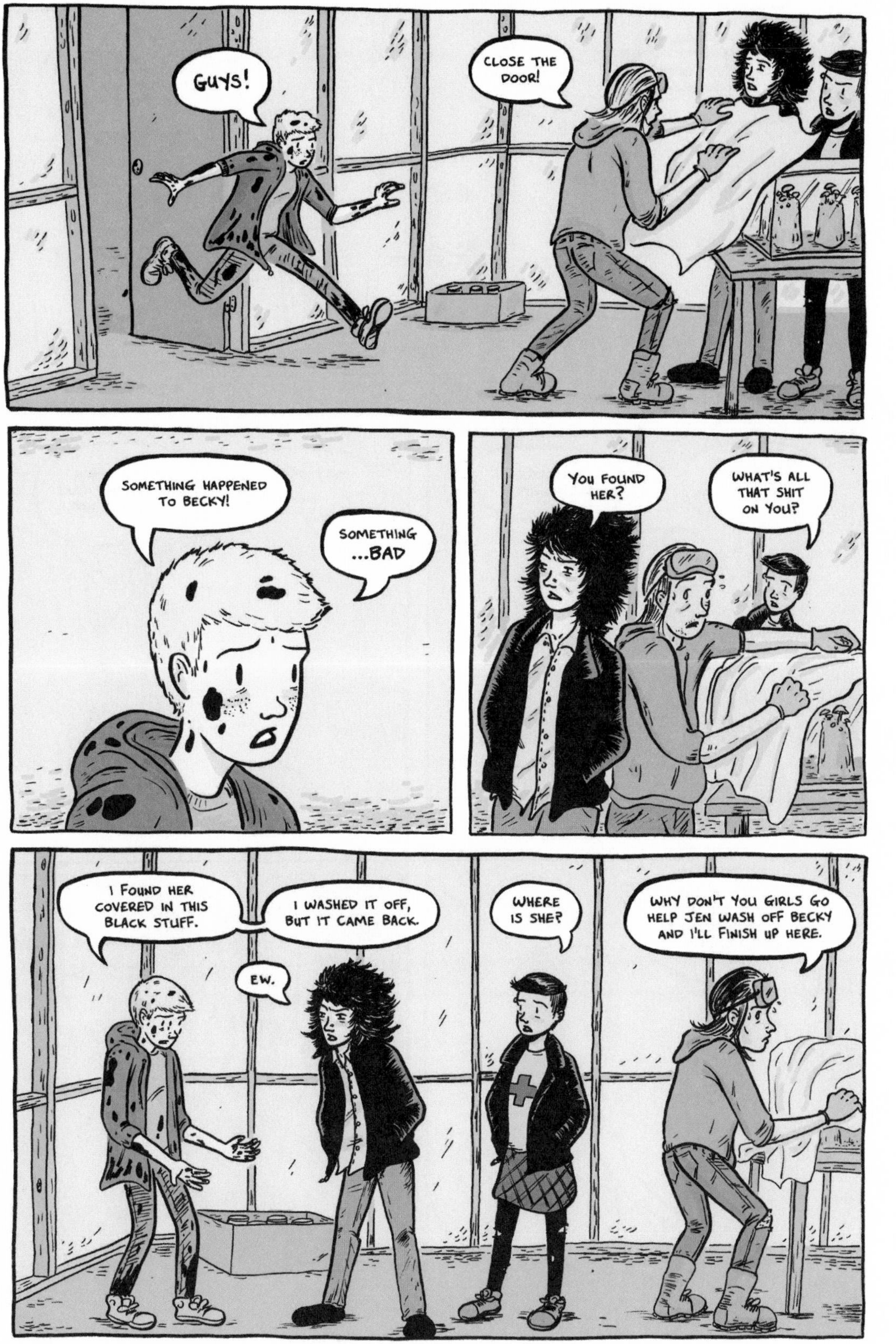
GUYS!
CLOSE THE DOOR!
SOMETHING HAPPENED TO BECKY!
SOMETHING ...BAD
YOU FOUND HER?
WHAT'S ALL THAT SHIT ON YOU?
I FOUND HER COVERED IN THIS BLACK STUFF.
I WASHED IT OFF, BUT IT CAME BACK.
EW.
WHERE IS SHE?
WHY DON'T YOU GIRLS GO HELP JEN WASH OFF BECKY AND I'LL FINISH UP HERE.

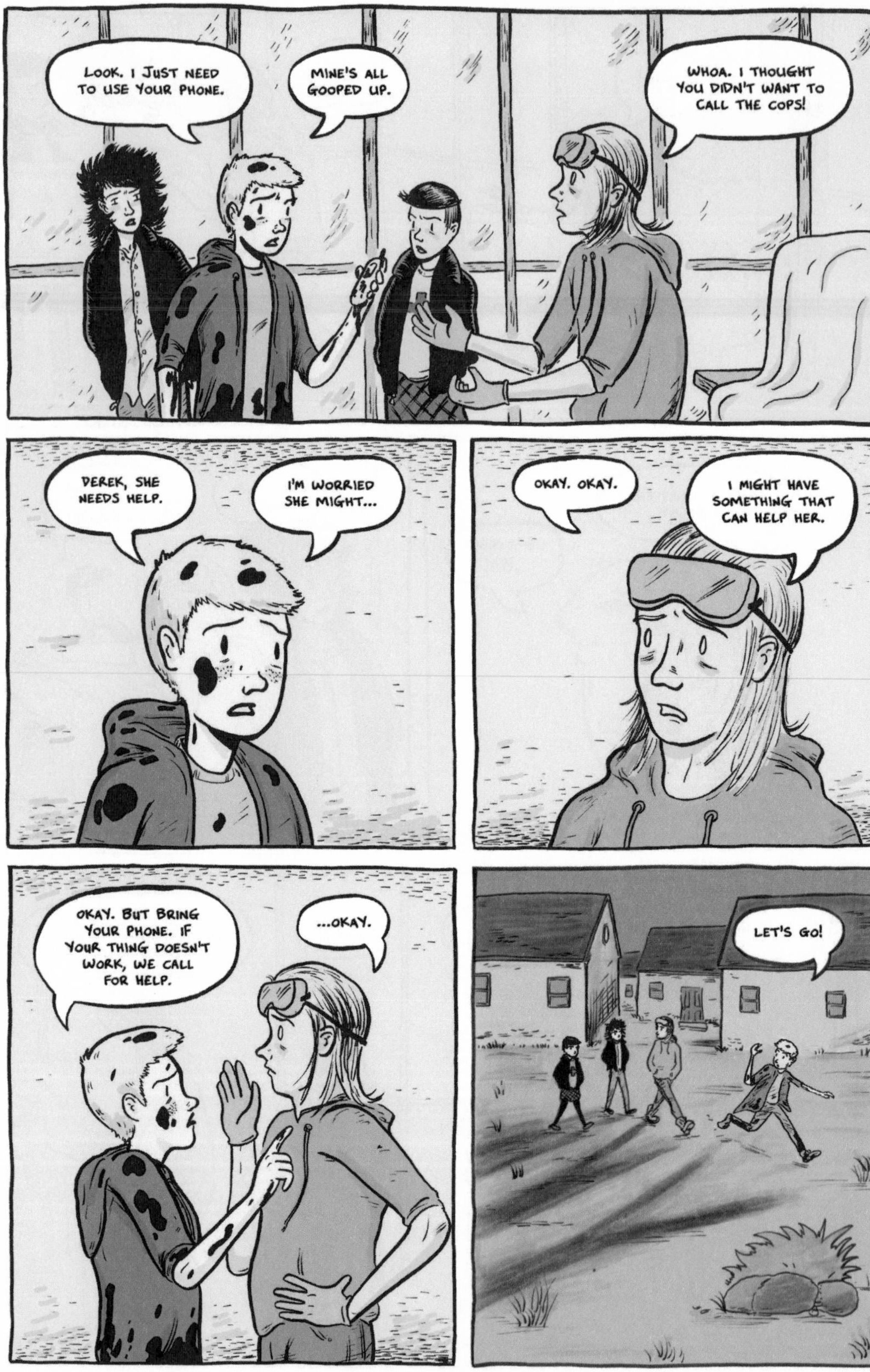
LOOK. I JUST NEED TO USE YOUR PHONE.
MINE'S ALL GOOPED UP.
WHOA. I THOUGHT YOU DIDN'T WANT TO CALL THE COPS!
DEREK, SHE NEEDS HELP.
I'M WORRIED SHE MIGHT...
OKAY. OKAY.
I MIGHT HAVE SOMETHING THAT CAN HELP HER.
OKAY. BUT BRING YOUR PHONE. IF YOUR THING DOESN'T WORK, WE CALL FOR HELP.
...OKAY.
LET'S GO!

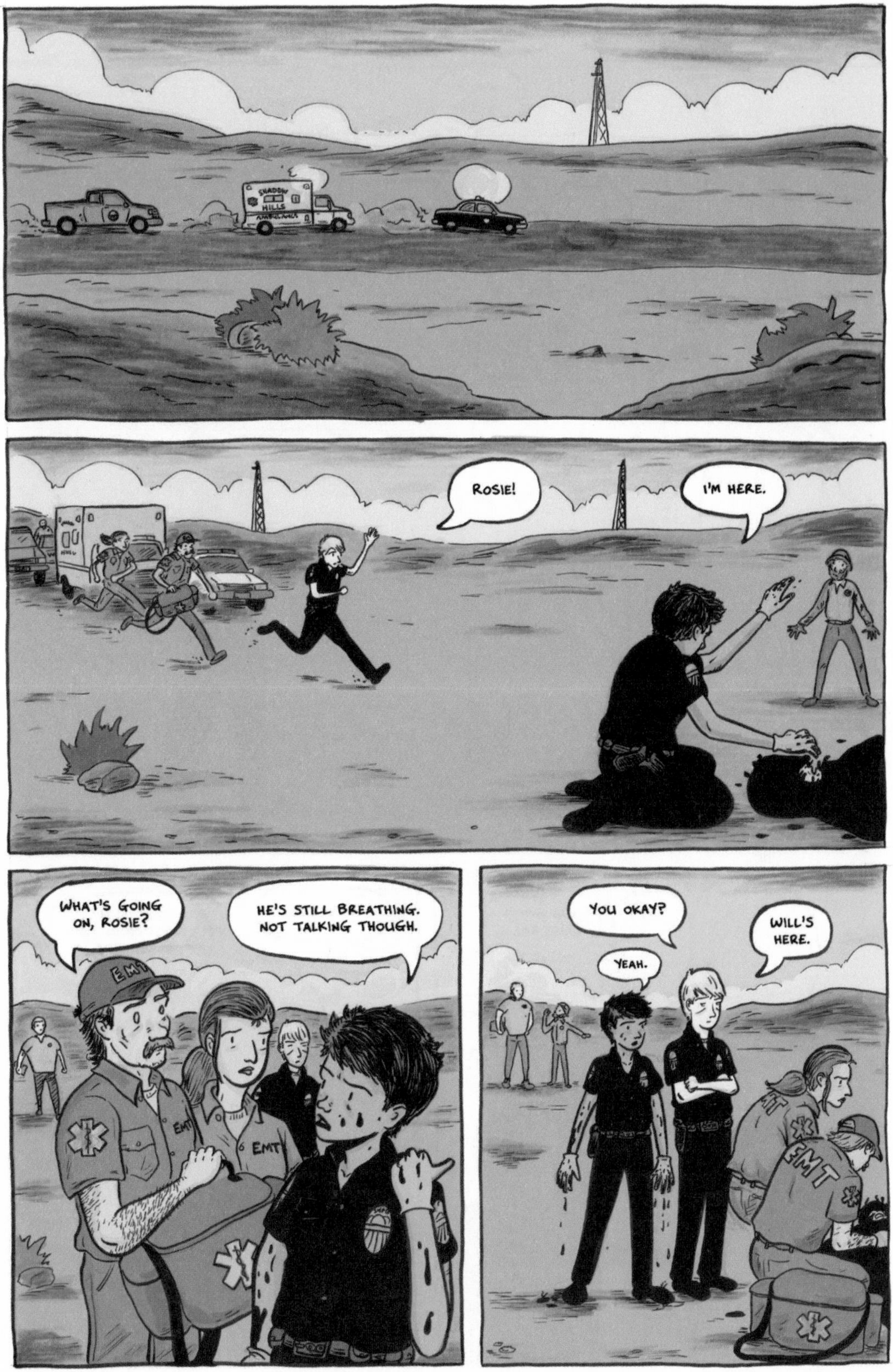
SHADOW HILLS AMBULANCE
ROSIE!
I'M HERE.
WHAT'S GOING ON, ROSIE?
HE'S STILL BREATHING. NOT TALKING THOUGH.
YOU OKAY?
YEAH.
WILL'S HERE.

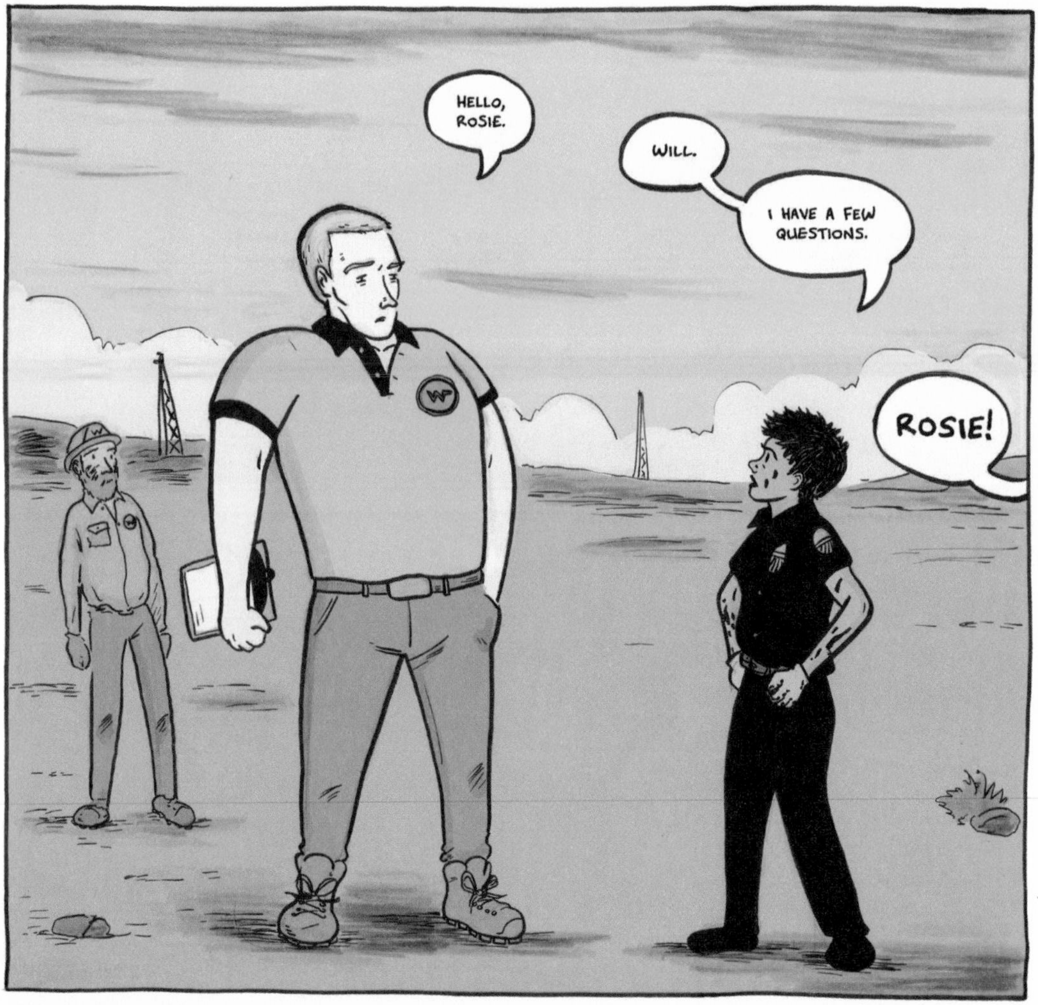
HELLO, ROSIE.
WILL.
I HAVE A FEW QUESTIONS.
ROSIE!

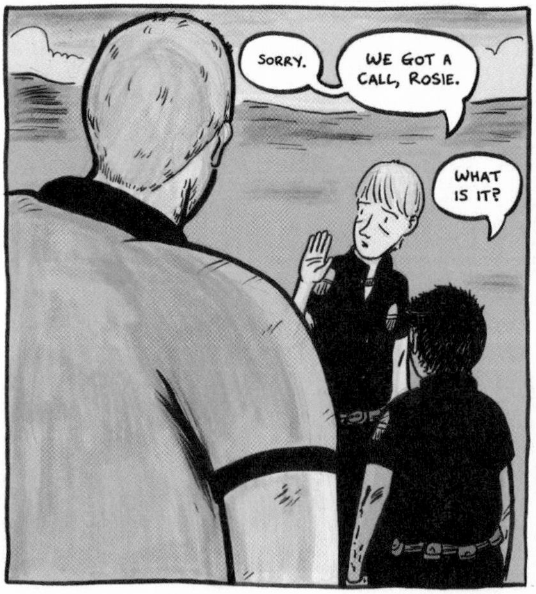
SORRY.
WE GOT A CALL, ROSIE.
WHAT IS IT?

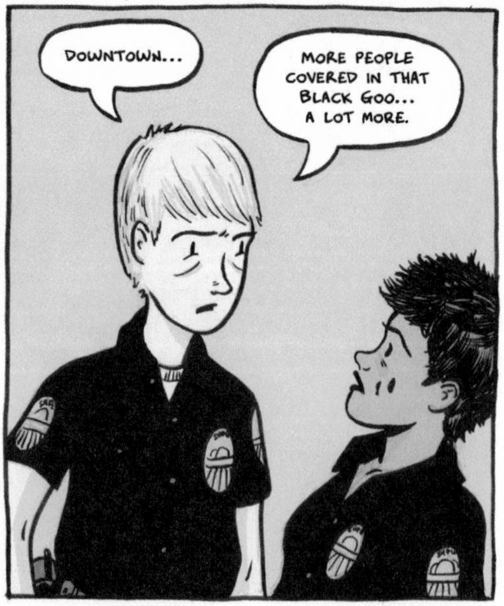
DOWNTOWN...
MORE PEOPLE COVERED IN THAT BLACK GOO... A LOT MORE.

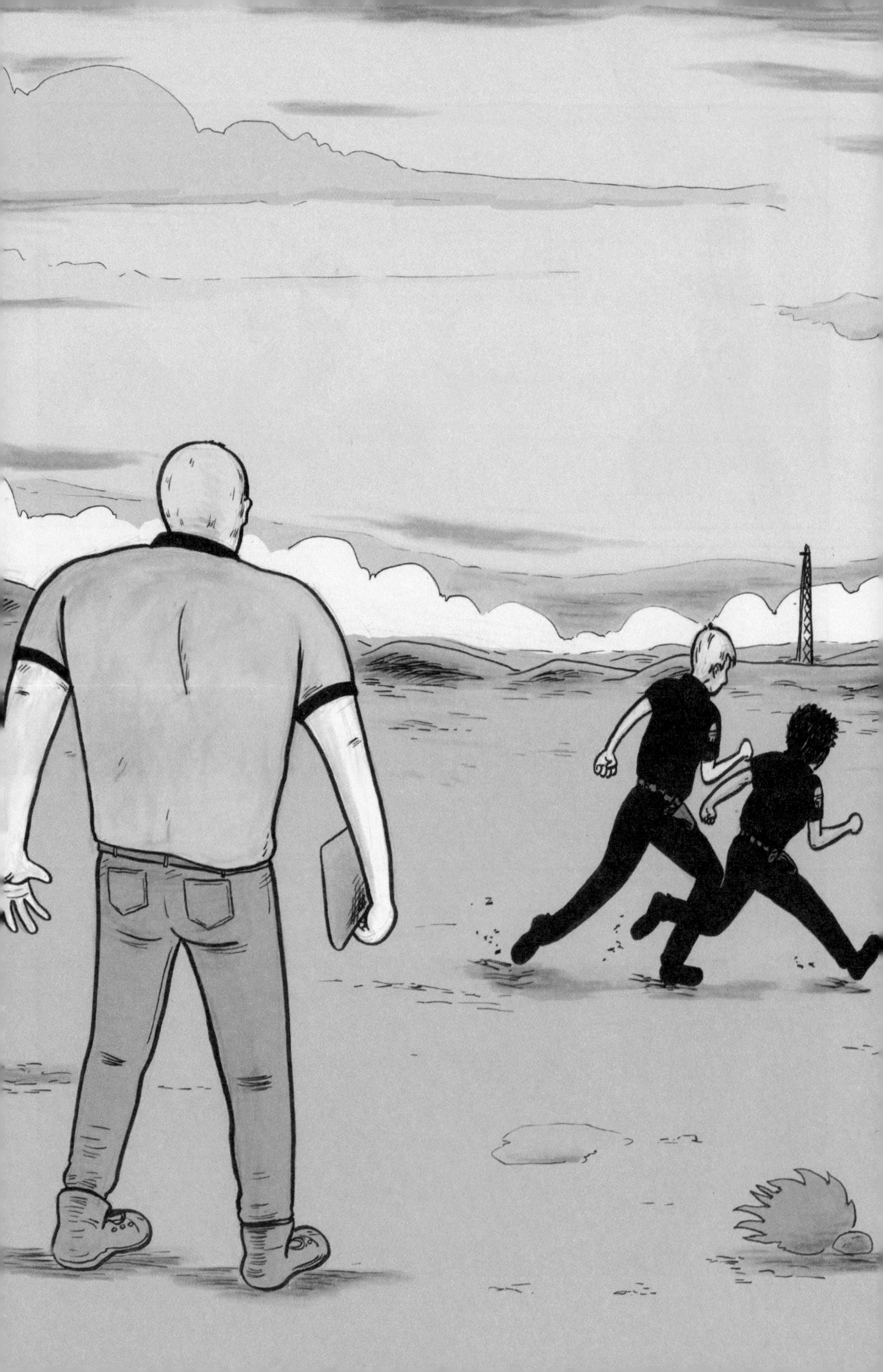

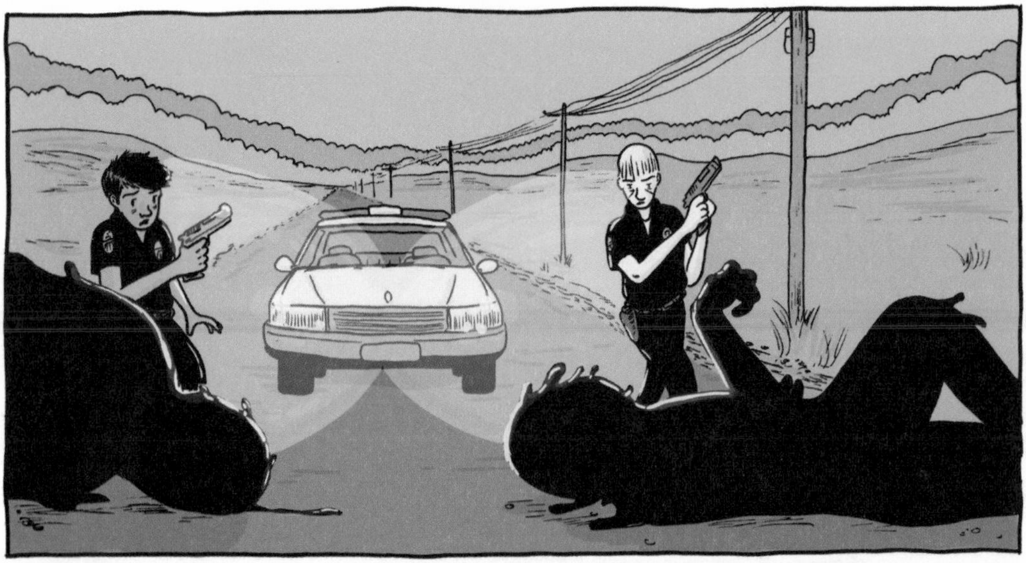

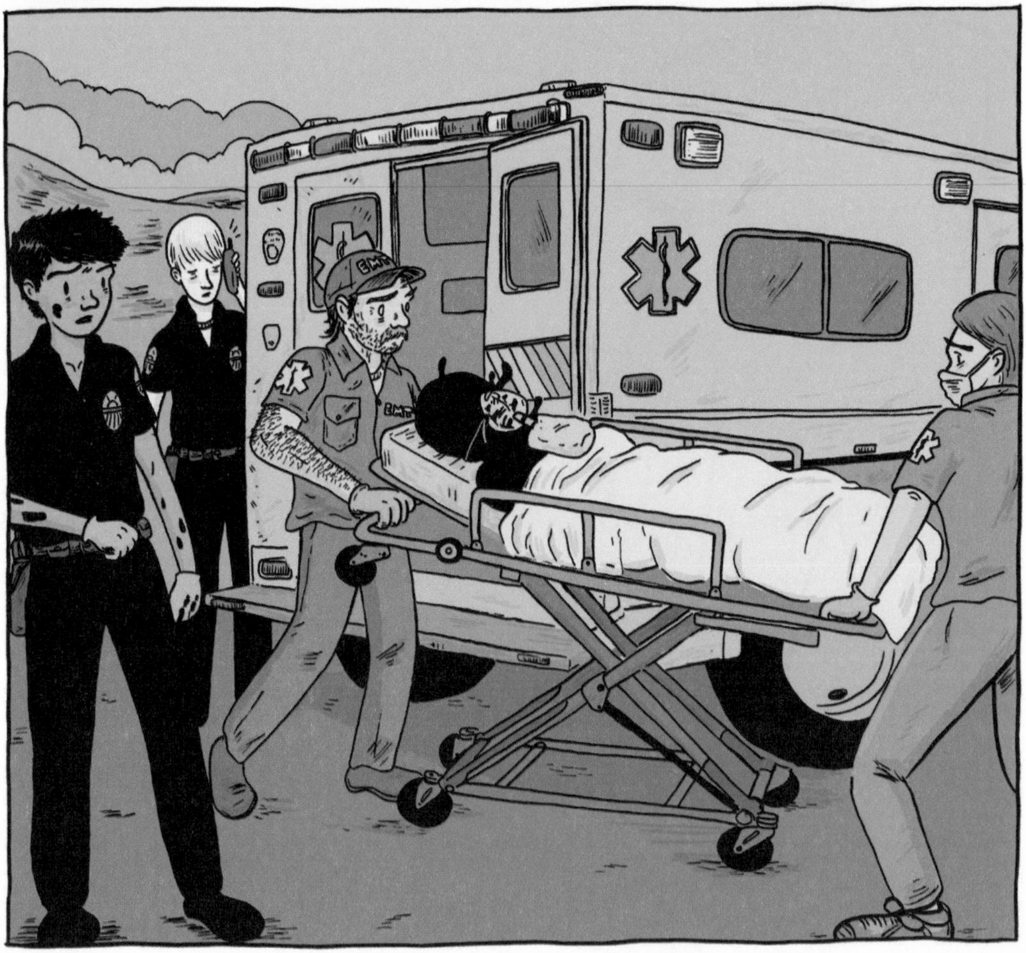

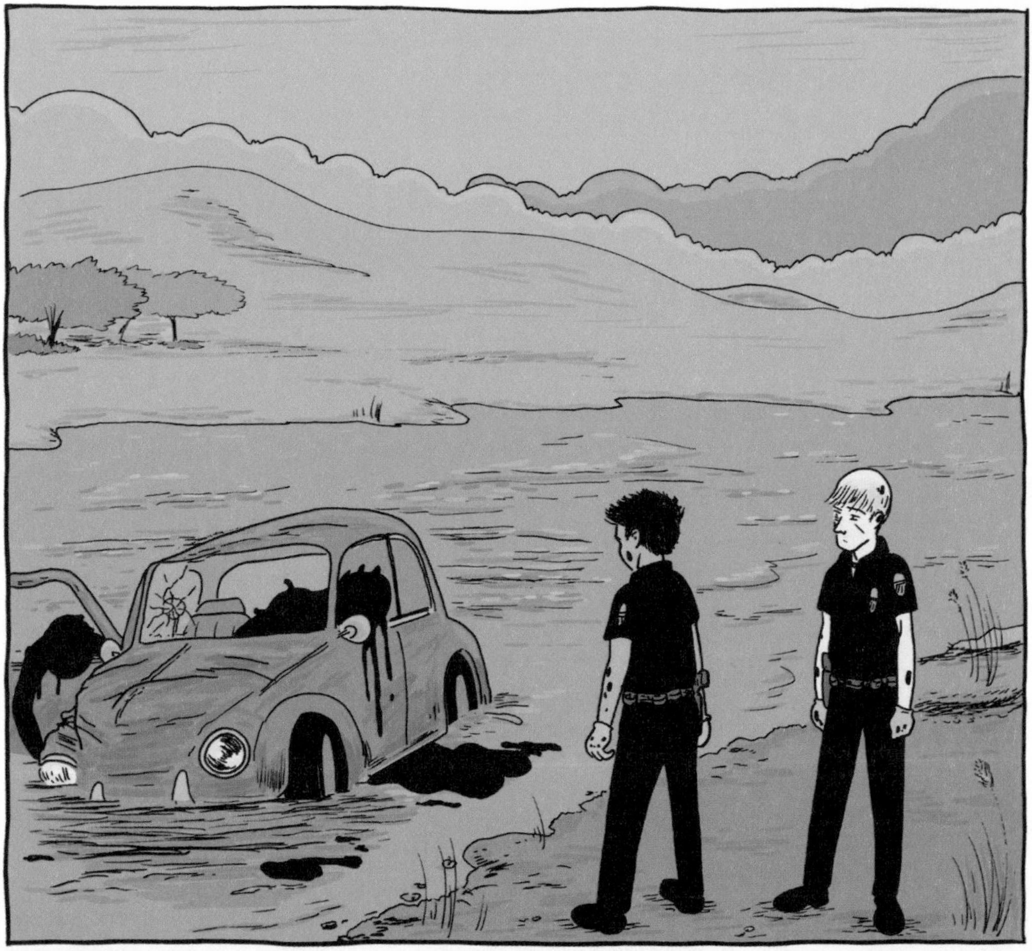

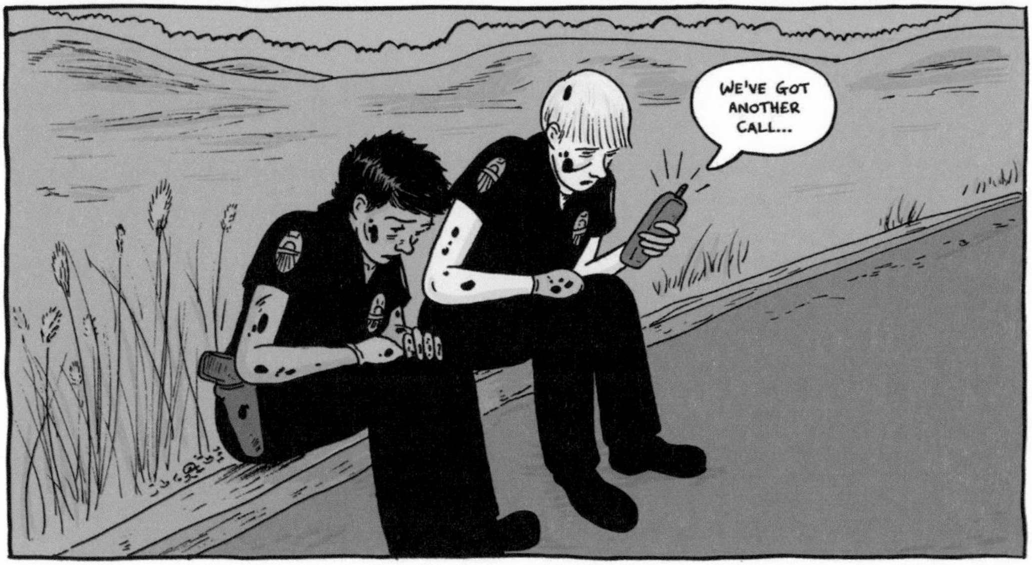
WE'VE GOT ANOTHER CALL...

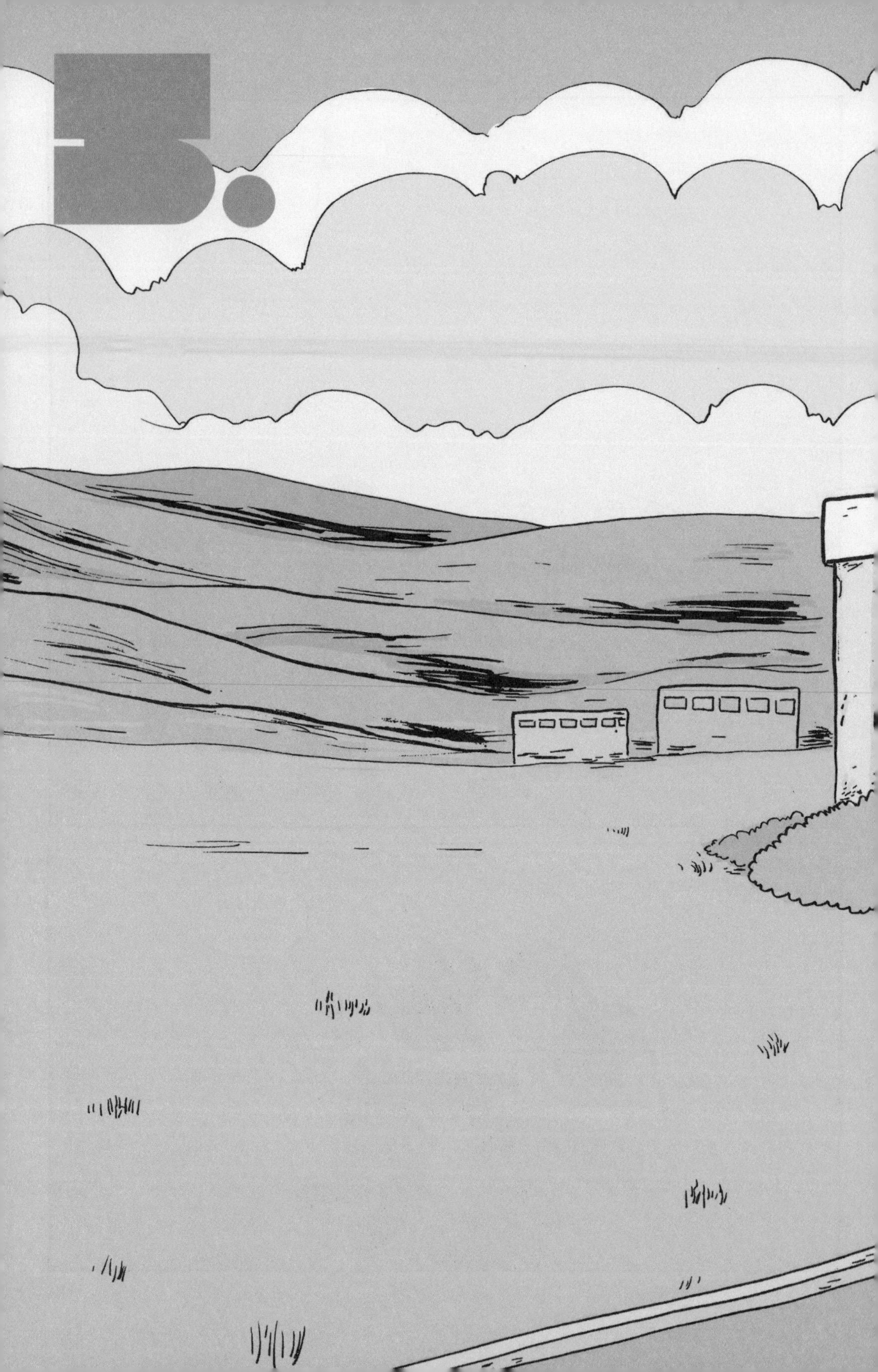
5.

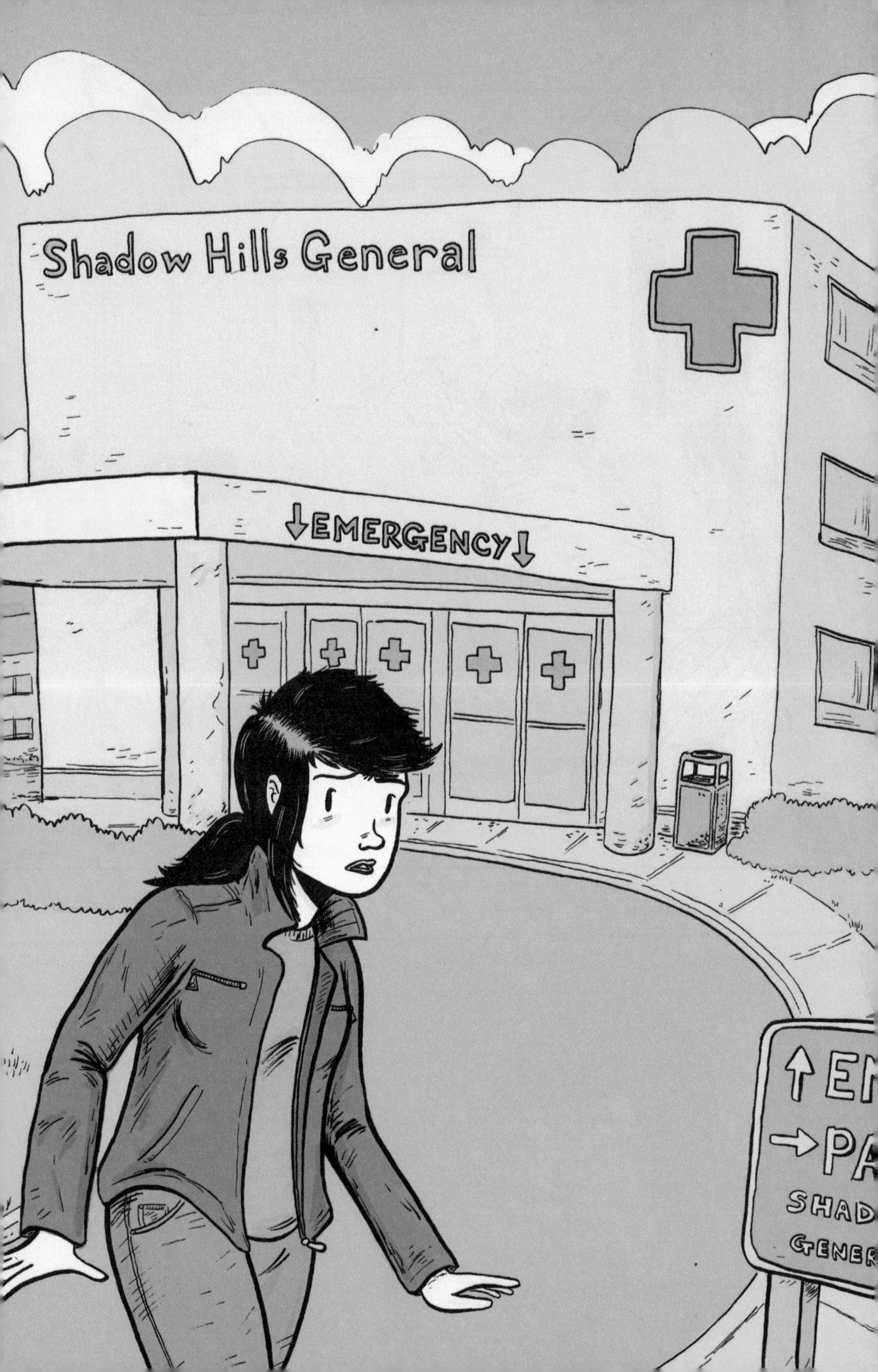
Shadow Hills General
EMERGENCY

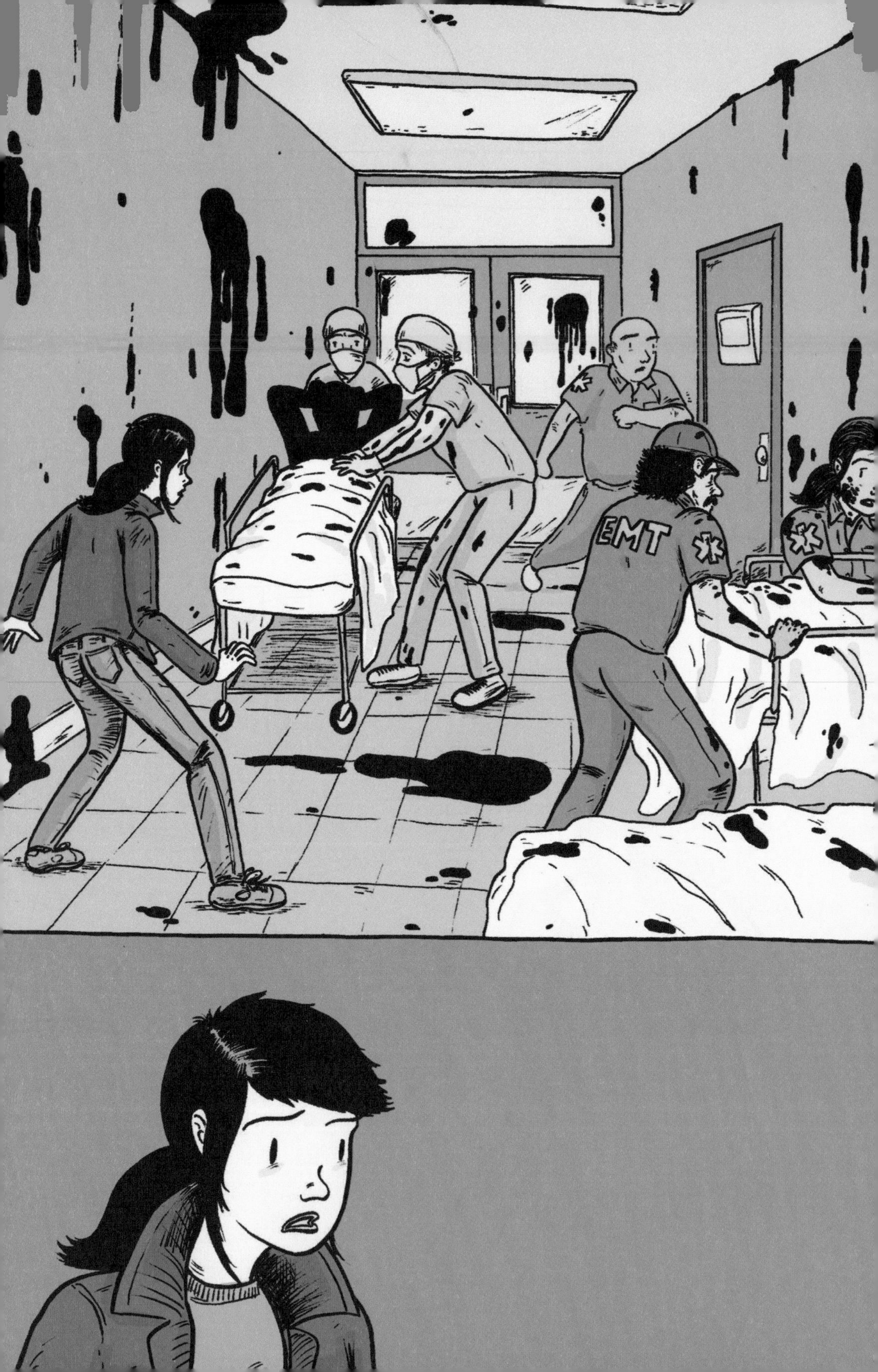
EMT

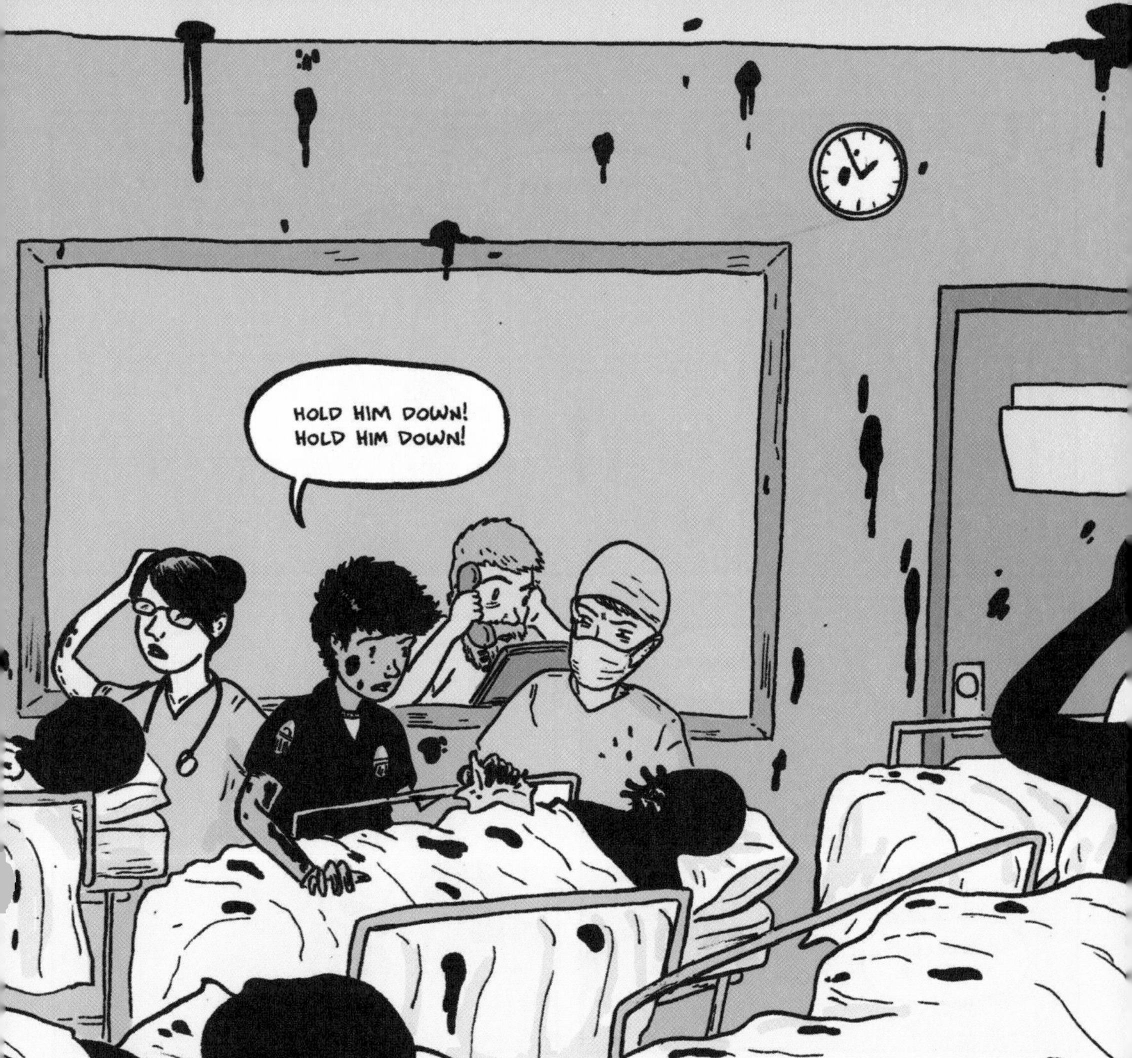
HOLD HIM DOWN!
HOLD HIM DOWN!

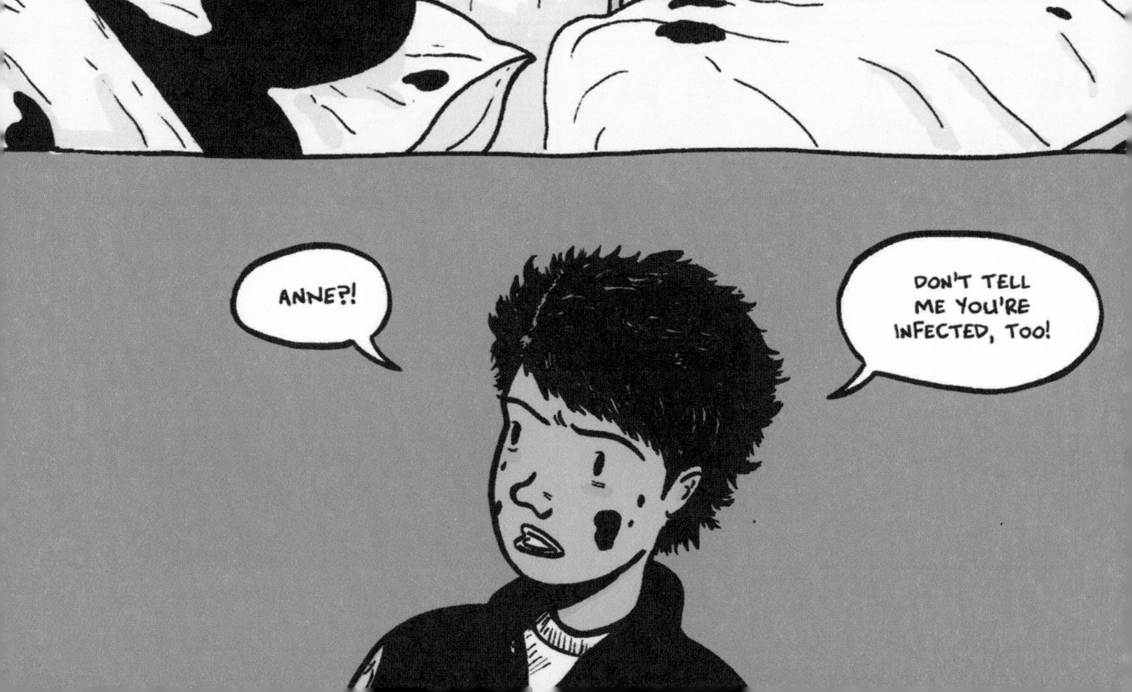
ANNE?!
DON'T TELL ME YOU'RE INFECTED, TOO!

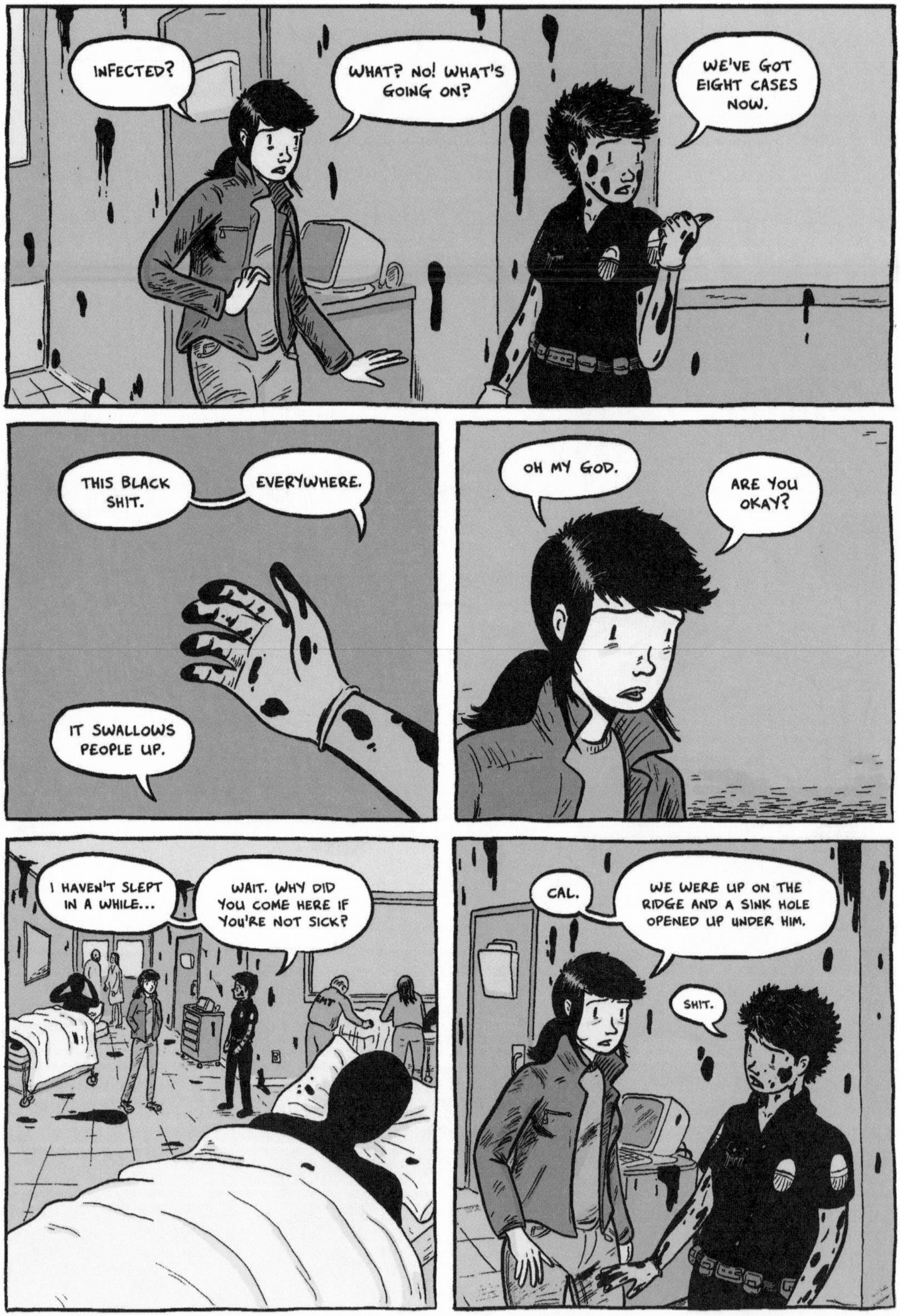
INFECTED?
WHAT? NO! WHAT'S GOING ON?
WE'VE GOT EIGHT CASES NOW.
THIS BLACK SHIT.
EVERYWHERE.
IT SWALLOWS PEOPLE UP.
OH MY GOD.
ARE YOU OKAY?
I HAVEN'T SLEPT IN A WHILE...
WAIT. WHY DID YOU COME HERE IF YOU'RE NOT SICK?
EMT
CAL.
WE WERE UP ON THE RIDGE AND A SINK HOLE OPENED UP UNDER HIM.
SHIT.

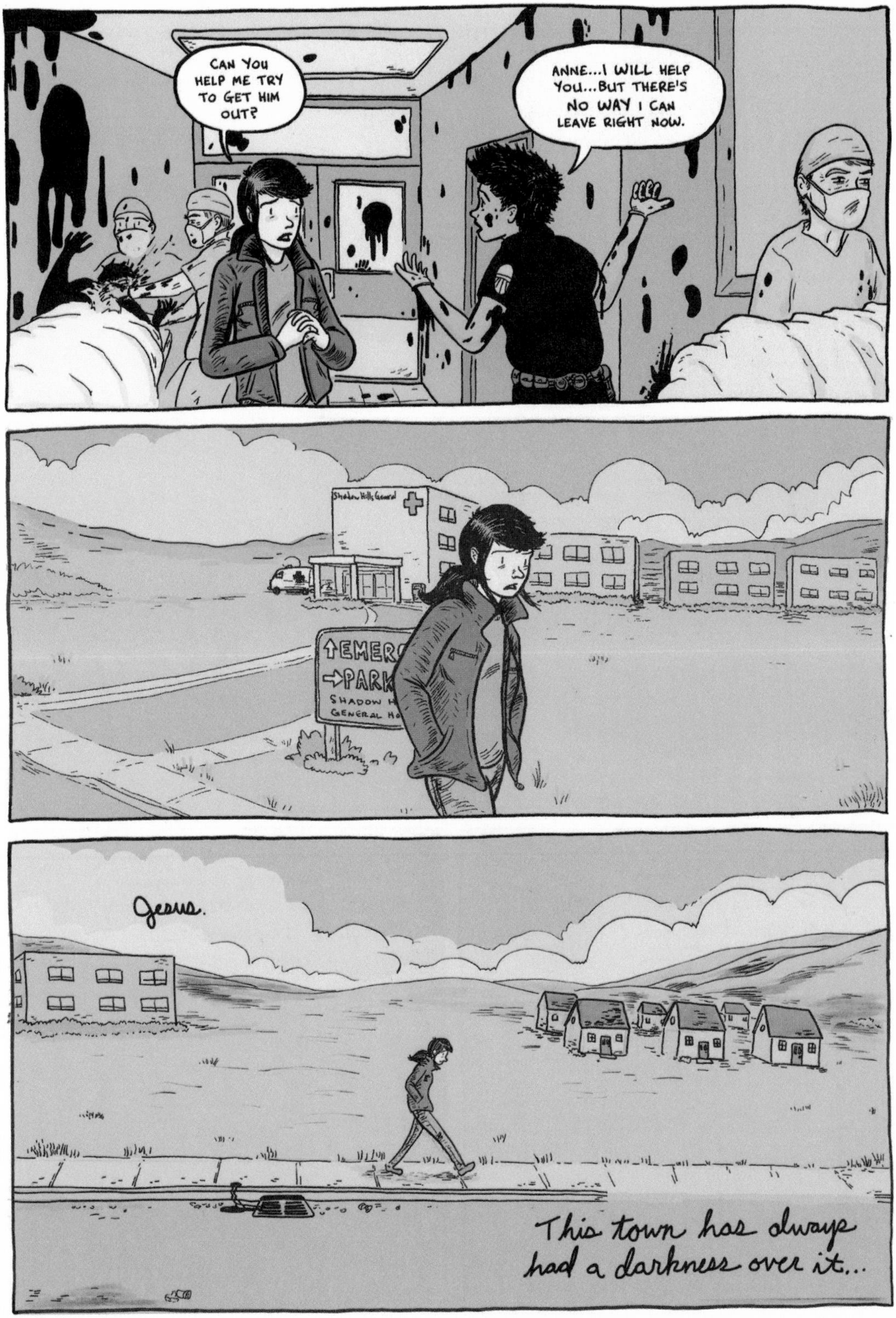
CAN YOU HELP ME TRY TO GET HIM OUT?
ANNE...I WILL HELP YOU...BUT THERE'S NO WAY I CAN LEAVE RIGHT NOW.
Shadow Hills General
EMERG
PARK
SHADOW H
GENERAL HO
Jesus.
This town has always had a darkness over it...

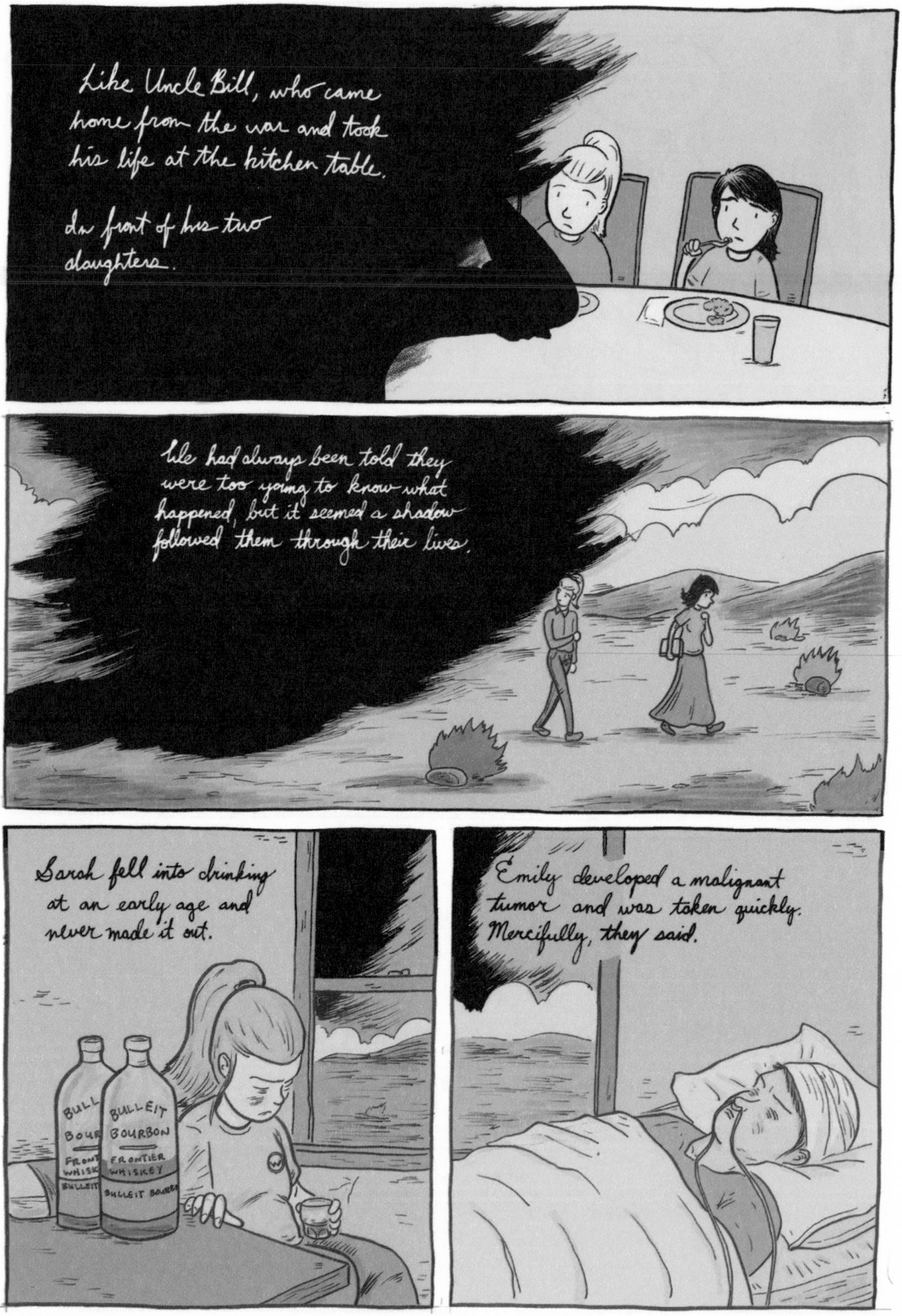
Like Uncle Bill, who came home from the war and took his life at the kitchen table.
In front of his two daughters.
We had always been told they were too young to know what happened, but it seemed a shadow followed them through their lives.
Sarah fell into drinking at an early age and never made it out.
BULLEIT BOURBON FRONTIER WHISKEY
BULLEIT BOURBON
Emily developed a malignant tumor and was taken quickly. Mercifully, they said.

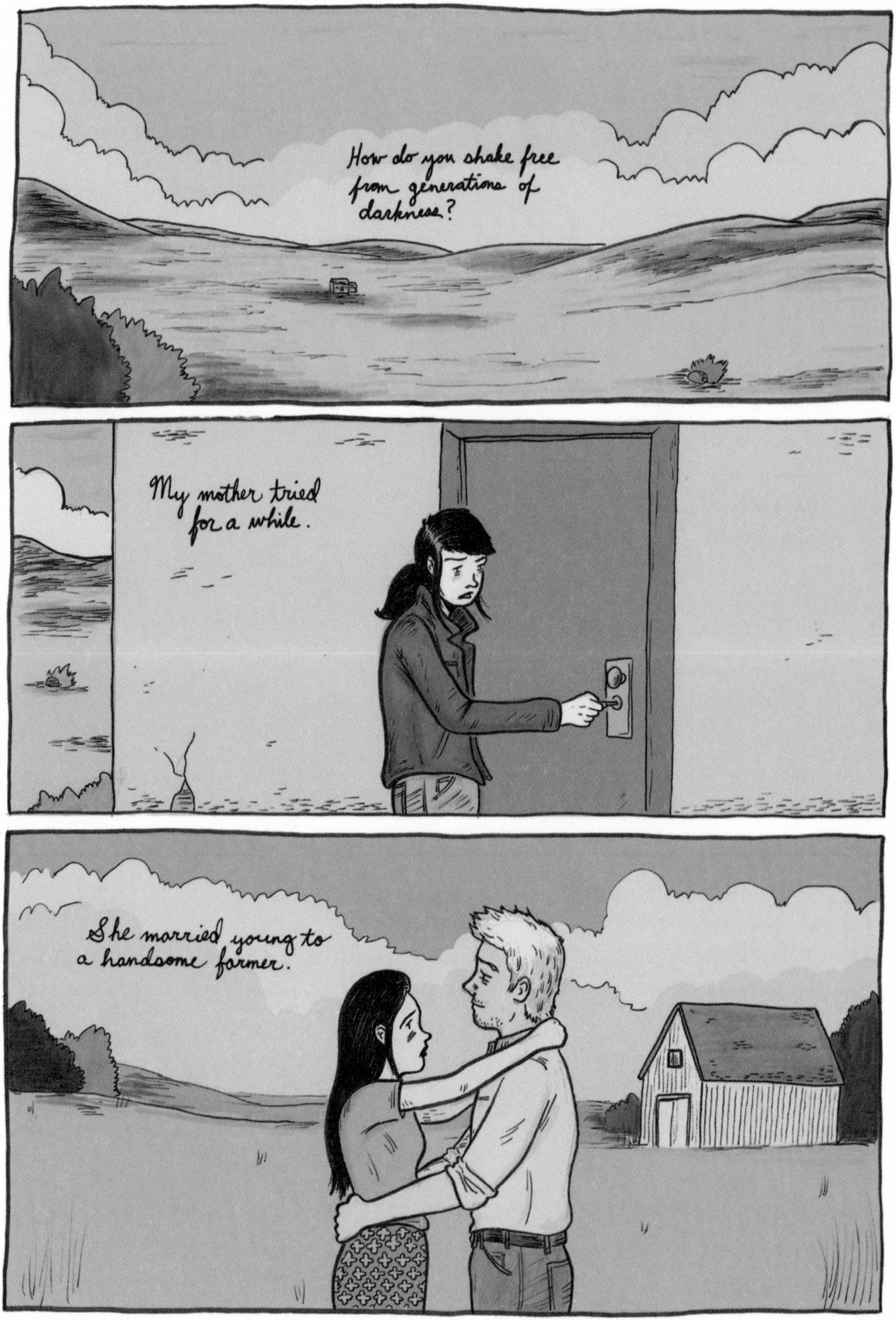
How do you shake free from generations of darkness?
My mother tried for a while.
She married young to a handsome farmer.

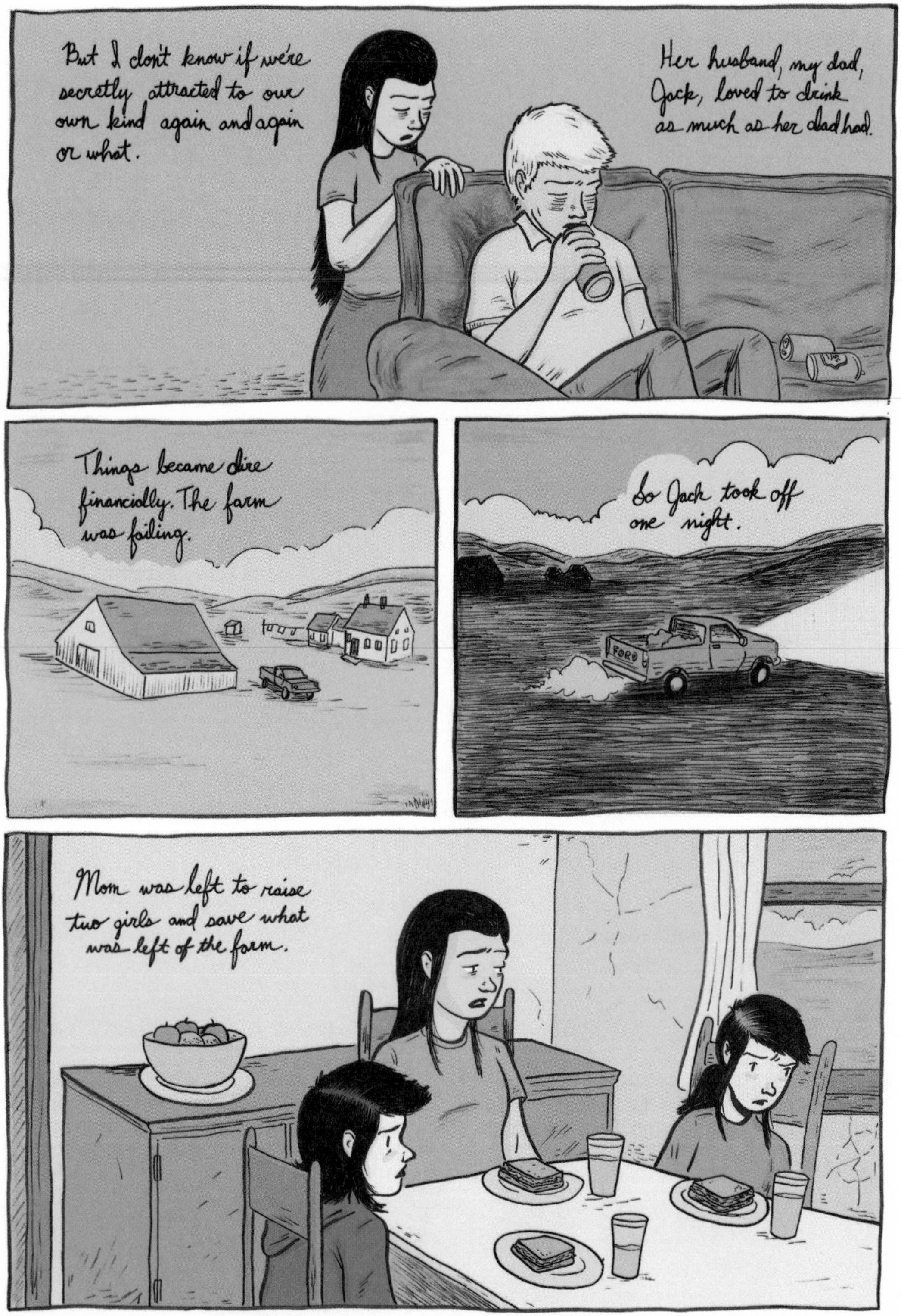
But I don't know if we're secretly attracted to our own kind again and again or what.
Her husband, my dad, Jack, loved to drink as much as her dad had.
Things became dire financially. The farm was failing.
So Jack took off one night.
FORD
Mom was left to raise two girls and save what was left of the farm.

She was able to lease parts of the farm to Will's company and keep a small piece that fed us and gave us produce to sell at the market.

We were happy enough. Thankful for the small gifts life gave us.

Then we found out my sister had a growth on her brain.

A tumor.

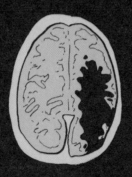

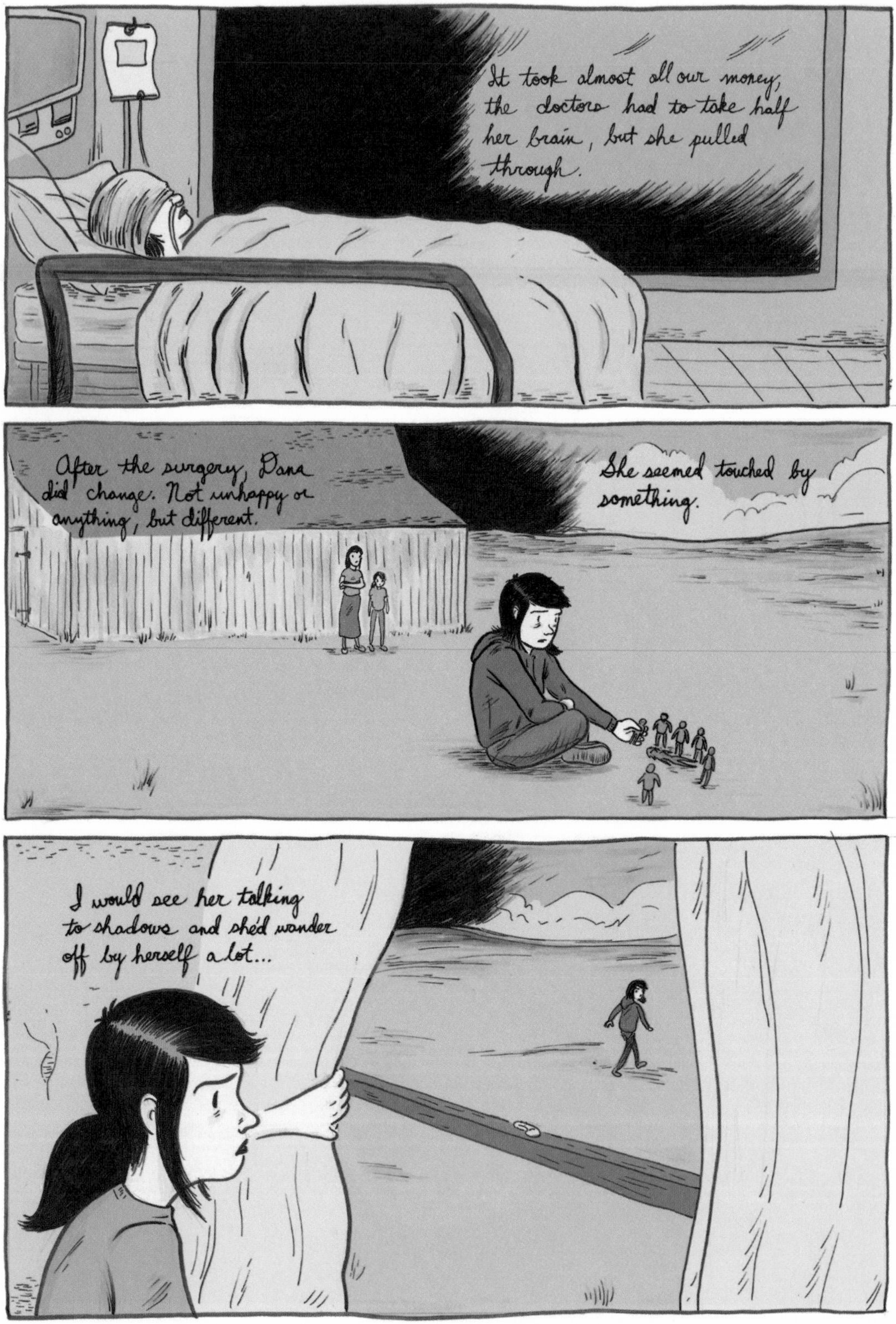

It took almost all our money, the doctors had to take half her brain, but she pulled through.
After the surgery, Dana did change. Not unhappy or anything, but different.
She seemed touched by something.
I would see her talking to shadows and she'd wander off by herself a lot...

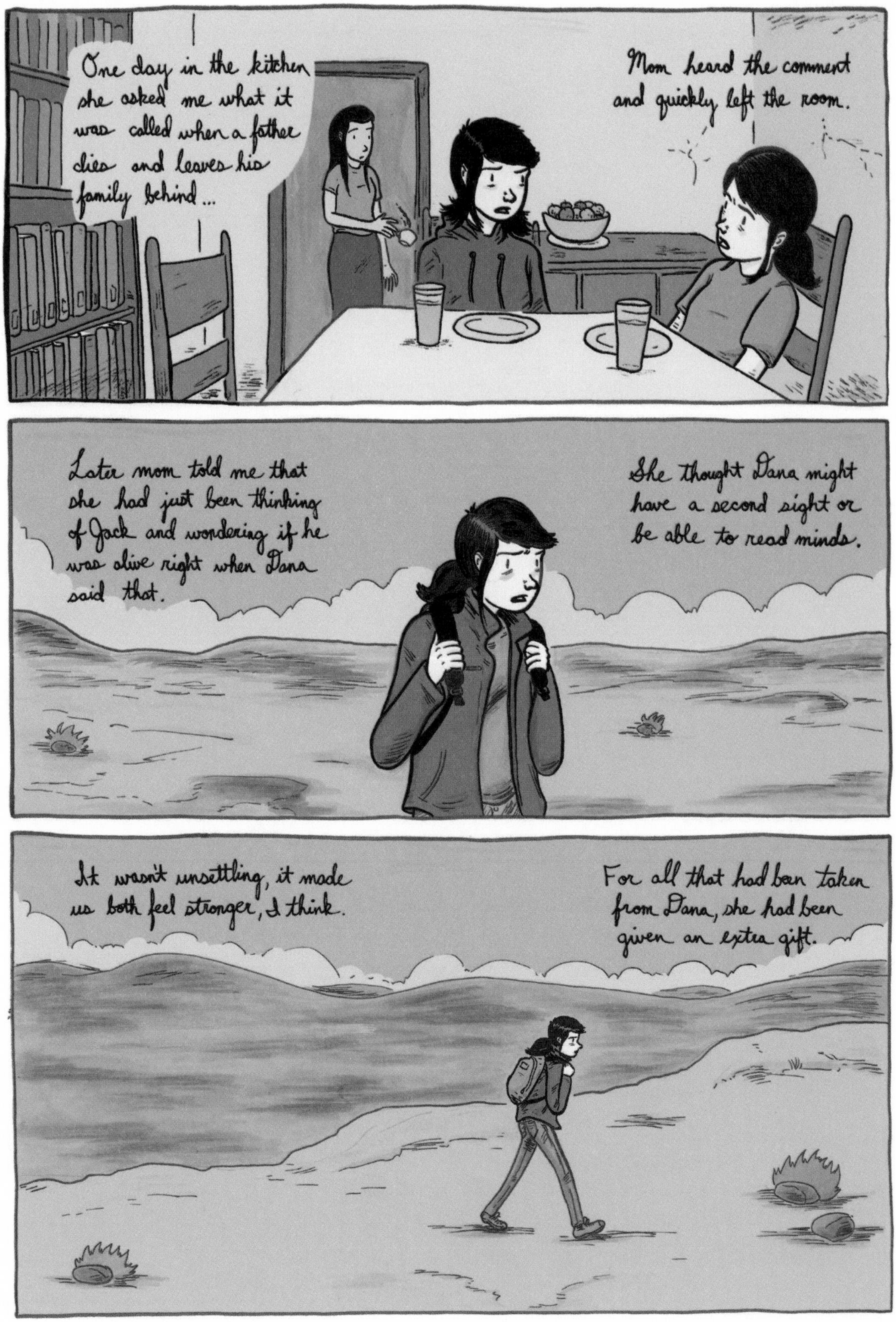
One day in the kitchen she asked me what it was called when a father dies and leaves his family behind...
Mom heard the comment and quickly left the room.
Later mom told me that she had just been thinking of Jack and wondering if he was alive right when Dana said that.
She thought Dana might have a second sight or be able to read minds.
It wasn't unsettling, it made us both feel stronger, I think.
For all that had been taken from Dana, she had been given an extra gift.

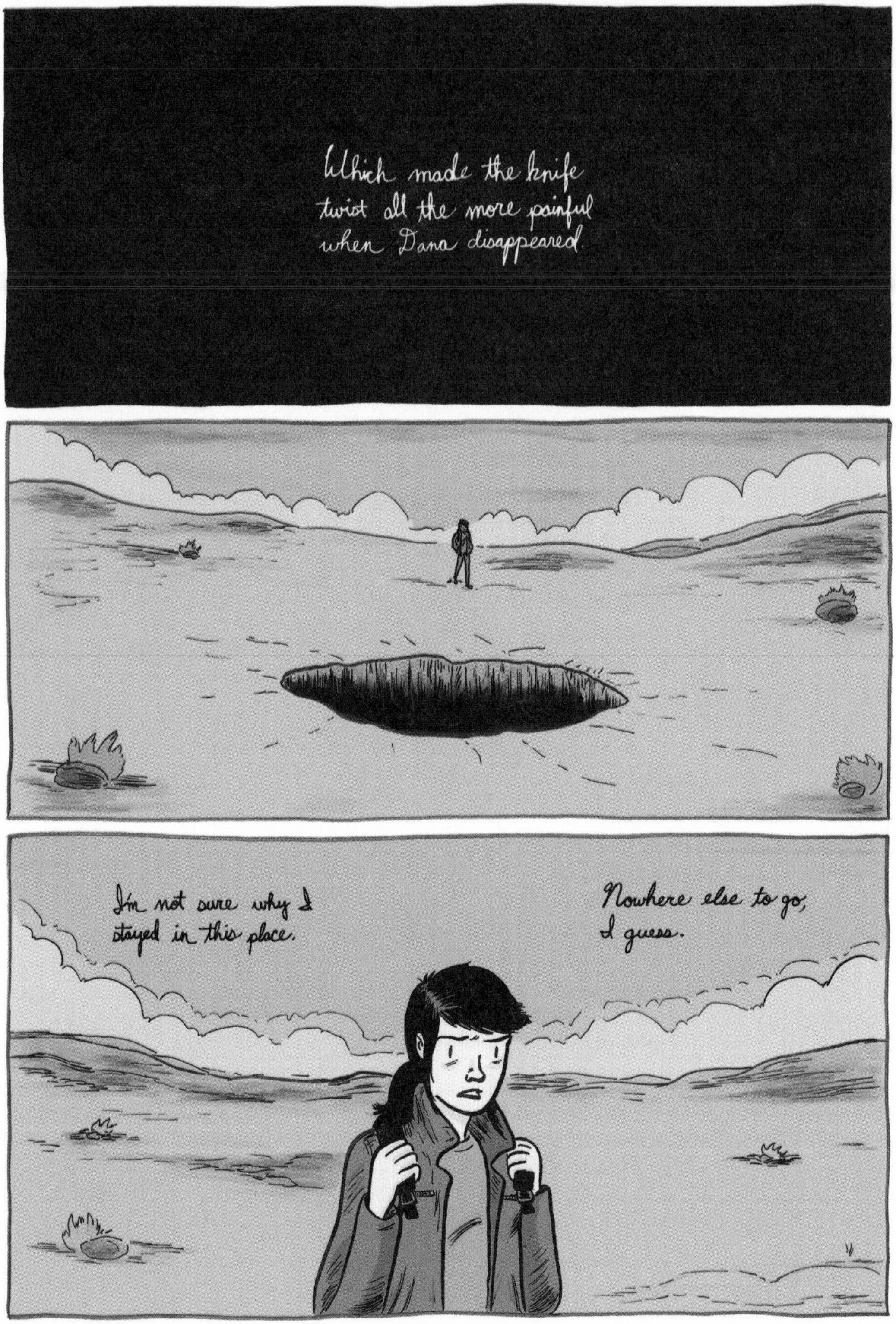
Which made the knife twist all the more painful when Dana disappeared.
I'm not sure why I stayed in this place.
Nowhere else to go, I guess.

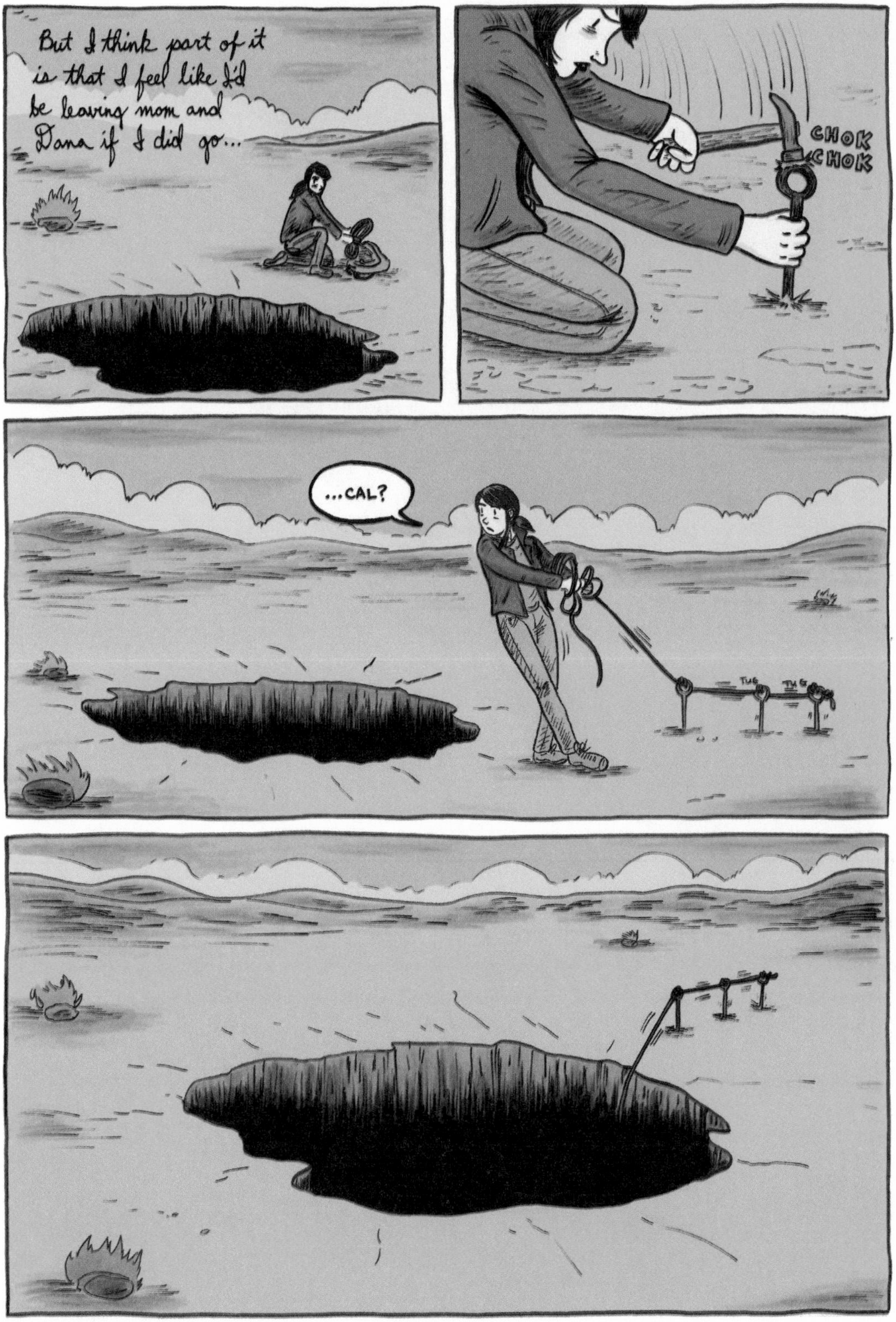
But I think part of it is that I feel like I'd be leaving mom and Dana if I did go...
CHOK CHOK
...CAL?
TUG TUG

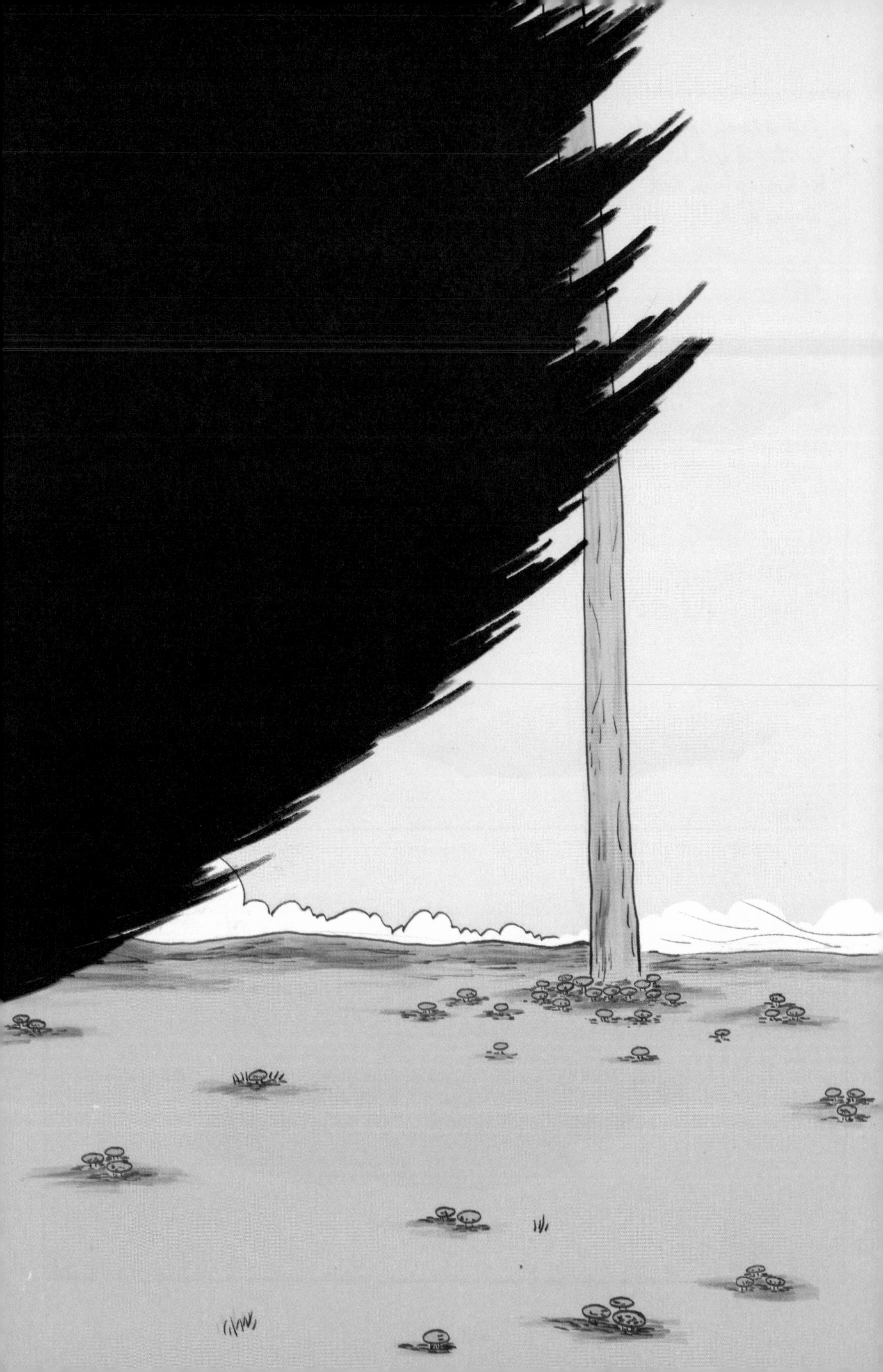

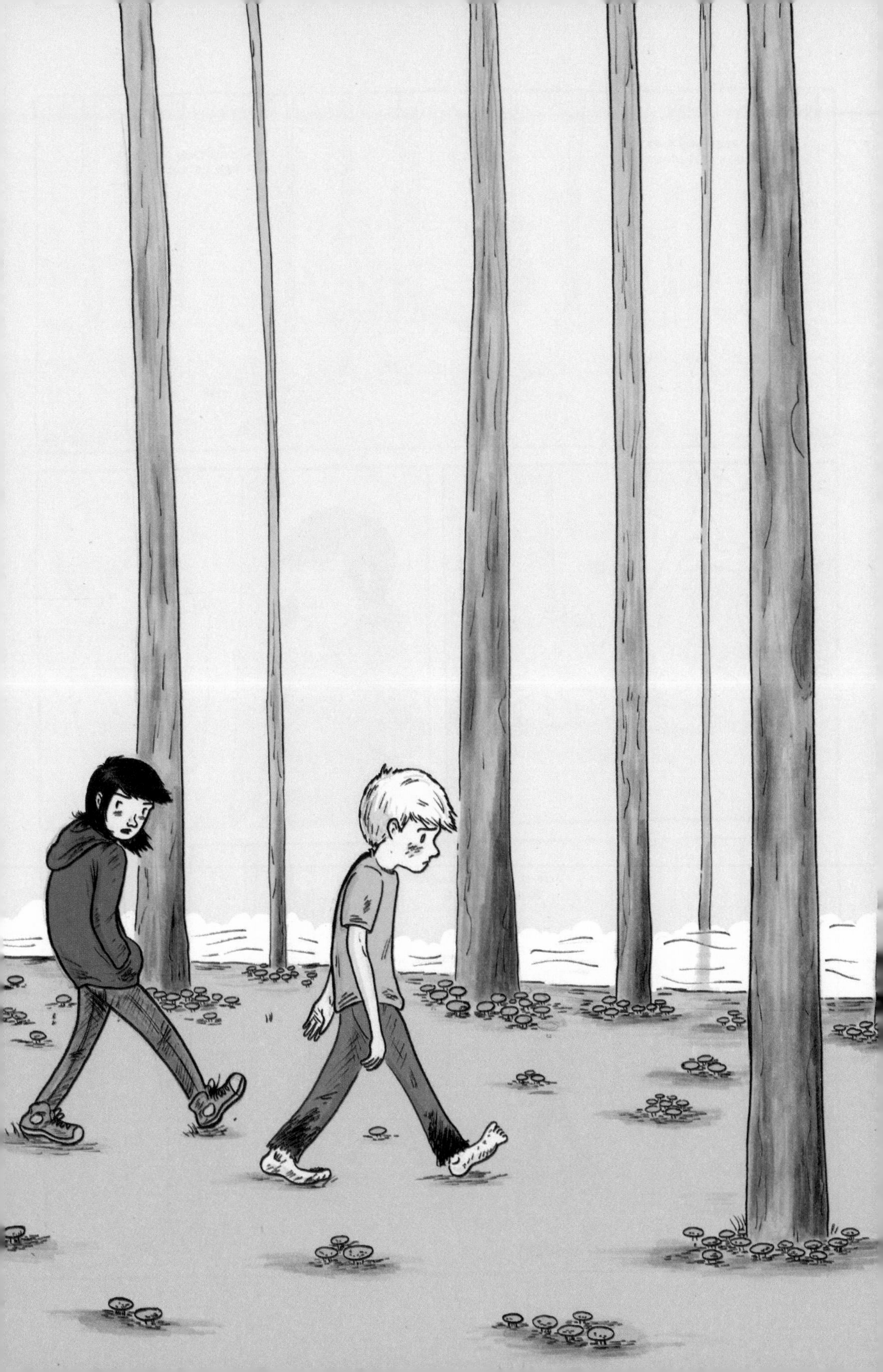

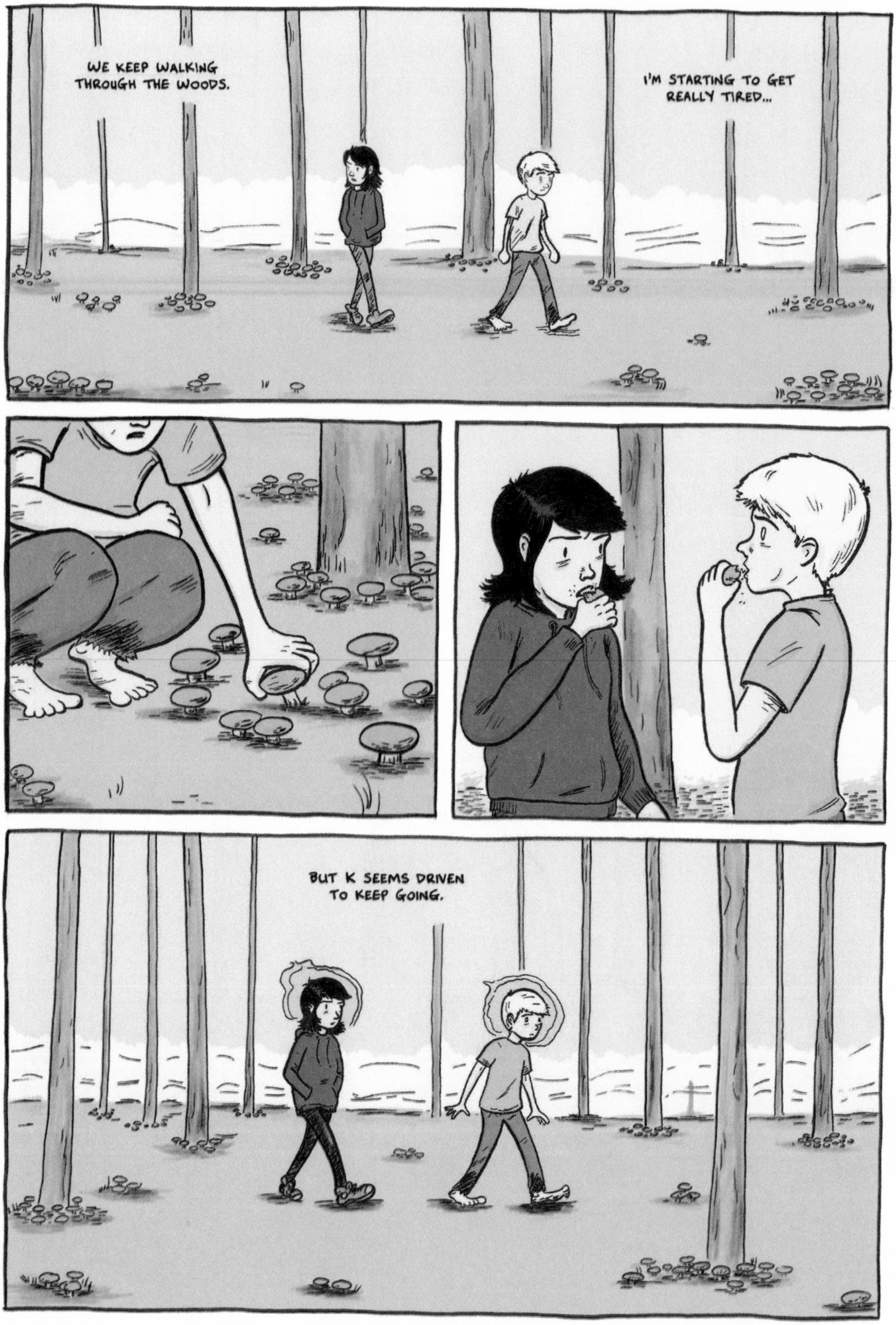
WE KEEP WALKING THROUGH THE WOODS.
I'M STARTING TO GET REALLY TIRED...
BUT K SEEMS DRIVEN TO KEEP GOING.

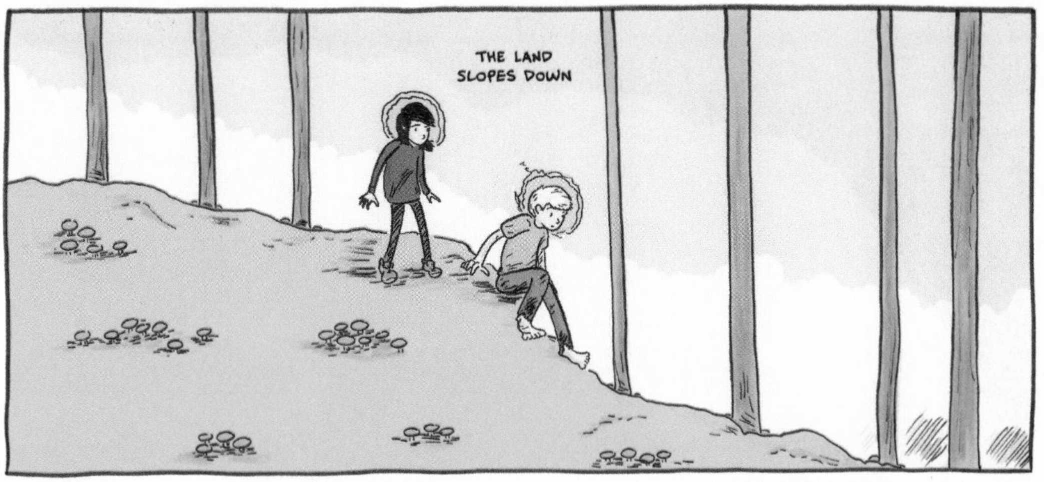
THE LAND
SLOPES DOWN

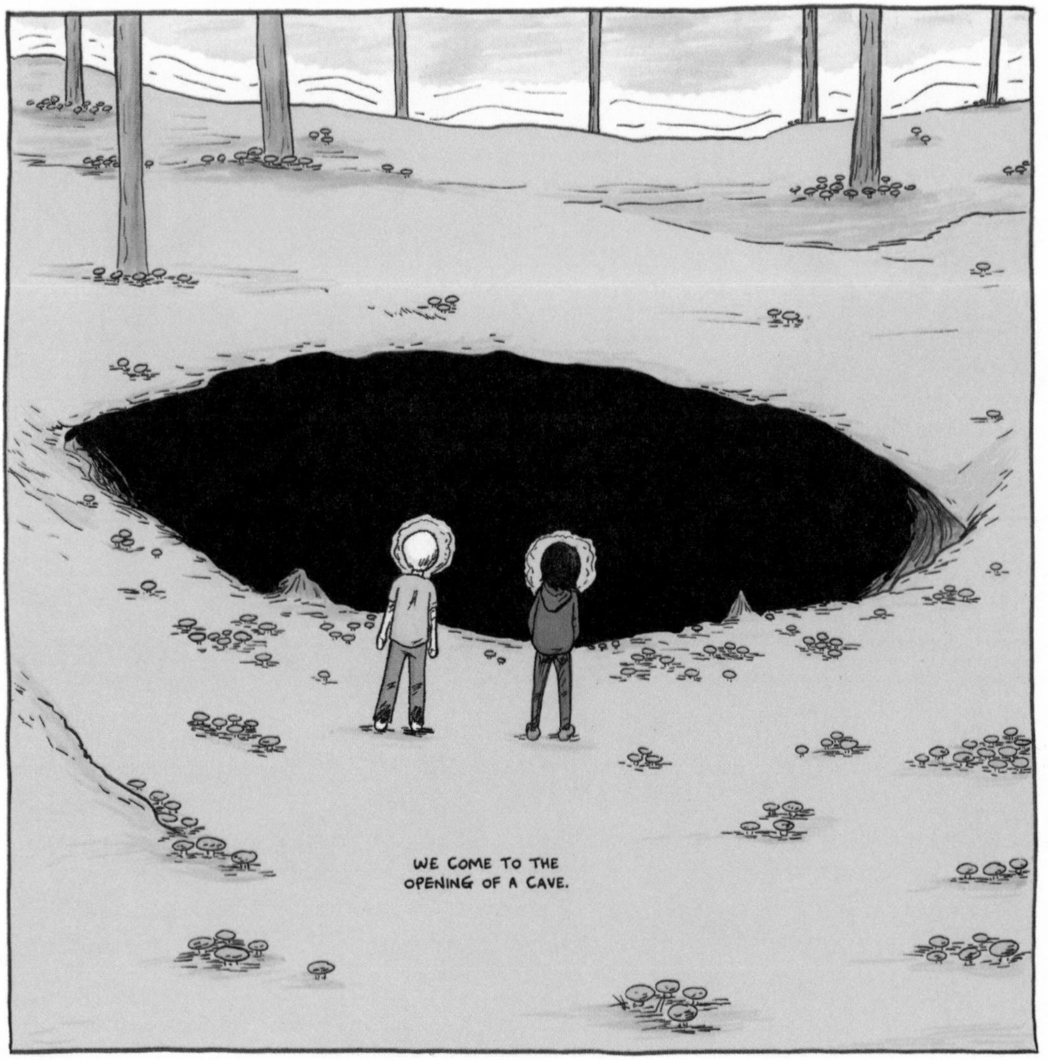
WE COME TO THE
OPENING OF A CAVE.

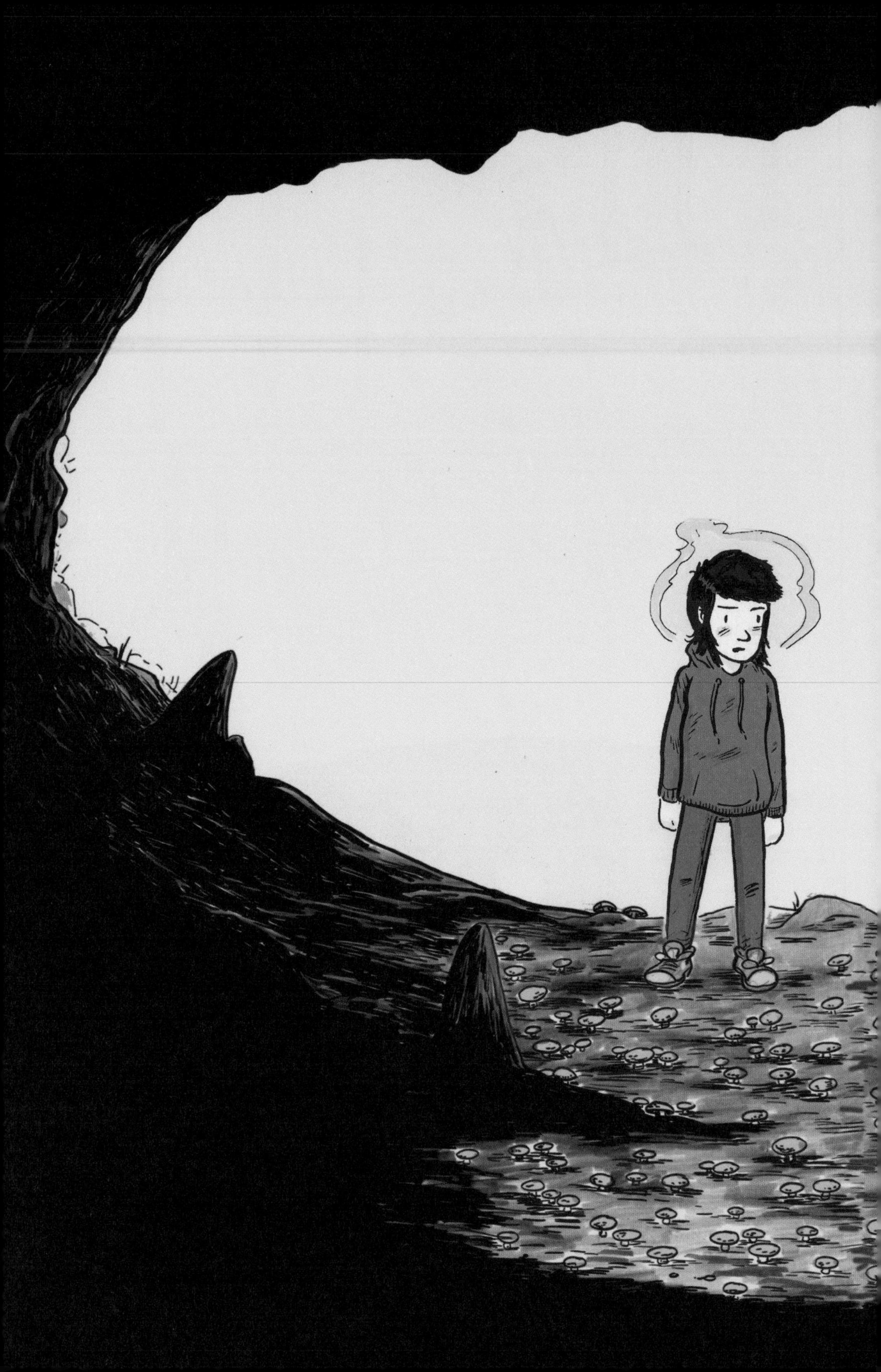

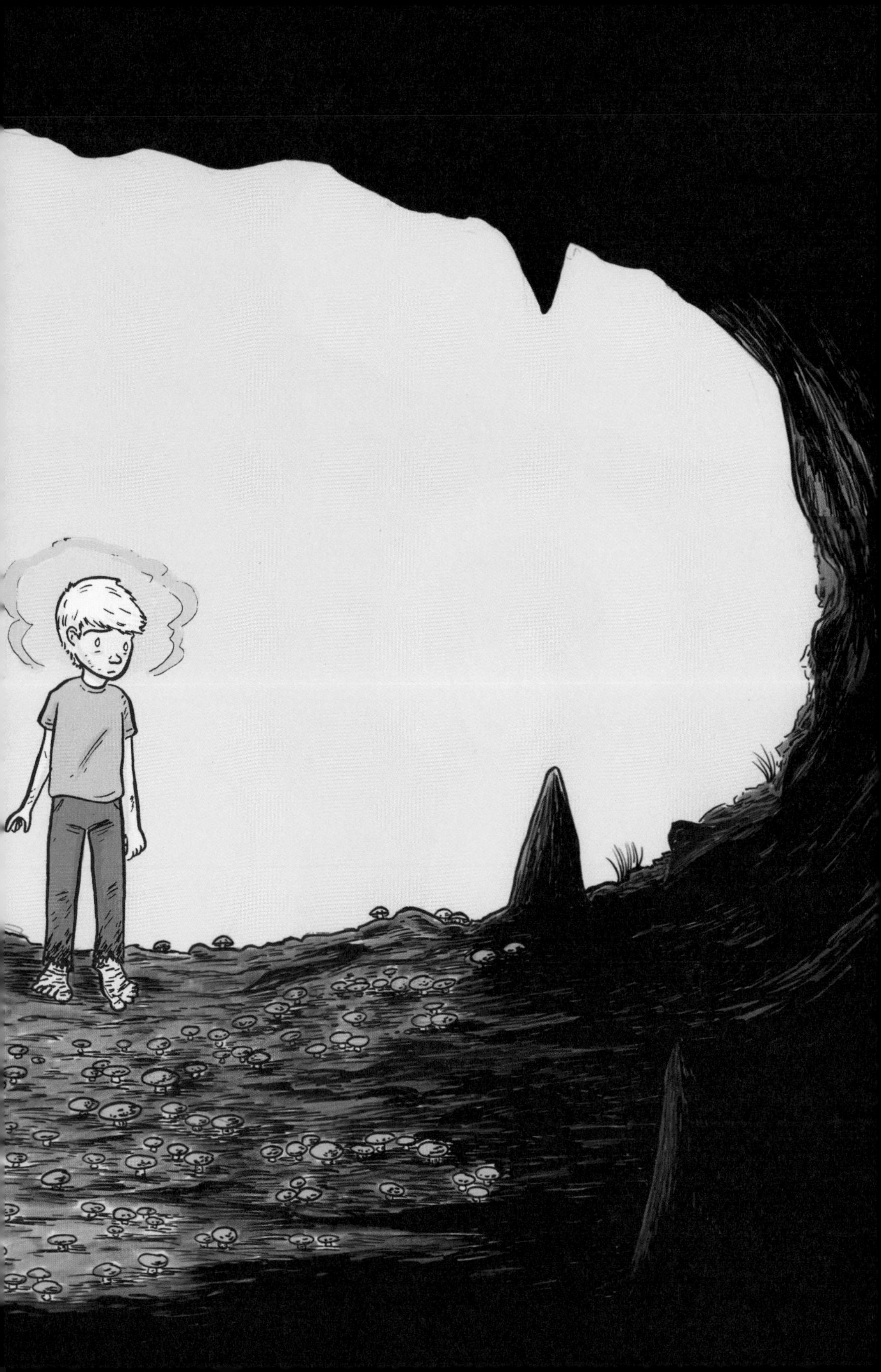

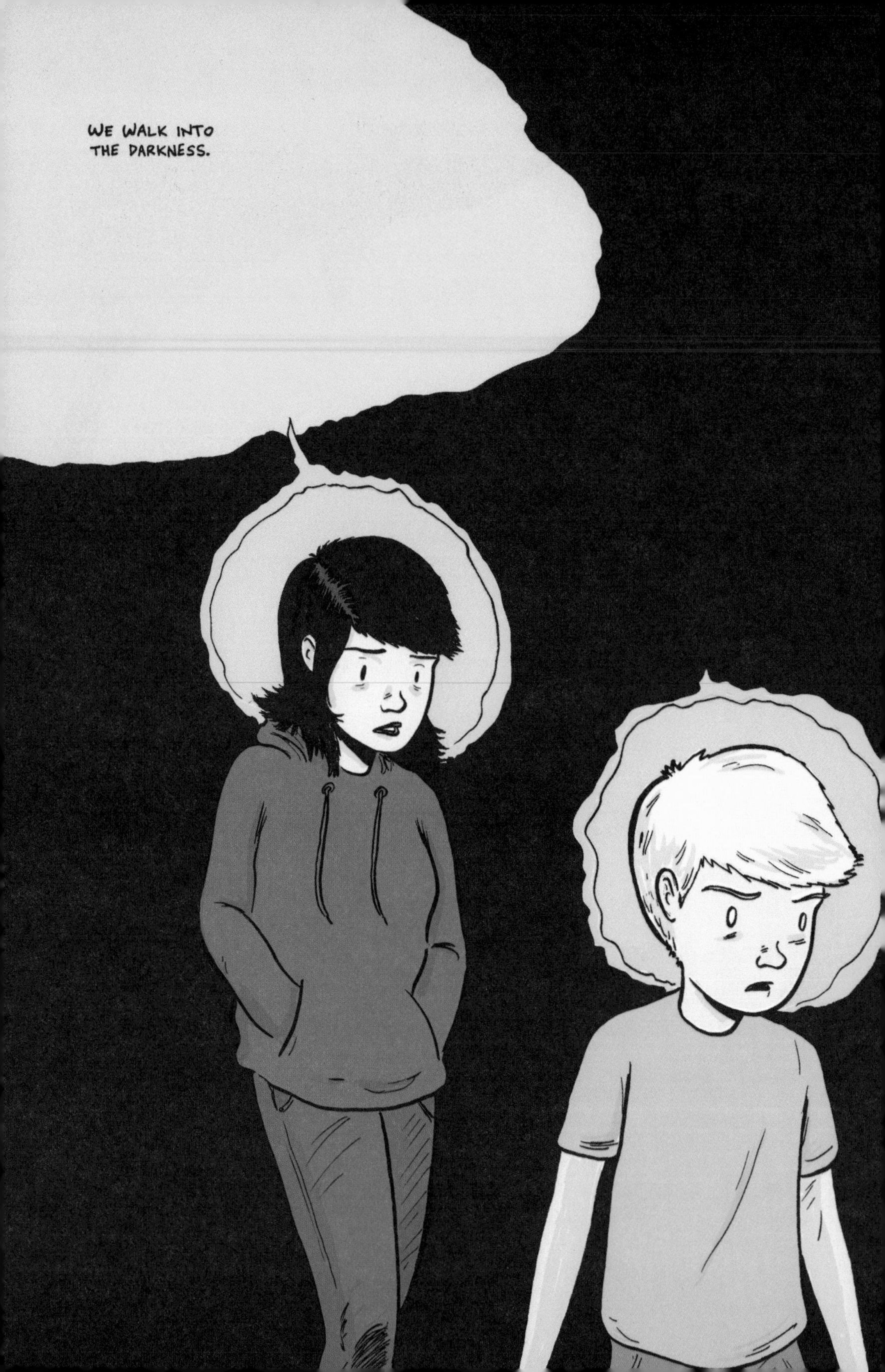
WE WALK INTO THE DARKNESS.

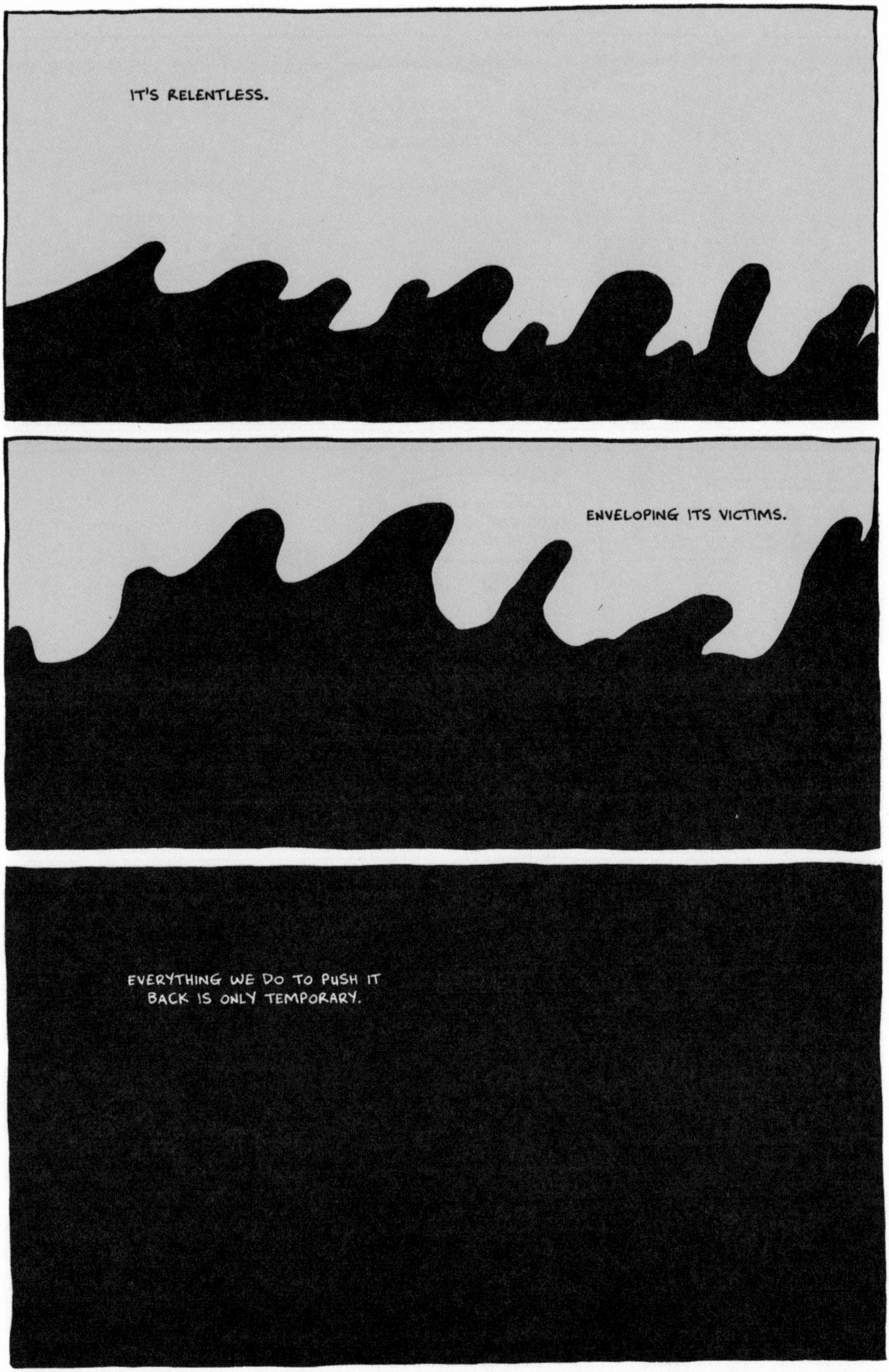
IT'S RELENTLESS.
ENVELOPING ITS VICTIMS.
EVERYTHING WE DO TO PUSH IT BACK IS ONLY TEMPORARY.

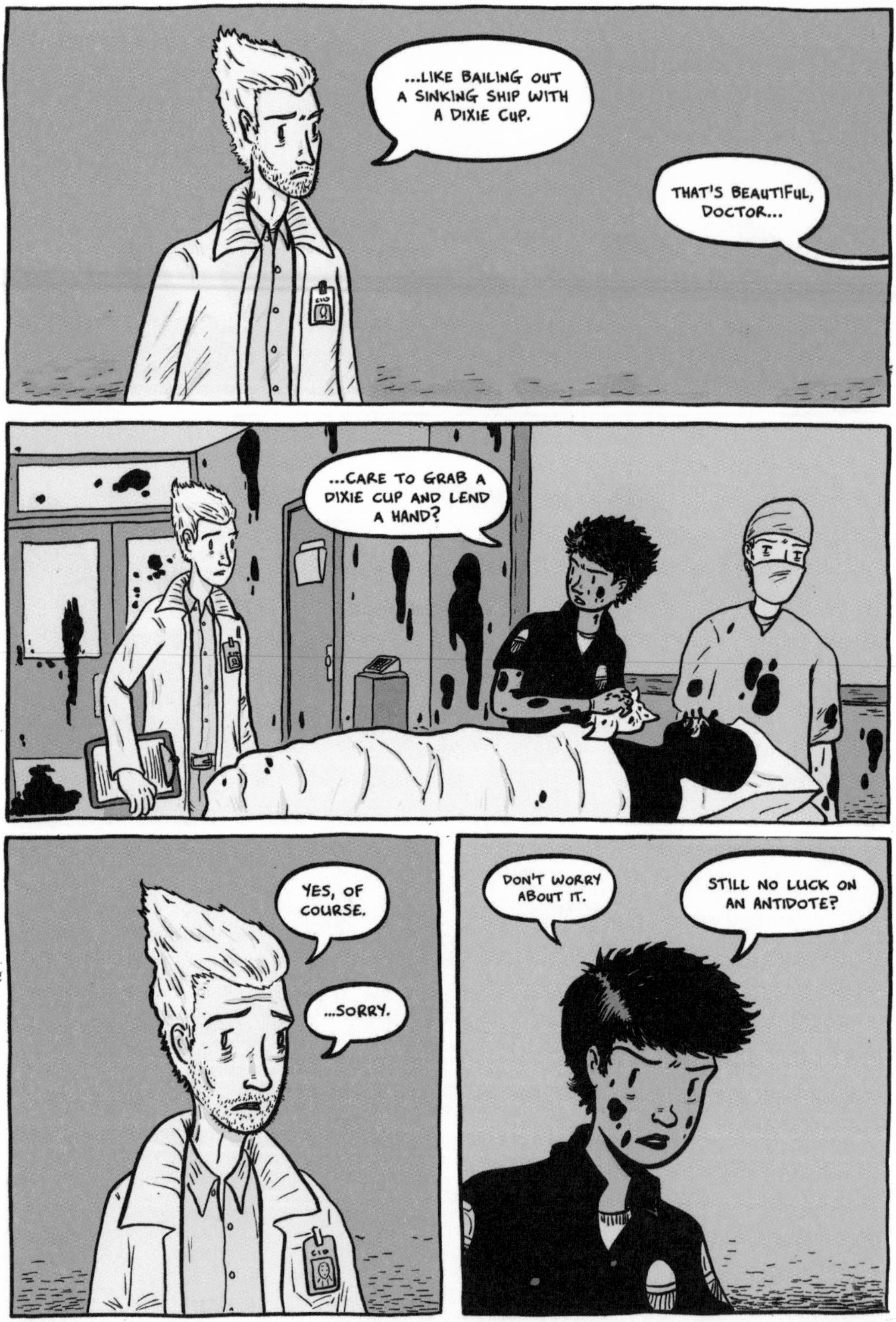
...LIKE BAILING OUT A SINKING SHIP WITH A DIXIE CUP.
THAT'S BEAUTIFUL, DOCTOR...
...CARE TO GRAB A DIXIE CUP AND LEND A HAND?
YES, OF COURSE.
...SORRY.
DON'T WORRY ABOUT IT.
STILL NO LUCK ON AN ANTIDOTE?

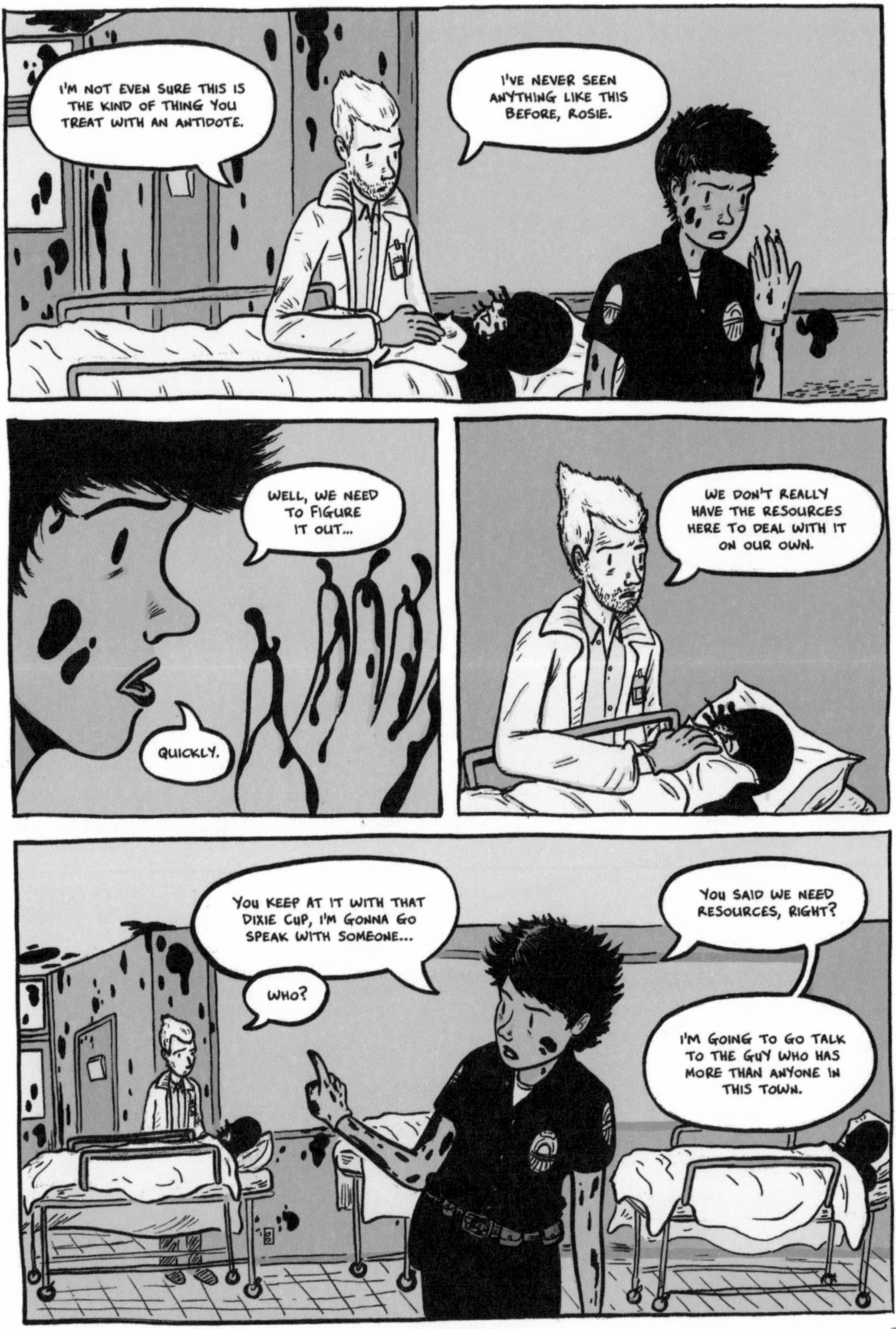
I'M NOT EVEN SURE THIS IS THE KIND OF THING YOU TREAT WITH AN ANTIDOTE.
I'VE NEVER SEEN ANYTHING LIKE THIS BEFORE, ROSIE.
WELL, WE NEED TO FIGURE IT OUT...
QUICKLY.
WE DON'T REALLY HAVE THE RESOURCES HERE TO DEAL WITH IT ON OUR OWN.
YOU KEEP AT IT WITH THAT DIXIE CUP, I'M GONNA GO SPEAK WITH SOMEONE...
WHO?
YOU SAID WE NEED RESOURCES, RIGHT?
I'M GOING TO GO TALK TO THE GUY WHO HAS MORE THAN ANYONE IN THIS TOWN.

6.

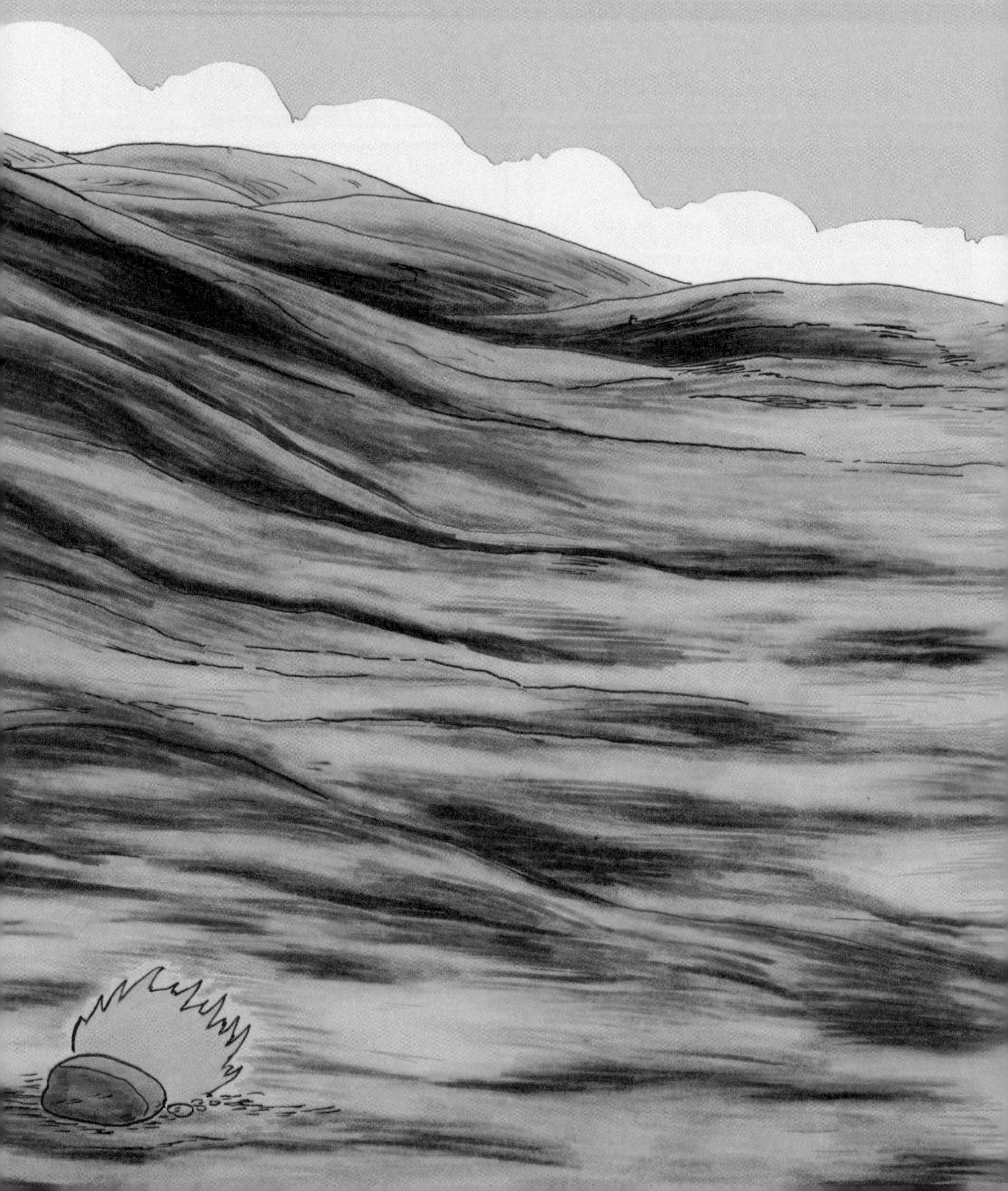

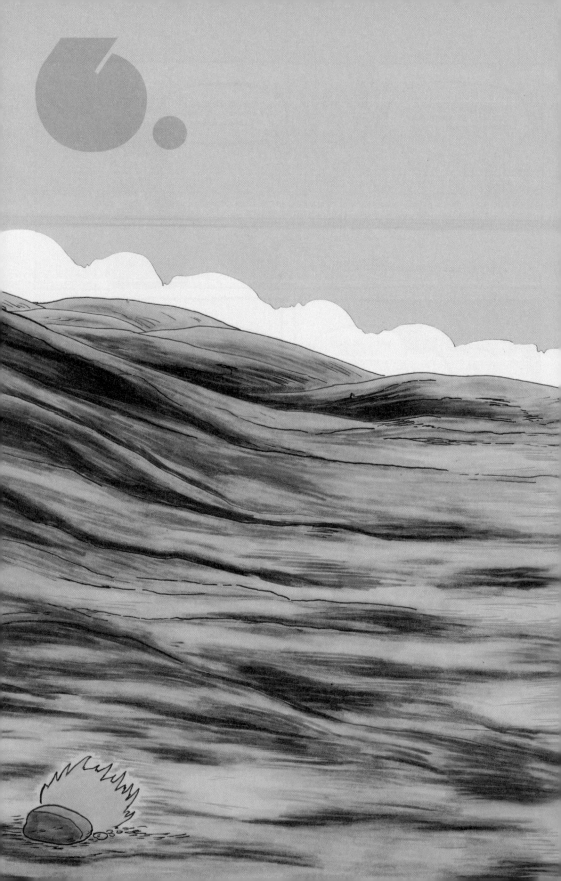

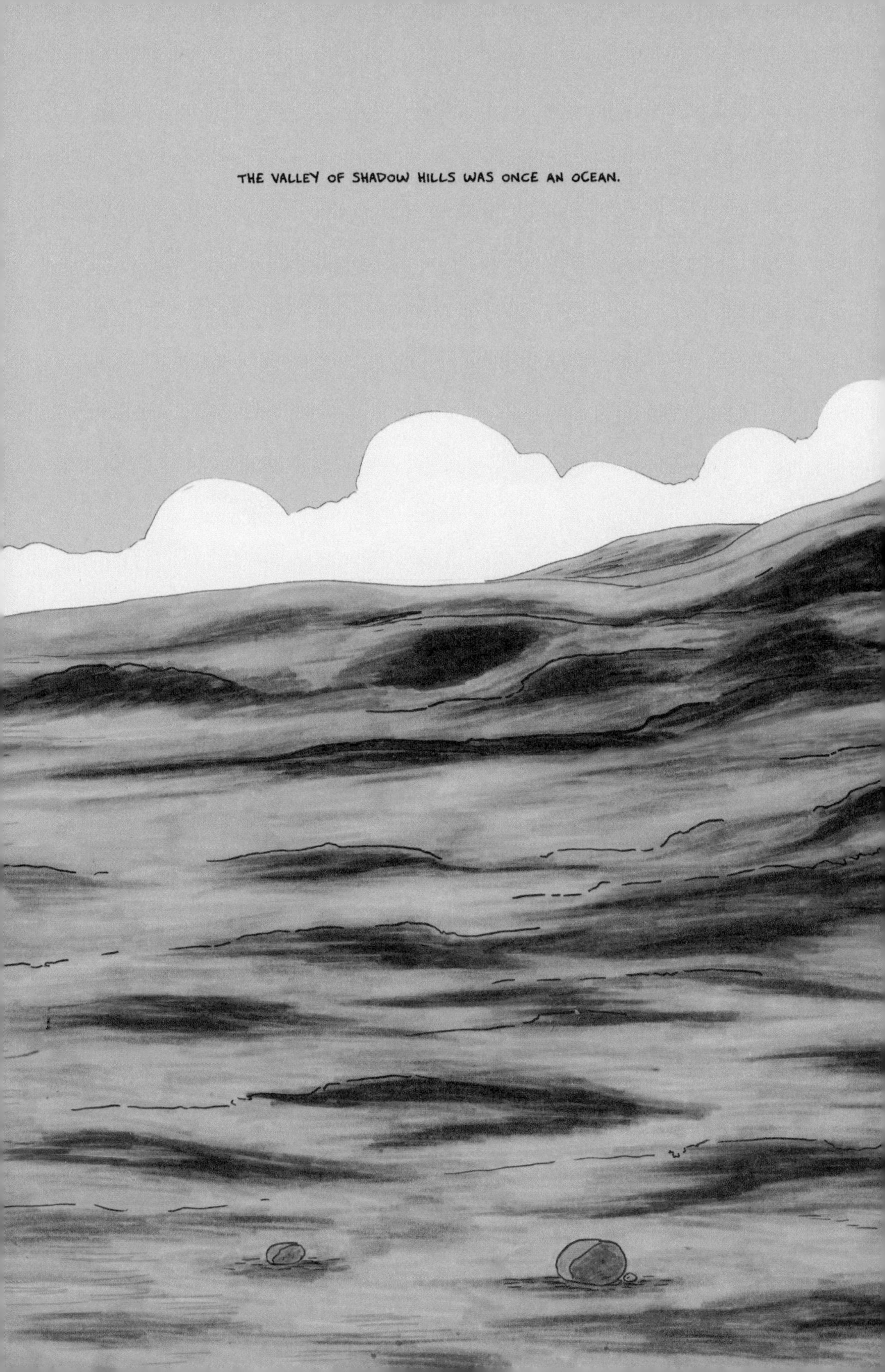
THE VALLEY OF SHADOW HILLS WAS ONCE AN OCEAN.

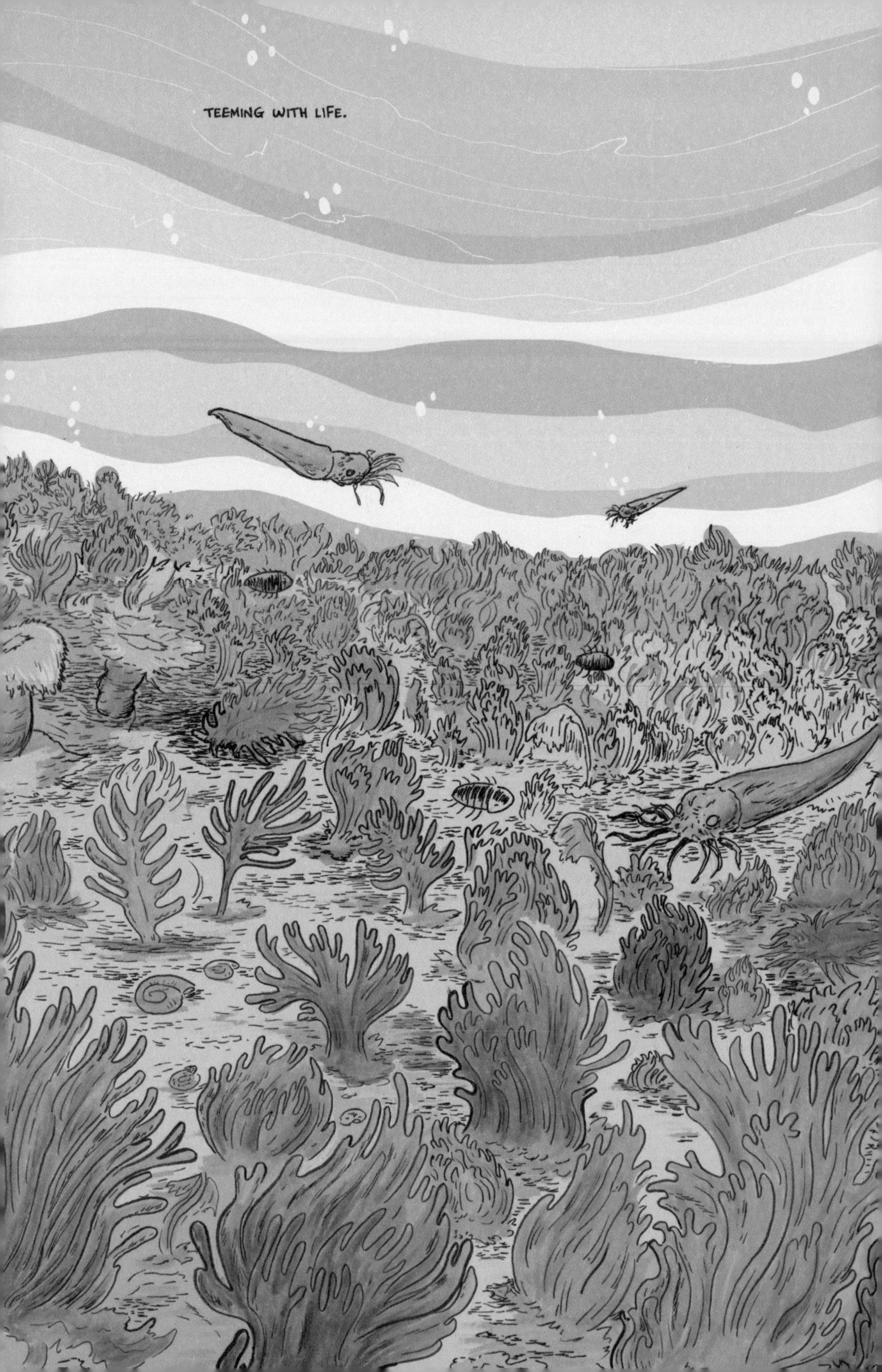
TEEMING WITH LIFE.

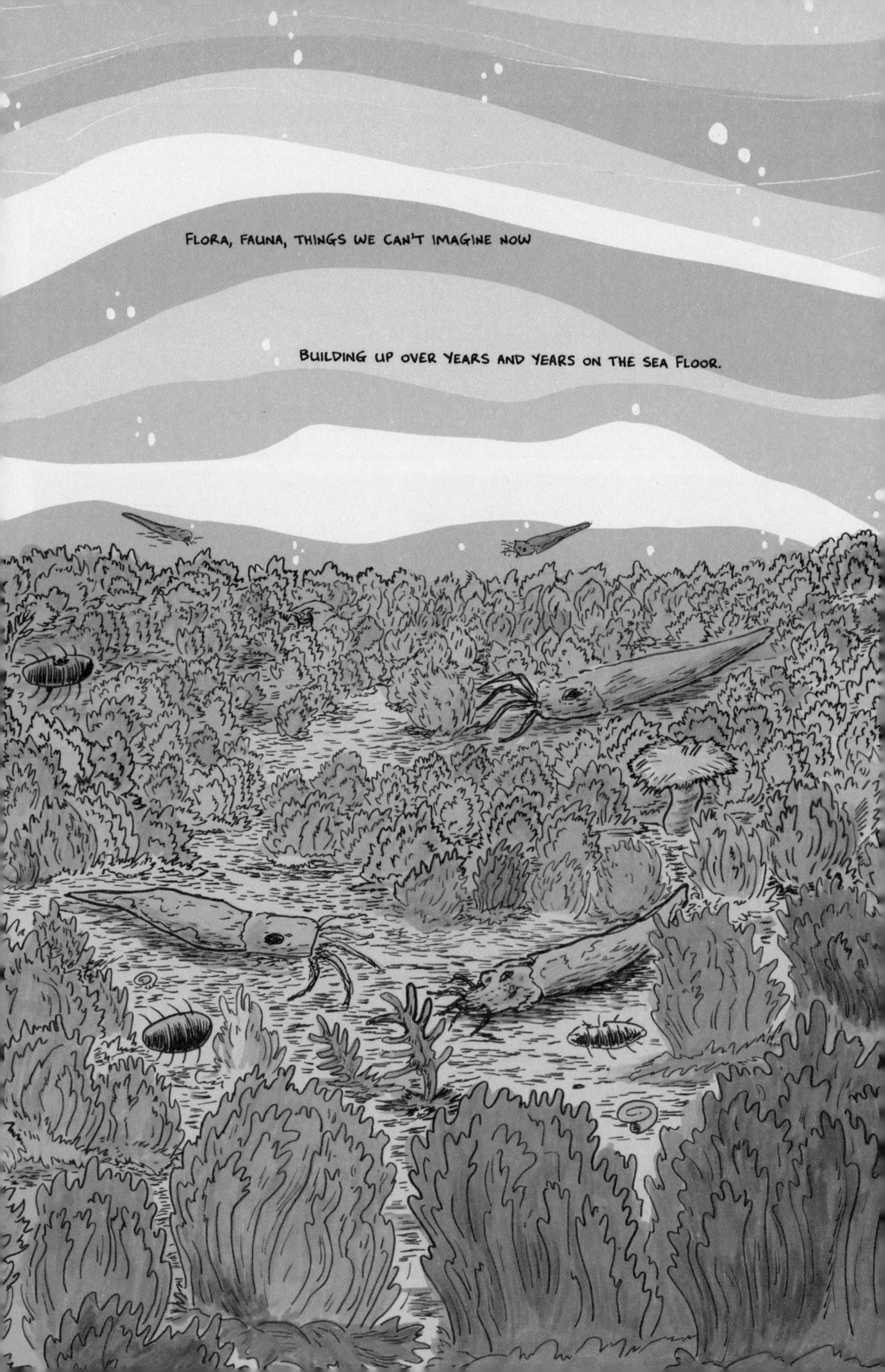
FLORA, FAUNA, THINGS WE CAN'T IMAGINE NOW
BUILDING UP OVER YEARS AND YEARS ON THE SEA FLOOR.

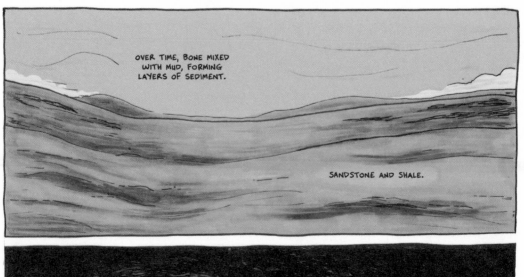

OVER TIME, BONE MIXED WITH MUD, FORMING LAYERS OF SEDIMENT.

SANDSTONE AND SHALE.

AS THE SEA RECEDED AND AN ICE AGE PASSED

DROPS OF MOISTURE CARVED AND ERODED

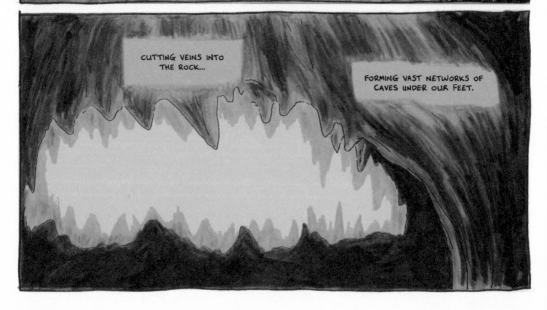

CUTTING VEINS INTO THE ROCK...

FORMING VAST NETWORKS OF CAVES UNDER OUR FEET.

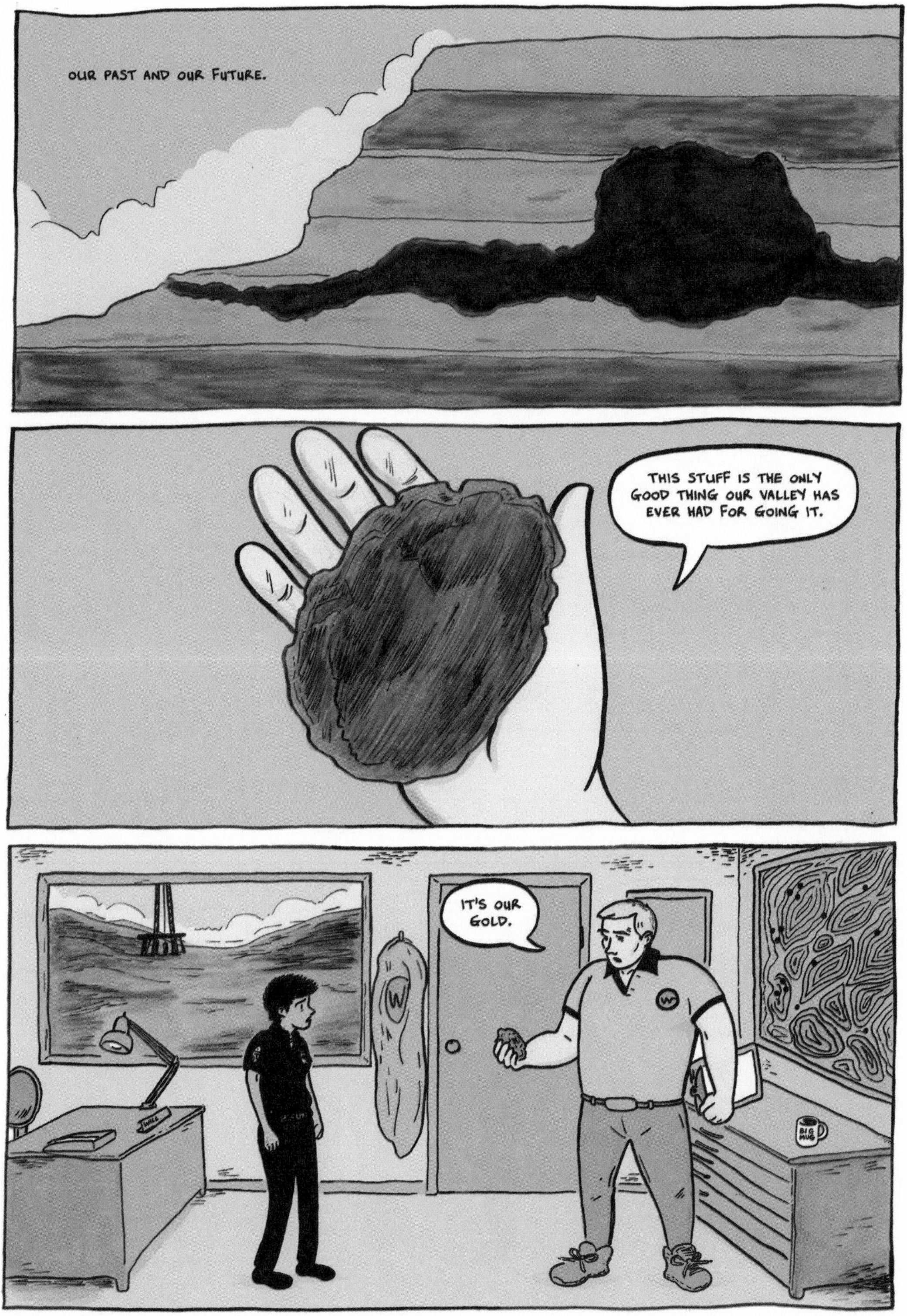
OUR PAST AND OUR FUTURE.
THIS STUFF IS THE ONLY GOOD THING OUR VALLEY HAS EVER HAD FOR GOING IT.
IT'S OUR GOLD.
BIG MUG

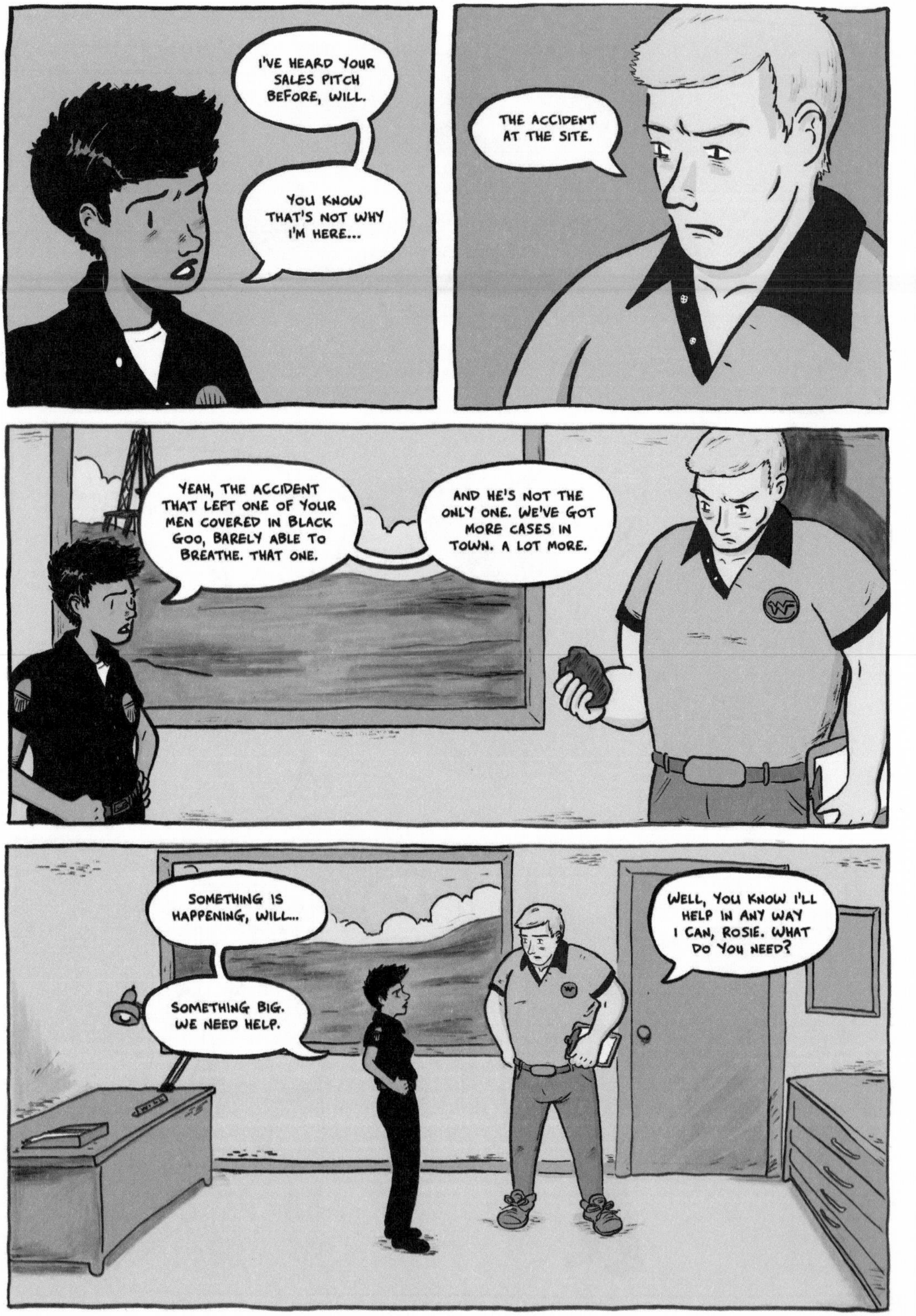
I'VE HEARD YOUR SALES PITCH BEFORE, WILL.
YOU KNOW THAT'S NOT WHY I'M HERE...
THE ACCIDENT AT THE SITE.
YEAH, THE ACCIDENT THAT LEFT ONE OF YOUR MEN COVERED IN BLACK GOO, BARELY ABLE TO BREATHE. THAT ONE.
AND HE'S NOT THE ONLY ONE. WE'VE GOT MORE CASES IN TOWN. A LOT MORE.
SOMETHING IS HAPPENING, WILL...
SOMETHING BIG. WE NEED HELP.
WELL, YOU KNOW I'LL HELP IN ANY WAY I CAN, ROSIE. WHAT DO YOU NEED?

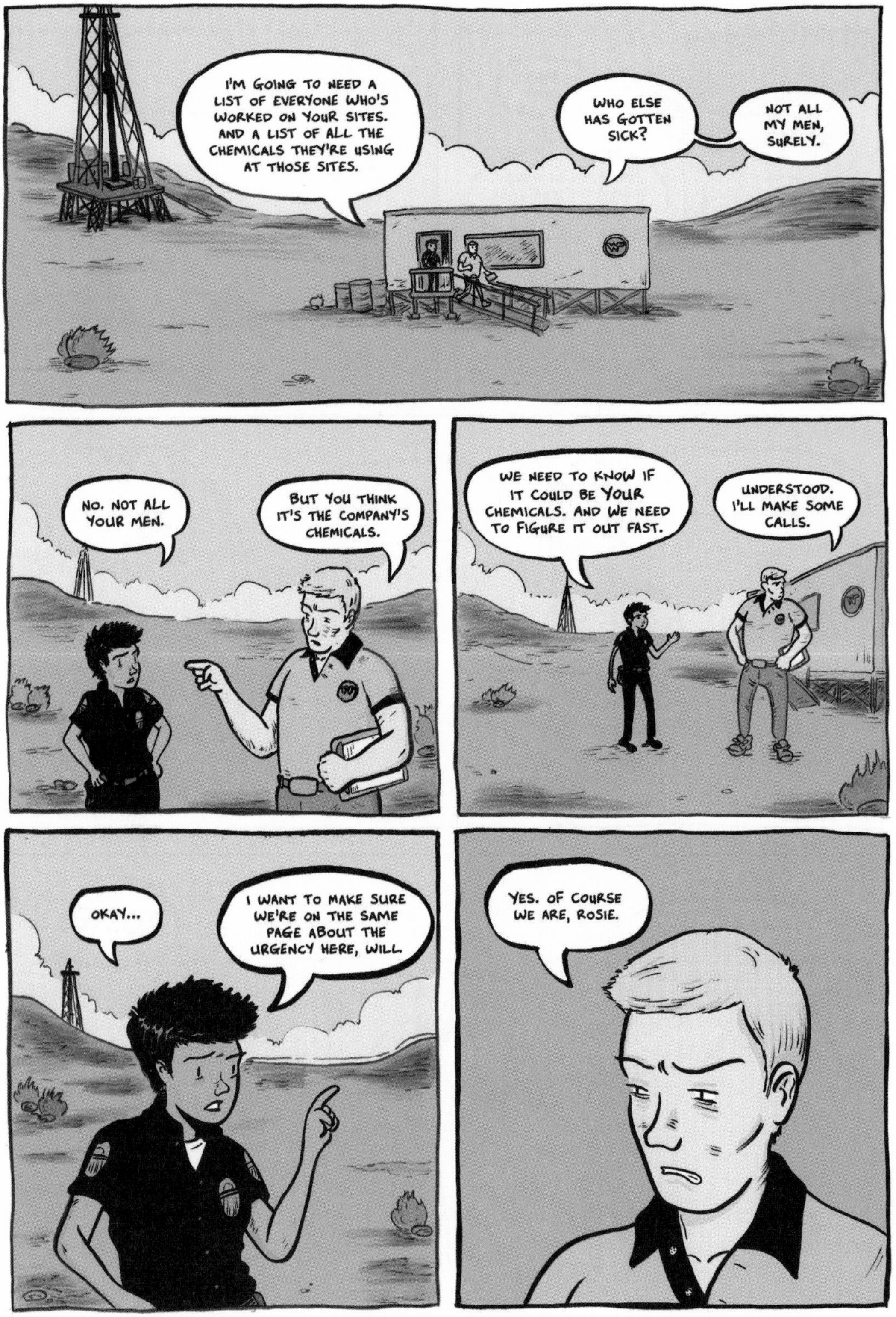
I'M GOING TO NEED A LIST OF EVERYONE WHO'S WORKED ON YOUR SITES. AND A LIST OF ALL THE CHEMICALS THEY'RE USING AT THOSE SITES.
WHO ELSE HAS GOTTEN SICK?
NOT ALL MY MEN, SURELY.
NO. NOT ALL YOUR MEN.
BUT YOU THINK IT'S THE COMPANY'S CHEMICALS.
WE NEED TO KNOW IF IT COULD BE YOUR CHEMICALS. AND WE NEED TO FIGURE IT OUT FAST.
UNDERSTOOD. I'LL MAKE SOME CALLS.
OKAY...
I WANT TO MAKE SURE WE'RE ON THE SAME PAGE ABOUT THE URGENCY HERE, WILL.
YES. OF COURSE WE ARE, ROSIE.

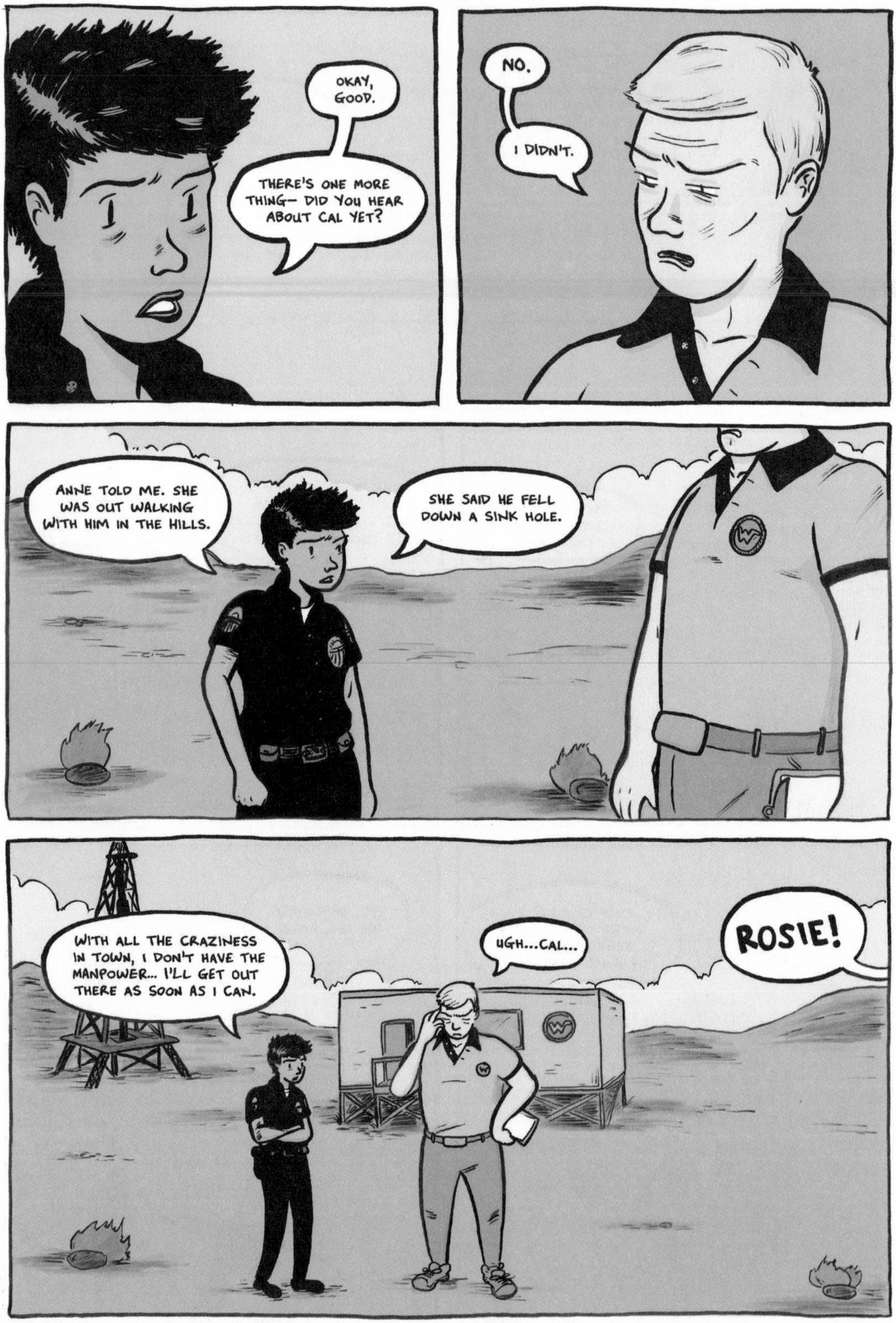
OKAY, GOOD.
THERE'S ONE MORE THING— DID YOU HEAR ABOUT CAL YET?
NO.
I DIDN'T.
ANNE TOLD ME. SHE WAS OUT WALKING WITH HIM IN THE HILLS.
SHE SAID HE FELL DOWN A SINK HOLE.
WITH ALL THE CRAZINESS IN TOWN, I DON'T HAVE THE MANPOWER... I'LL GET OUT THERE AS SOON AS I CAN.
UGH...CAL...
ROSIE!

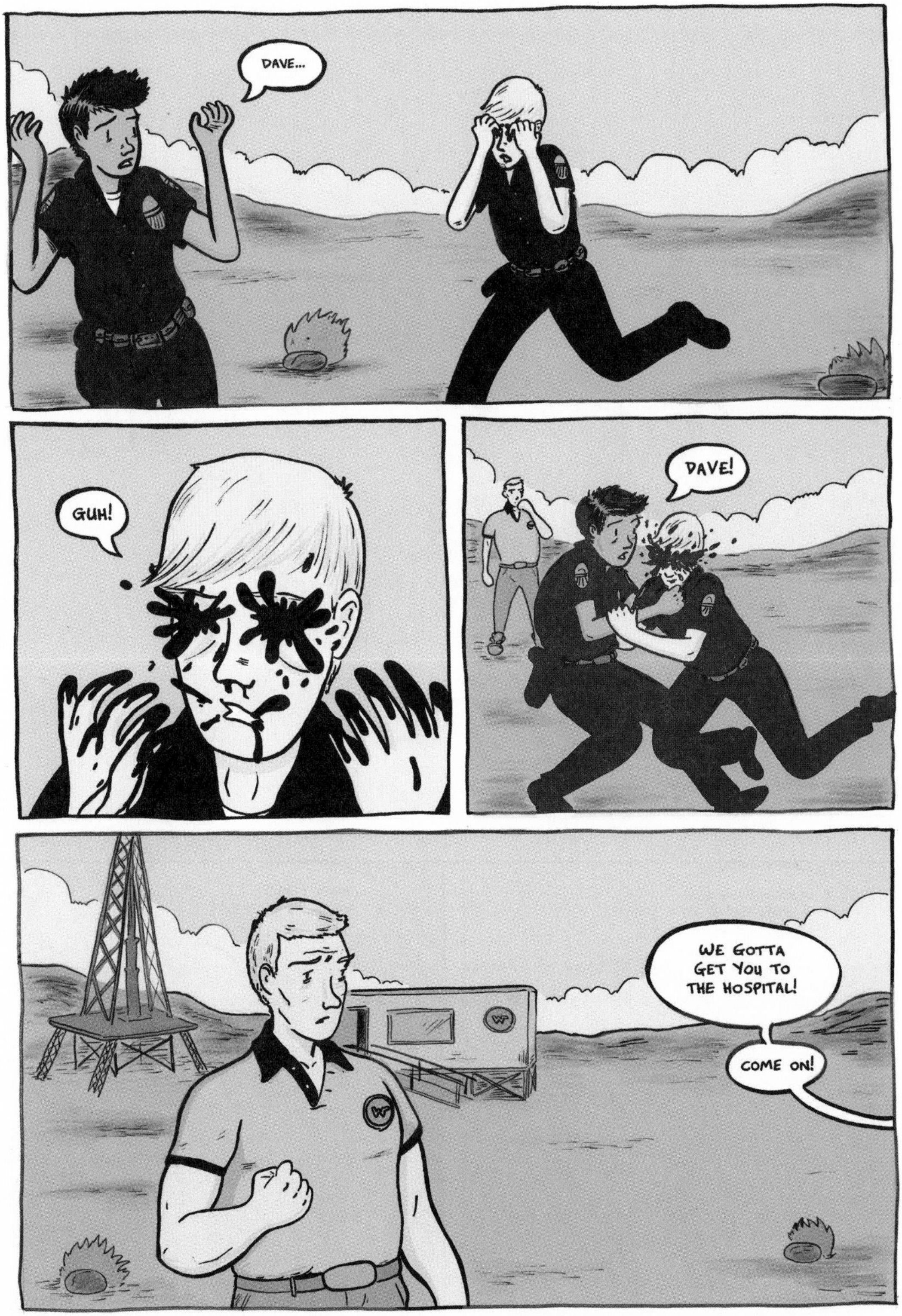
DAVE...
GUH!
DAVE!
WE GOTTA GET YOU TO THE HOSPITAL!
COME ON!

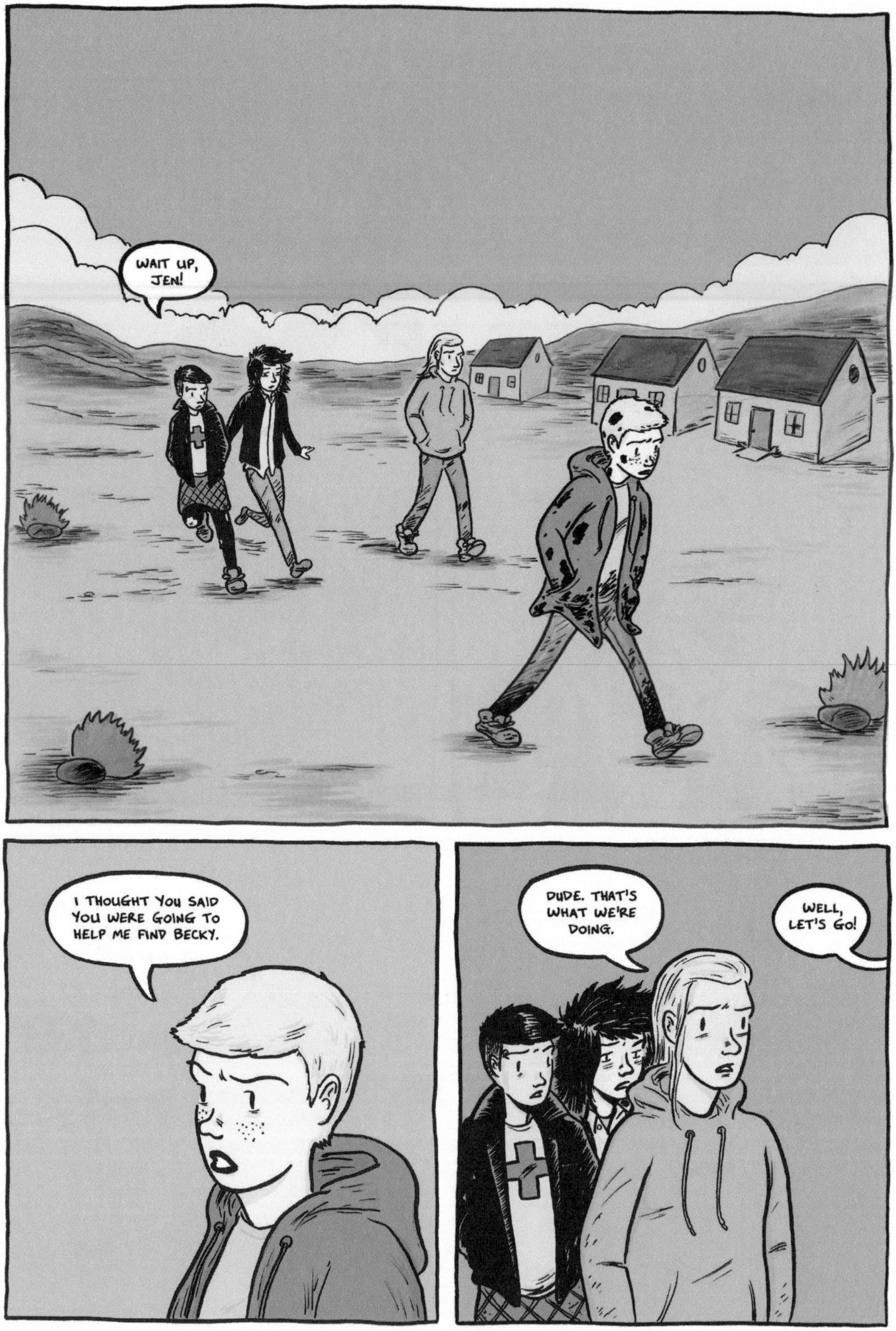
WAIT UP, JEN!
I THOUGHT YOU SAID YOU WERE GOING TO HELP ME FIND BECKY.
DUDE. THAT'S WHAT WE'RE DOING.
WELL, LET'S GO!

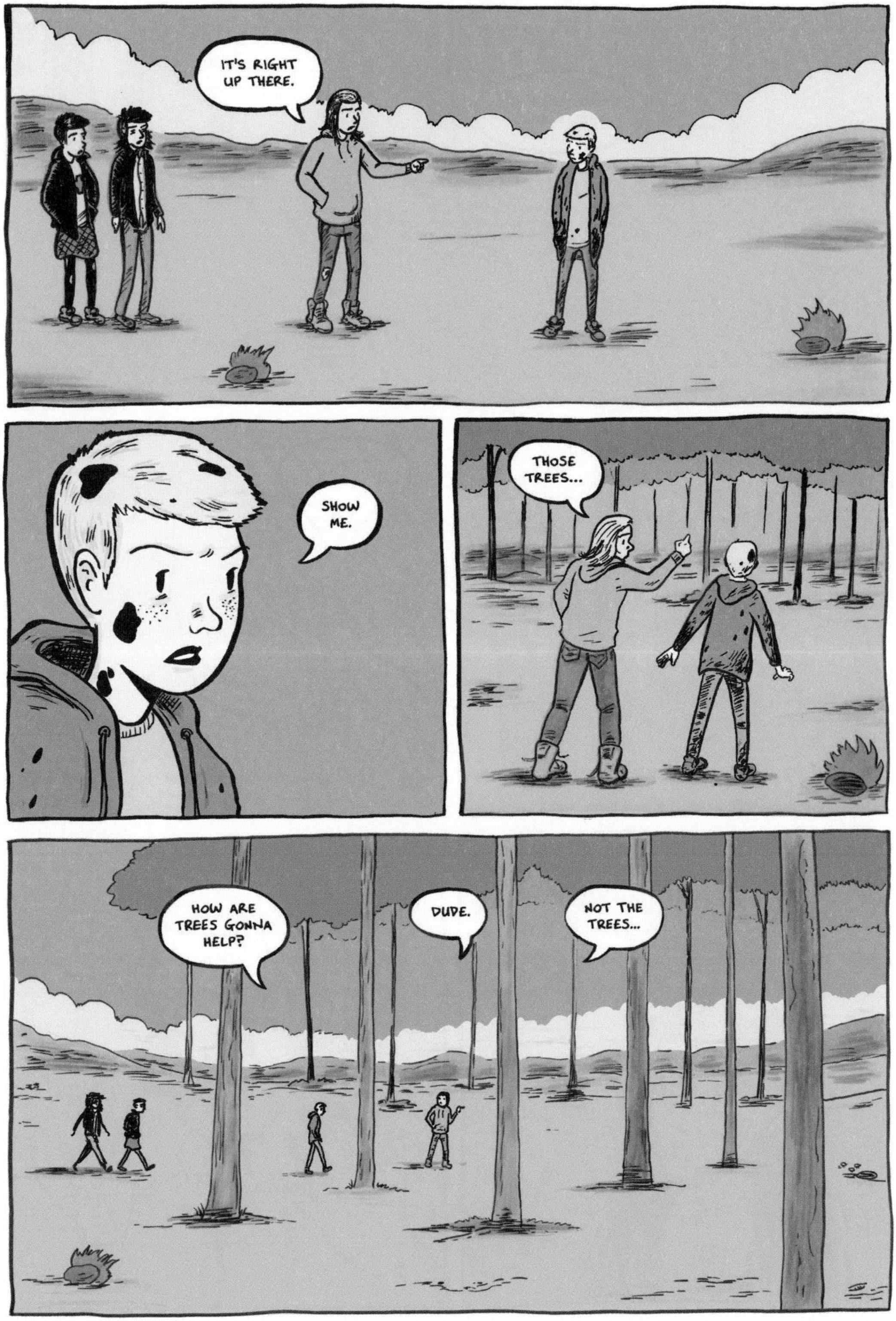
IT'S RIGHT UP THERE.
SHOW ME.
THOSE TREES...
HOW ARE TREES GONNA HELP?
DUDE.
NOT THE TREES...

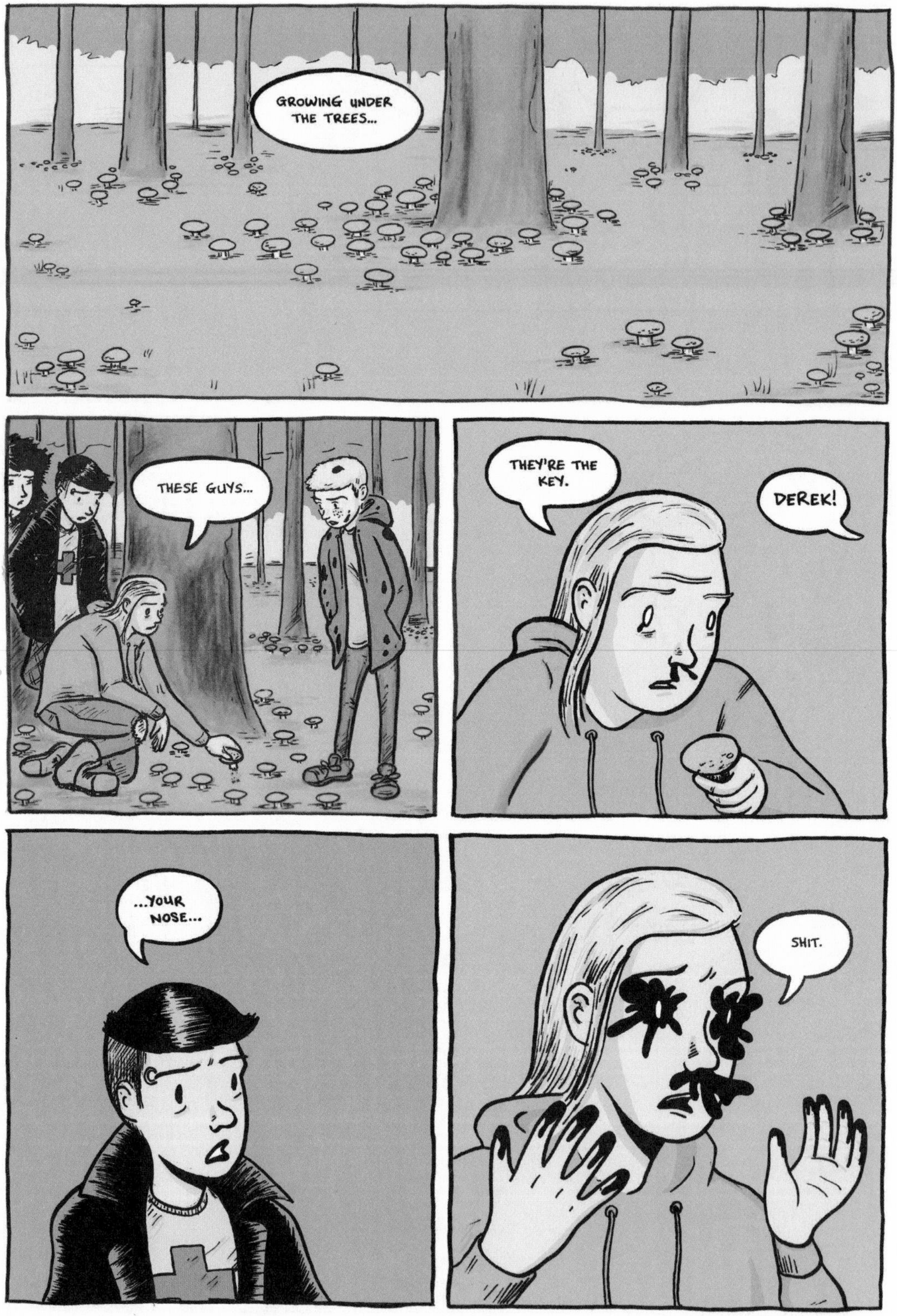
GROWING UNDER THE TREES...
THESE GUYS...
THEY'RE THE KEY.
DEREK!
...YOUR NOSE...
SHIT.

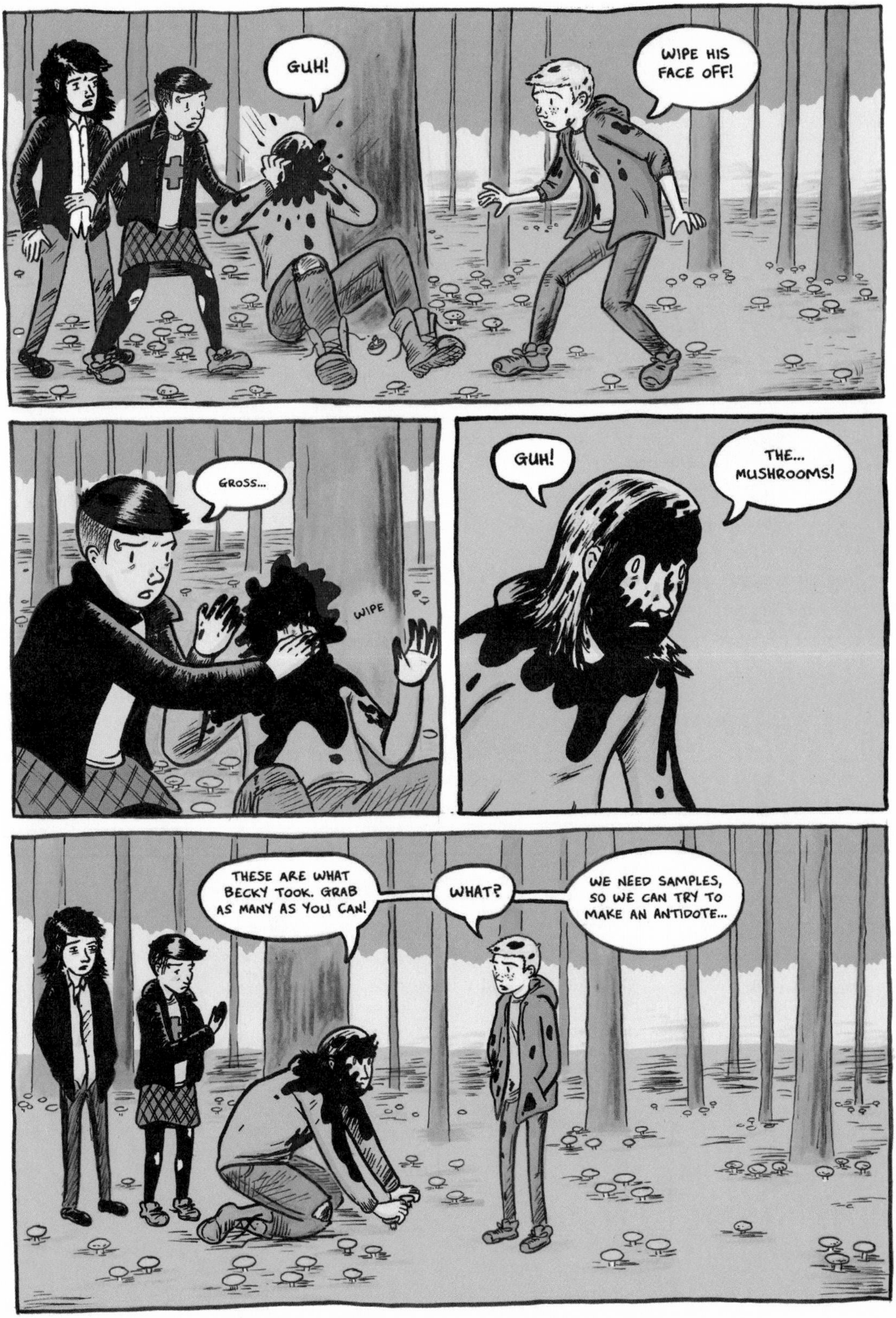
GUH!
WIPE HIS FACE OFF!
GROSS...
WIPE
GUH!
THE... MUSHROOMS!
THESE ARE WHAT BECKY TOOK. GRAB AS MANY AS YOU CAN!
WHAT?
WE NEED SAMPLES, SO WE CAN TRY TO MAKE AN ANTIDOTE...

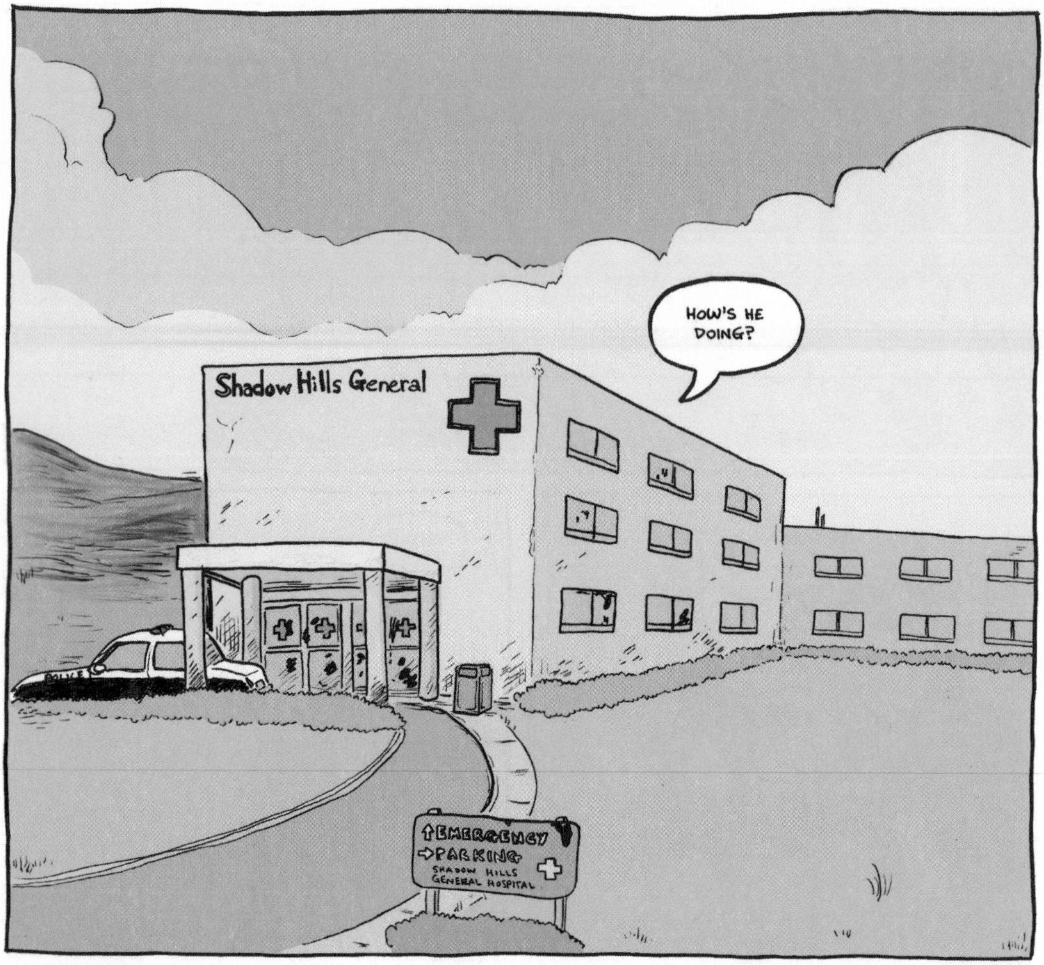
Shadow Hills General
HOW'S HE DOING?
EMERGENCY
PARKING
SHADOW HILLS GENERAL HOSPITAL

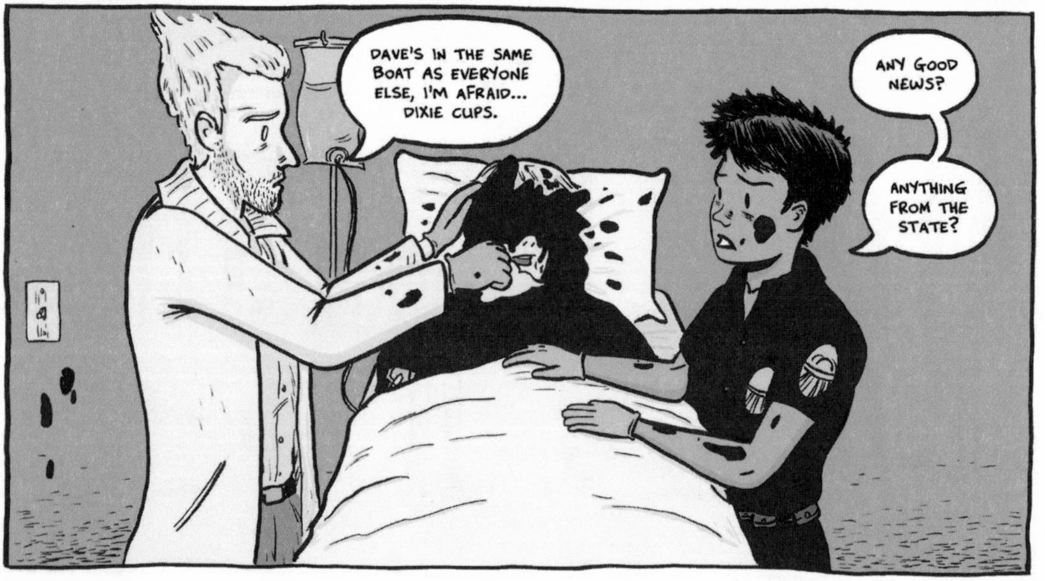
DAVE'S IN THE SAME BOAT AS EVERYONE ELSE, I'M AFRAID... DIXIE CUPS.
ANY GOOD NEWS?
ANYTHING FROM THE STATE?

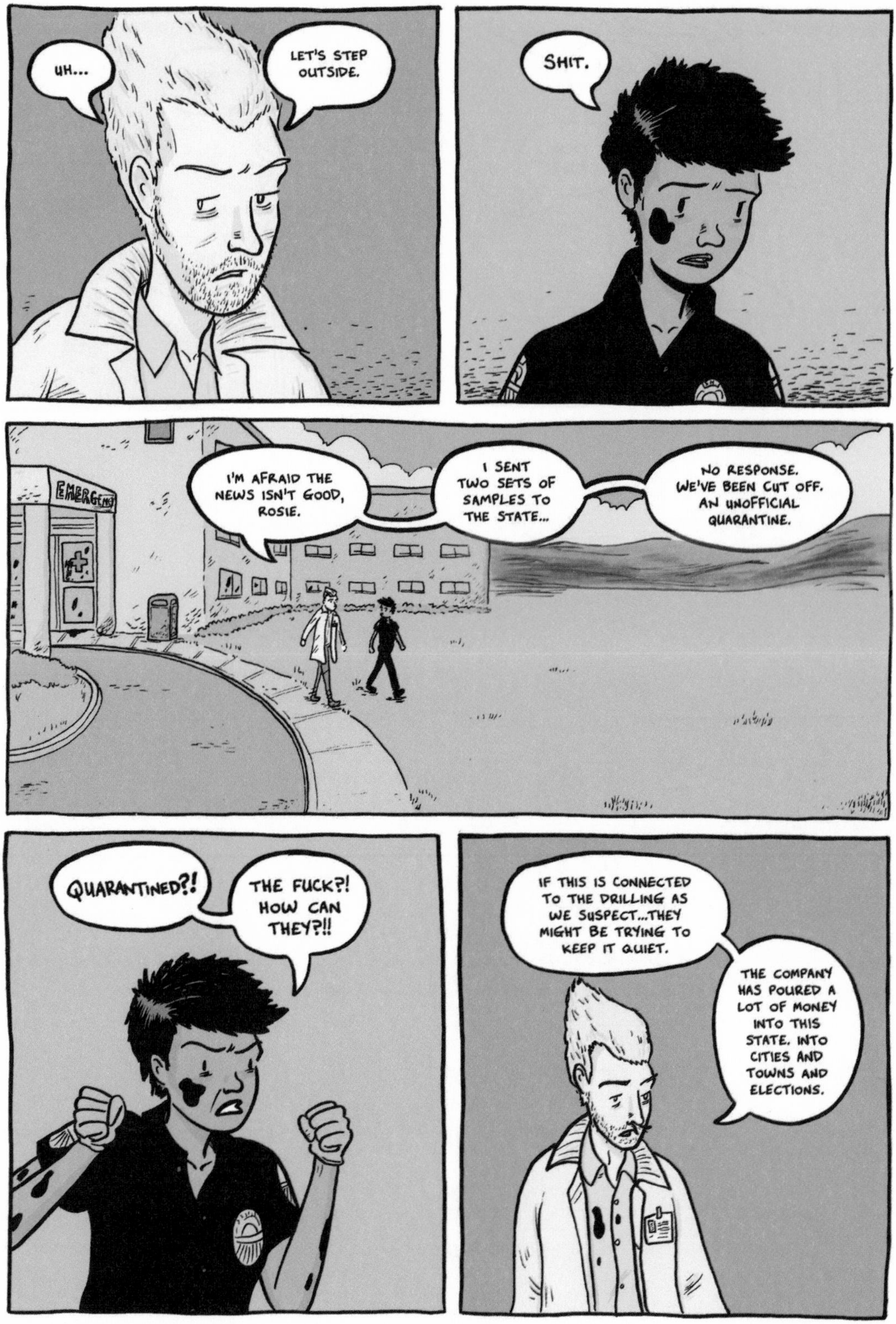
UH...
LET'S STEP OUTSIDE.
SHIT.
EMERGENCY
I'M AFRAID THE NEWS ISN'T GOOD, ROSIE.
I SENT TWO SETS OF SAMPLES TO THE STATE...
NO RESPONSE. WE'VE BEEN CUT OFF. AN UNOFFICIAL QUARANTINE.
QUARANTINED?!
THE FUCK?! HOW CAN THEY?!!
IF THIS IS CONNECTED TO THE DRILLING AS WE SUSPECT...THEY MIGHT BE TRYING TO KEEP IT QUIET.
THE COMPANY HAS POURED A LOT OF MONEY INTO THIS STATE. INTO CITIES AND TOWNS AND ELECTIONS.

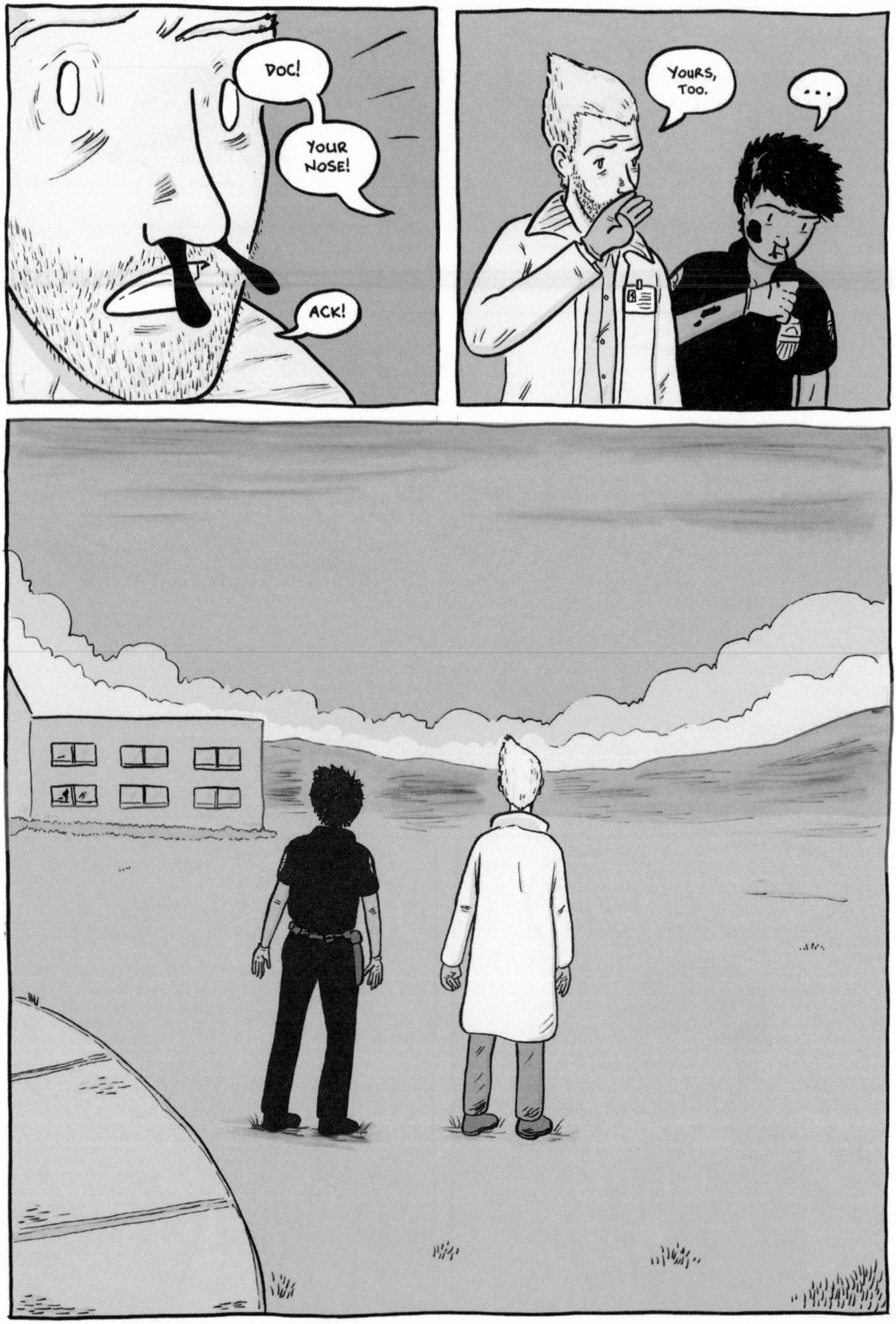
DOC!
YOUR NOSE!
ACK!
YOURS, TOO.
...

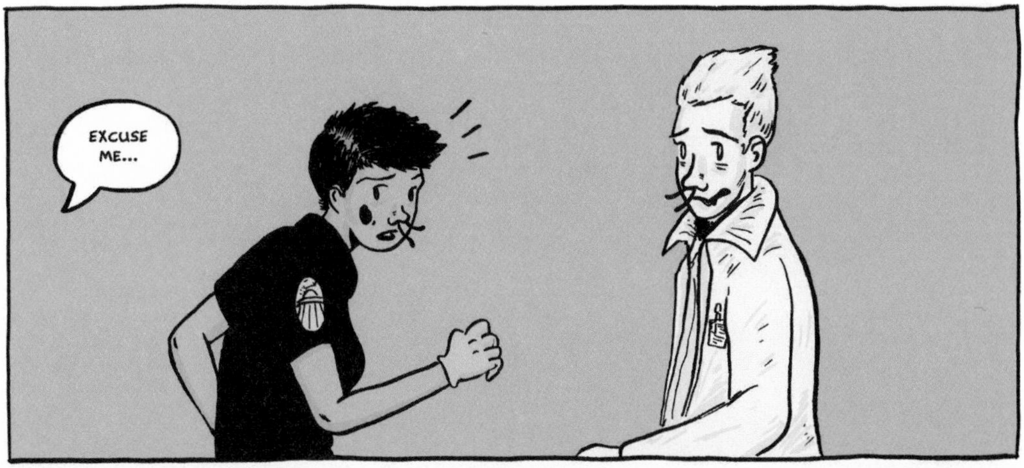
EXCUSE ME...

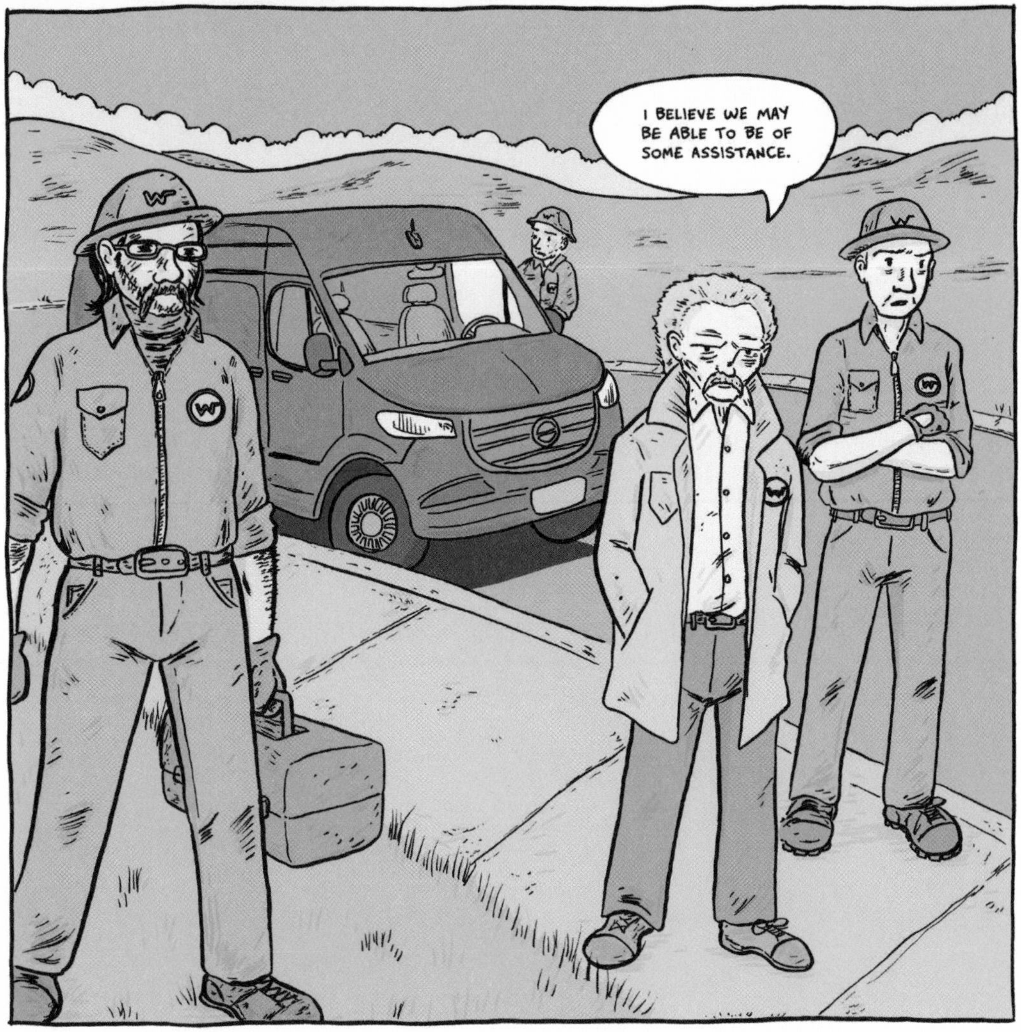
I BELIEVE WE MAY BE ABLE TO BE OF SOME ASSISTANCE.

7.

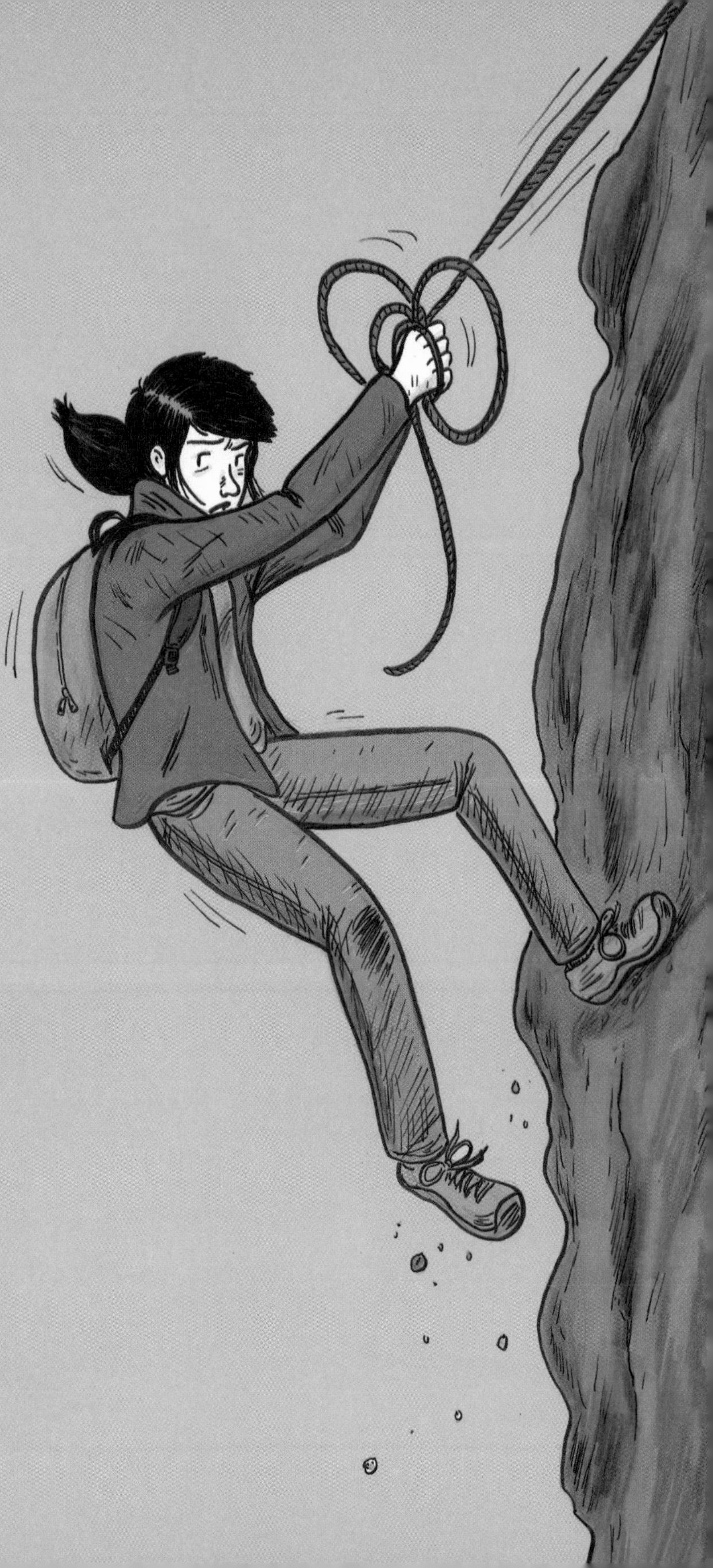

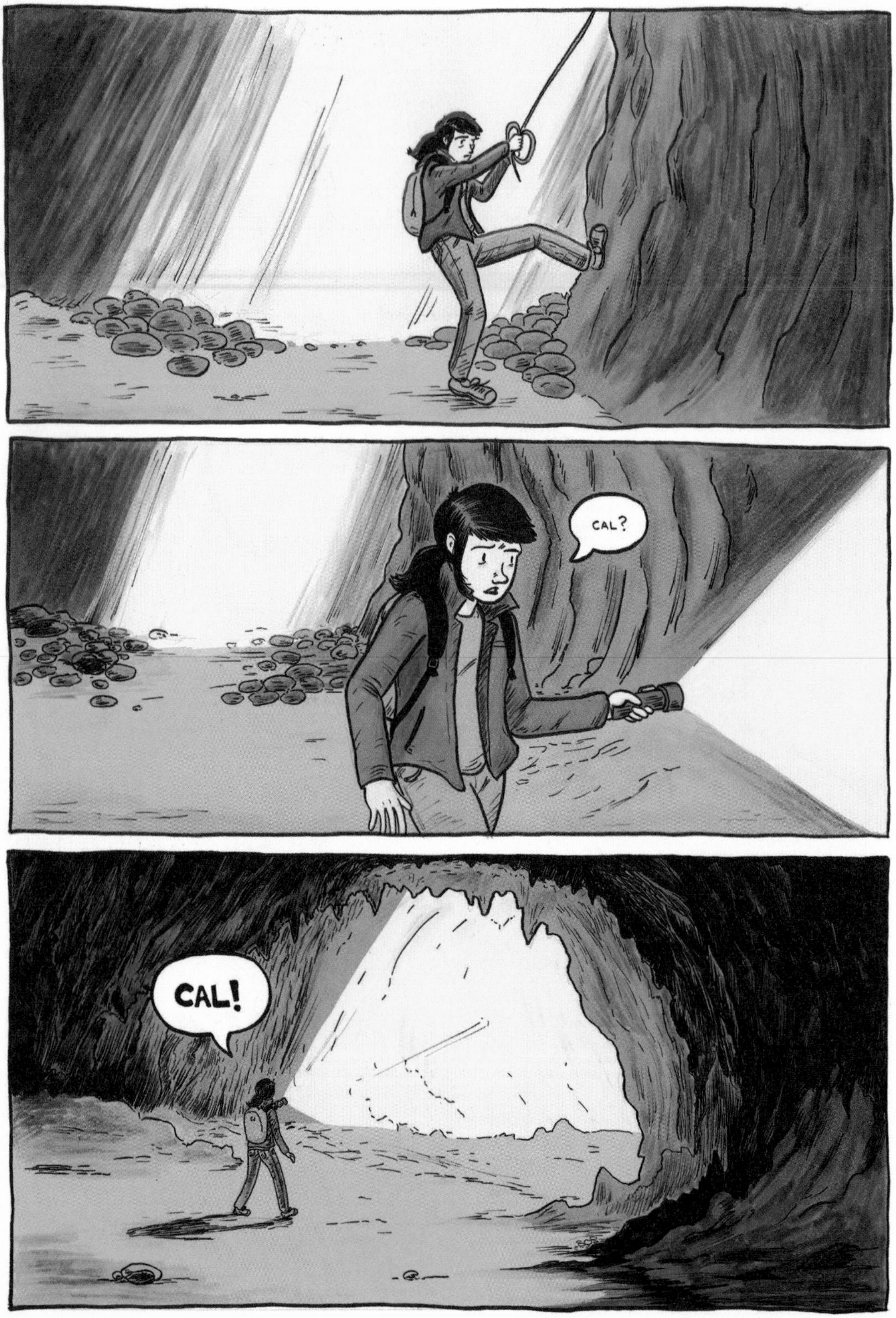
CAL?
CAL!

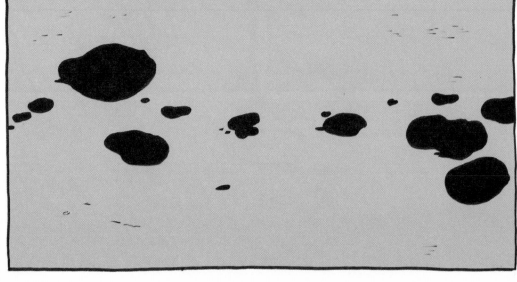

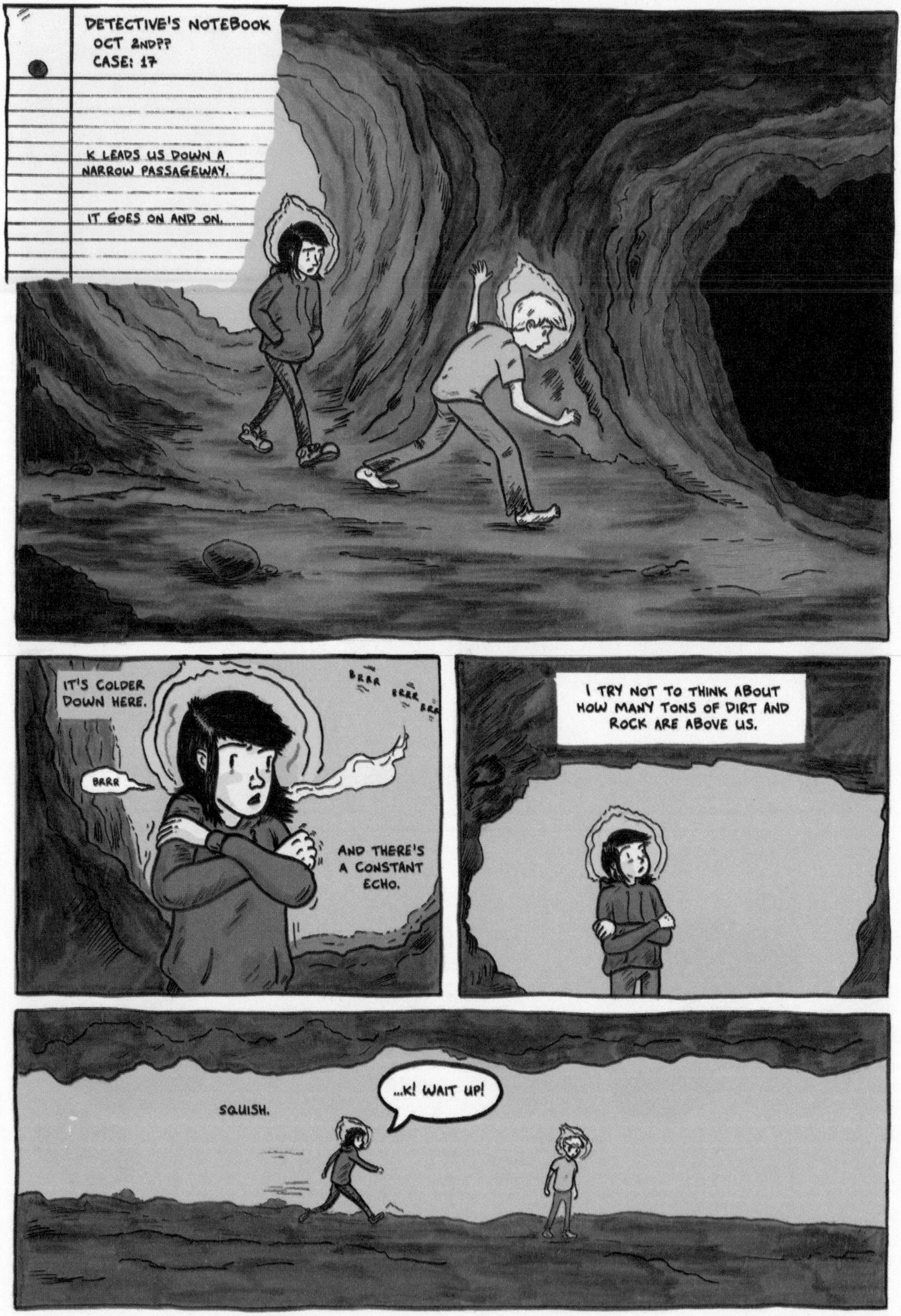
DETECTIVE'S NOTEBOOK
OCT 2ND??
CASE: 17
K LEADS US DOWN A NARROW PASSAGEWAY.
IT GOES ON AND ON.
IT'S COLDER DOWN HERE.
BRRR
BRRR
BRRR
BRRR
AND THERE'S A CONSTANT ECHO.
I TRY NOT TO THINK ABOUT HOW MANY TONS OF DIRT AND ROCK ARE ABOVE US.
SQUISH.
...K! WAIT UP!

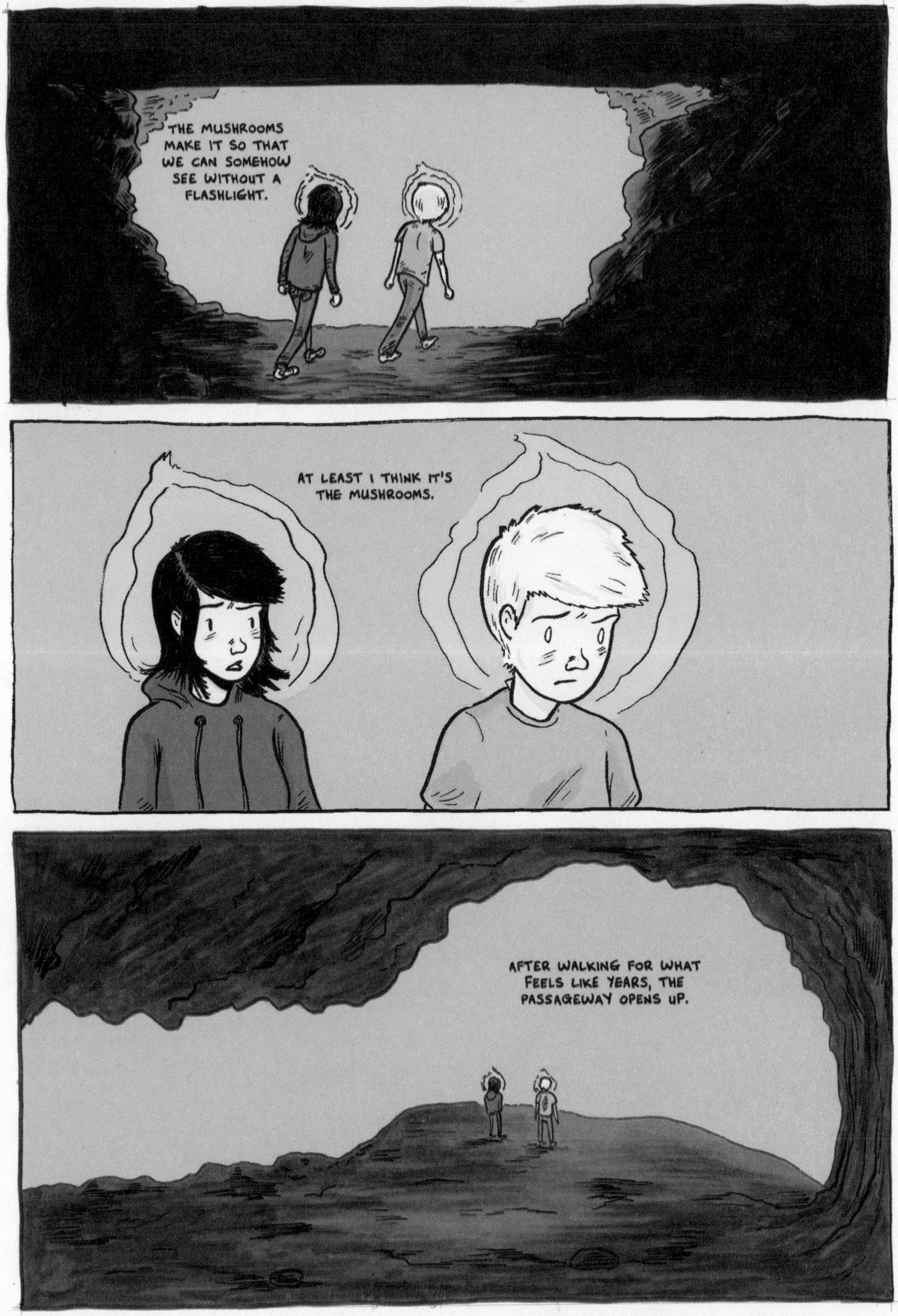
THE MUSHROOMS MAKE IT SO THAT WE CAN SOMEHOW SEE WITHOUT A FLASHLIGHT.
AT LEAST I THINK IT'S THE MUSHROOMS.
AFTER WALKING FOR WHAT FEELS LIKE YEARS, THE PASSAGEWAY OPENS UP.

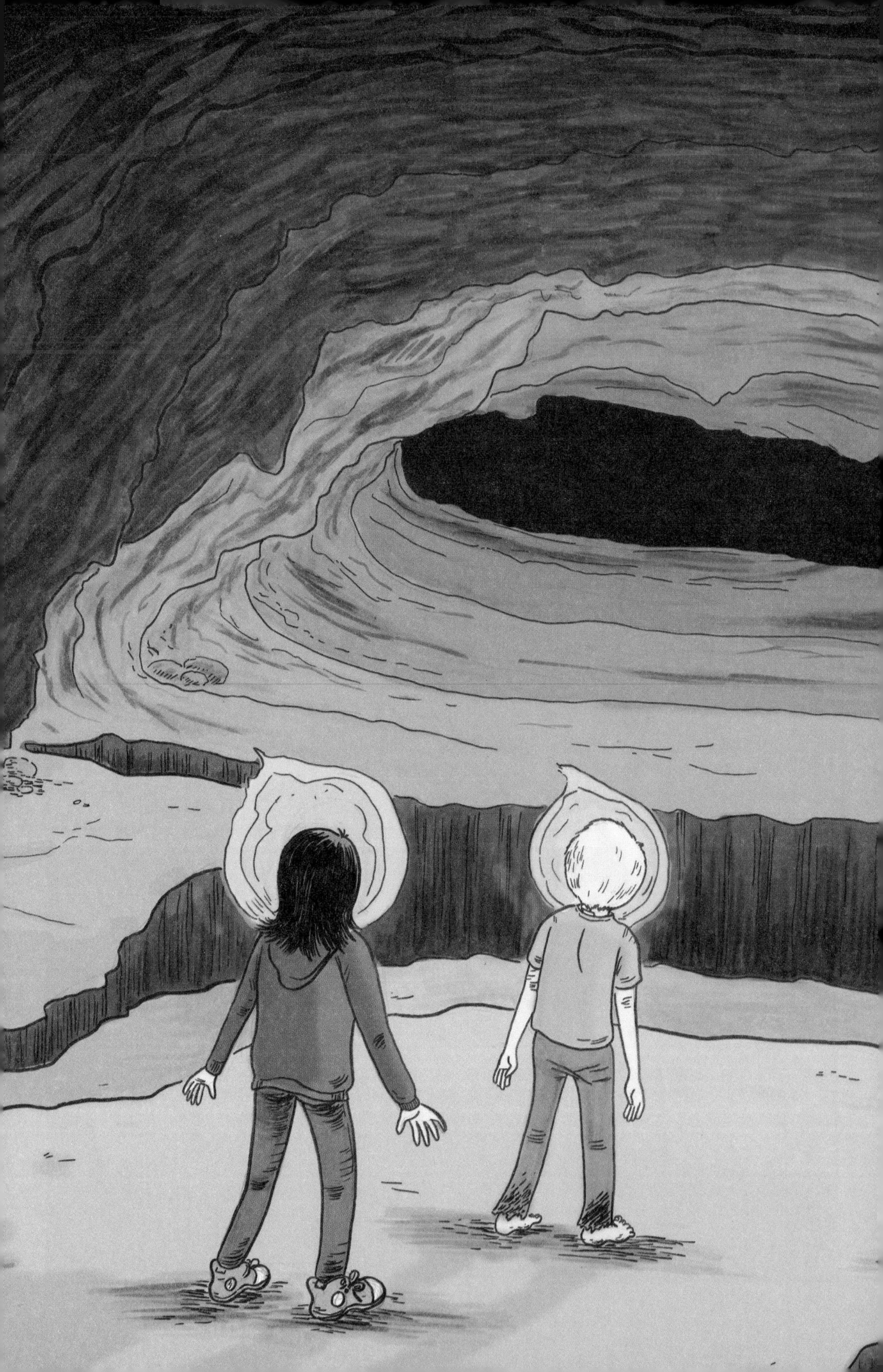

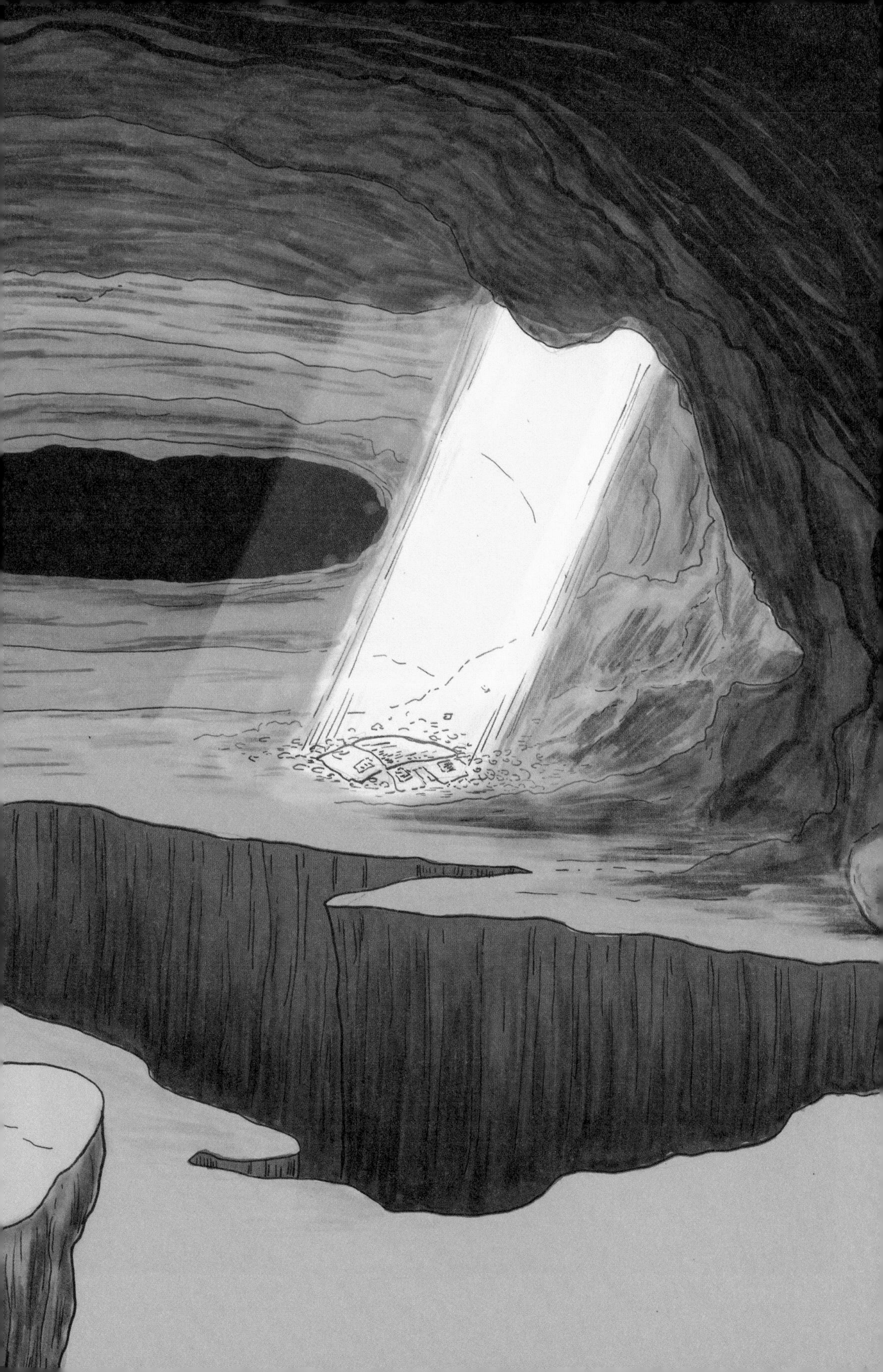

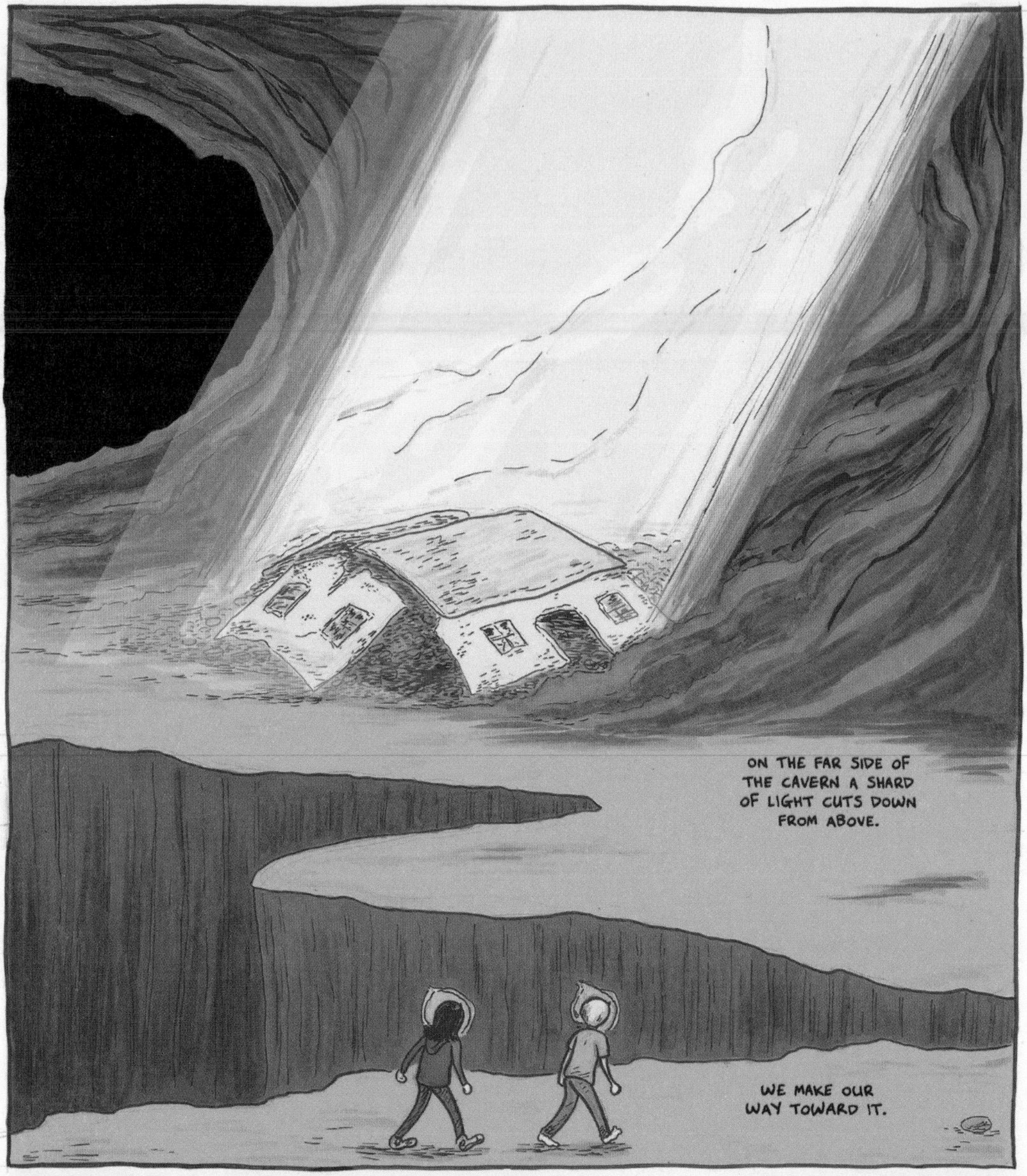
ON THE FAR SIDE OF THE CAVERN A SHARD OF LIGHT CUTS DOWN FROM ABOVE.
WE MAKE OUR WAY TOWARD IT.

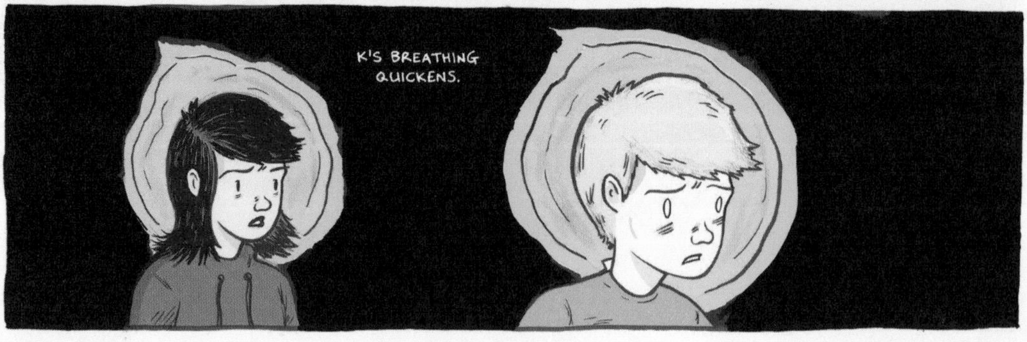
K'S BREATHING QUICKENS.

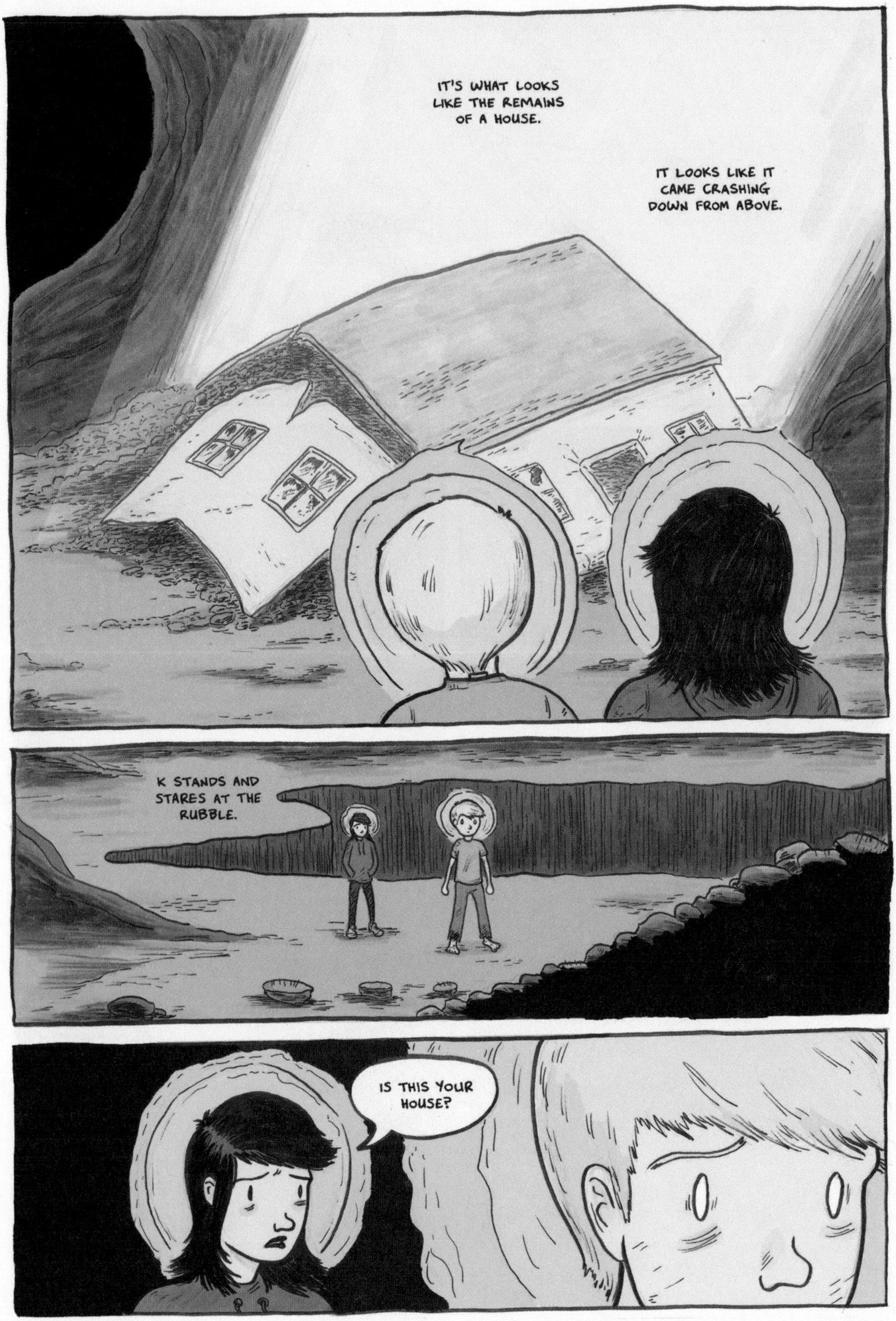
IT'S WHAT LOOKS LIKE THE REMAINS OF A HOUSE.
IT LOOKS LIKE IT CAME CRASHING DOWN FROM ABOVE.
K STANDS AND STARES AT THE RUBBLE.
IS THIS YOUR HOUSE?

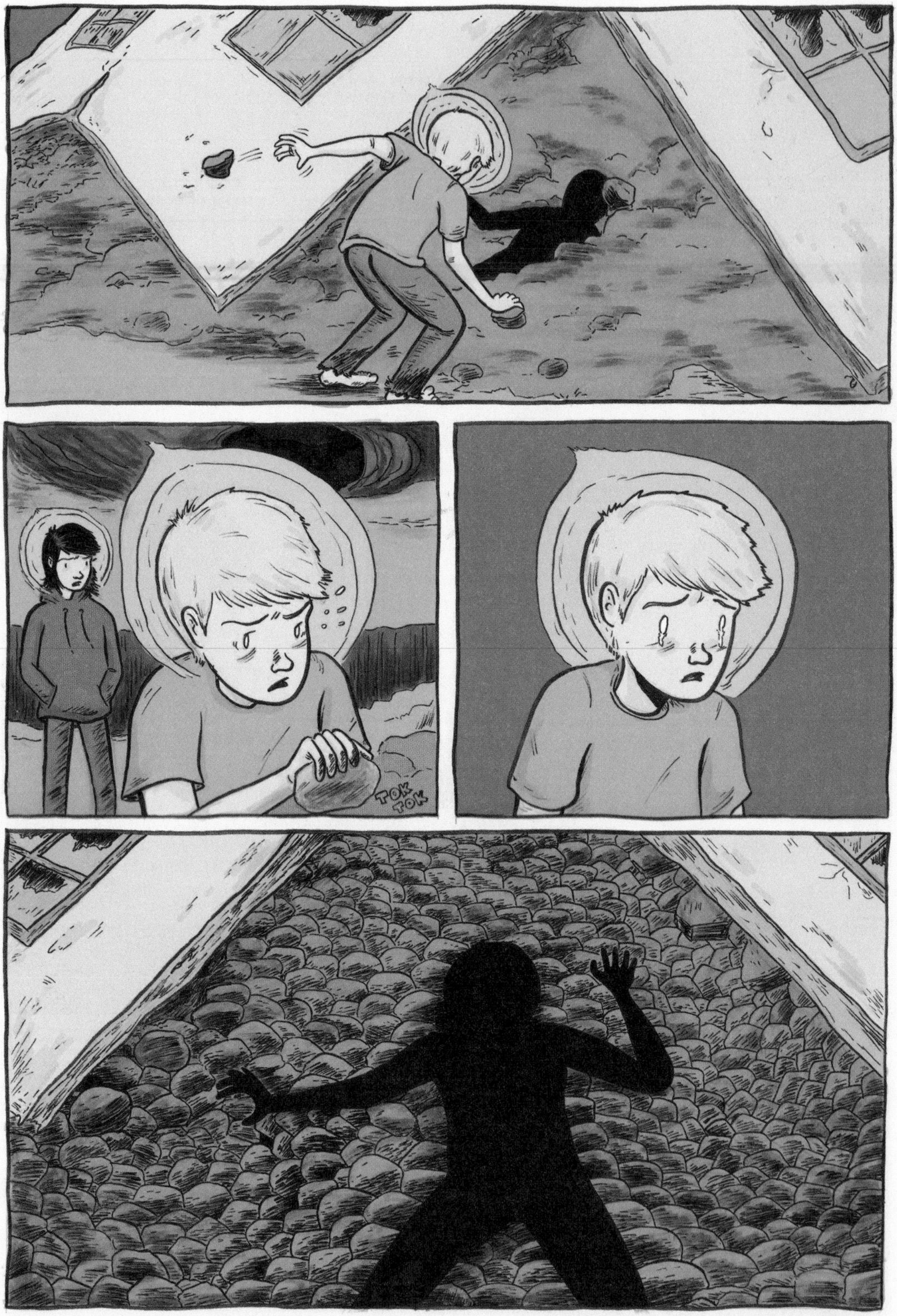
TOK
TOK

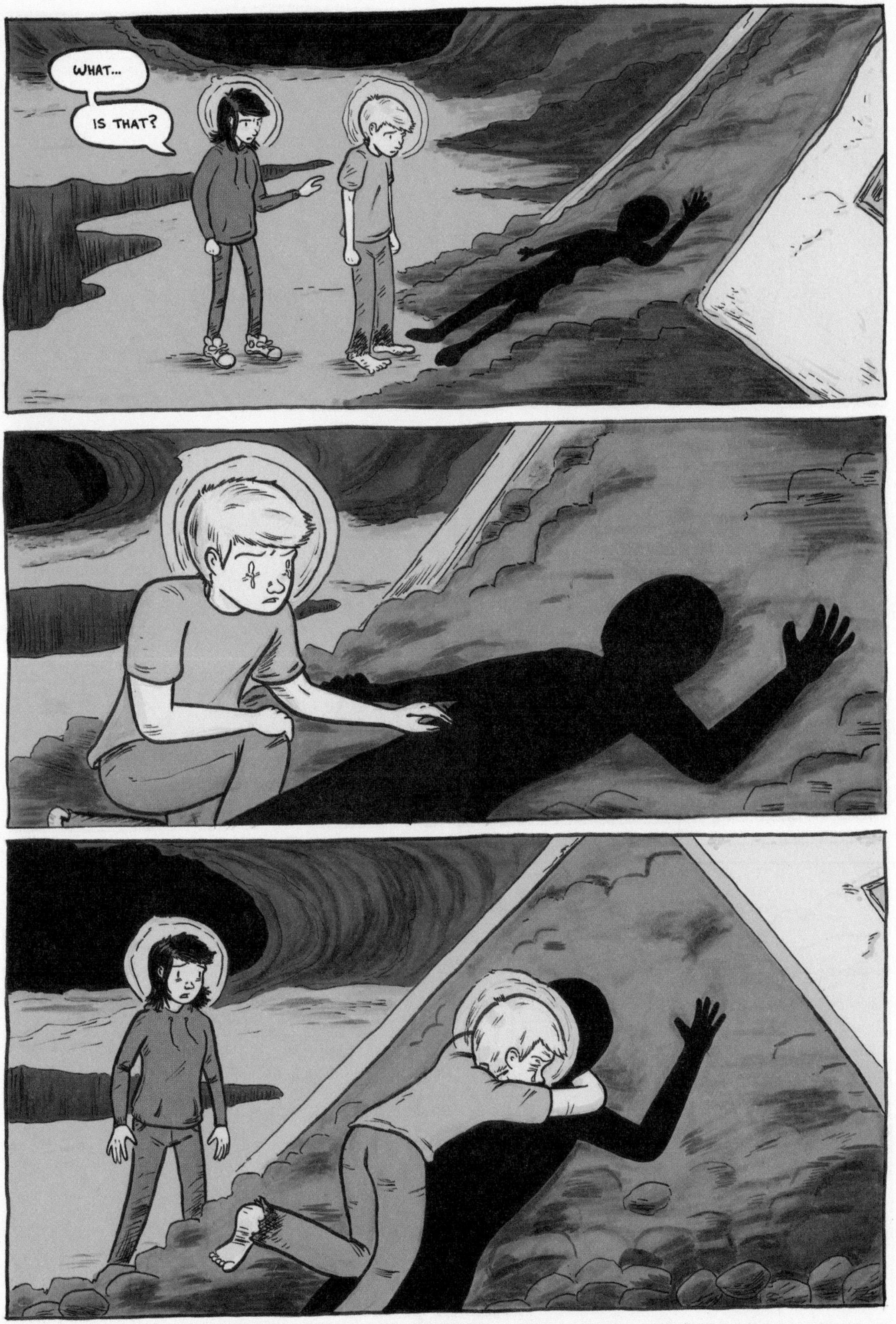
WHAT...
IS THAT?

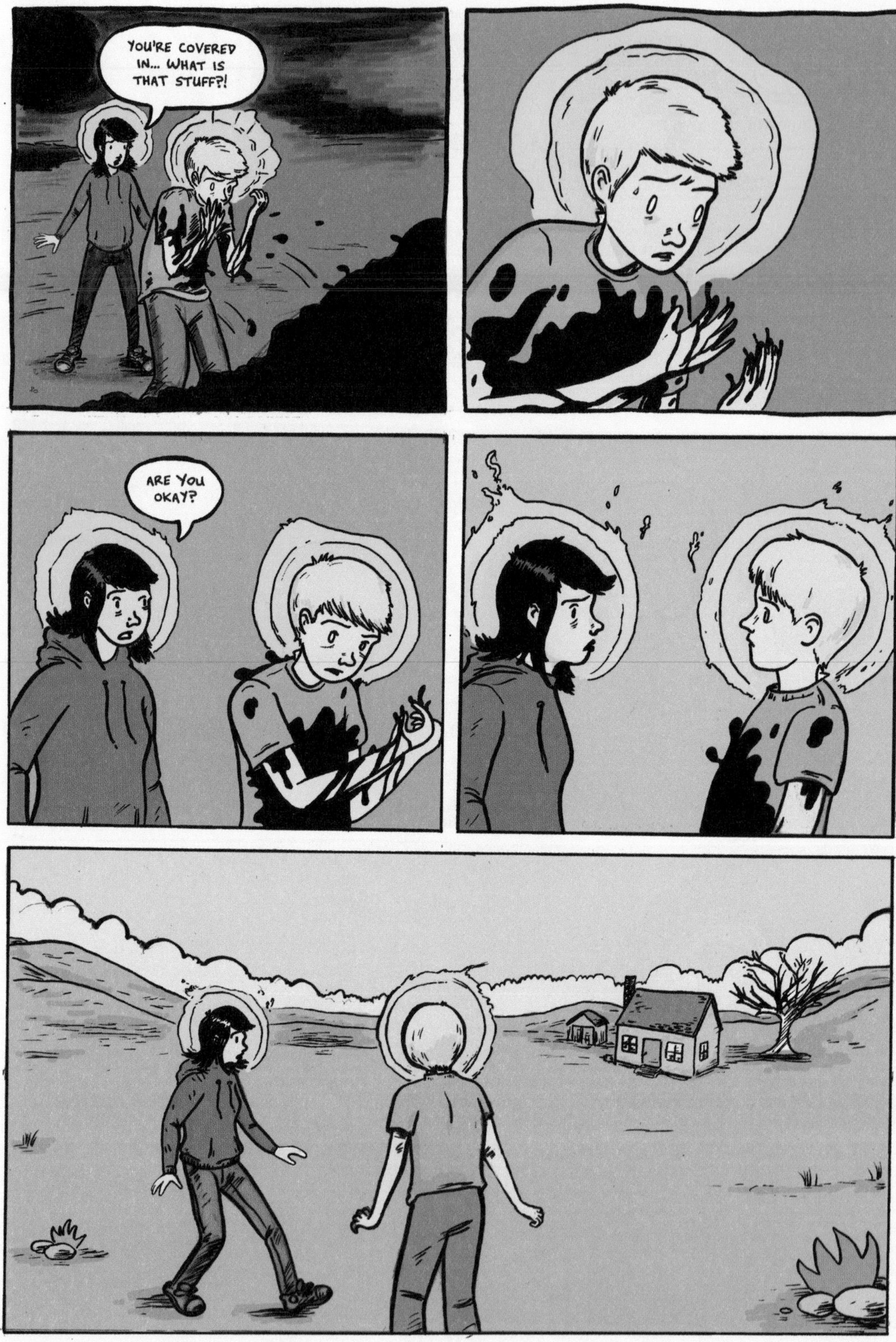
YOU'RE COVERED IN... WHAT IS THAT STUFF?!
ARE YOU OKAY?

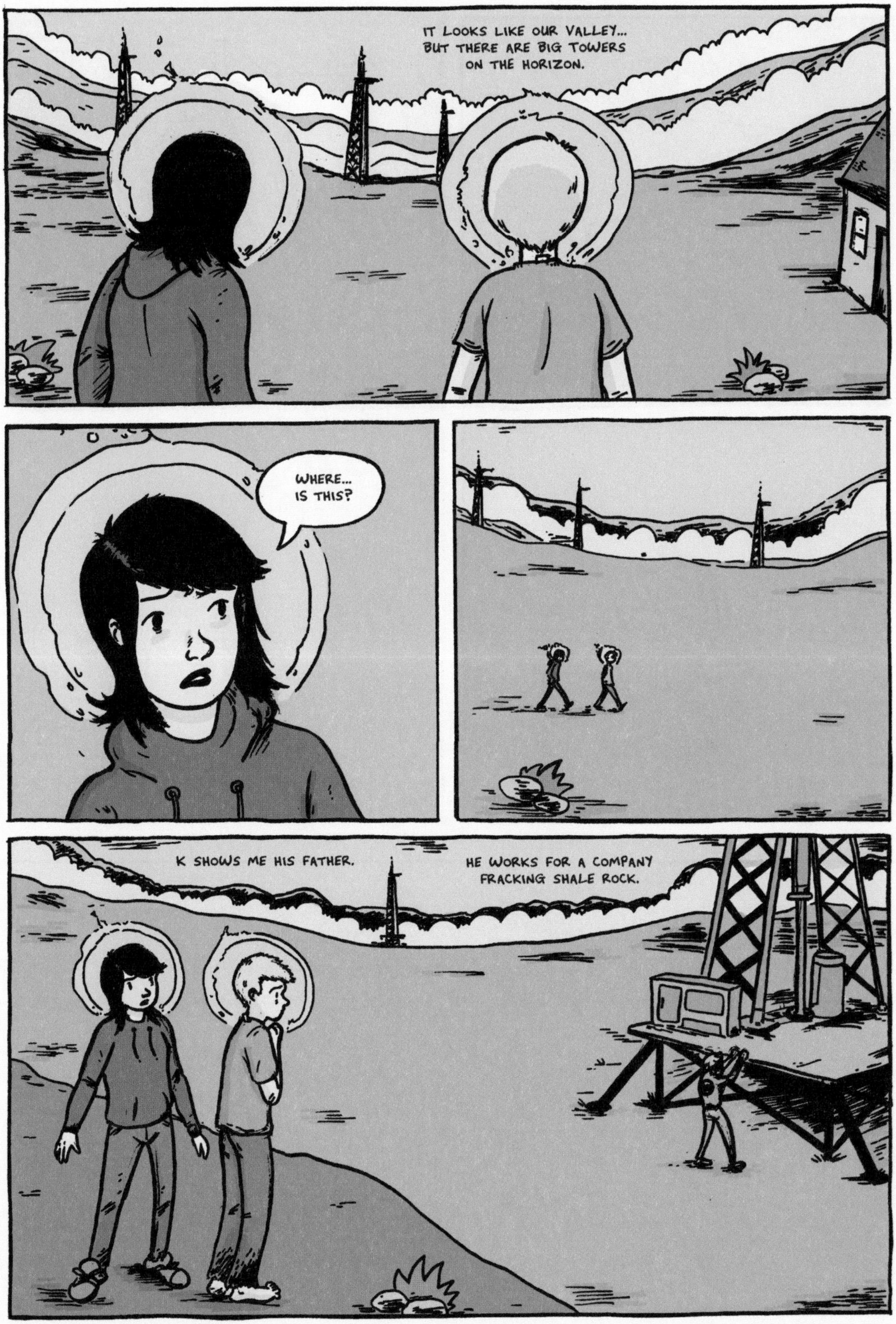
IT LOOKS LIKE OUR VALLEY... BUT THERE ARE BIG TOWERS ON THE HORIZON.
WHERE... IS THIS?
K SHOWS ME HIS FATHER.
HE WORKS FOR A COMPANY FRACKING SHALE ROCK.

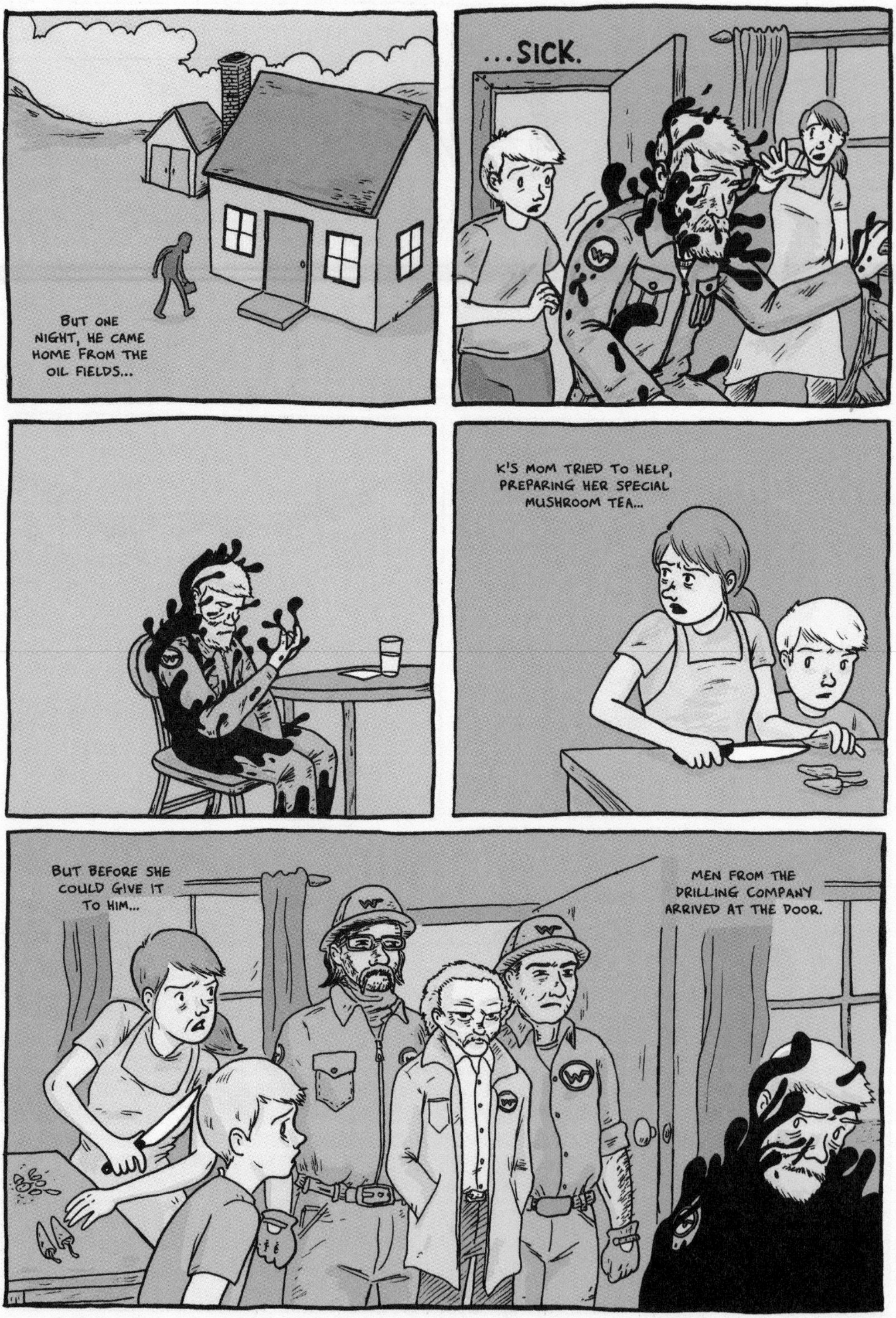
BUT ONE NIGHT, HE CAME HOME FROM THE OIL FIELDS...
...SICK.
K'S MOM TRIED TO HELP, PREPARING HER SPECIAL MUSHROOM TEA...
BUT BEFORE SHE COULD GIVE IT TO HIM...
MEN FROM THE DRILLING COMPANY ARRIVED AT THE DOOR.

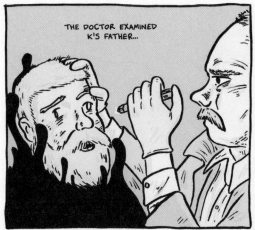

THE DOCTOR EXAMINED K'S FATHER...

HE SAID HE HAD SOMETHING TO HELP IN HIS TRUCK.

K'S MOTHER LOOKED OUT IN THE YARD AND...

SAW THE MEN LAYING WIRE AND WHAT LOOKED LIKE...

SHE TRIED TO RUSH K OUT THE BACK DOOR...

BUT...

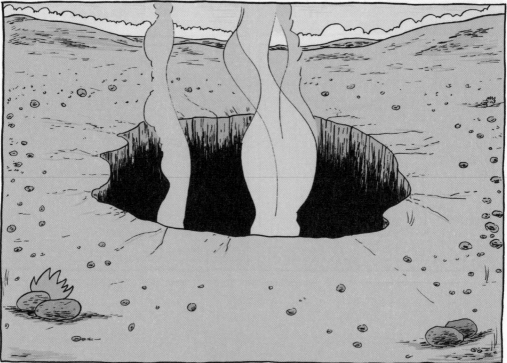

I'M SORRY.

K LOOKS AROUND AND
TAKES OFF RUNNING...

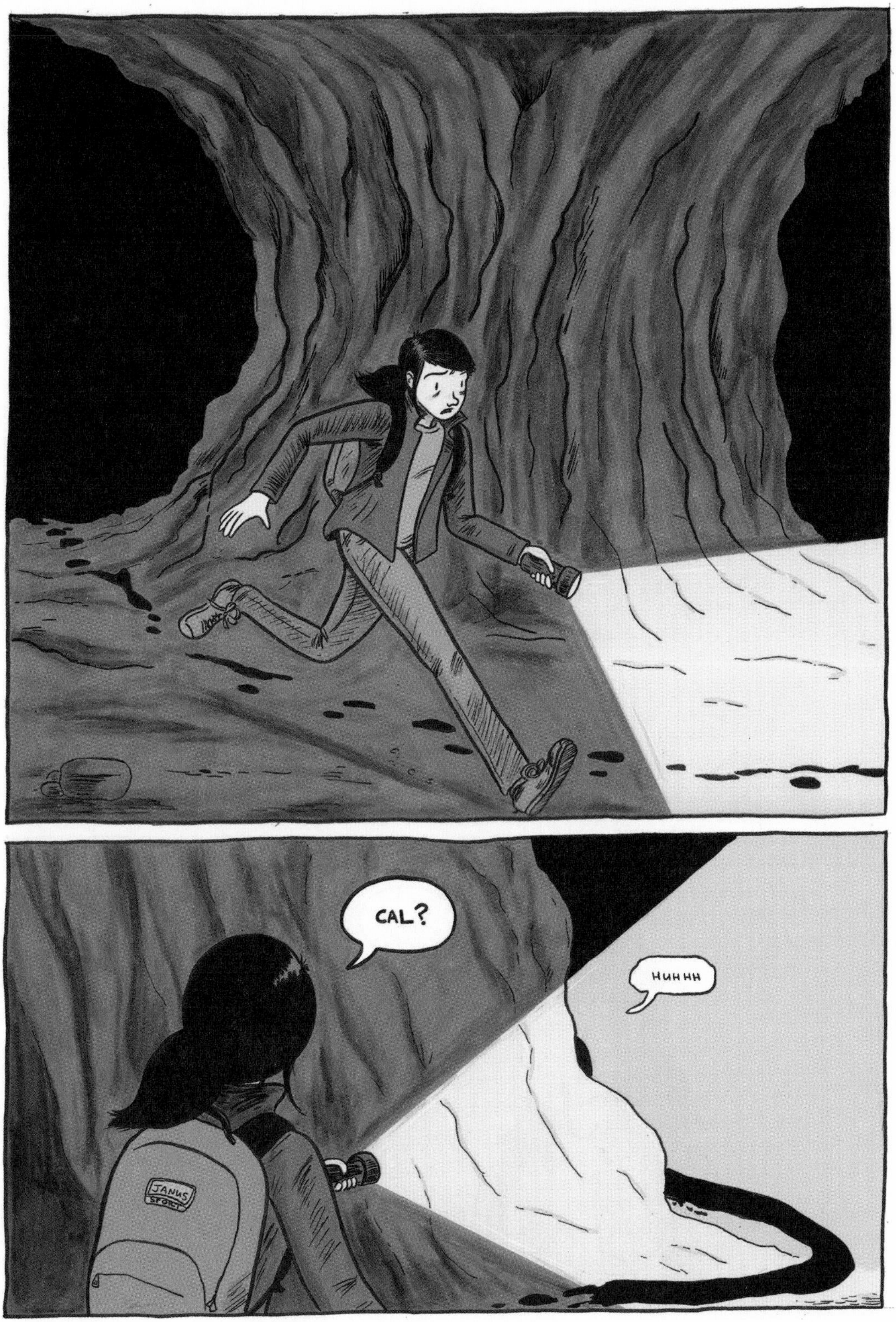
CAL?
HUHHH
JANUS

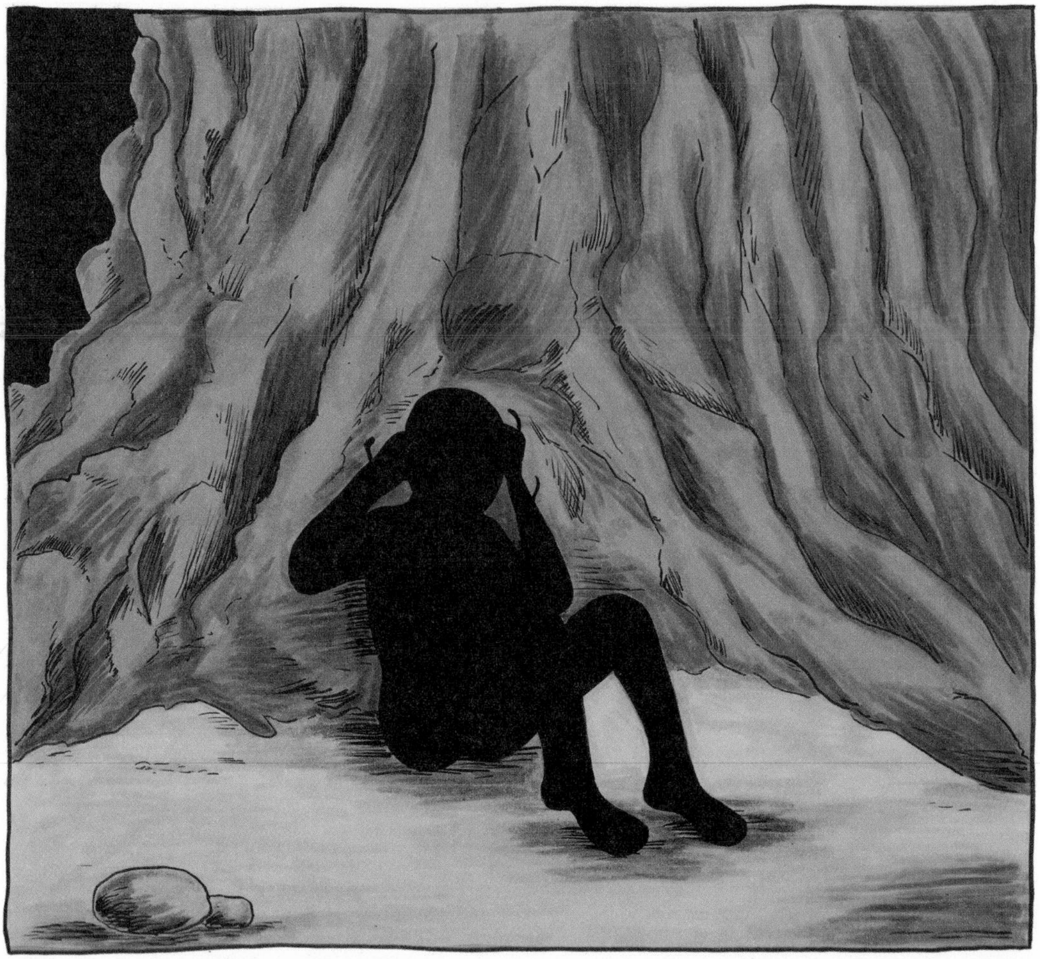

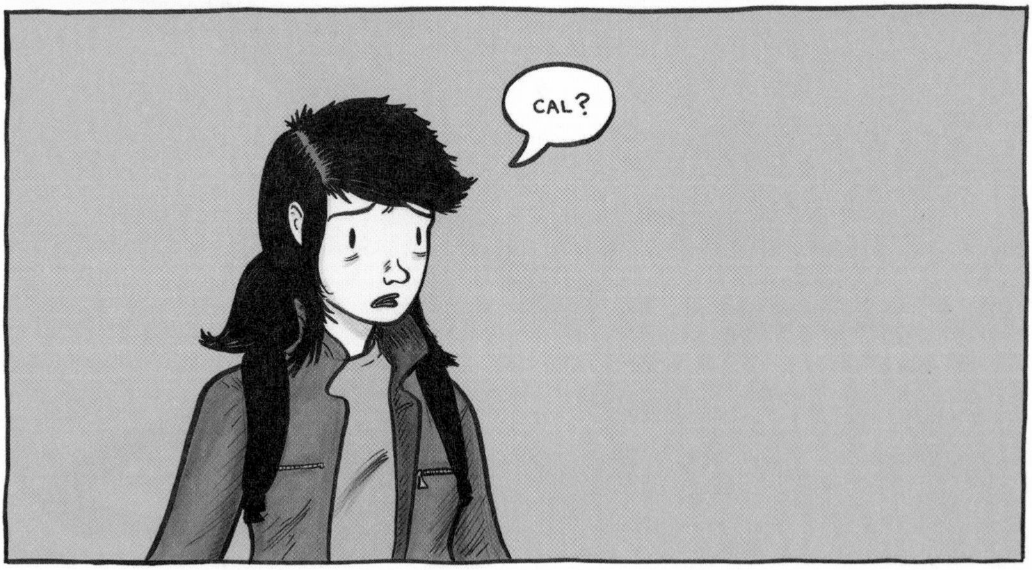
CAL?

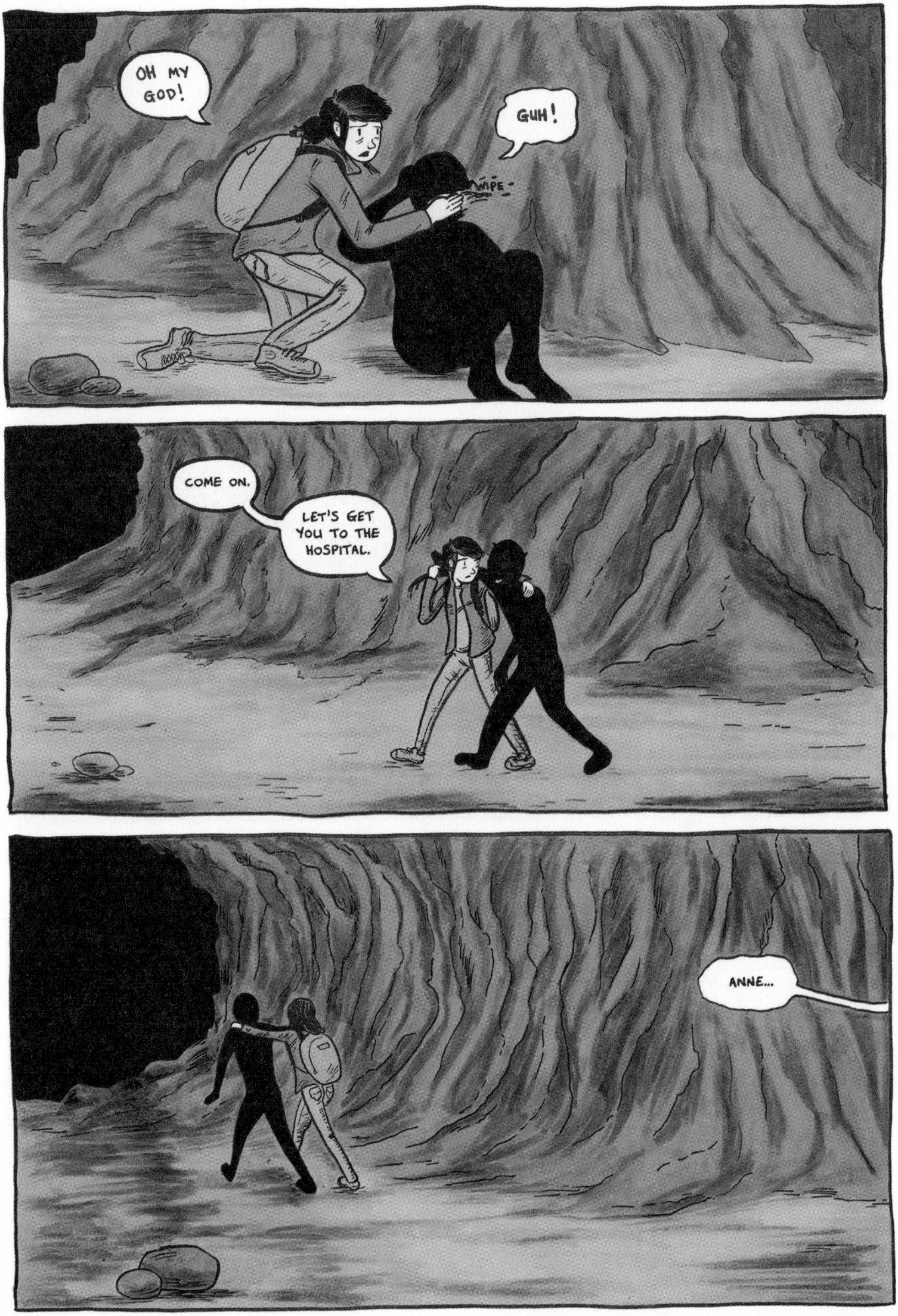
OH MY GOD!
GUH!
WIPE
COME ON.
LET'S GET YOU TO THE HOSPITAL.
ANNE...

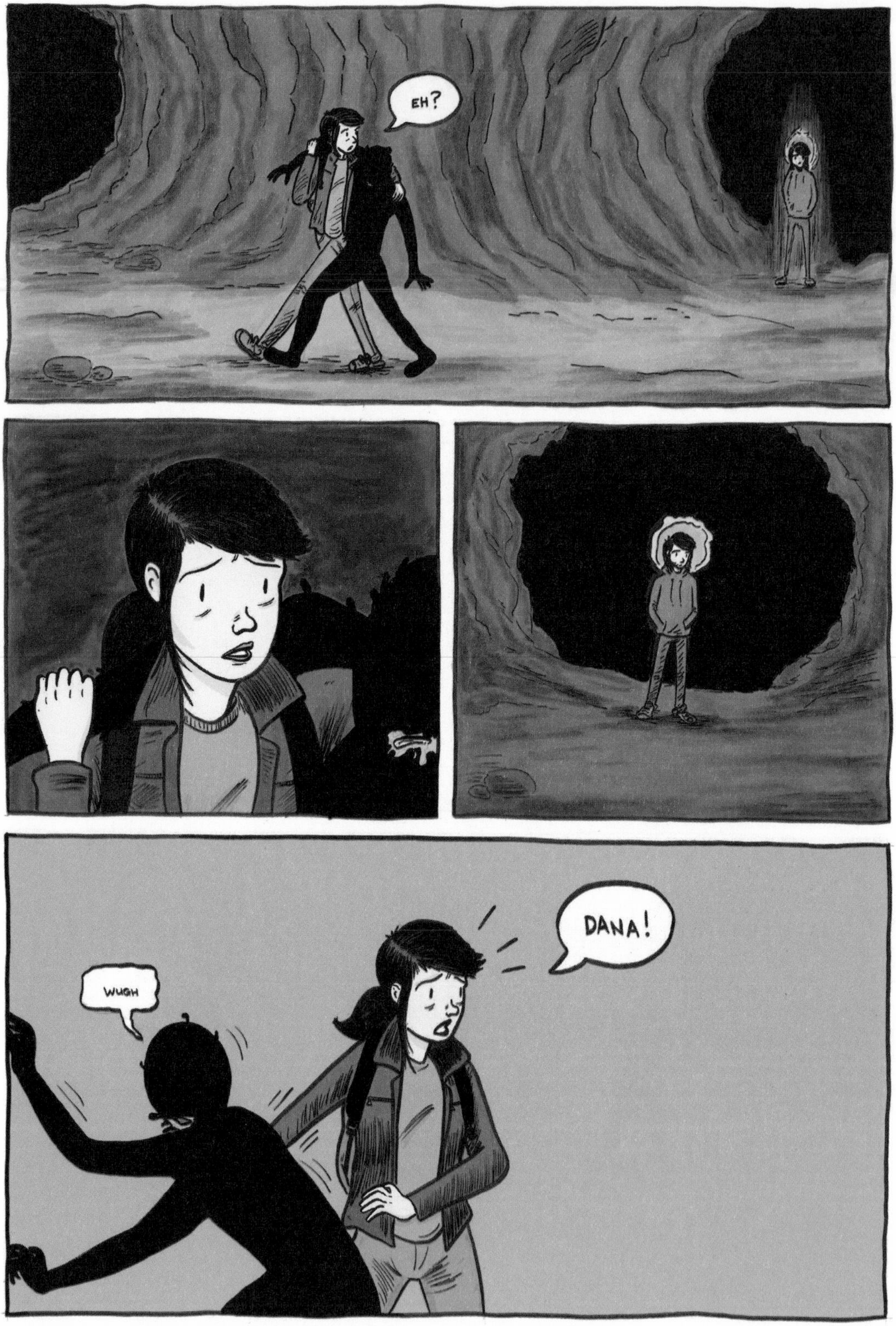
EH?
WUGH
DANA!

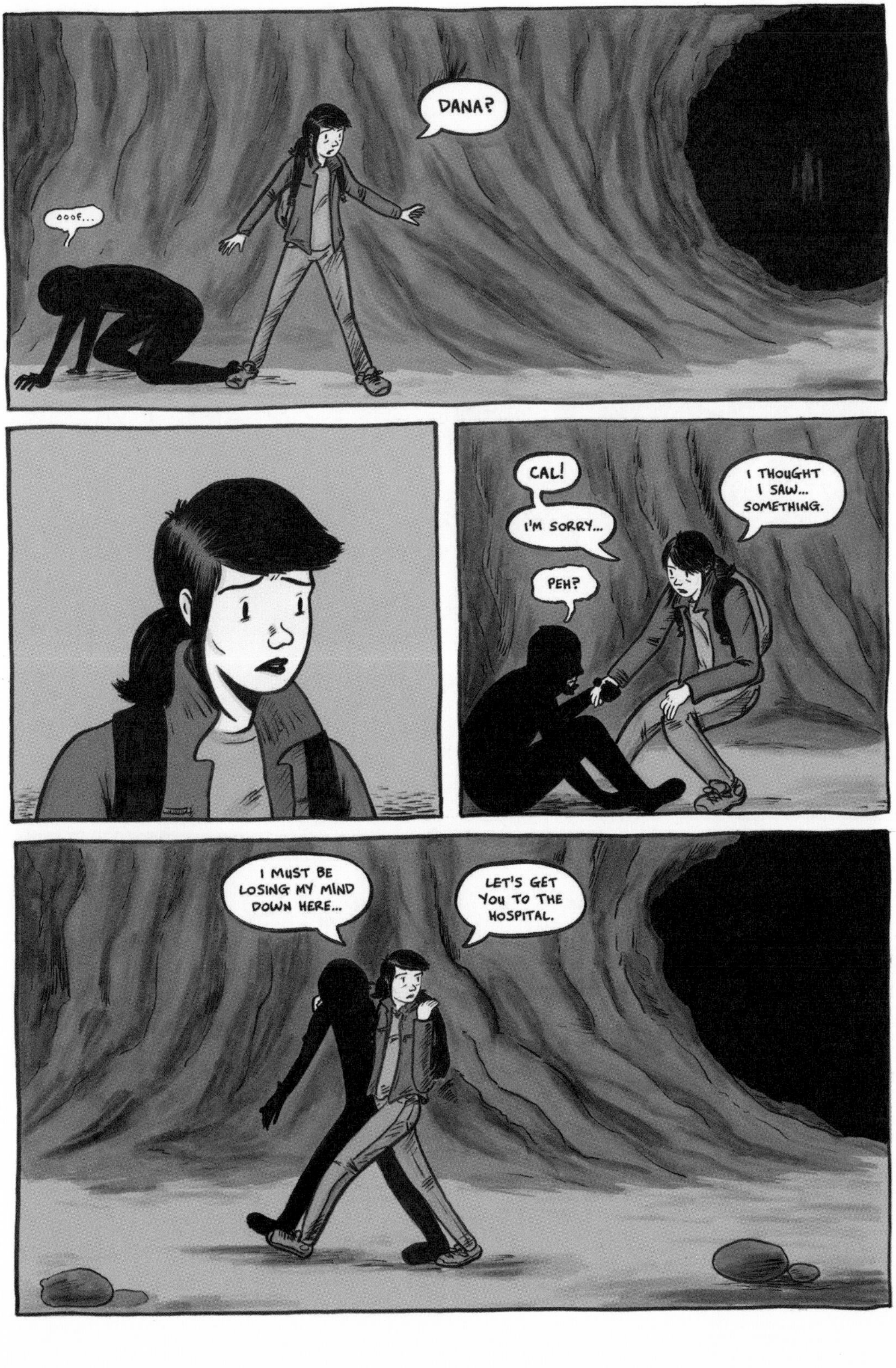
DANA?
OOOF...
CAL!
I'M SORRY...
PEH?
I THOUGHT I SAW... SOMETHING.
I MUST BE LOSING MY MIND DOWN HERE...
LET'S GET YOU TO THE HOSPITAL.

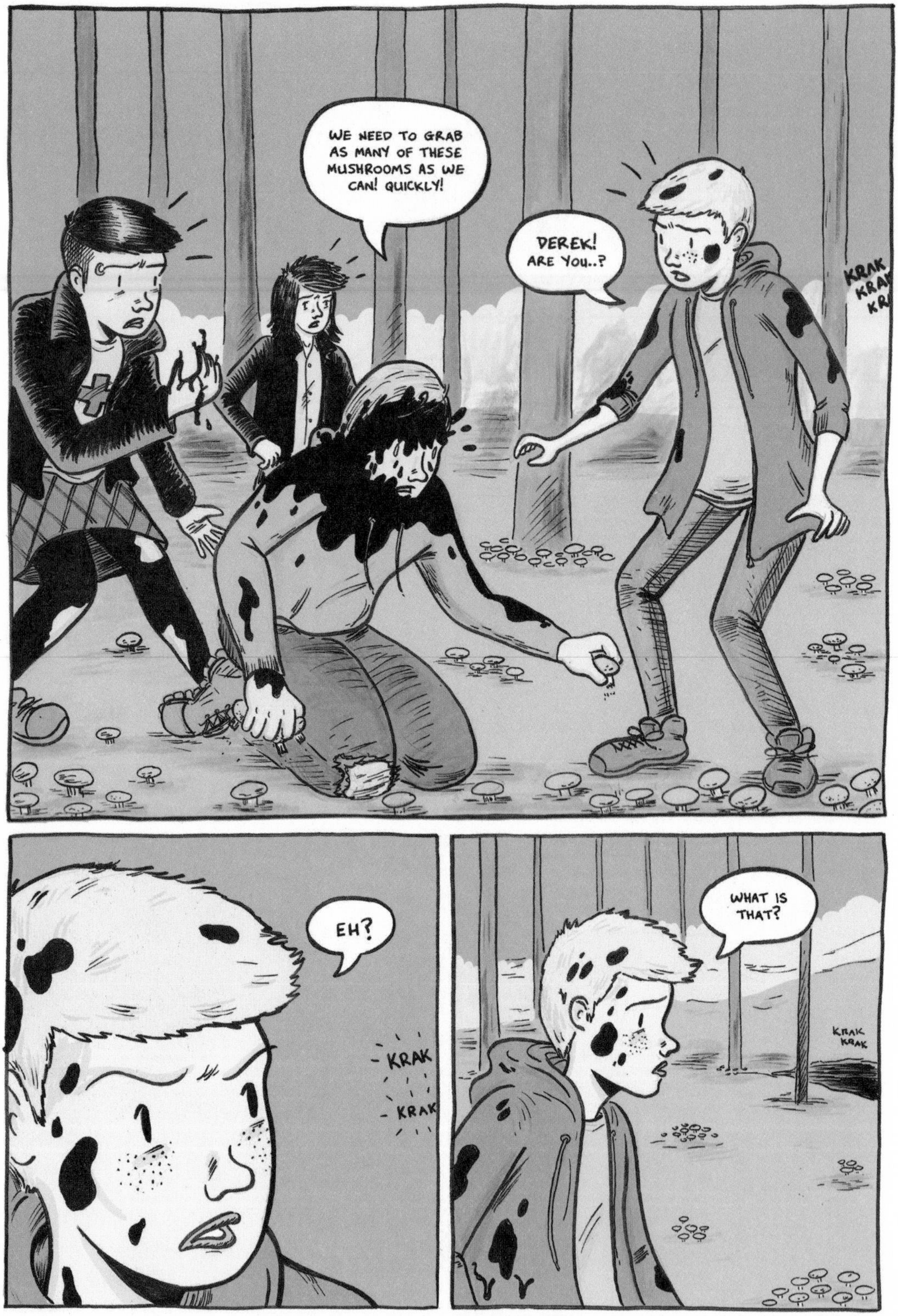
WE NEED TO GRAB AS MANY OF THESE MUSHROOMS AS WE CAN! QUICKLY!
DEREK! ARE YOU..?
KRAK KRAK KRA
EH?
KRAK
KRAK
WHAT IS THAT?
KRAK KRAK

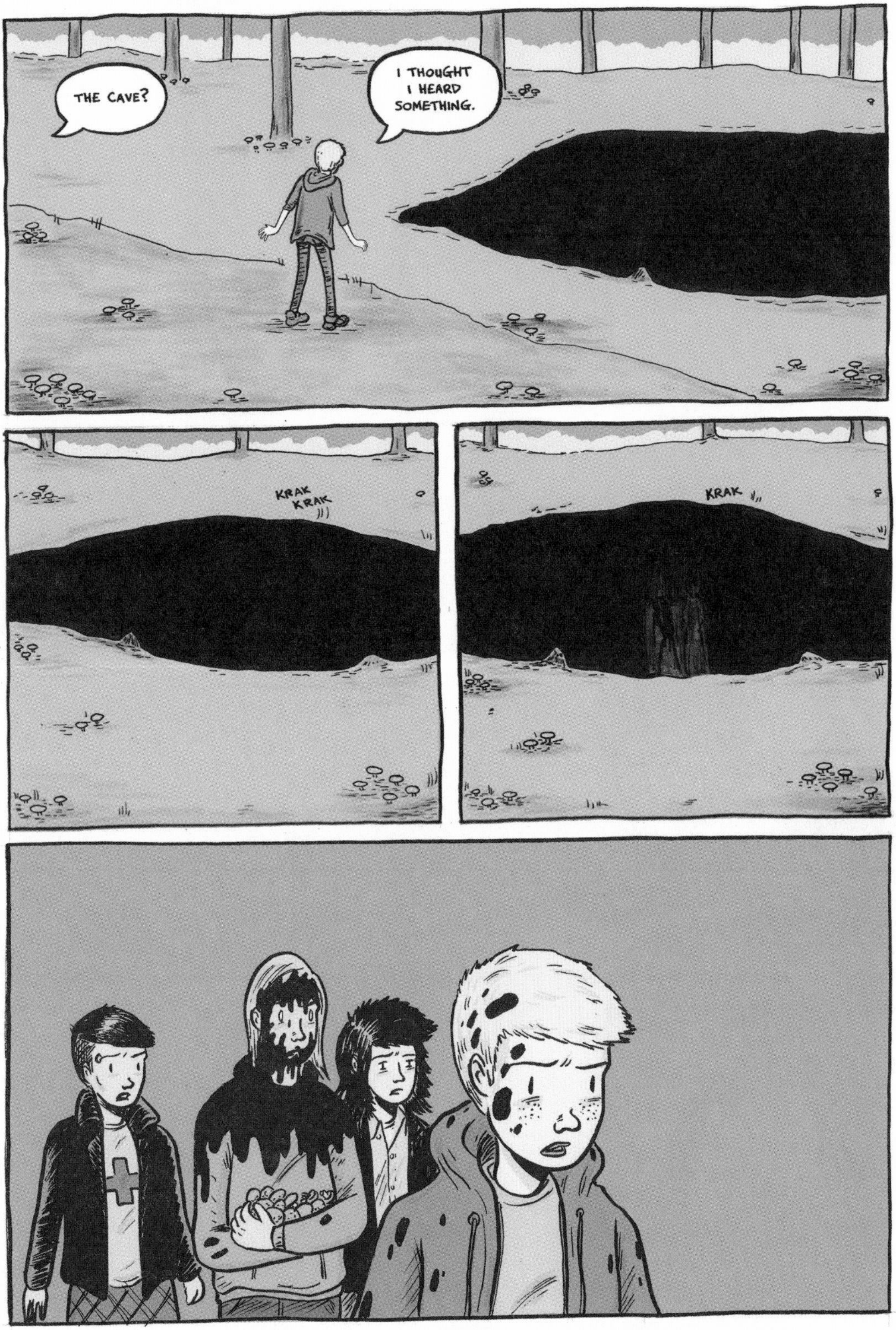
THE CAVE?
I THOUGHT I HEARD SOMETHING.
KRAK KRAK
KRAK

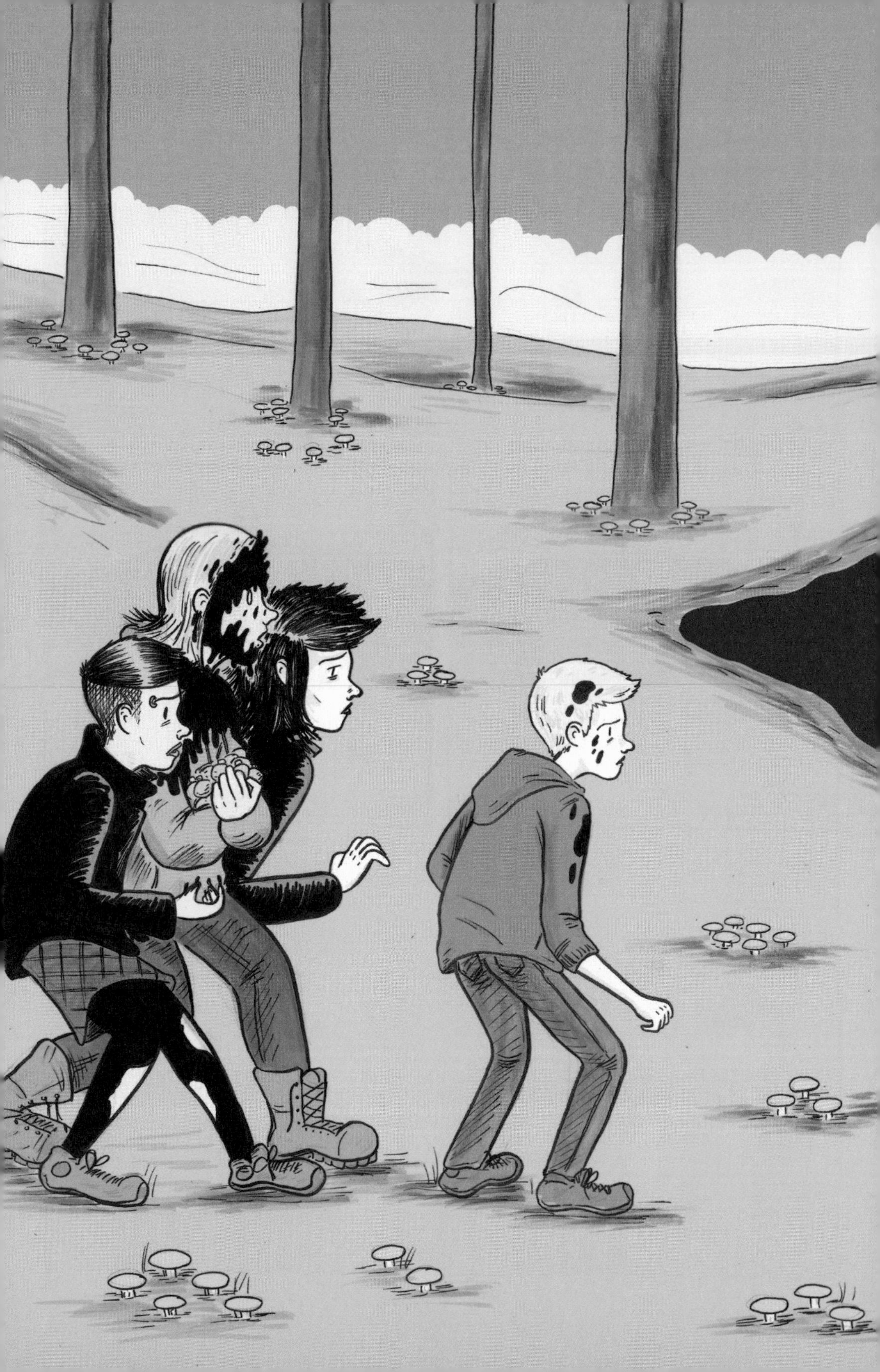

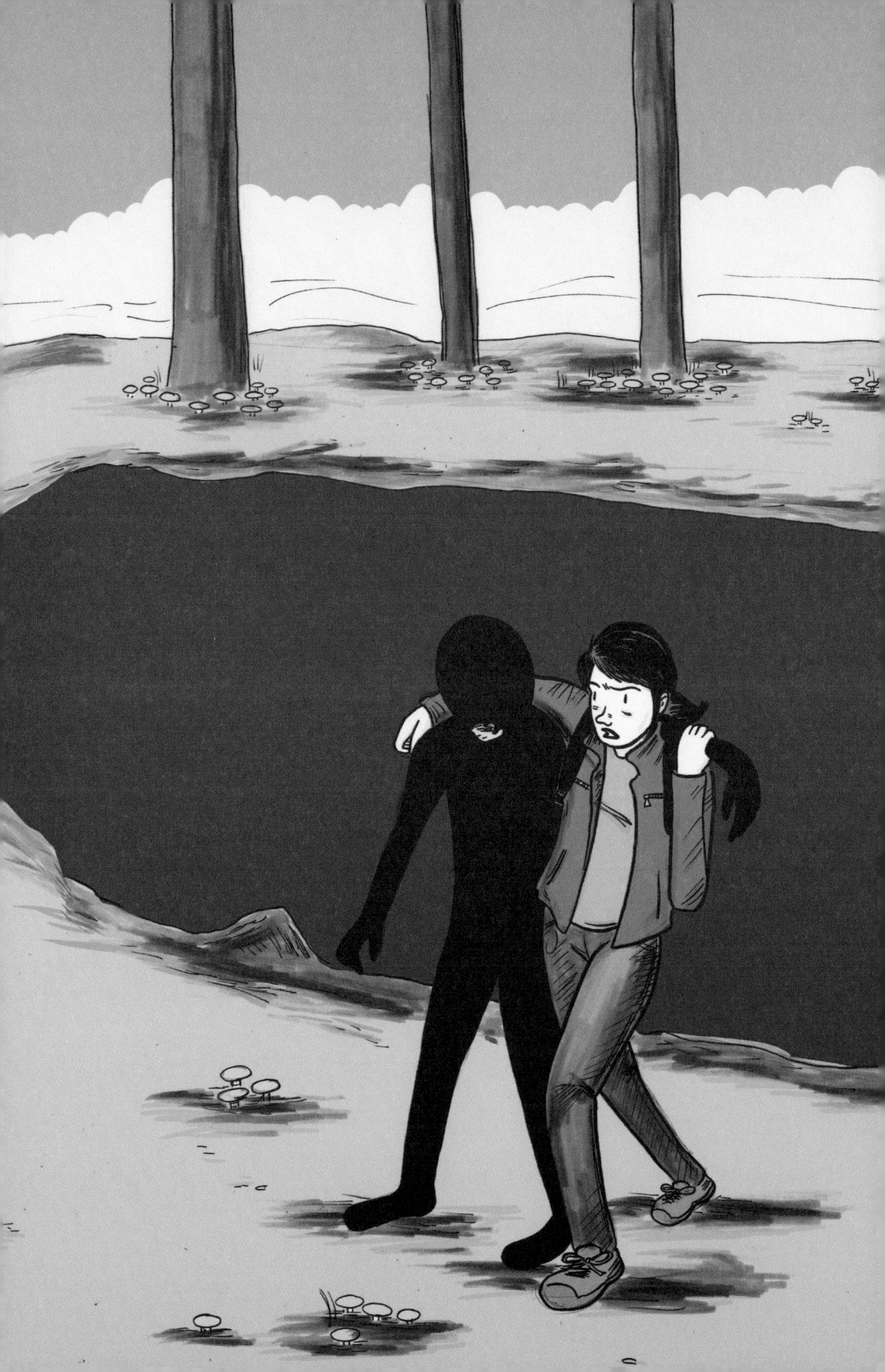

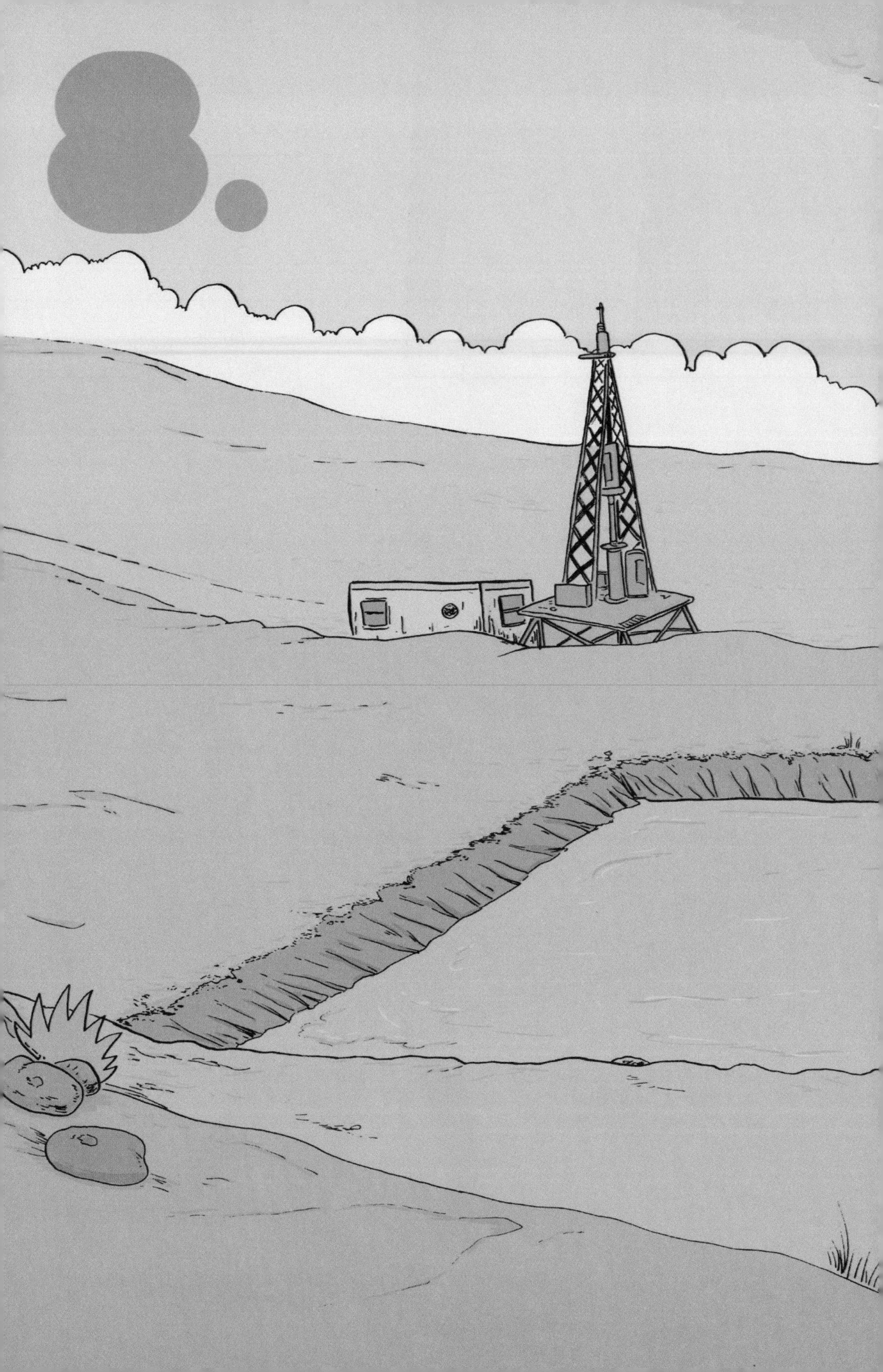
8.

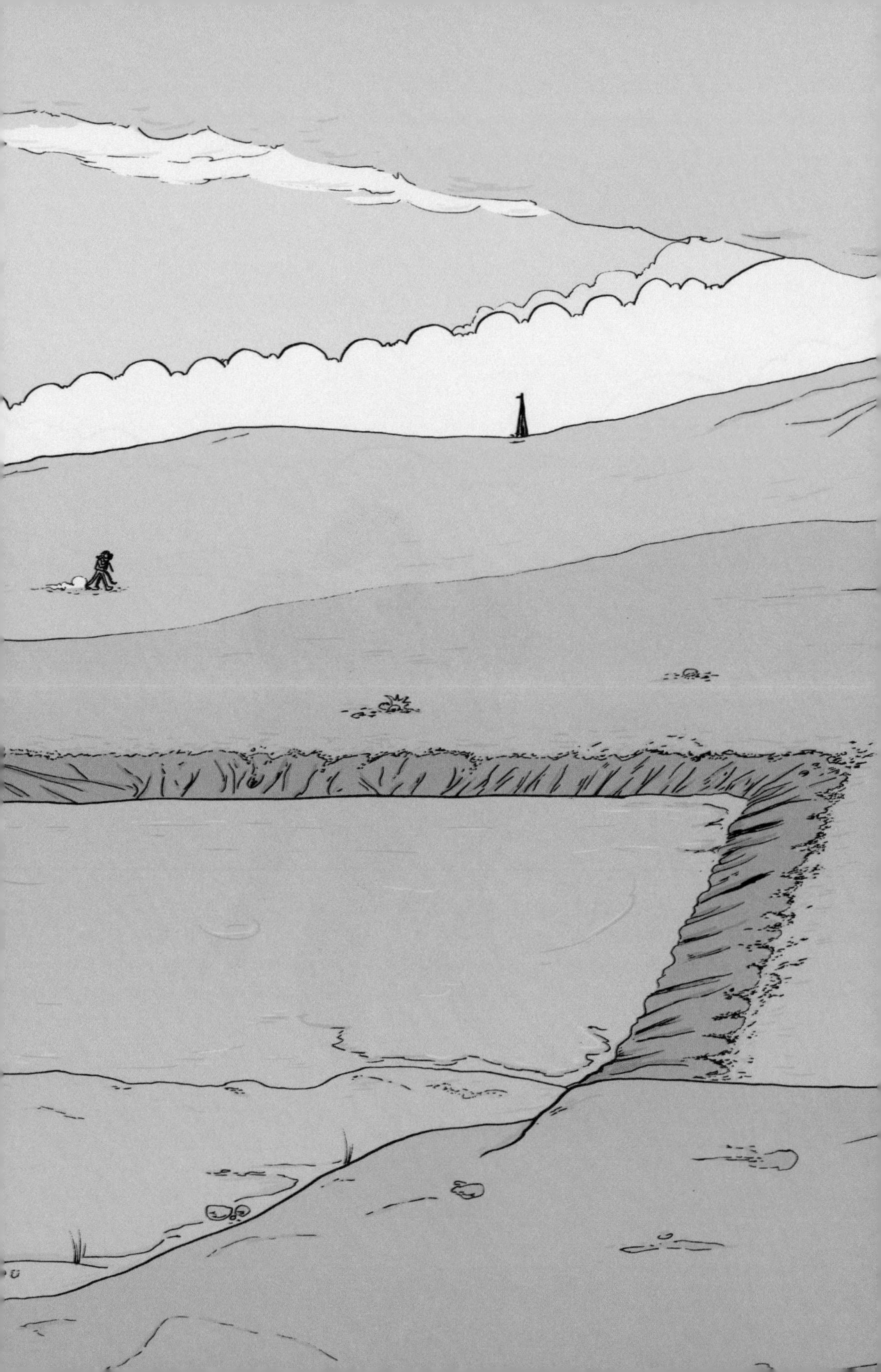

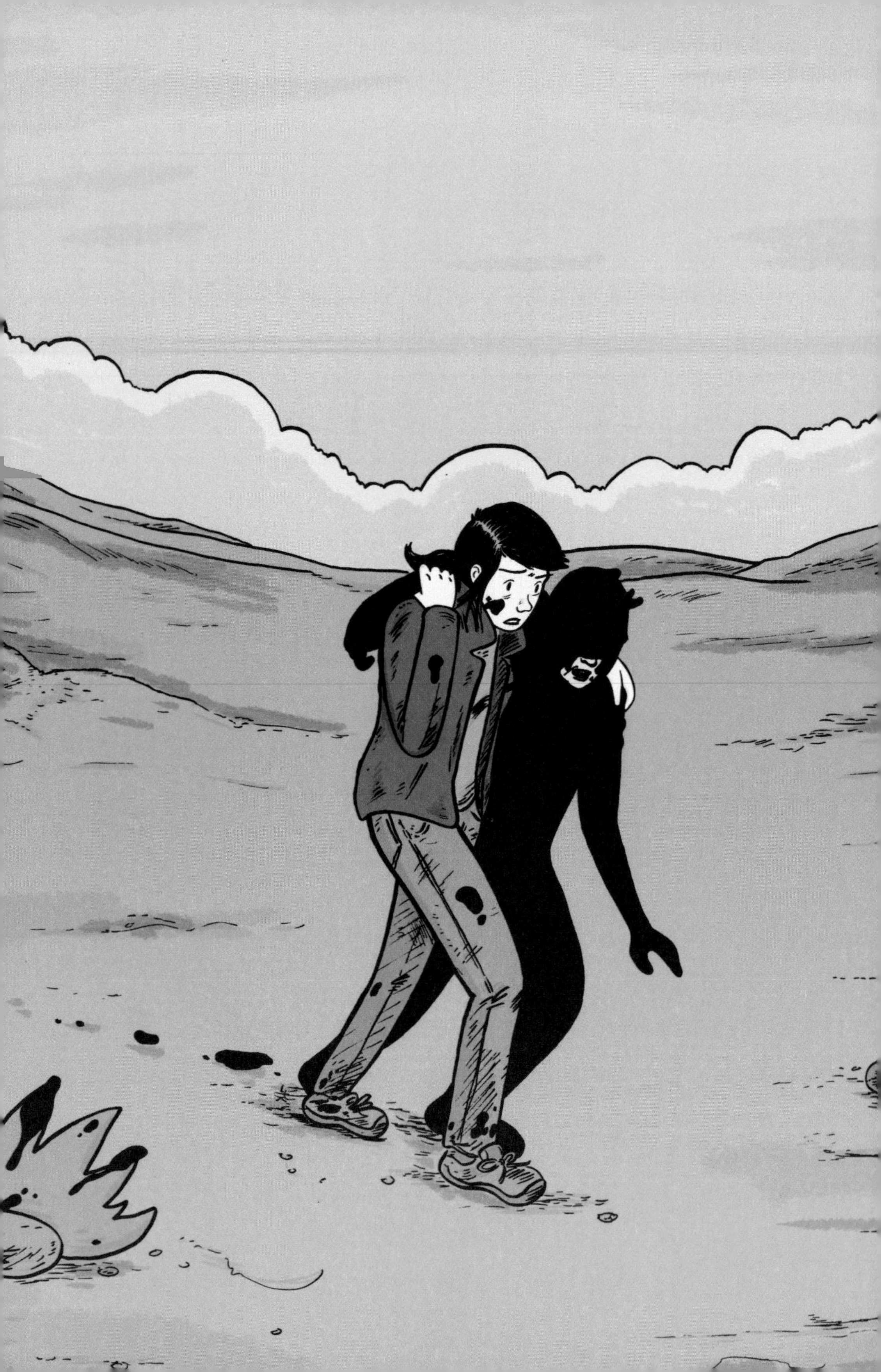

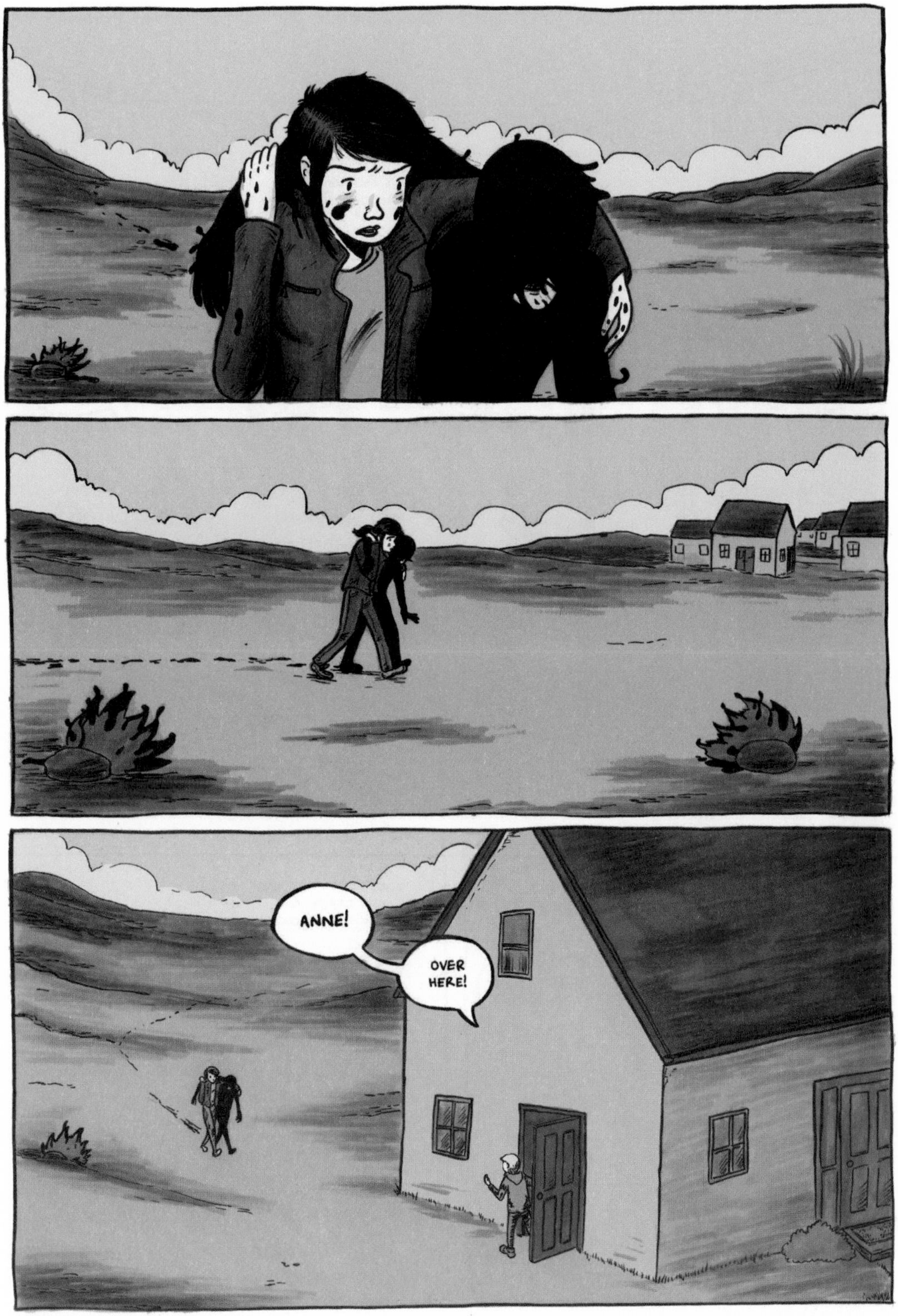
ANNE!
OVER HERE!

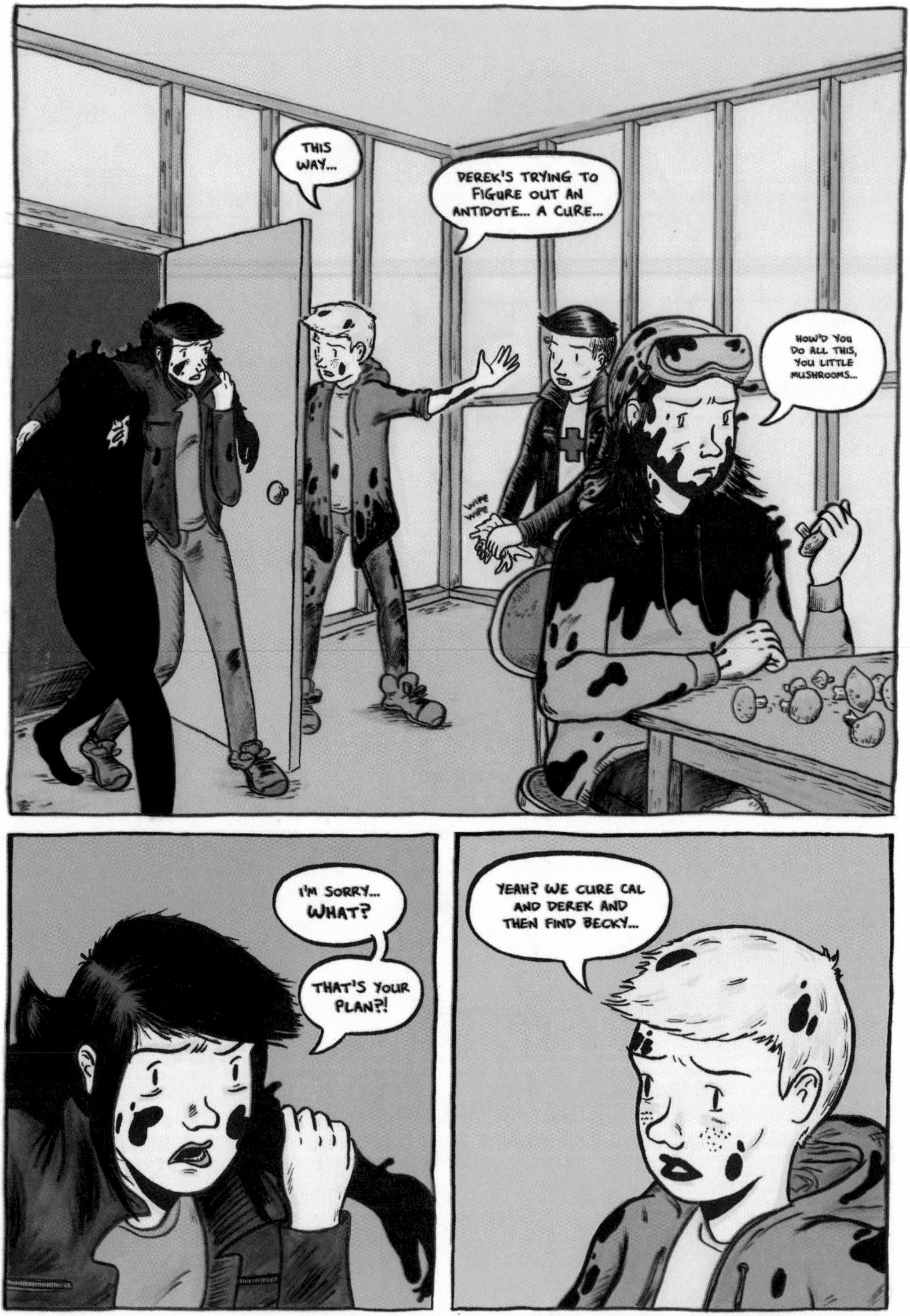
THIS WAY...
DEREK'S TRYING TO FIGURE OUT AN ANTIDOTE... A CURE...
HOW'D YOU DO ALL THIS, YOU LITTLE MUSHROOMS...
WIPE WIPE
I'M SORRY... WHAT?
THAT'S YOUR PLAN?!
YEAH? WE CURE CAL AND DEREK AND THEN FIND BECKY...

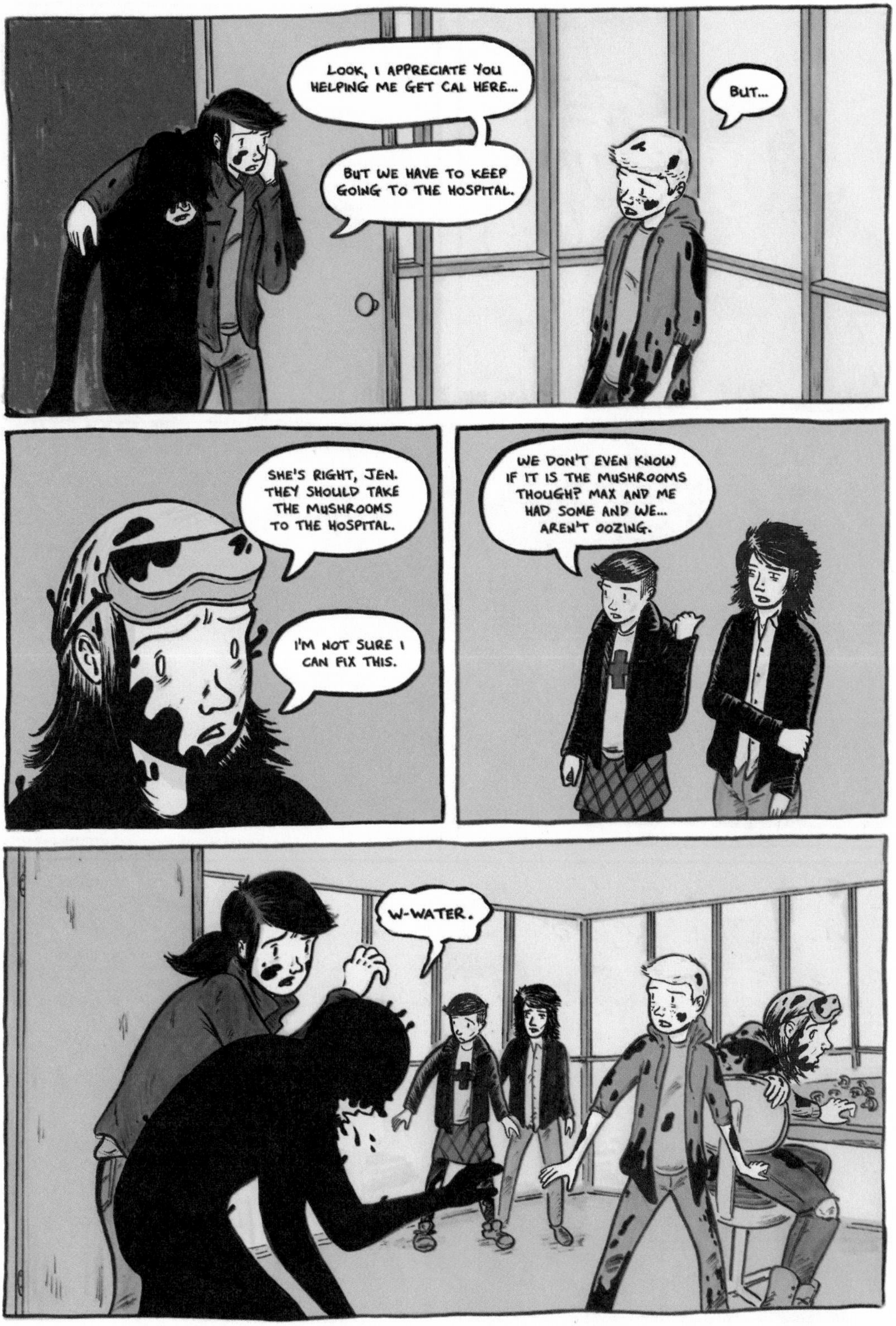
LOOK, I APPRECIATE YOU HELPING ME GET CAL HERE...
BUT WE HAVE TO KEEP GOING TO THE HOSPITAL.
BUT...
SHE'S RIGHT, JEN. THEY SHOULD TAKE THE MUSHROOMS TO THE HOSPITAL.
I'M NOT SURE I CAN FIX THIS.
WE DON'T EVEN KNOW IF IT IS THE MUSHROOMS THOUGH? MAX AND ME HAD SOME AND WE... AREN'T OOZING.
W-WATER.

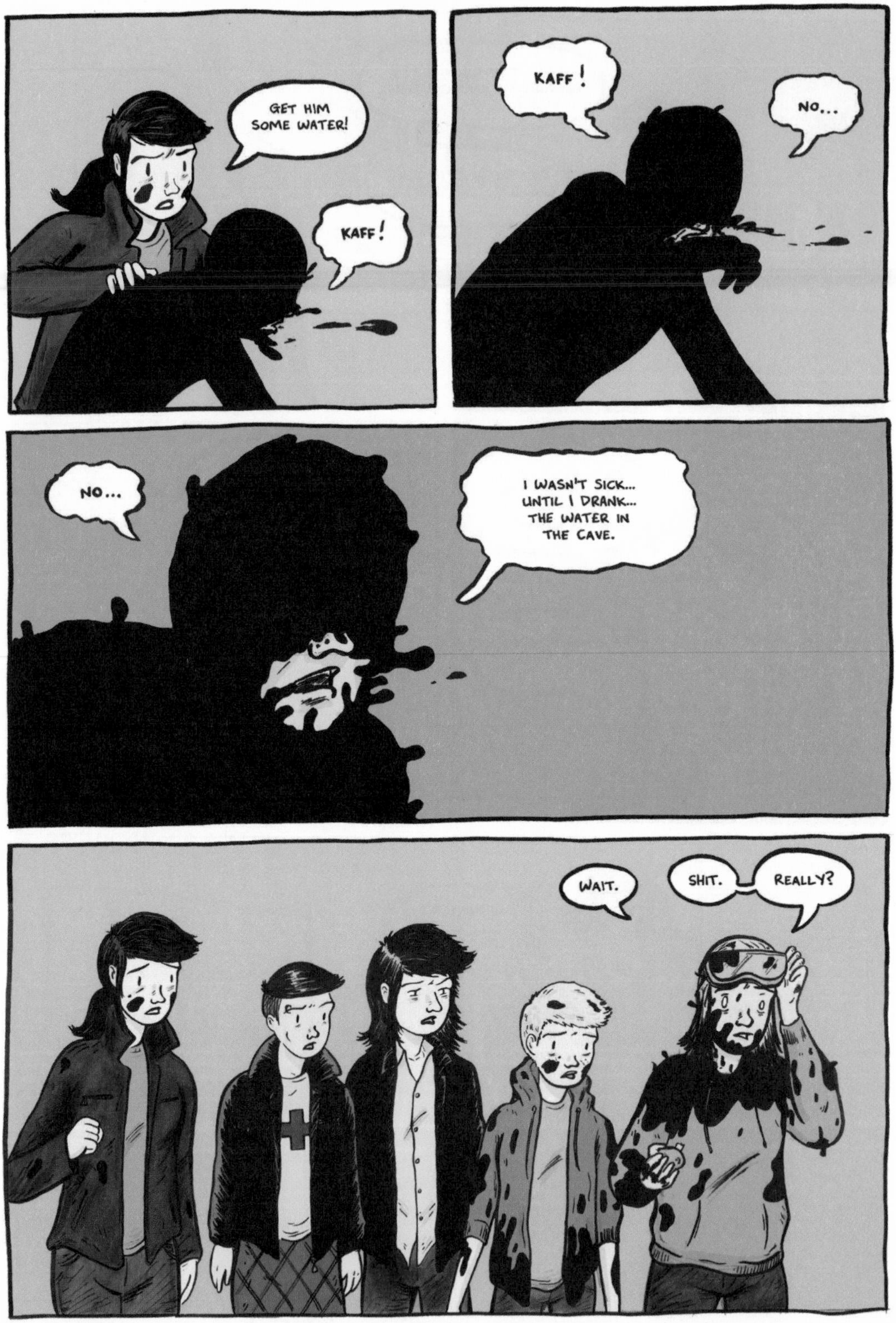
GET HIM SOME WATER!
KAFF!
KAFF!
NO...
NO...
I WASN'T SICK... UNTIL I DRANK... THE WATER IN THE CAVE.
WAIT.
SHIT.
REALLY?

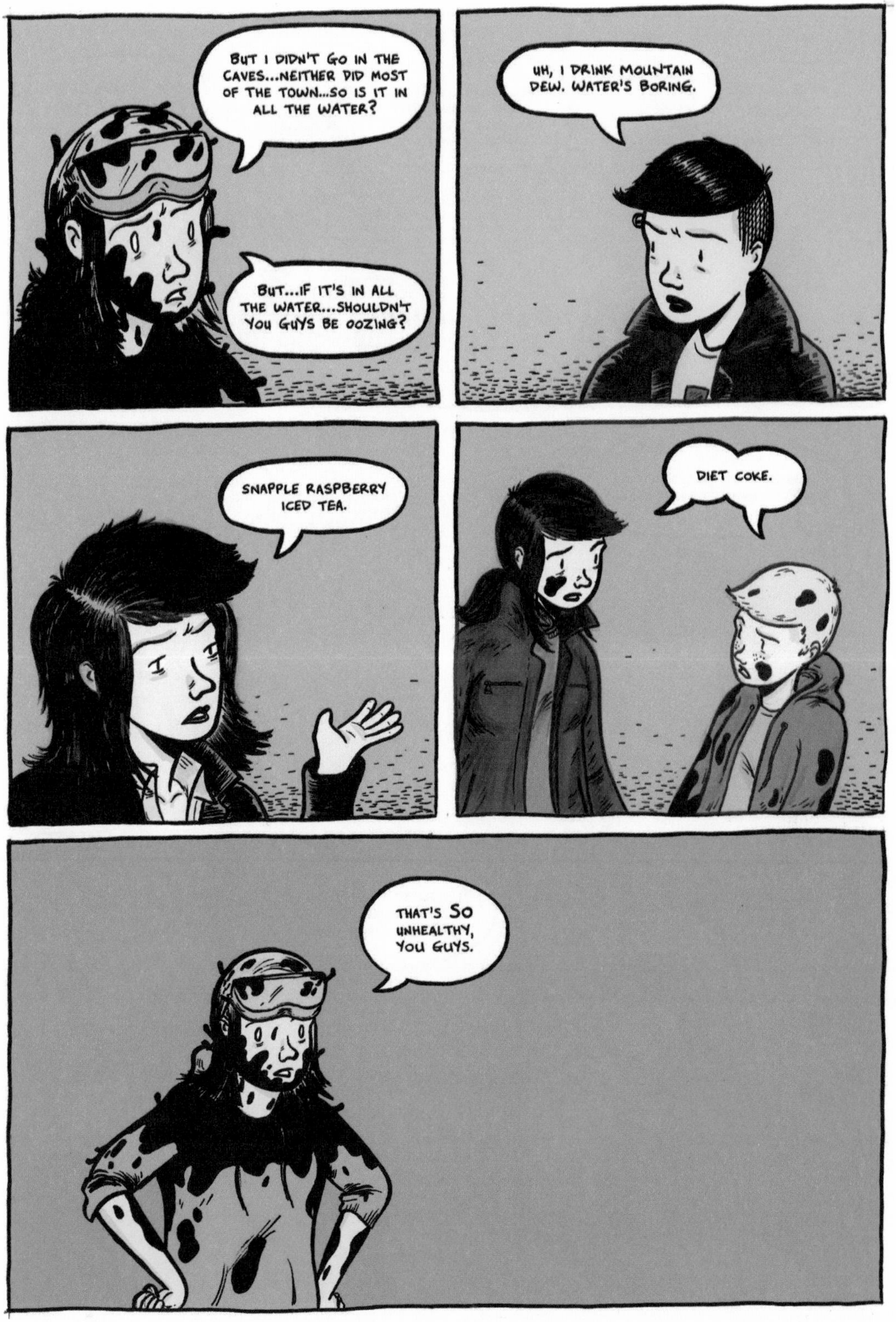
BUT I DIDN'T GO IN THE CAVES...NEITHER DID MOST OF THE TOWN...SO IS IT IN ALL THE WATER?
BUT...IF IT'S IN ALL THE WATER...SHOULDN'T YOU GUYS BE OOZING?
UH, I DRINK MOUNTAIN DEW. WATER'S BORING.
SNAPPLE RASPBERRY ICED TEA.
DIET COKE.
THAT'S SO UNHEALTHY, YOU GUYS.

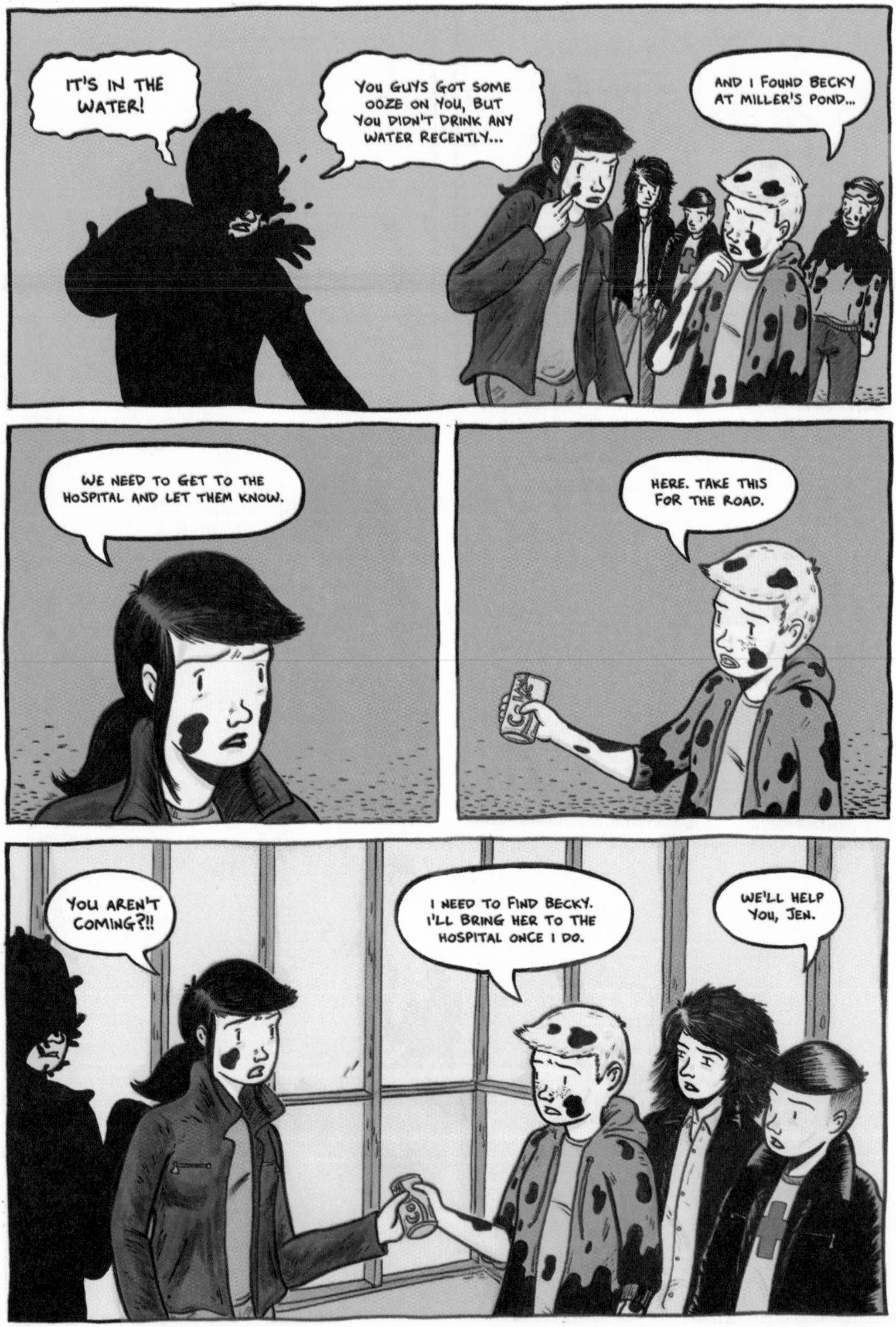
IT'S IN THE WATER!
YOU GUYS GOT SOME OOZE ON YOU, BUT YOU DIDN'T DRINK ANY WATER RECENTLY...
AND I FOUND BECKY AT MILLER'S POND...
WE NEED TO GET TO THE HOSPITAL AND LET THEM KNOW.
HERE. TAKE THIS FOR THE ROAD.
YOU AREN'T COMING?!!
I NEED TO FIND BECKY. I'LL BRING HER TO THE HOSPITAL ONCE I DO.
WE'LL HELP YOU, JEN.

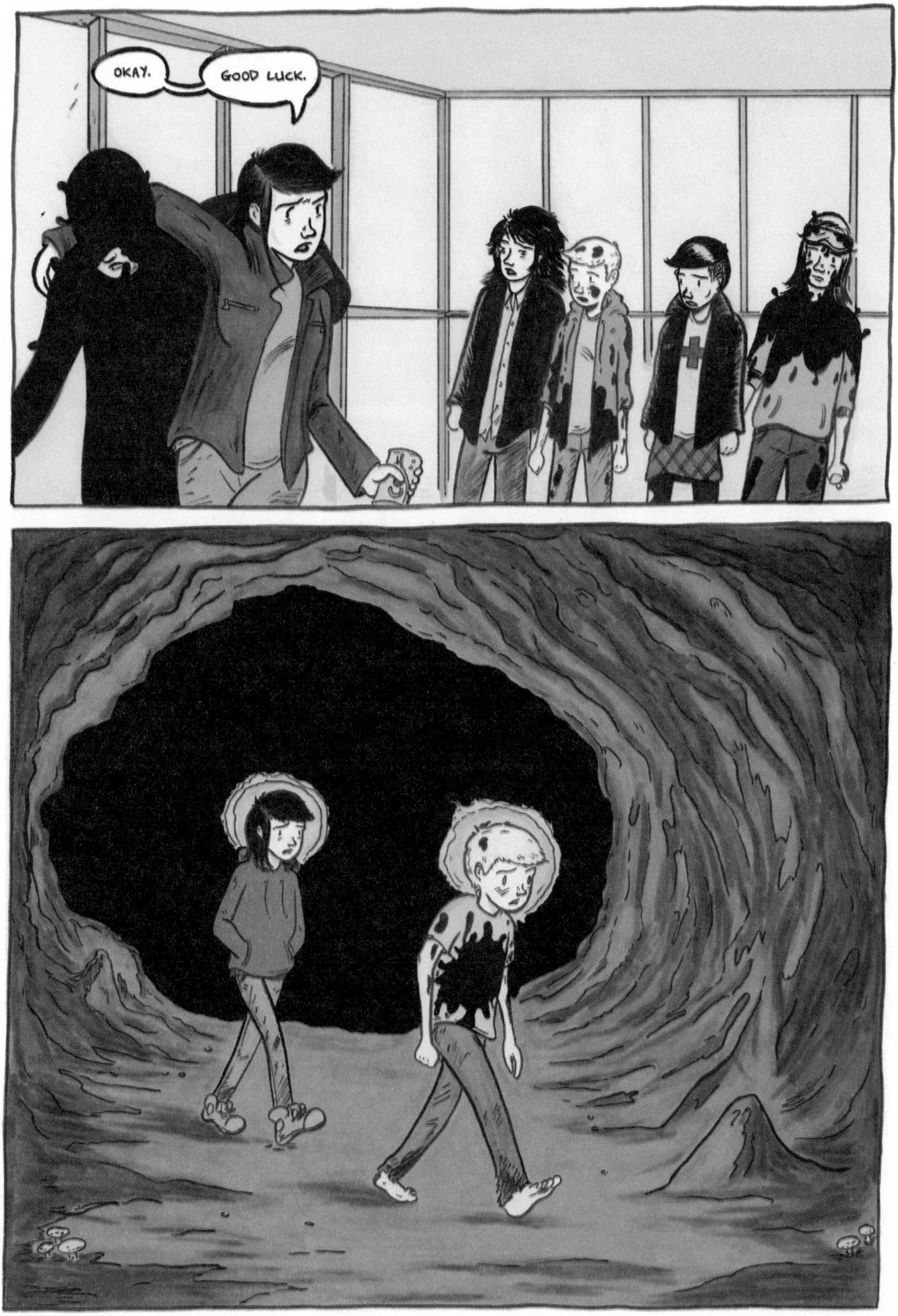
OKAY.
GOOD LUCK.

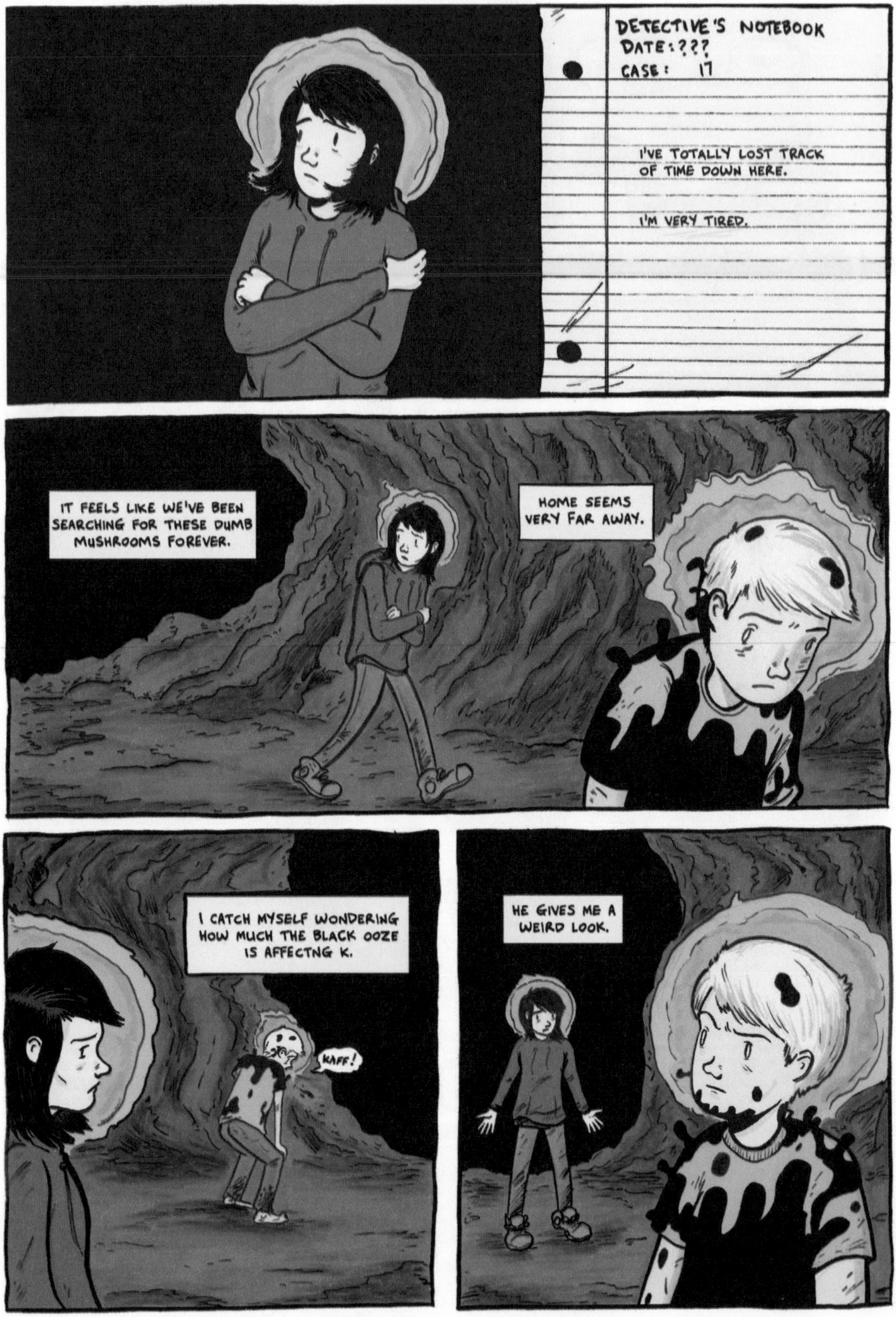
DETECTIVE'S NOTEBOOK
DATE: ???
CASE: 17
I'VE TOTALLY LOST TRACK OF TIME DOWN HERE.
I'M VERY TIRED.
IT FEELS LIKE WE'VE BEEN SEARCHING FOR THESE DUMB MUSHROOMS FOREVER.
HOME SEEMS VERY FAR AWAY.
I CATCH MYSELF WONDERING HOW MUCH THE BLACK OOZE IS AFFECTNG K.
KAFF!
HE GIVES ME A WEIRD LOOK.

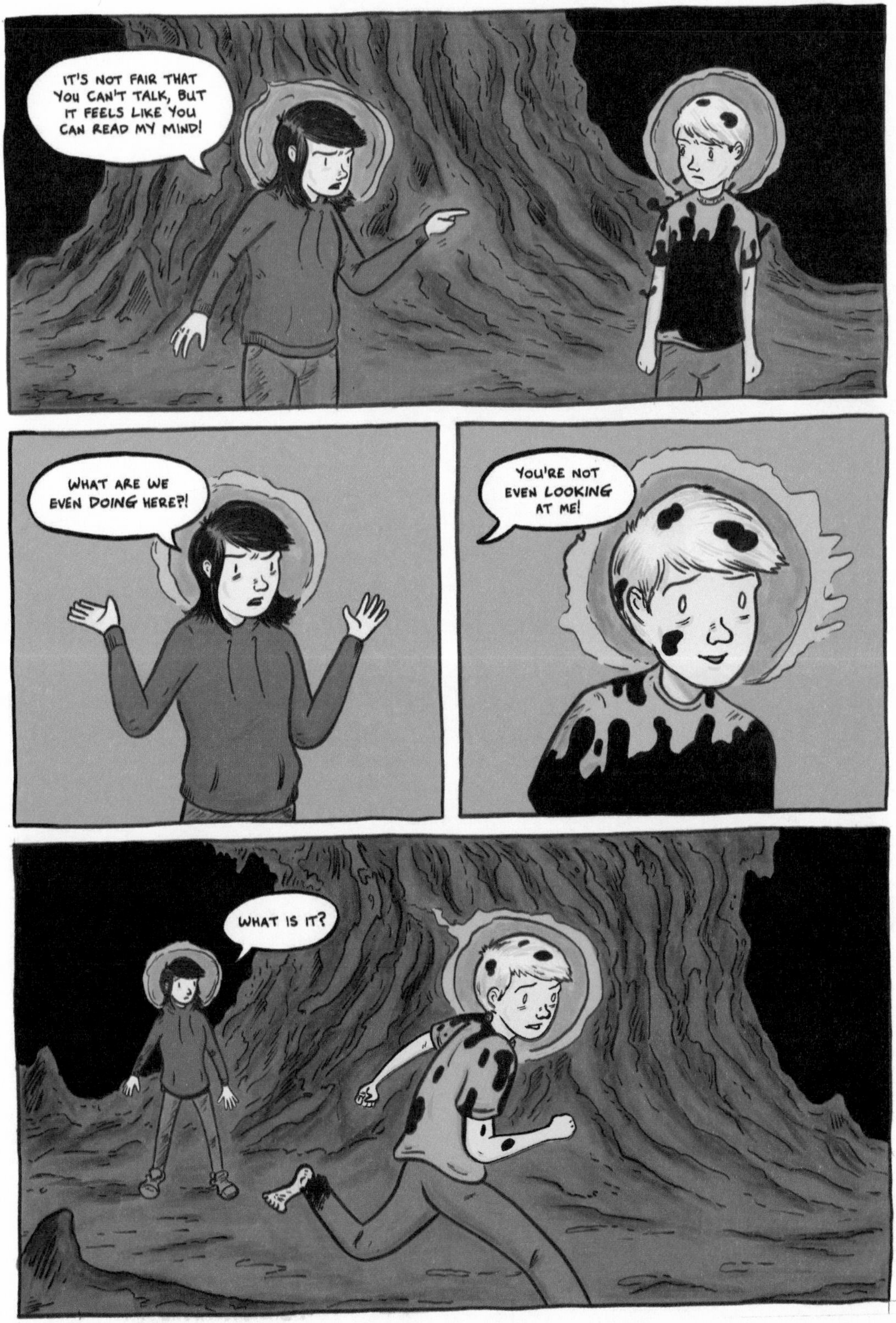
IT'S NOT FAIR THAT YOU CAN'T TALK, BUT IT FEELS LIKE YOU CAN READ MY MIND!
WHAT ARE WE EVEN DOING HERE?!
YOU'RE NOT EVEN LOOKING AT ME!
WHAT IS IT?

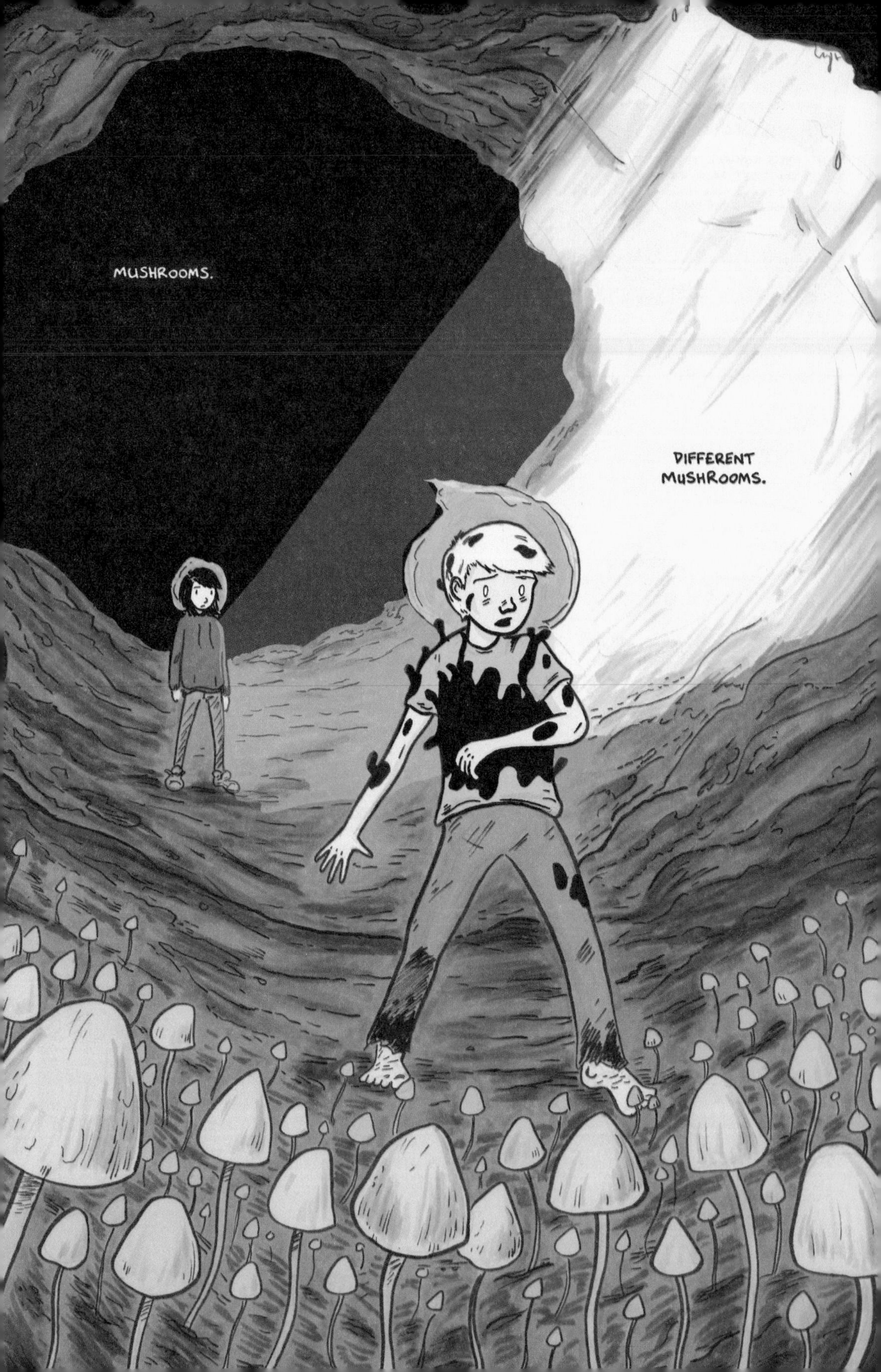
MUSHROOMS.
DIFFERENT MUSHROOMS.

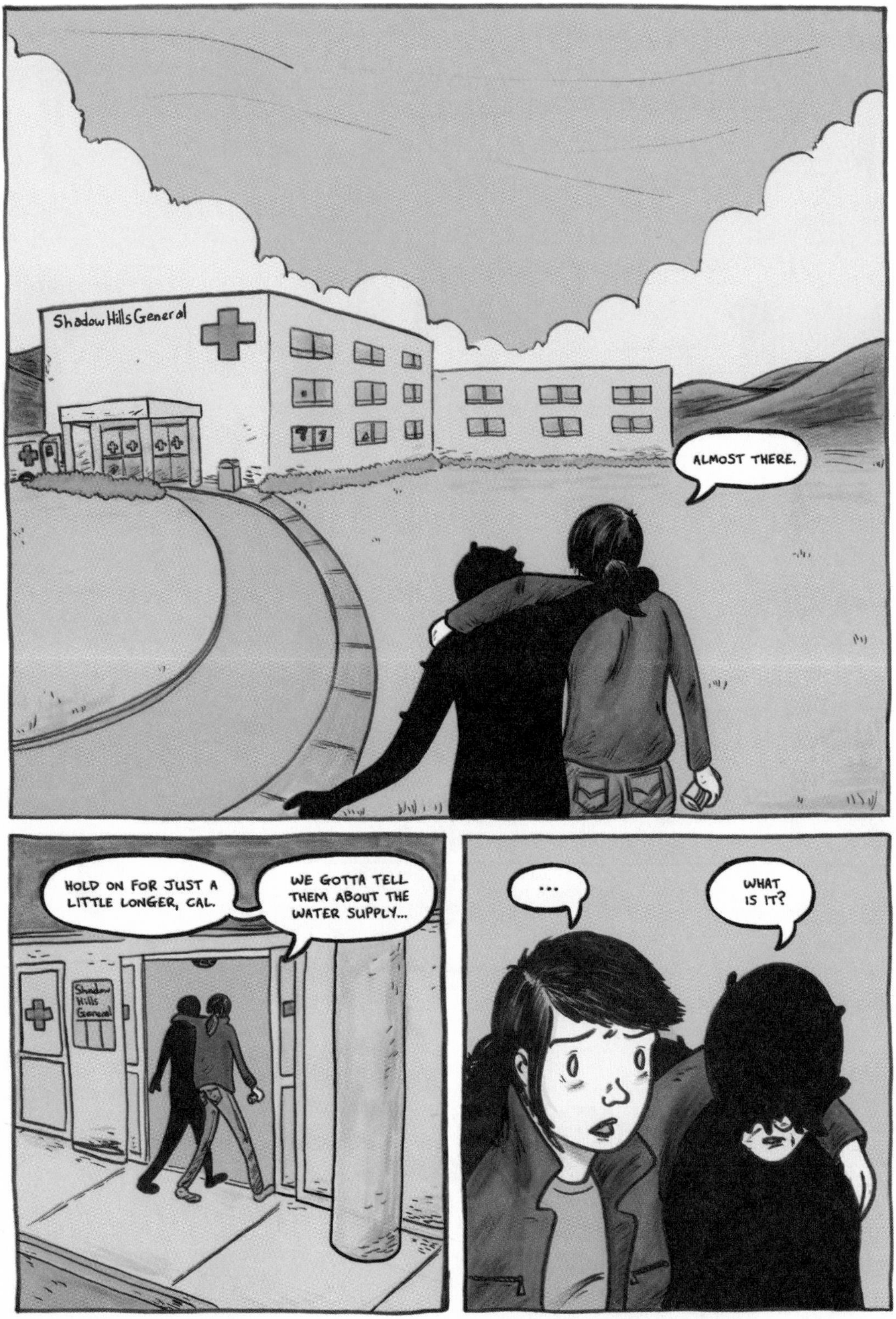
Shadow Hills General
ALMOST THERE.
HOLD ON FOR JUST A LITTLE LONGER, CAL.
WE GOTTA TELL THEM ABOUT THE WATER SUPPLY...
Shadow Hills General
...
WHAT IS IT?

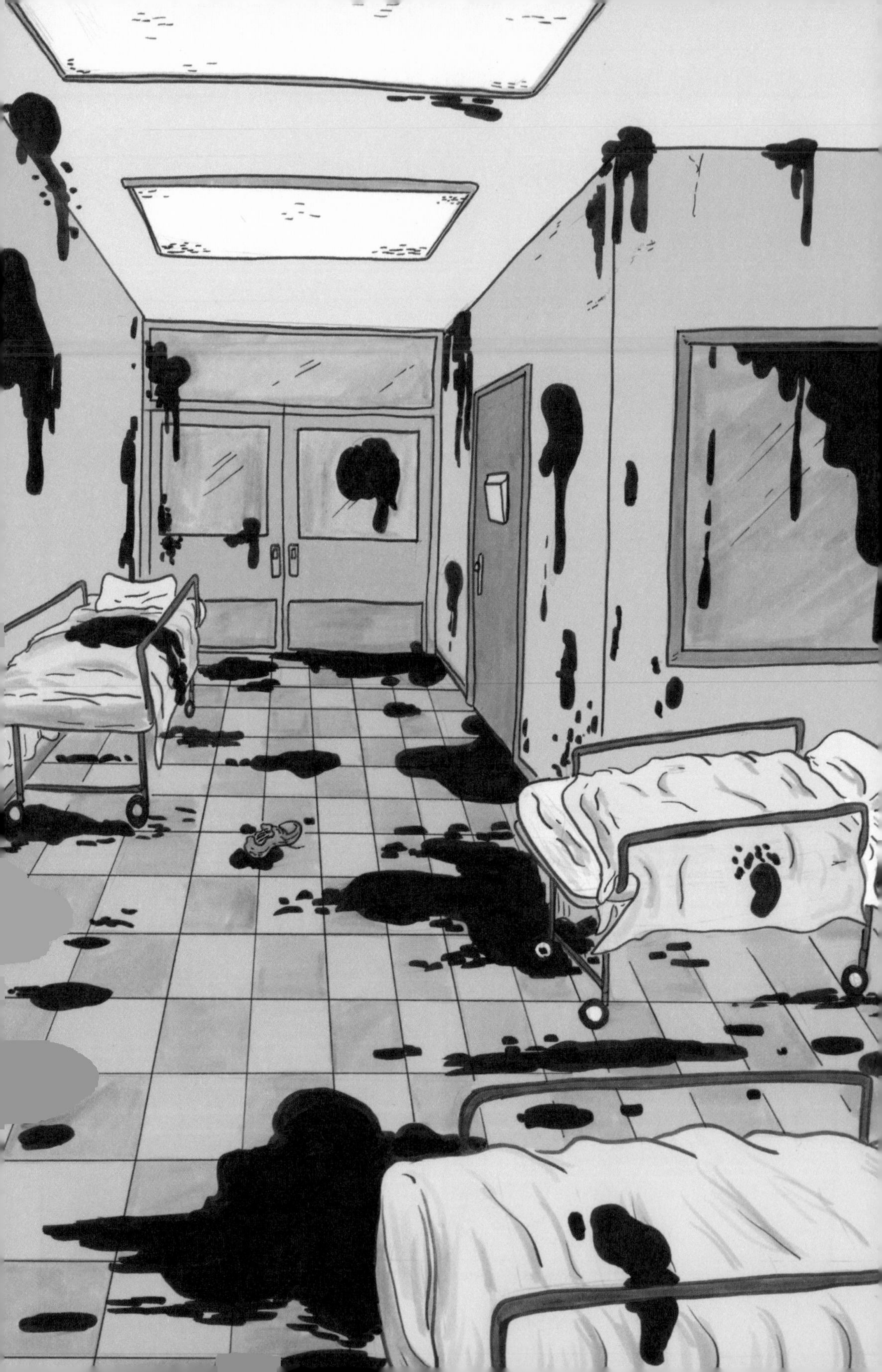

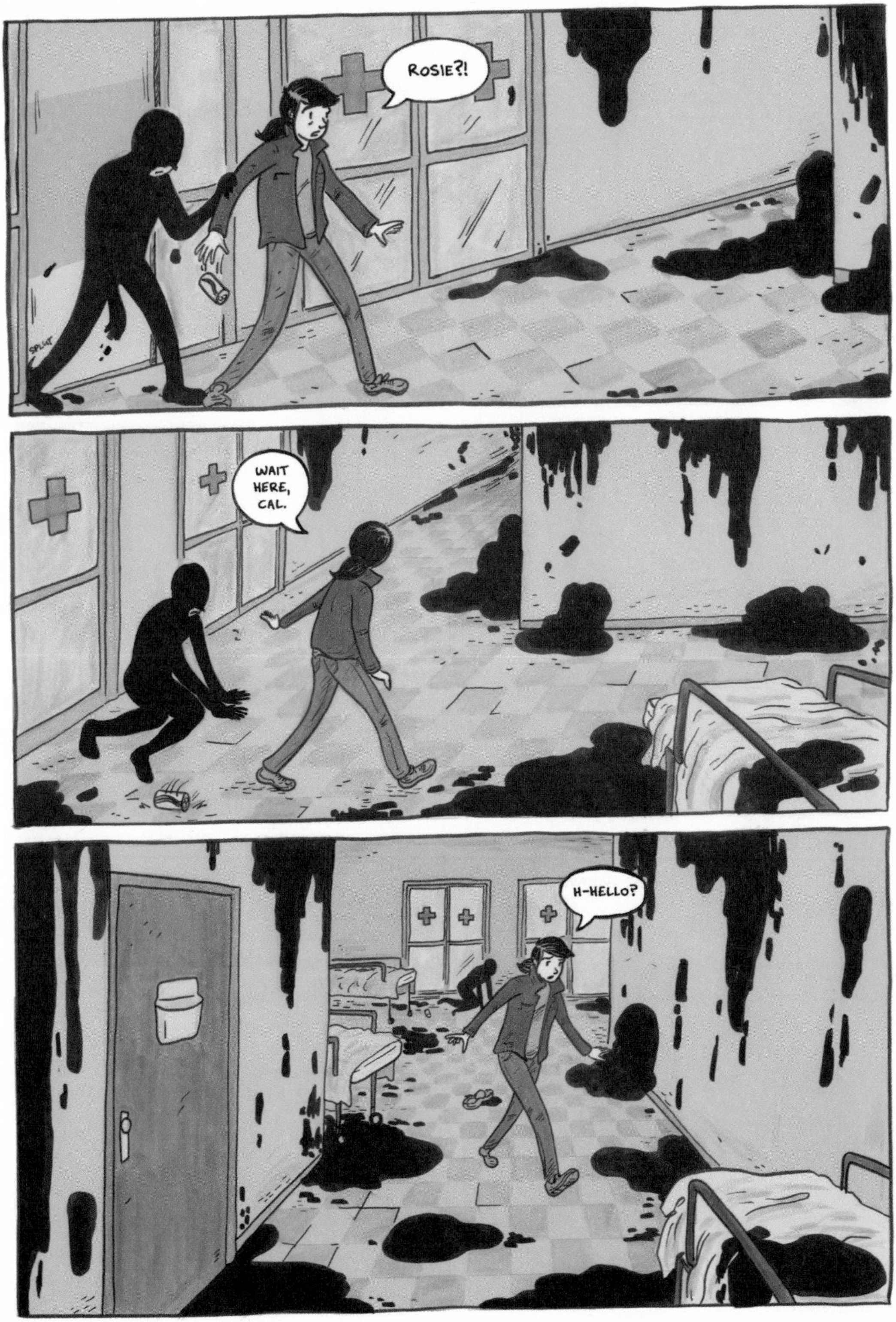
ROSIE?!
SPLUT
WAIT HERE, CAL.
H-HELLO?

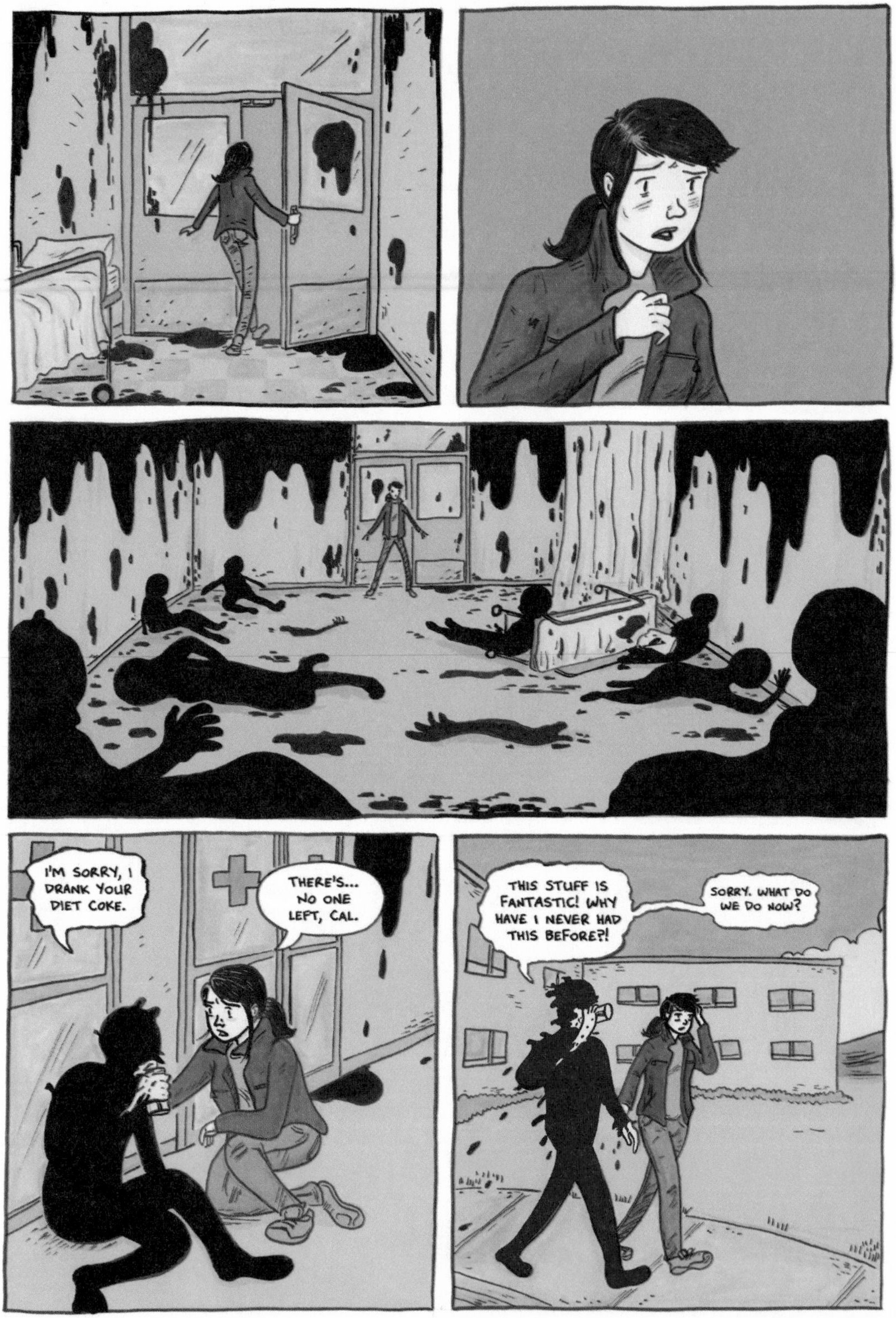
I'M SORRY, I DRANK YOUR DIET COKE.
THERE'S... NO ONE LEFT, CAL.
THIS STUFF IS FANTASTIC! WHY HAVE I NEVER HAD THIS BEFORE?!
SORRY. WHAT DO WE DO NOW?

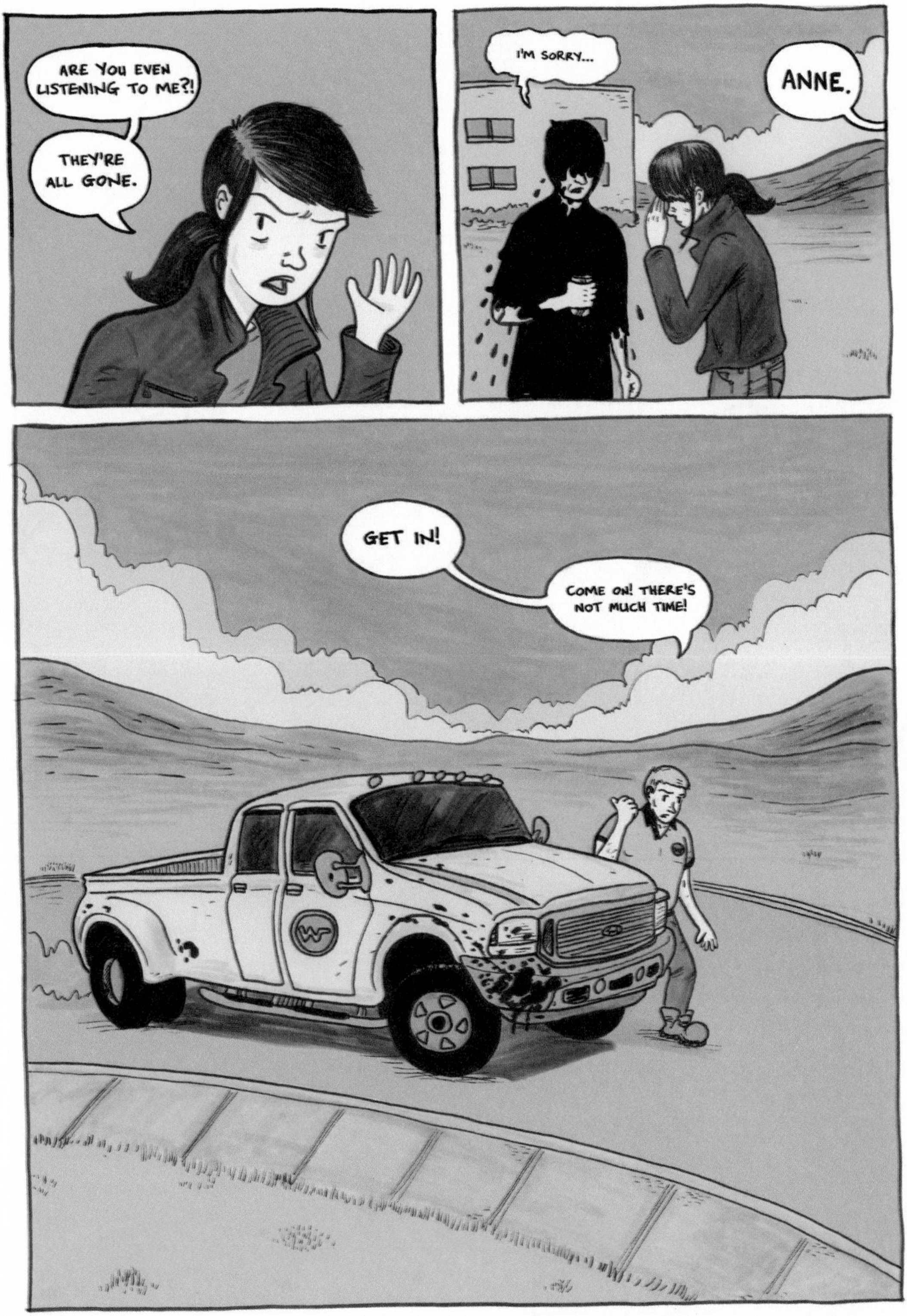
ARE YOU EVEN LISTENING TO ME?!
THEY'RE ALL GONE.
I'M SORRY...
ANNE.
GET IN!
COME ON! THERE'S NOT MUCH TIME!

9.

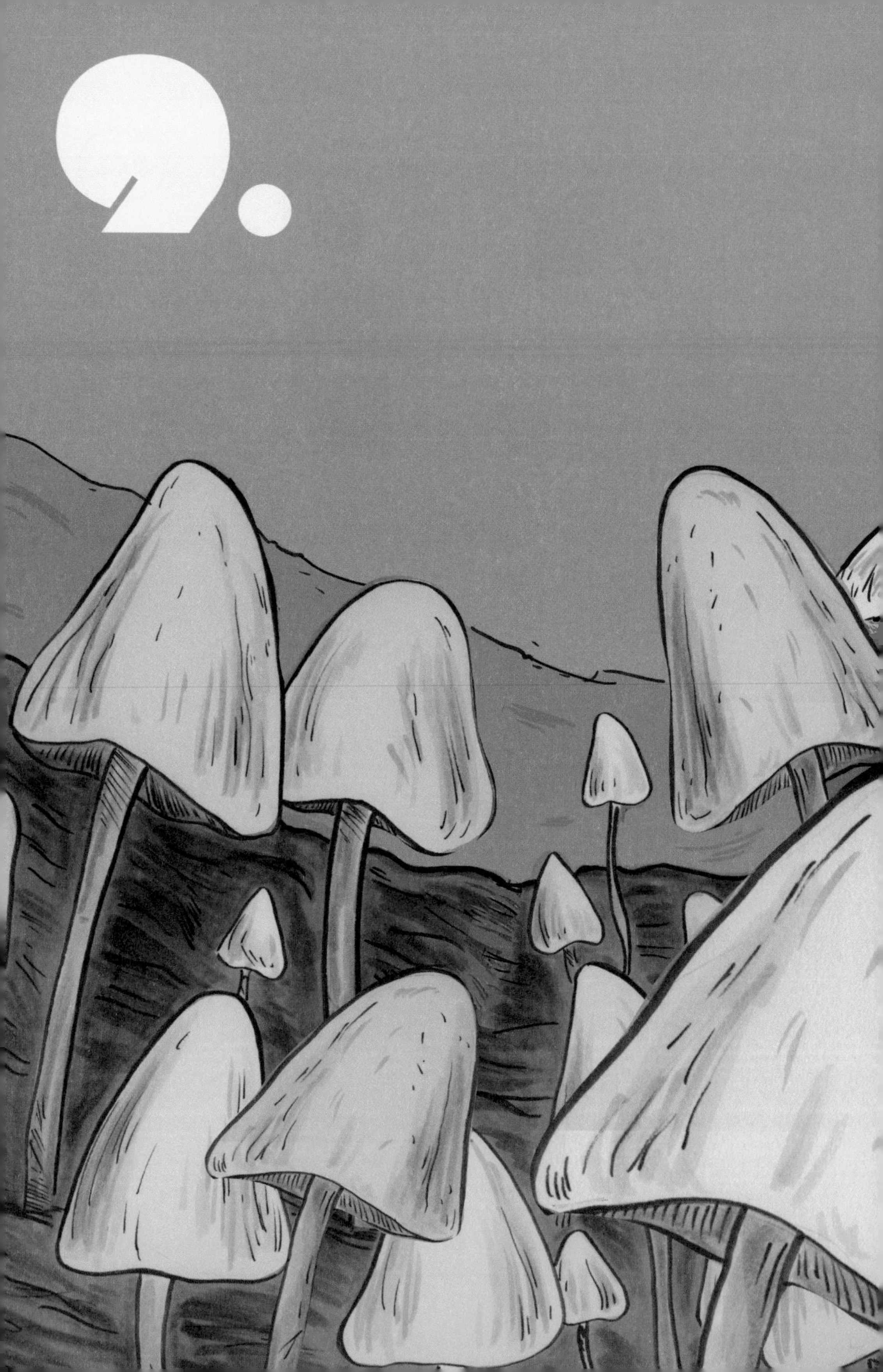

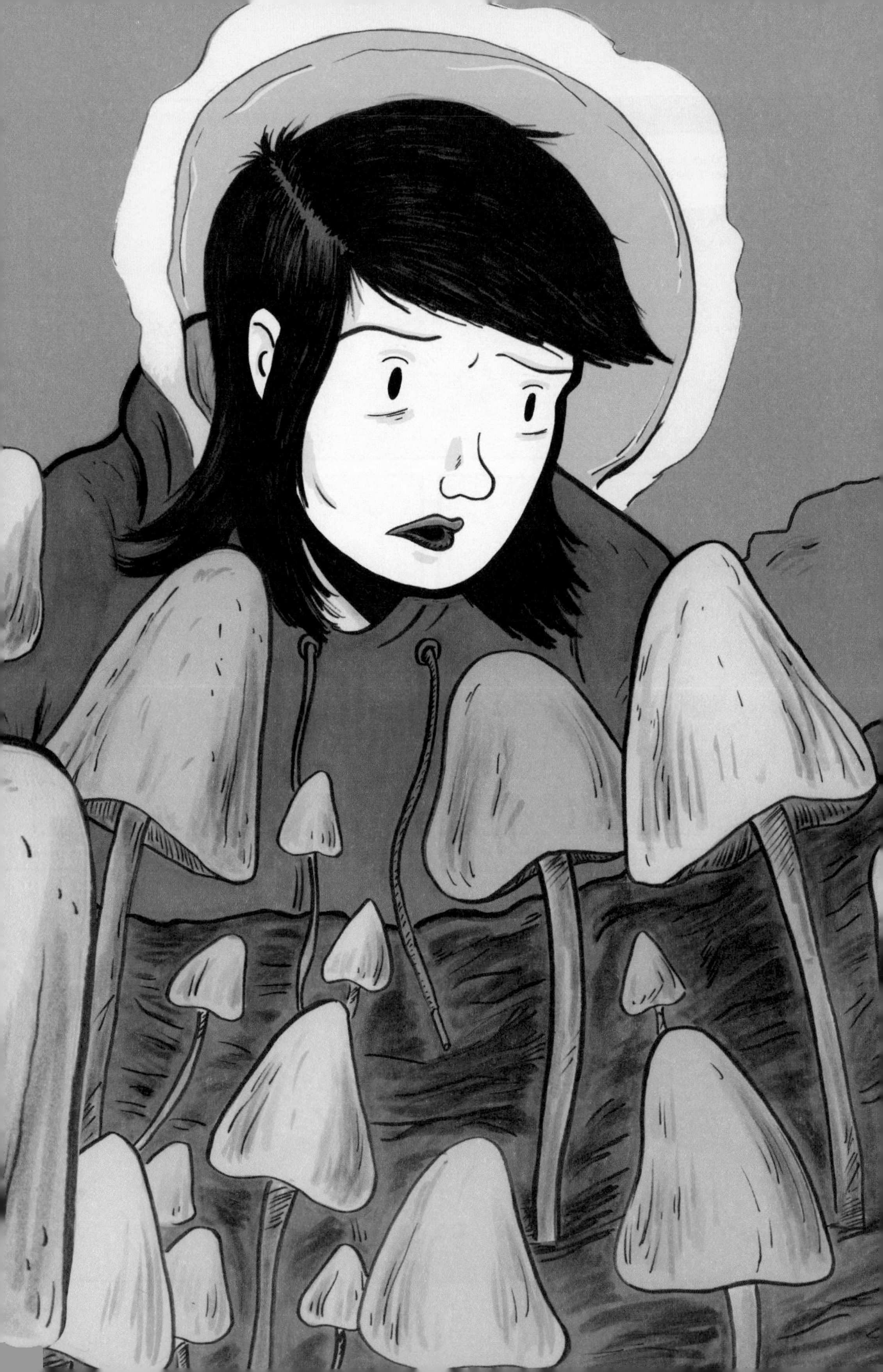

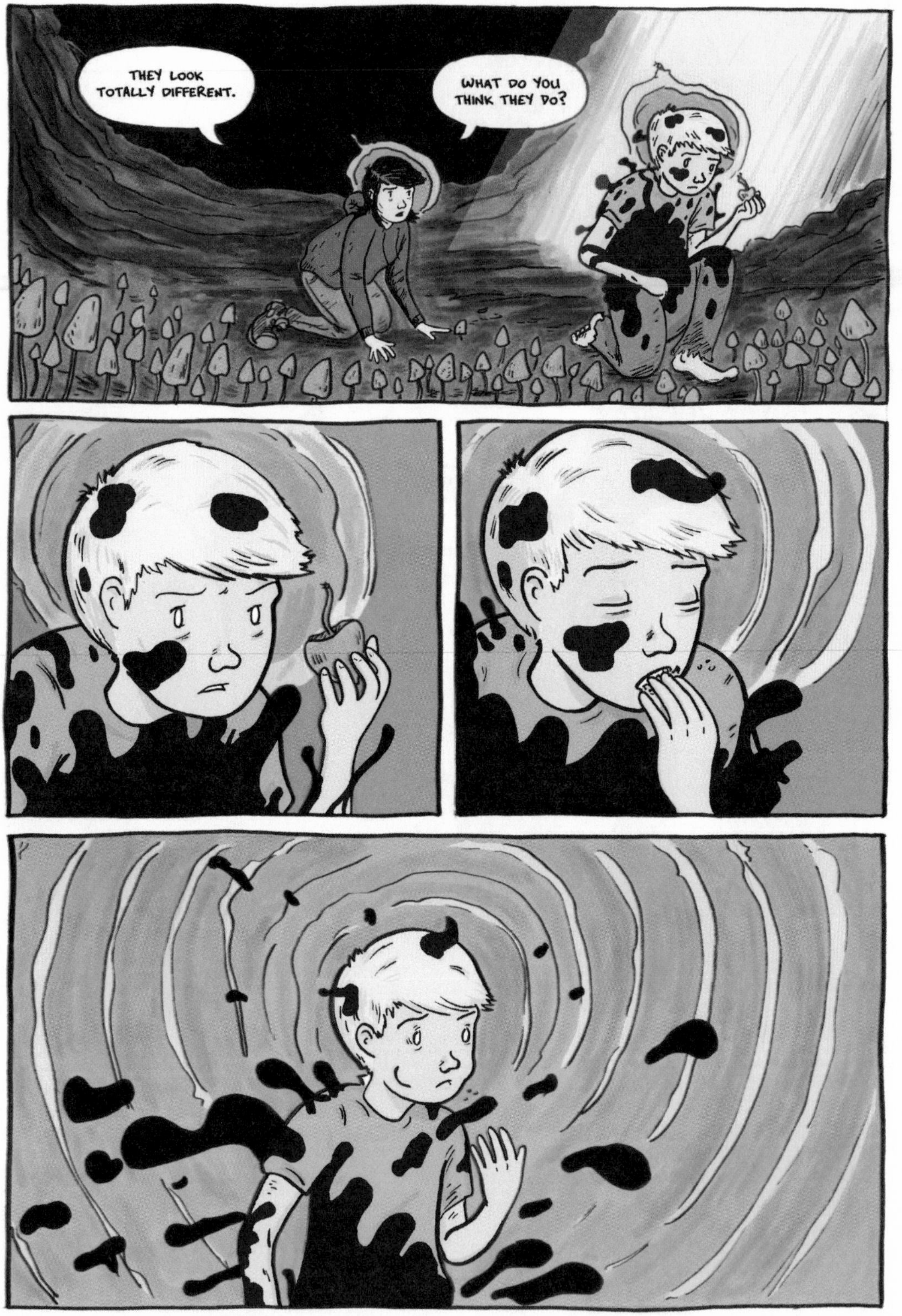
THEY LOOK TOTALLY DIFFERENT.
WHAT DO YOU THINK THEY DO?

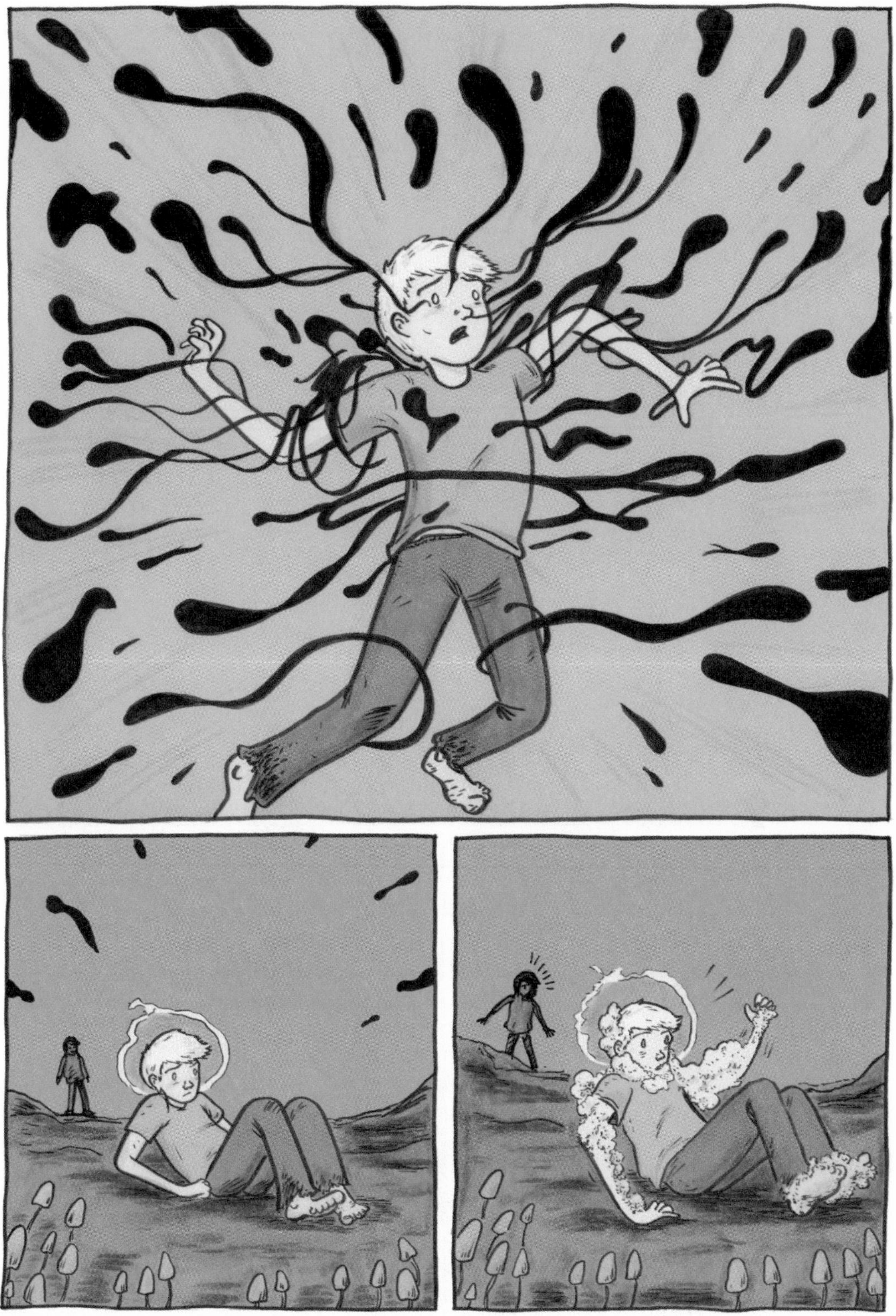

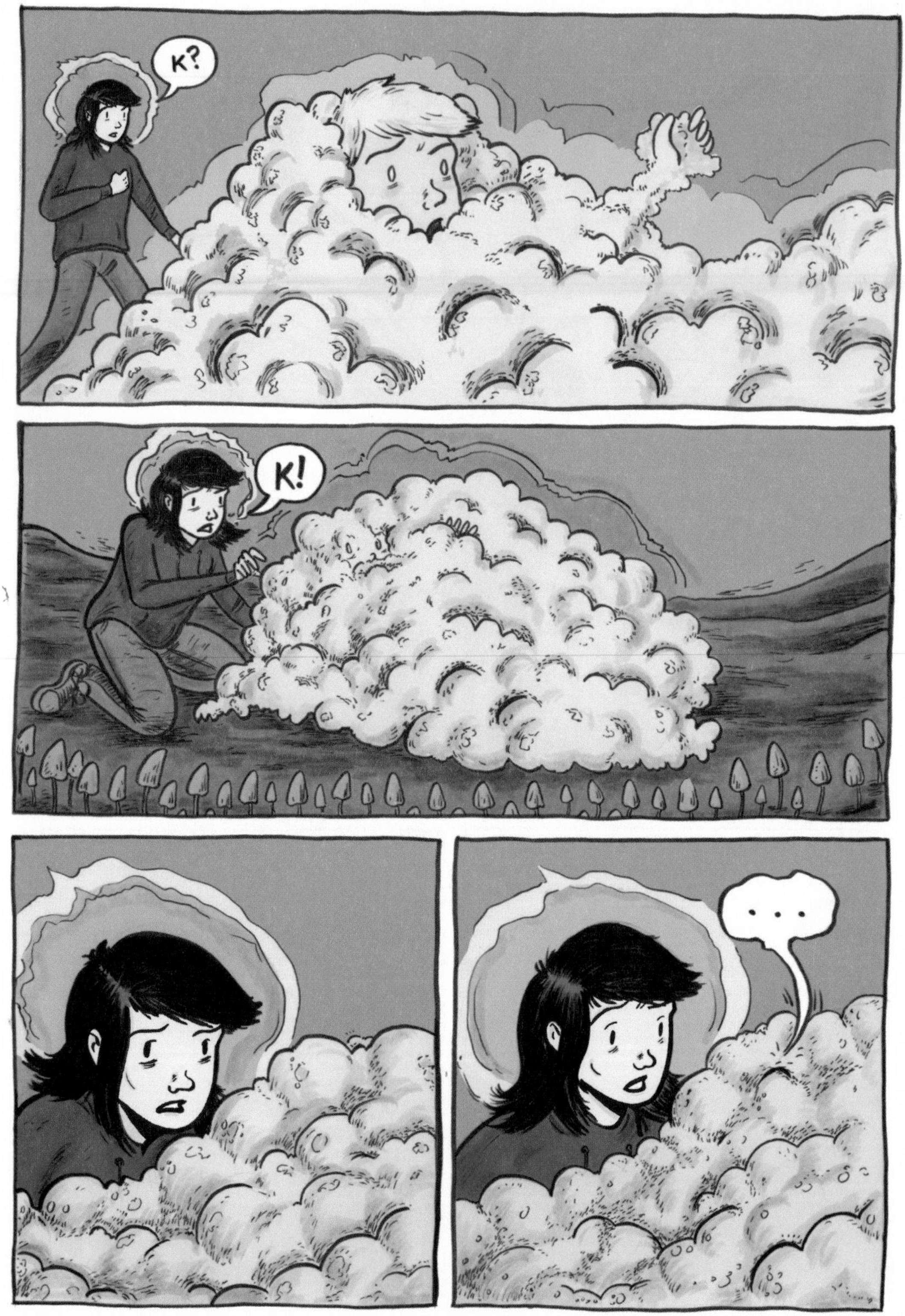
K?
K!
. . .

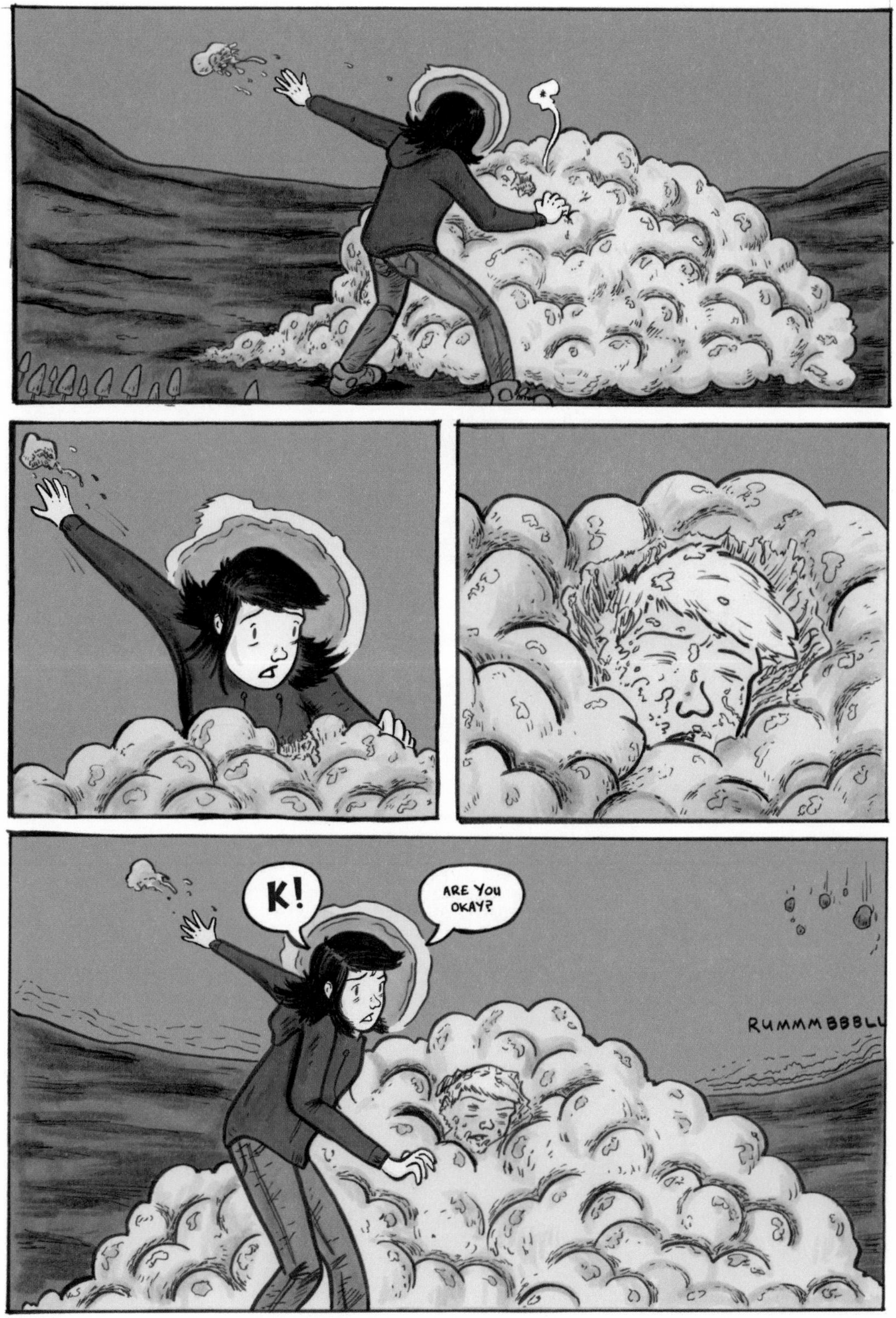
K!
ARE YOU OKAY?
RUMMMBBBLL

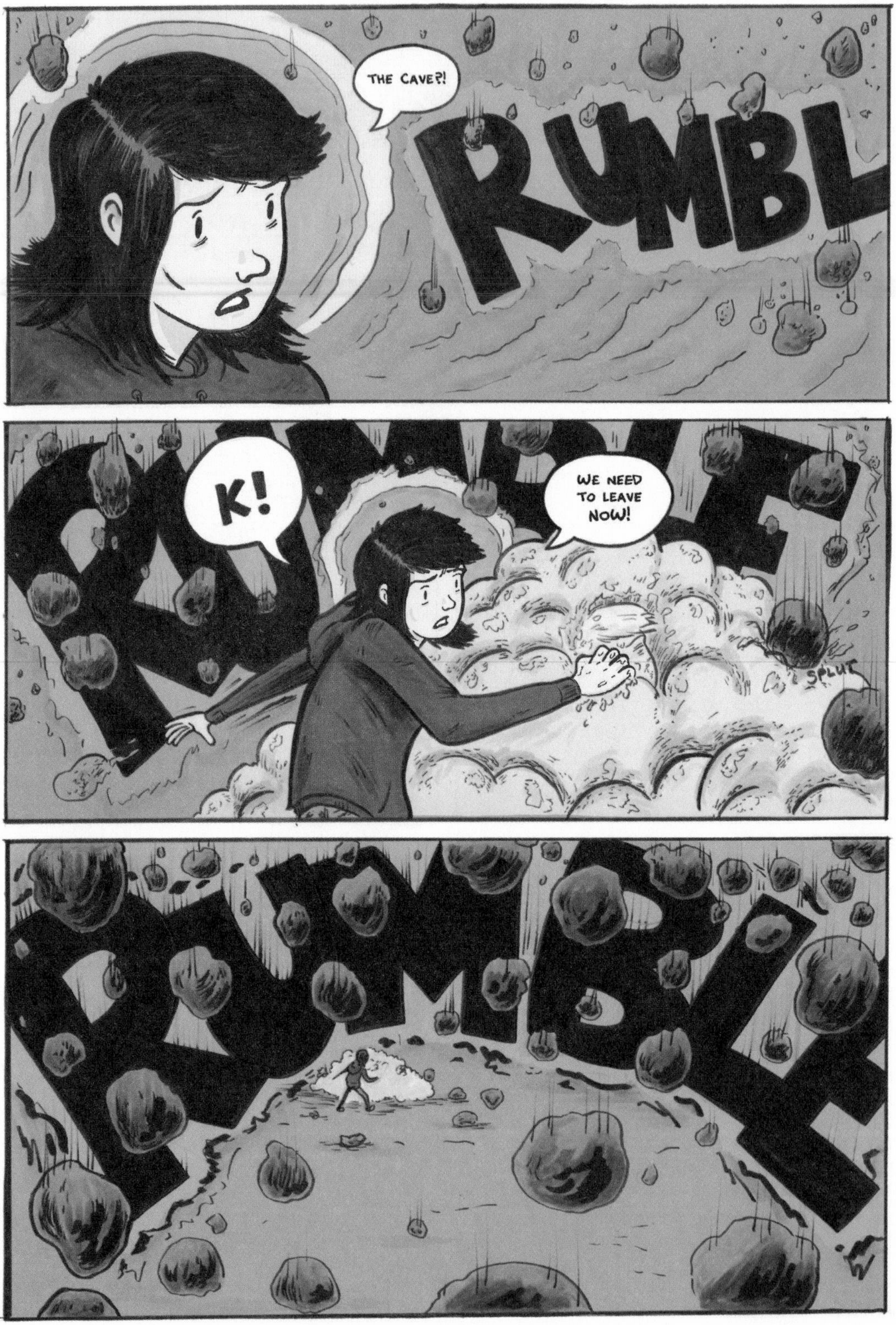
THE CAVE?!
RUMBL
K!
WE NEED TO LEAVE NOW!
SPLUT

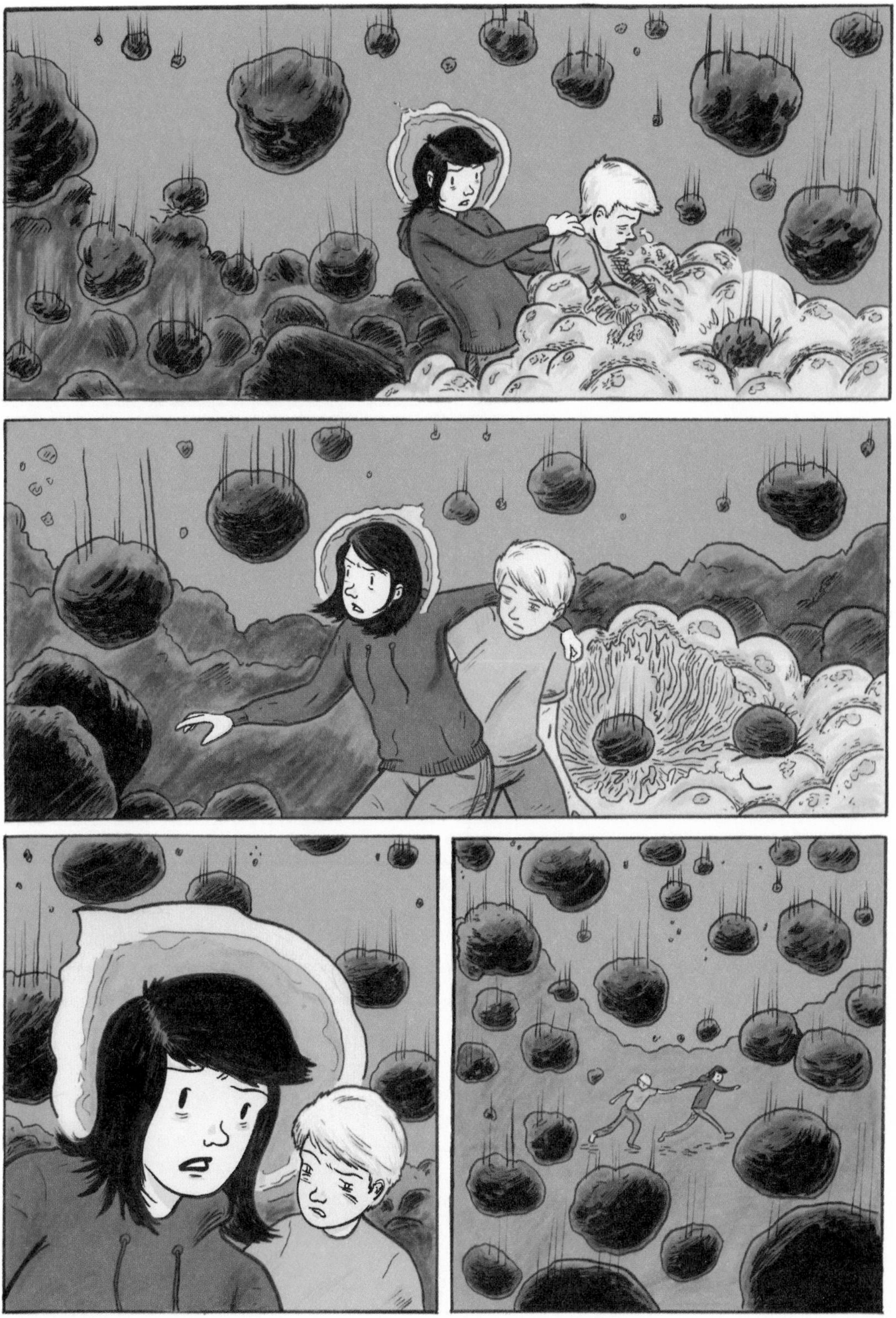

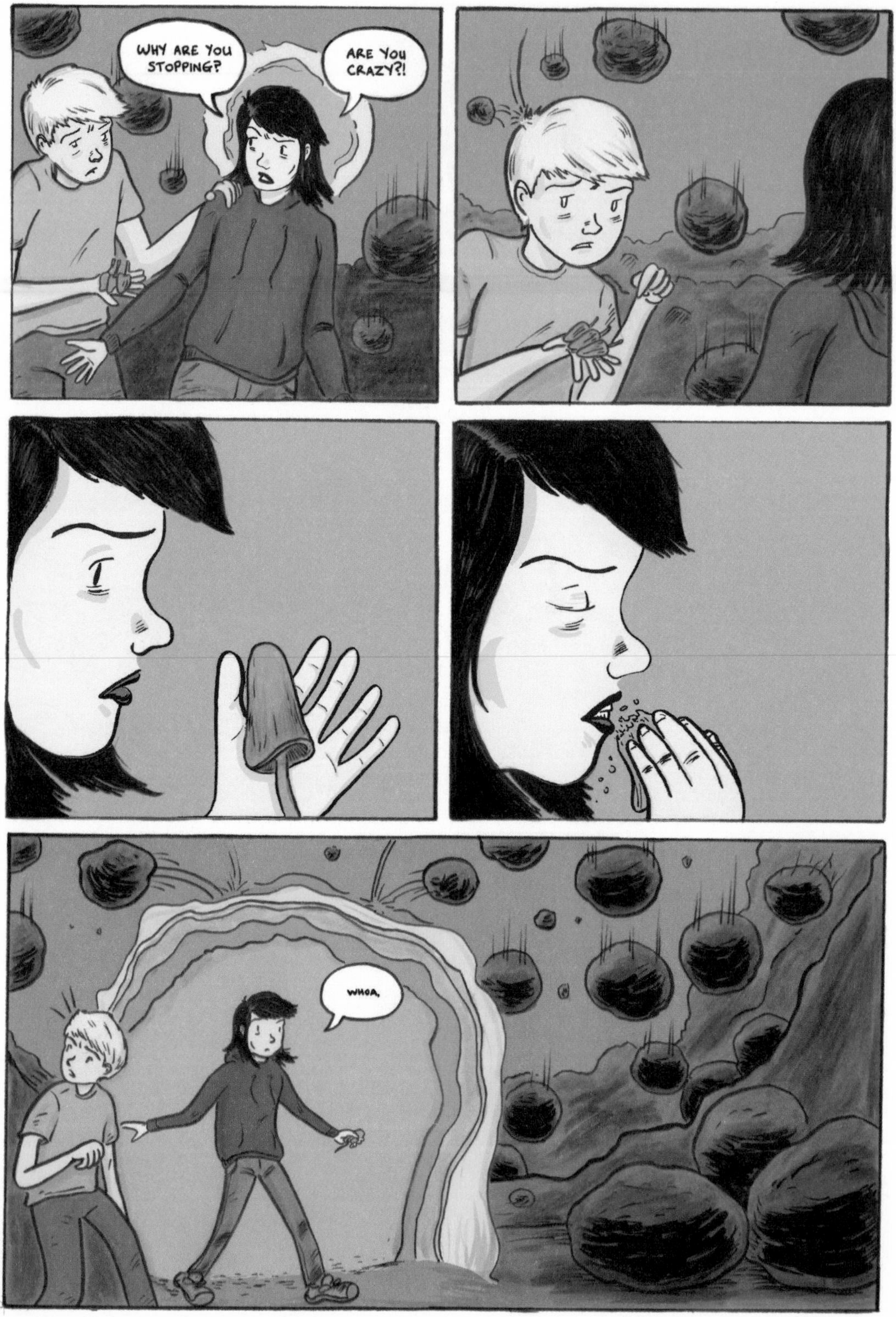
WHY ARE YOU STOPPING?
ARE YOU CRAZY?!
WHOA,

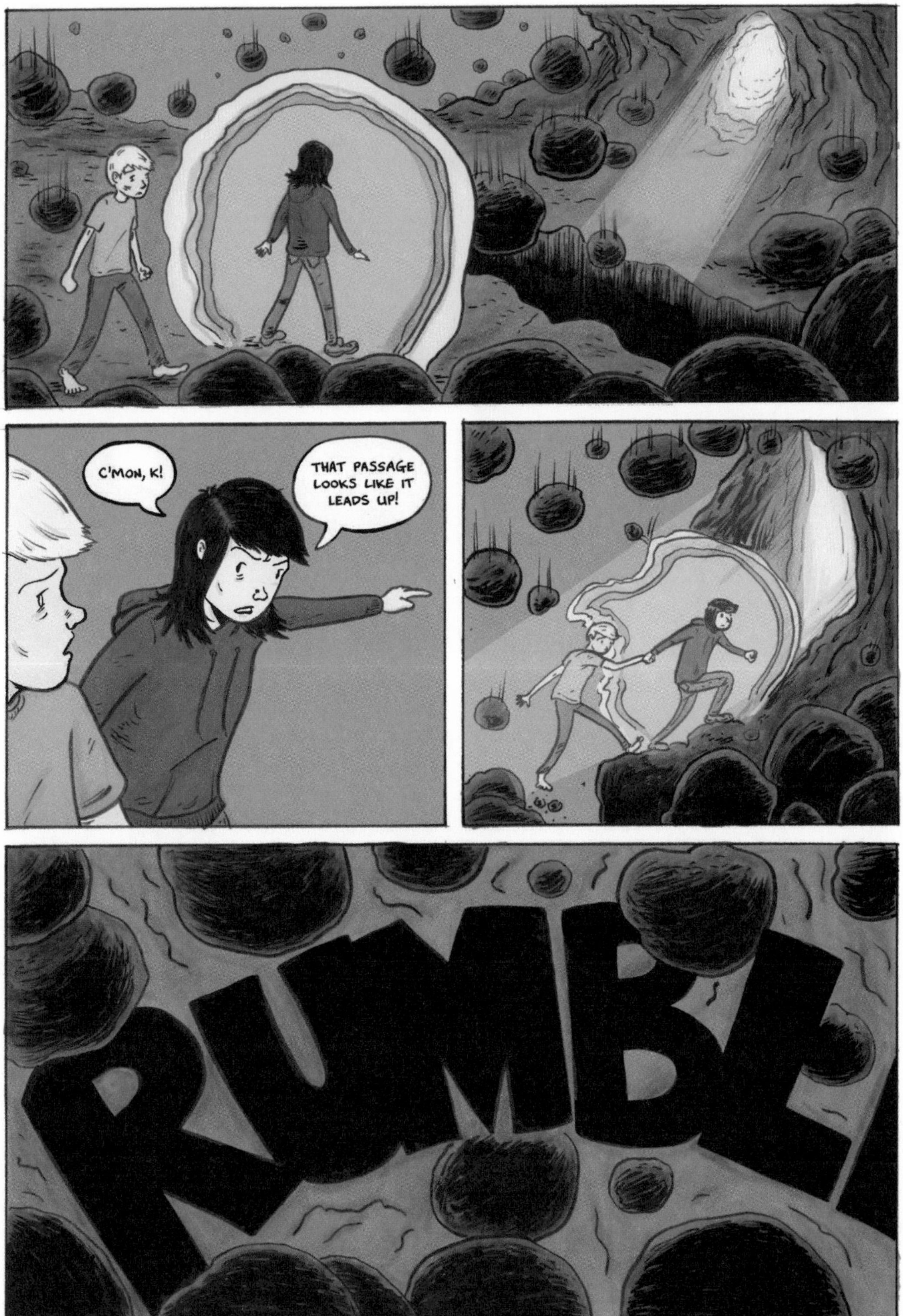
C'MON, K!
THAT PASSAGE LOOKS LIKE IT LEADS UP!
RUMBLE

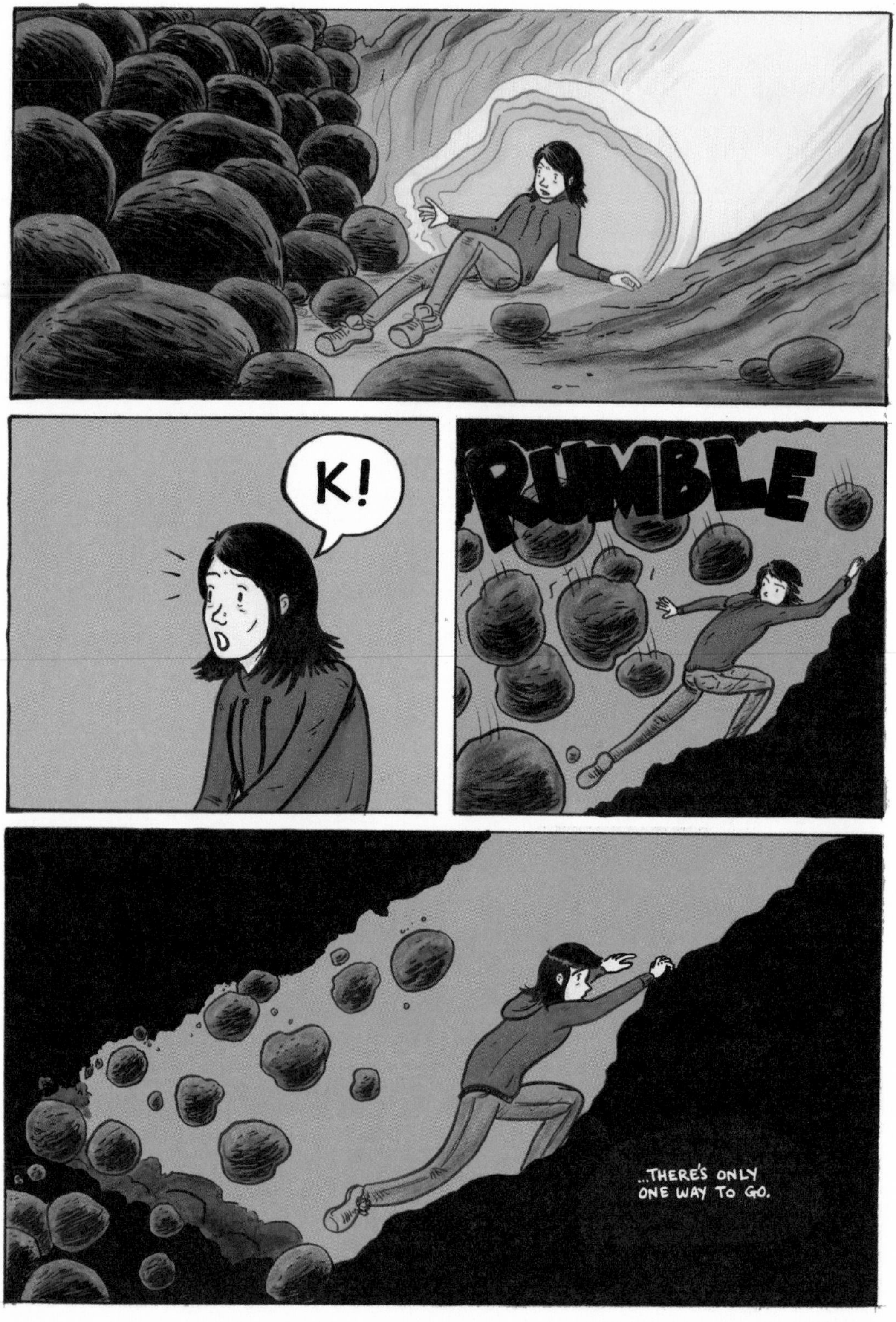
K!
RUMBLE
...THERE'S ONLY ONE WAY TO GO.

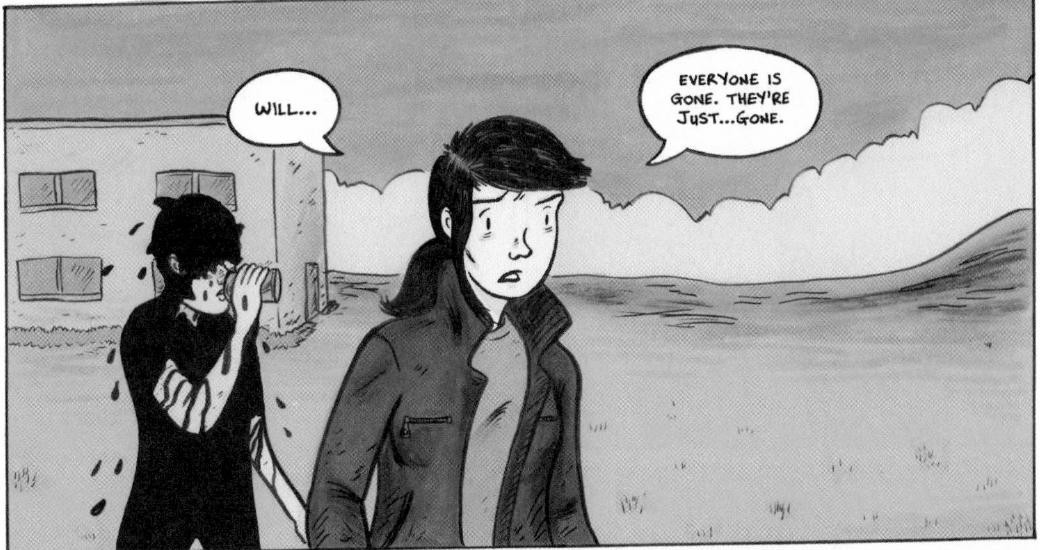
WILL...
EVERYONE IS GONE. THEY'RE JUST...GONE.

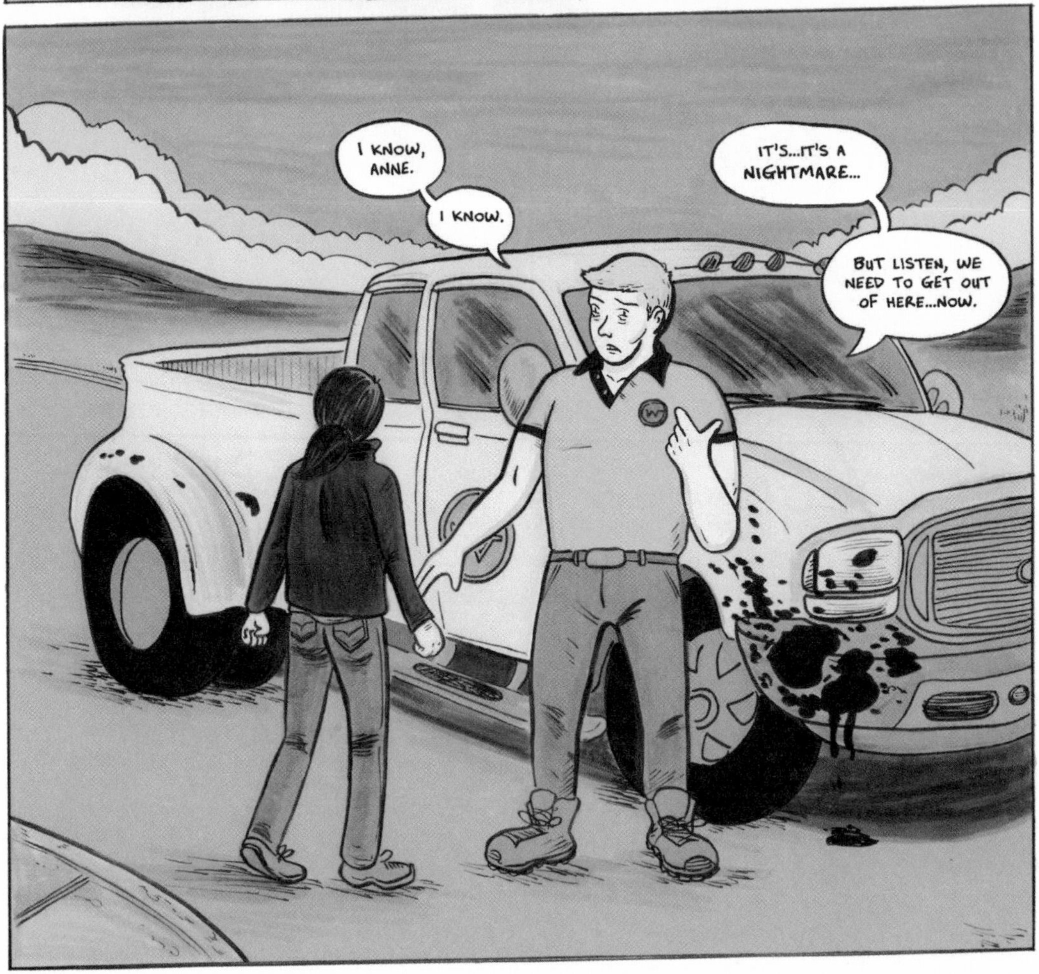
I KNOW, ANNE.
I KNOW.
IT'S...IT'S A NIGHTMARE...
BUT LISTEN, WE NEED TO GET OUT OF HERE...NOW.

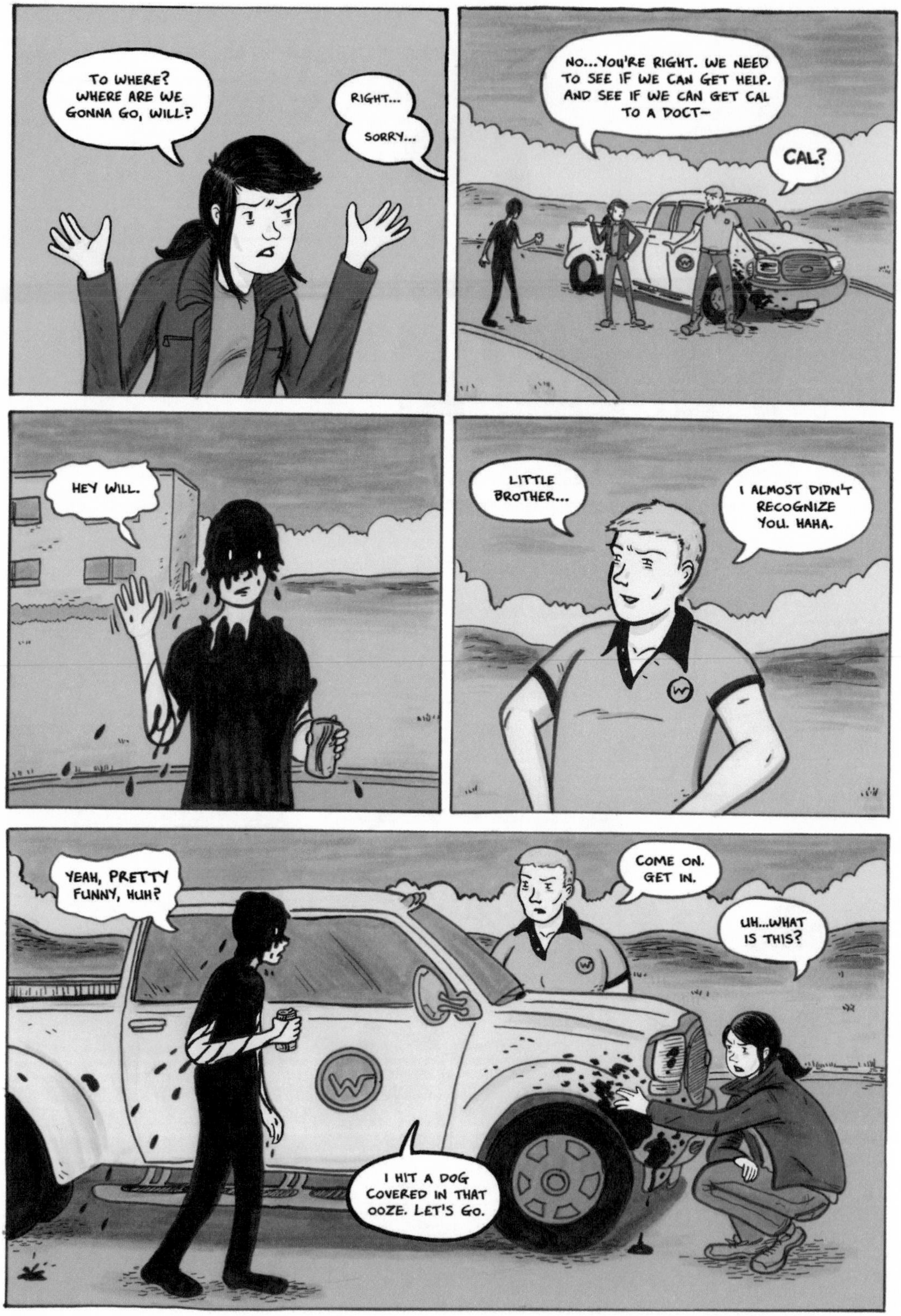
TO WHERE? WHERE ARE WE GONNA GO, WILL?
RIGHT...
SORRY...
NO...YOU'RE RIGHT. WE NEED TO SEE IF WE CAN GET HELP. AND SEE IF WE CAN GET CAL TO A DOCT—
CAL?
HEY WILL.
LITTLE BROTHER...
I ALMOST DIDN'T RECOGNIZE YOU. HAHA.
YEAH, PRETTY FUNNY, HUH?
COME ON. GET IN.
UH...WHAT IS THIS?
I HIT A DOG COVERED IN THAT OOZE. LET'S GO.

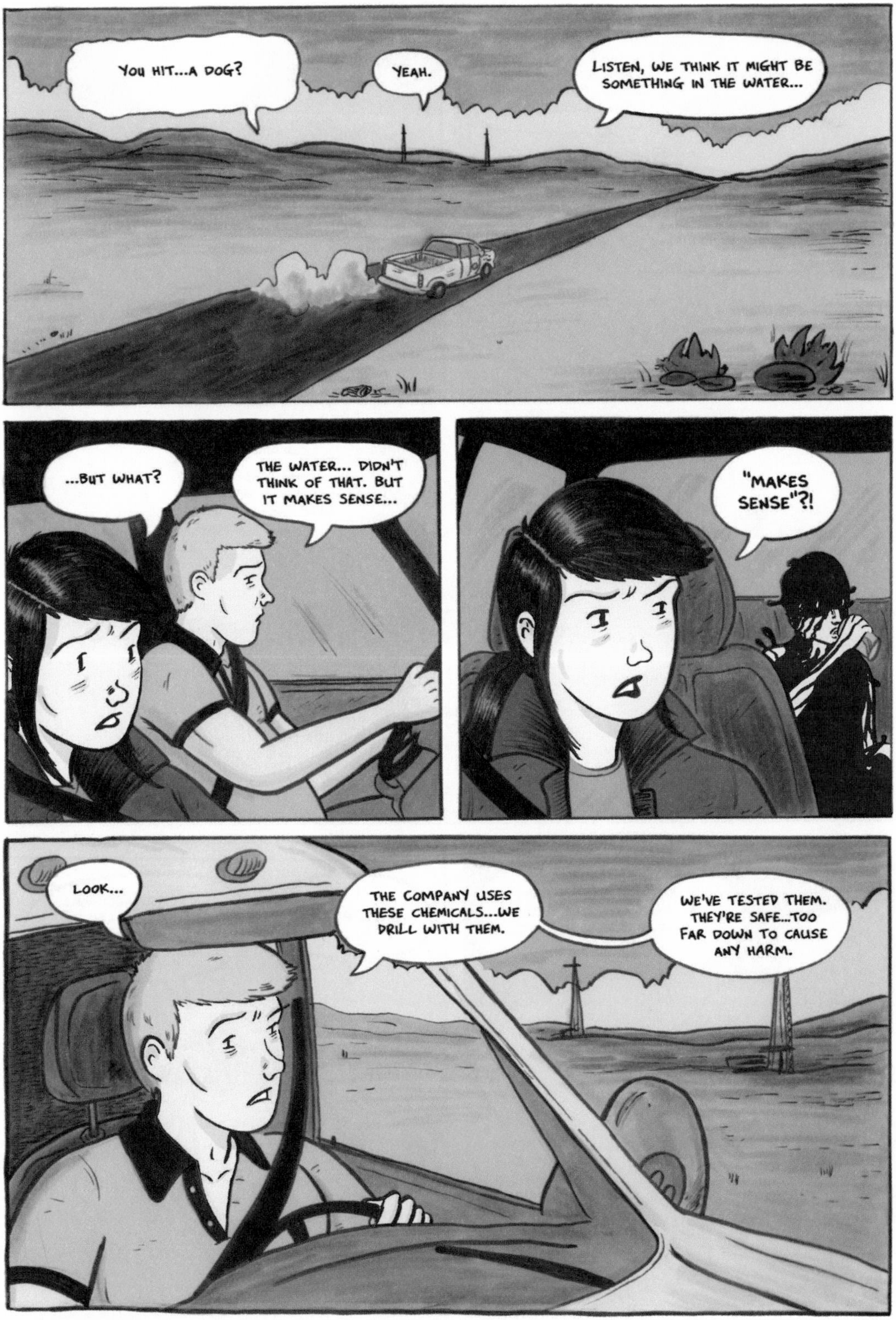
YOU HIT...A DOG?
YEAH.
LISTEN, WE THINK IT MIGHT BE SOMETHING IN THE WATER...
...BUT WHAT?
THE WATER... DIDN'T THINK OF THAT. BUT IT MAKES SENSE...
"MAKES SENSE"?!
LOOK...
THE COMPANY USES THESE CHEMICALS...WE DRILL WITH THEM.
WE'VE TESTED THEM. THEY'RE SAFE...TOO FAR DOWN TO CAUSE ANY HARM.

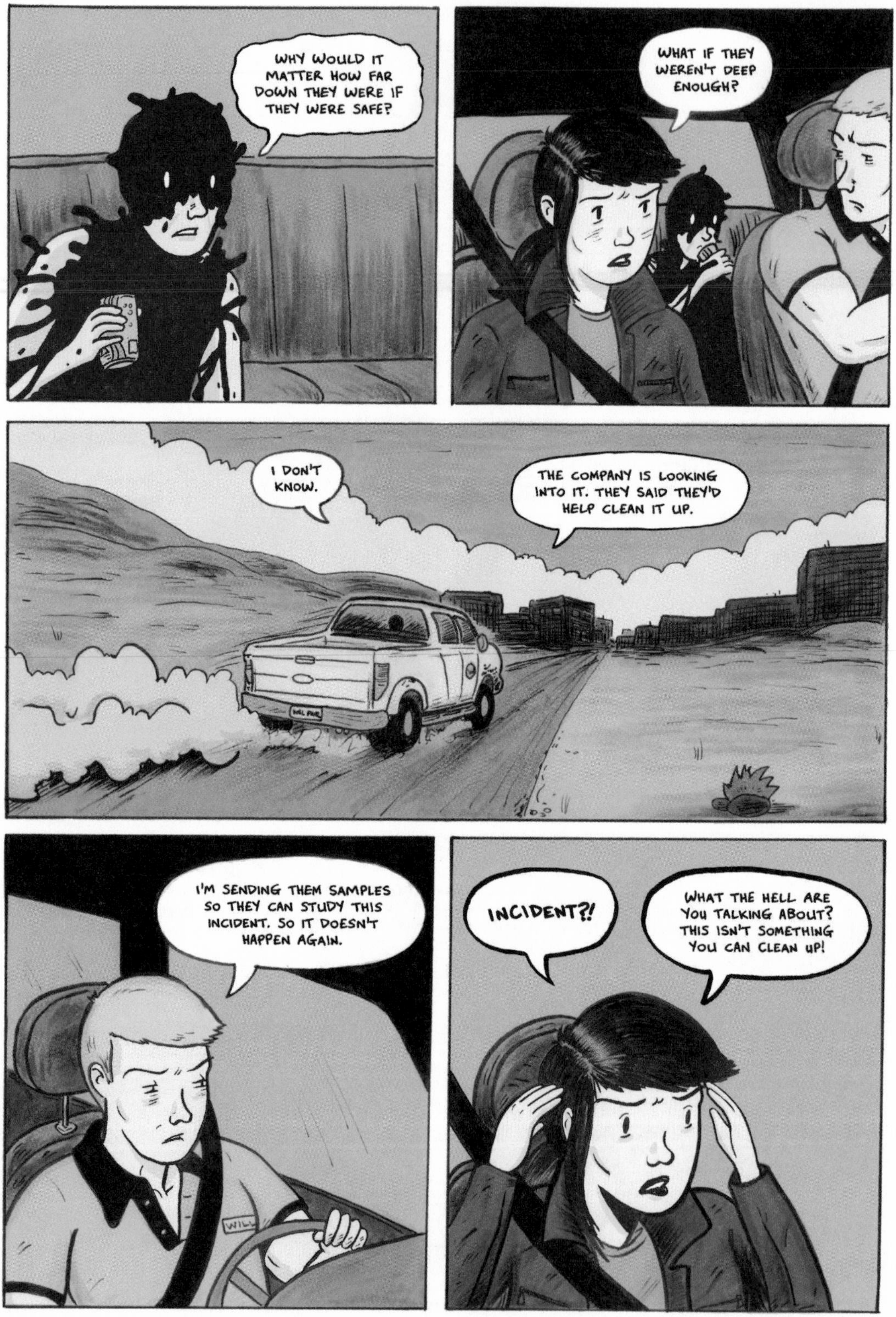
WHY WOULD IT MATTER HOW FAR DOWN THEY WERE IF THEY WERE SAFE?
WHAT IF THEY WEREN'T DEEP ENOUGH?
I DON'T KNOW.
THE COMPANY IS LOOKING INTO IT. THEY SAID THEY'D HELP CLEAN IT UP.
I'M SENDING THEM SAMPLES SO THEY CAN STUDY THIS INCIDENT. SO IT DOESN'T HAPPEN AGAIN.
INCIDENT?!
WHAT THE HELL ARE YOU TALKING ABOUT? THIS ISN'T SOMETHING YOU CAN CLEAN UP!

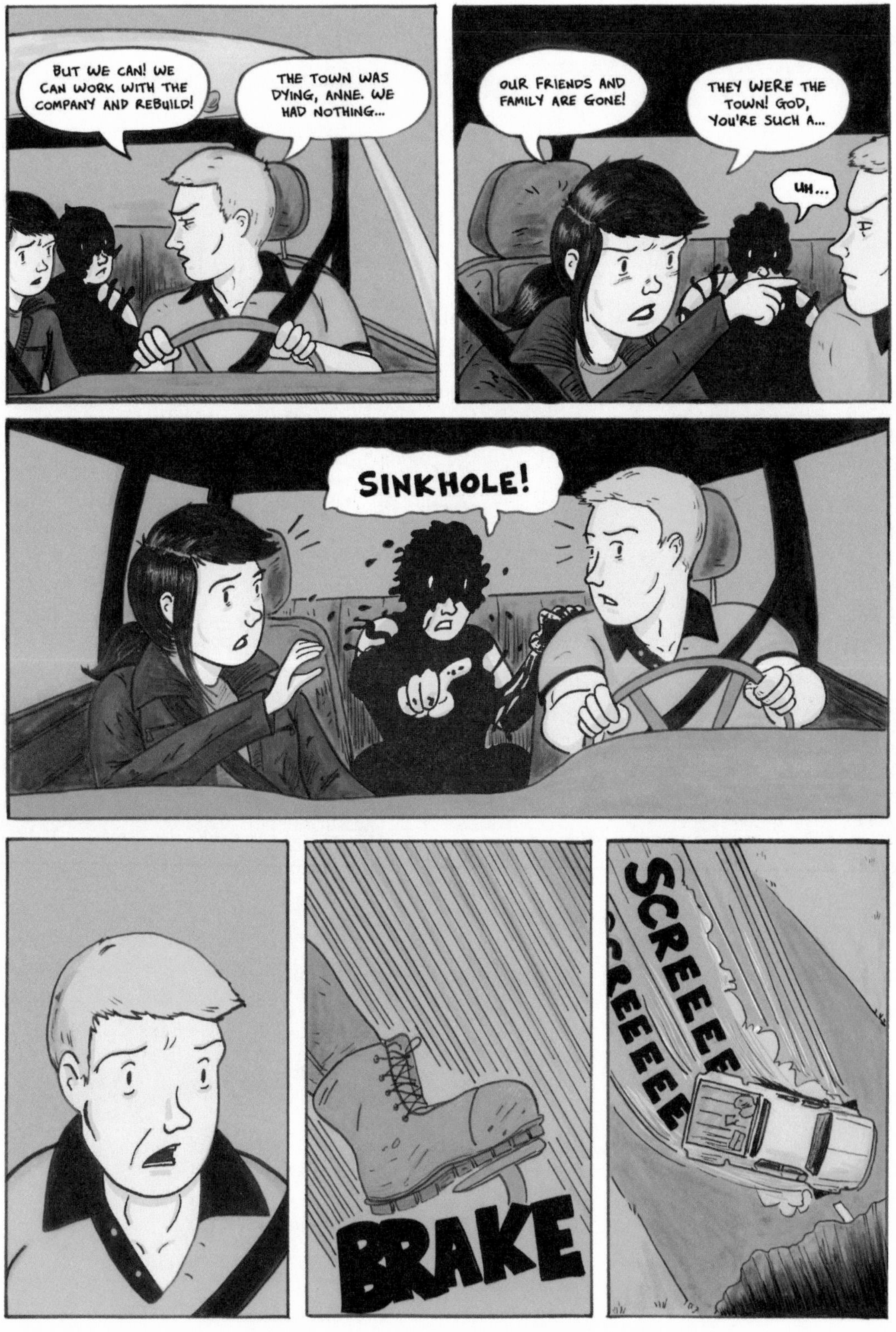
BUT WE CAN! WE CAN WORK WITH THE COMPANY AND REBUILD!
THE TOWN WAS DYING, ANNE. WE HAD NOTHING...
OUR FRIENDS AND FAMILY ARE GONE!
THEY WERE THE TOWN! GOD, YOU'RE SUCH A...
UH...
SINKHOLE!
BRAKE
SCREEEE
REEEEEE

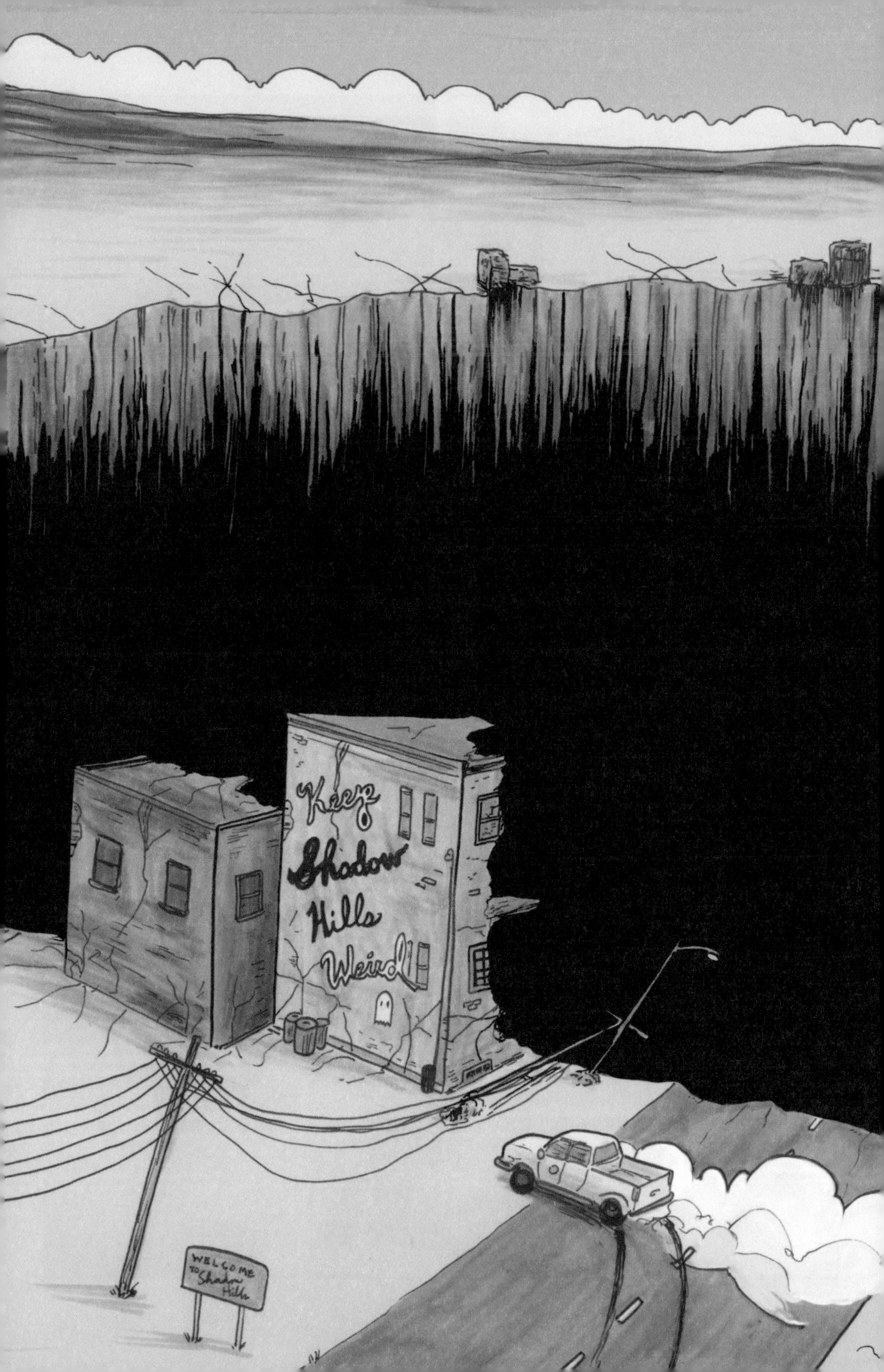
Keep Shadow Hills Weird
WELCOME TO Shadow Hills

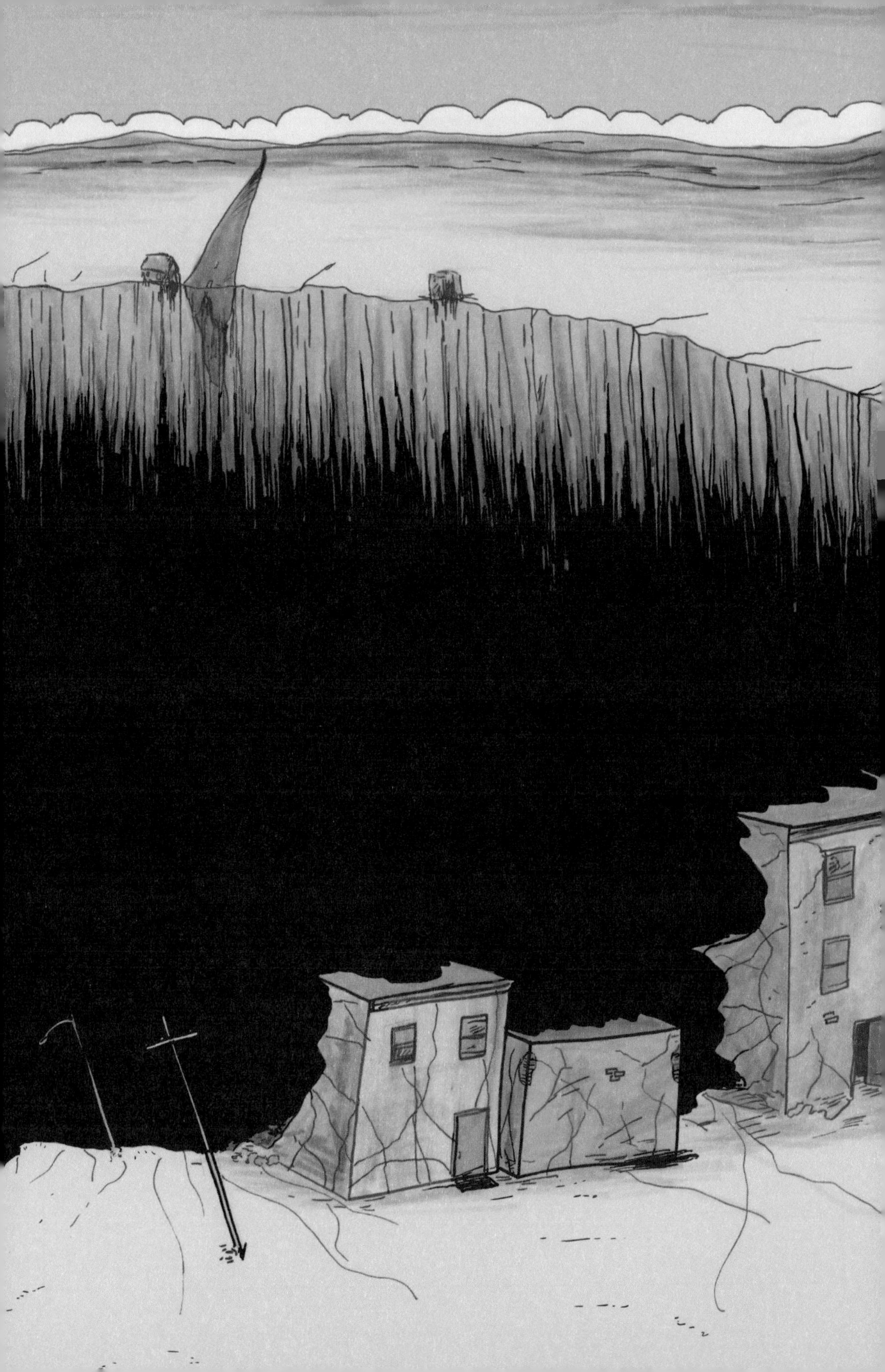

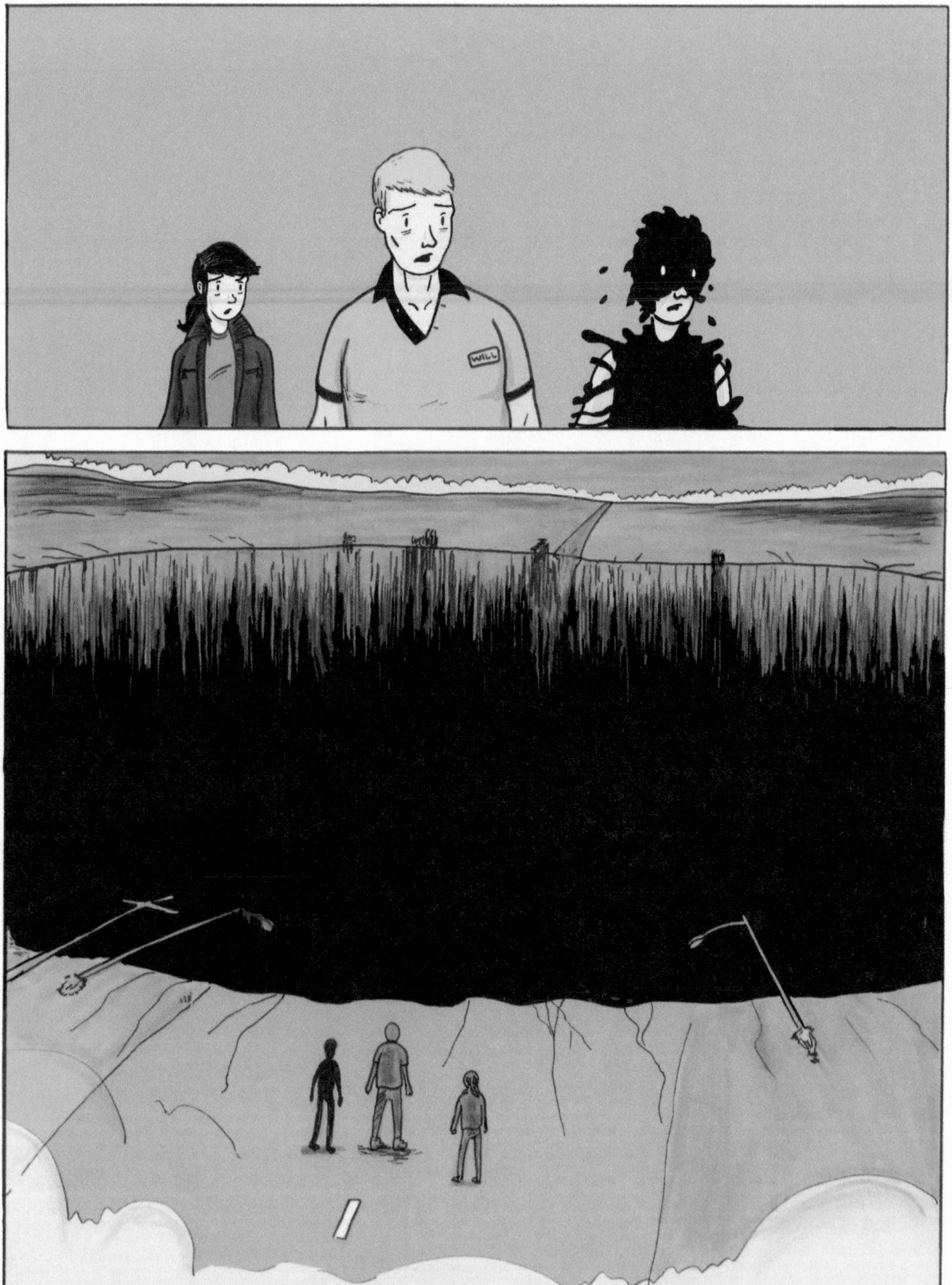
WILL

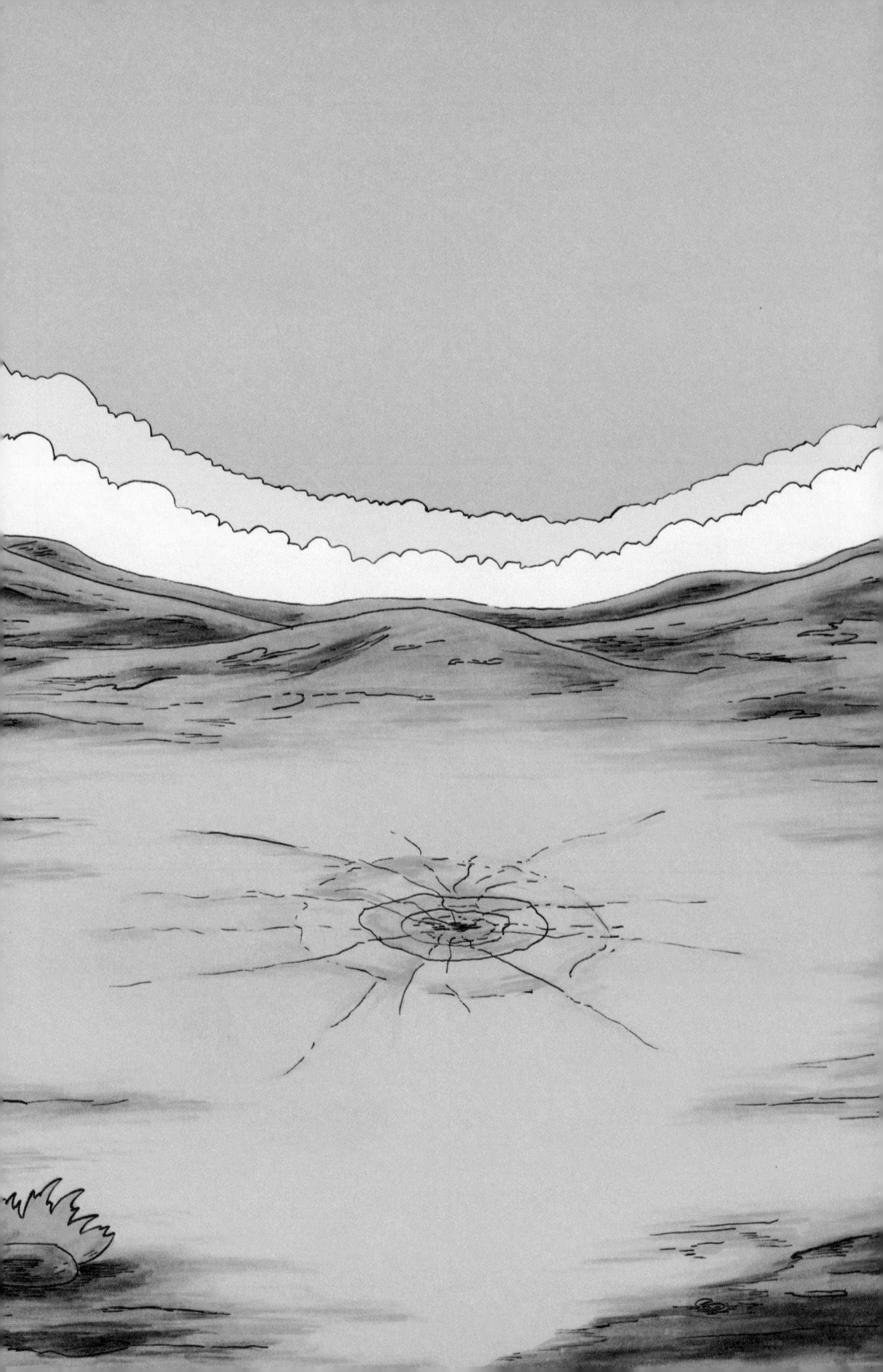

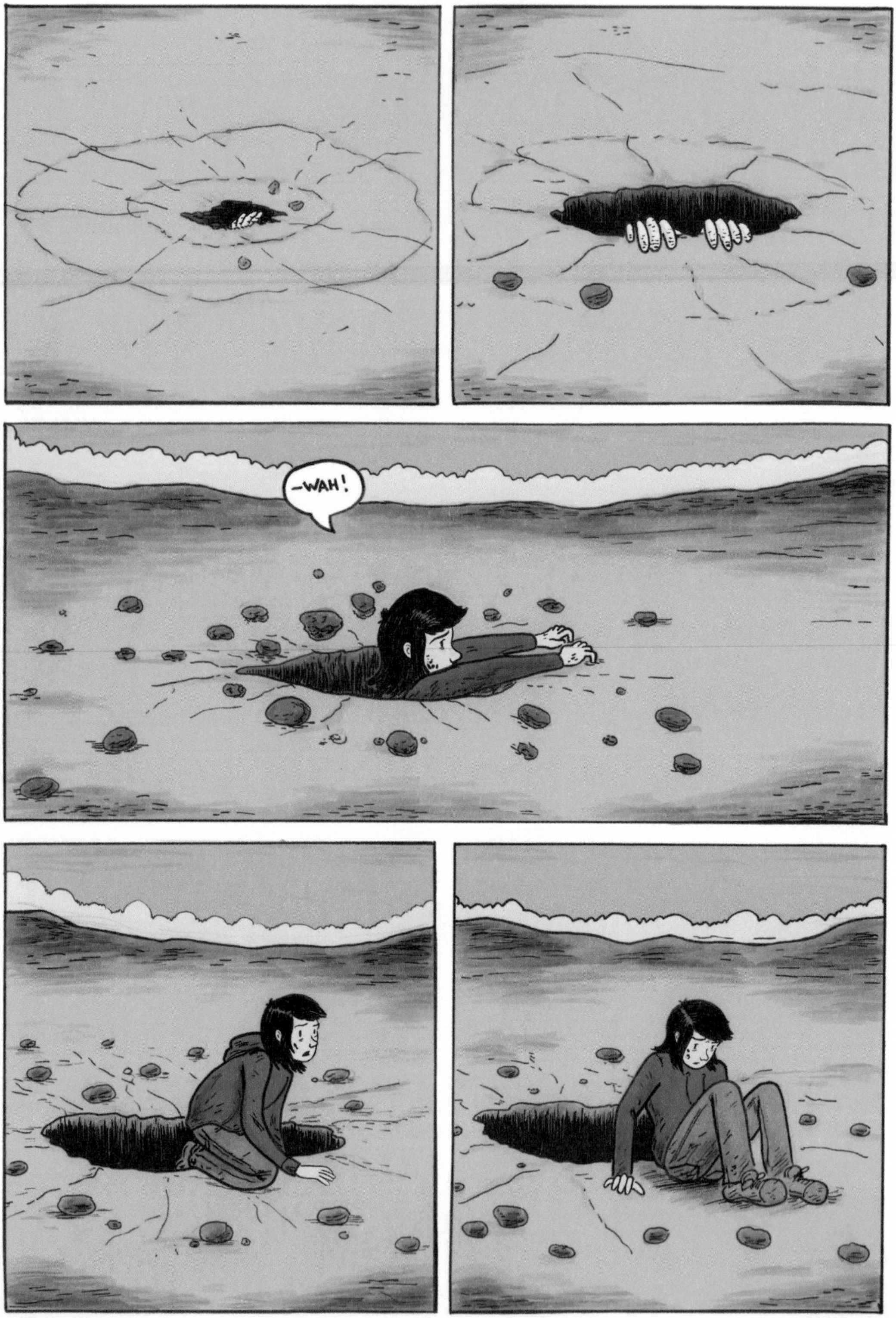
-WAH!

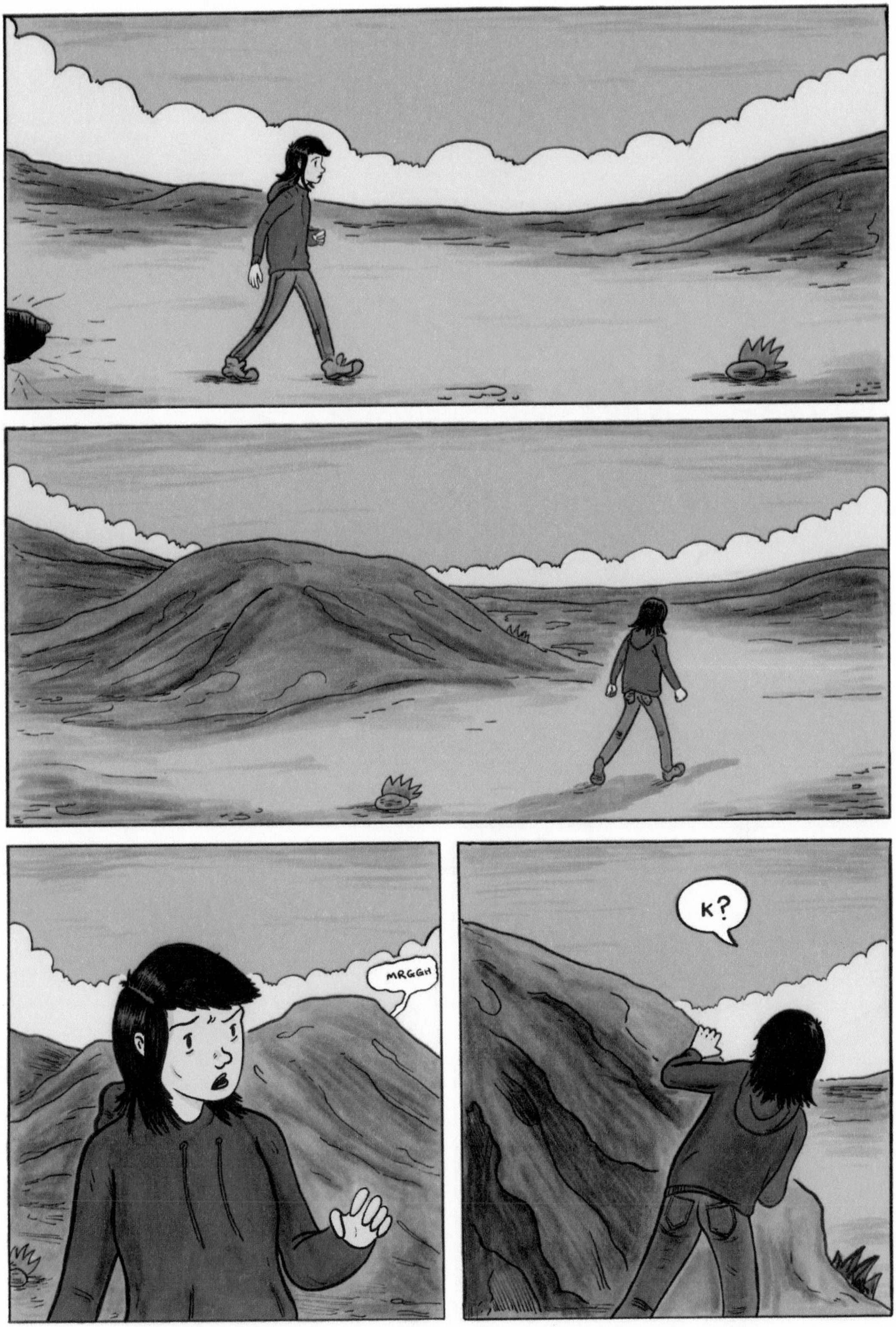
MRGGH
K?

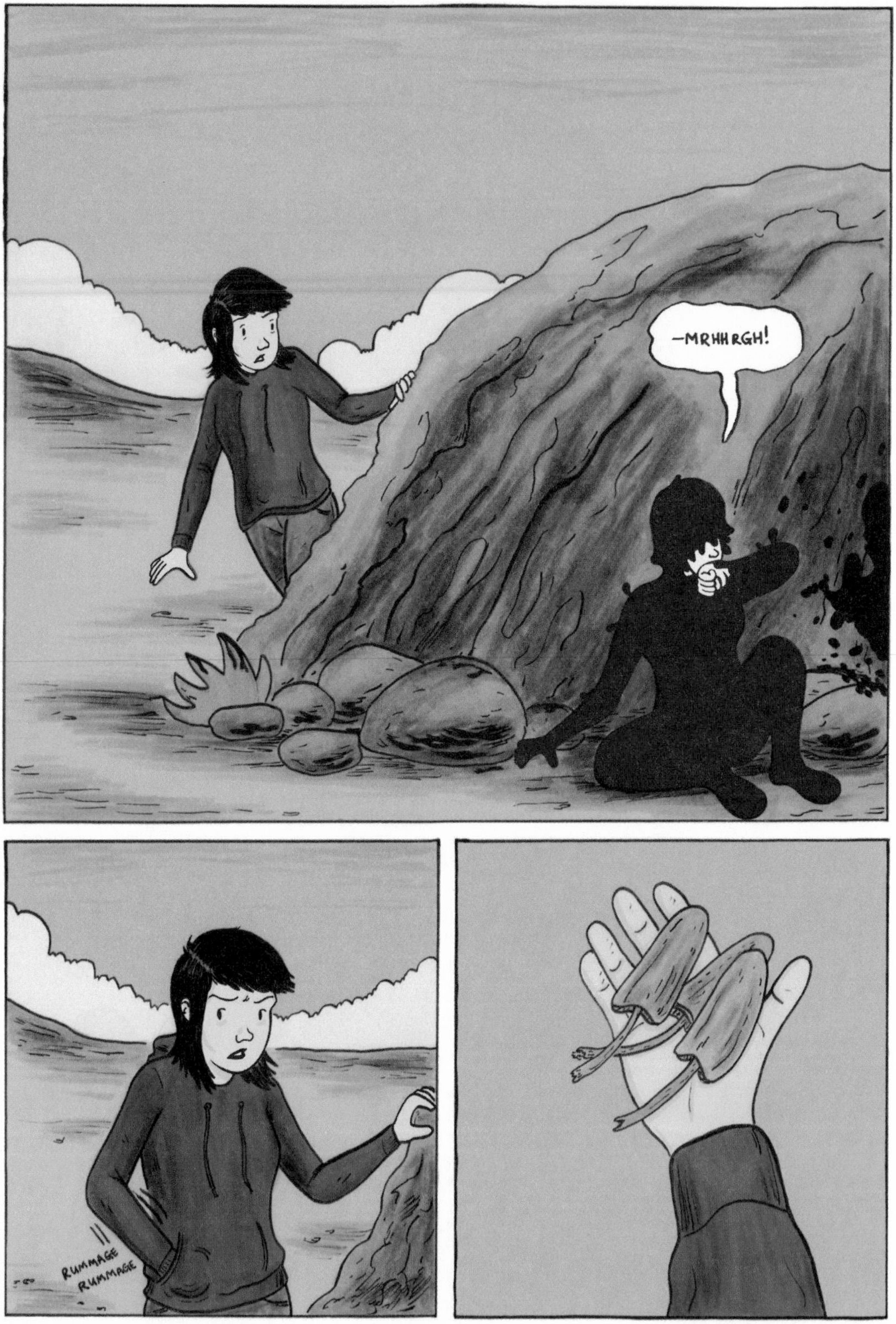
–MRHHRGH!
RUMMAGE RUMMAGE

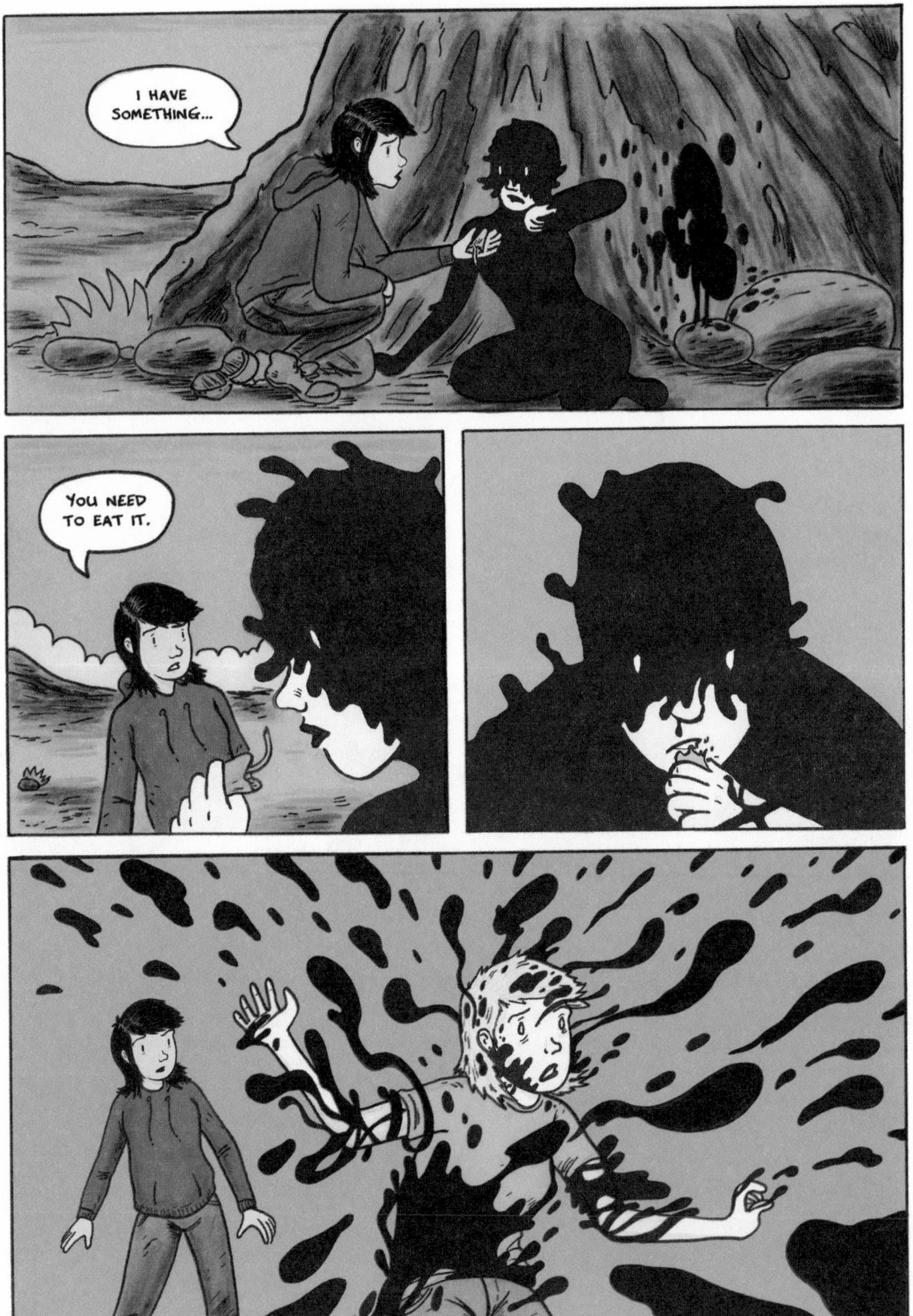
I HAVE SOMETHING...
YOU NEED TO EAT IT.

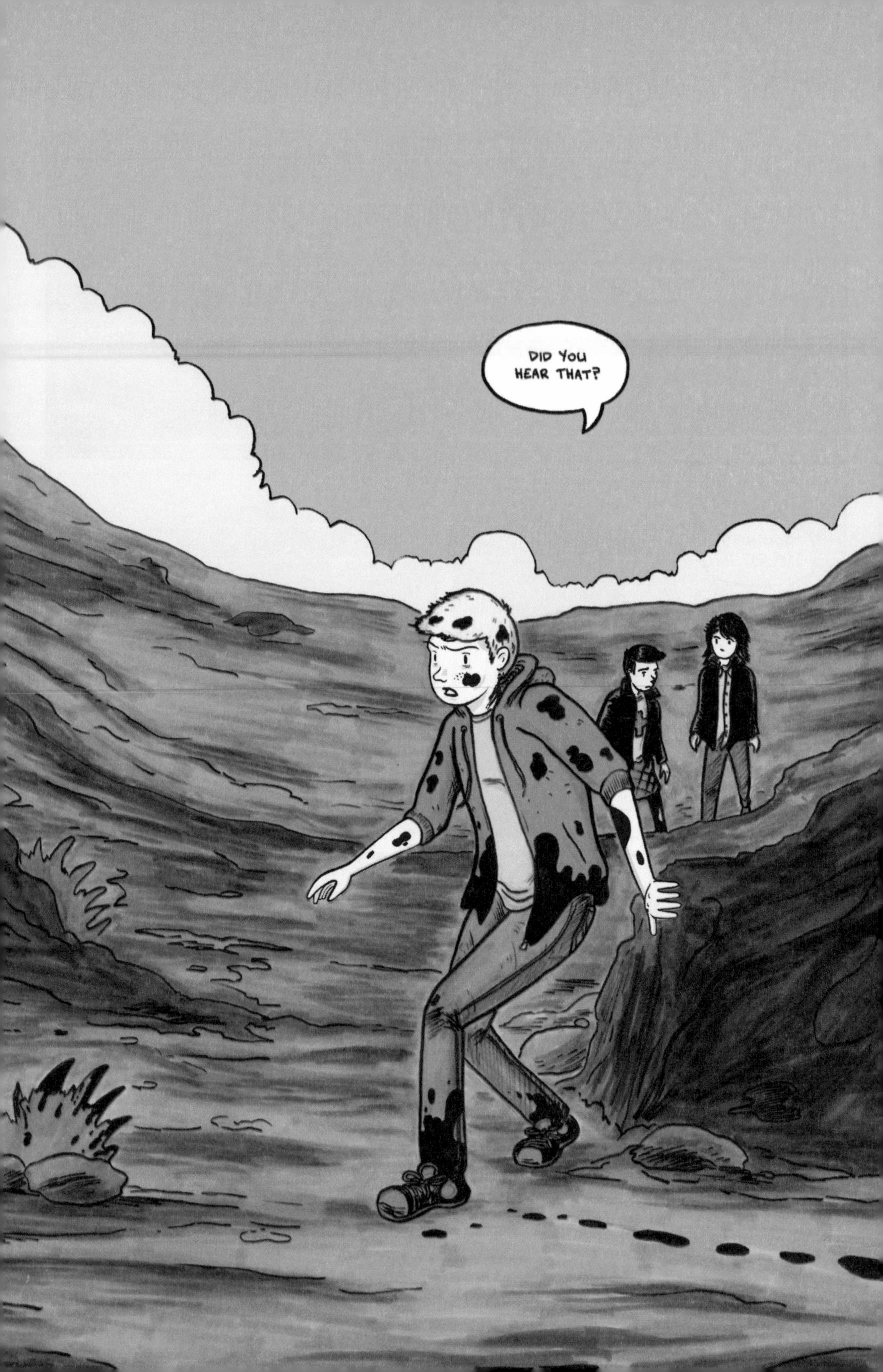
DID YOU HEAR THAT?

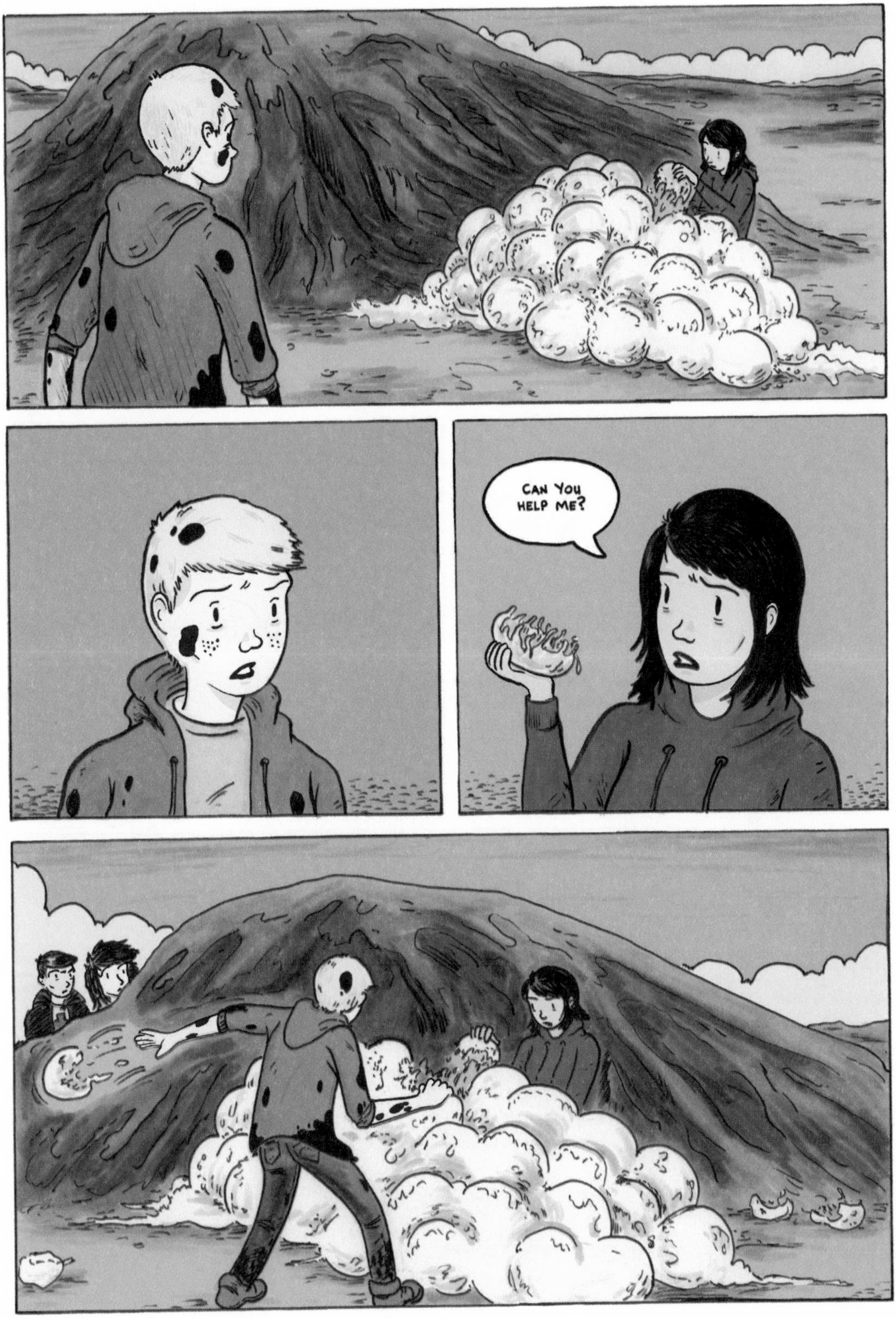
CAN YOU HELP ME?

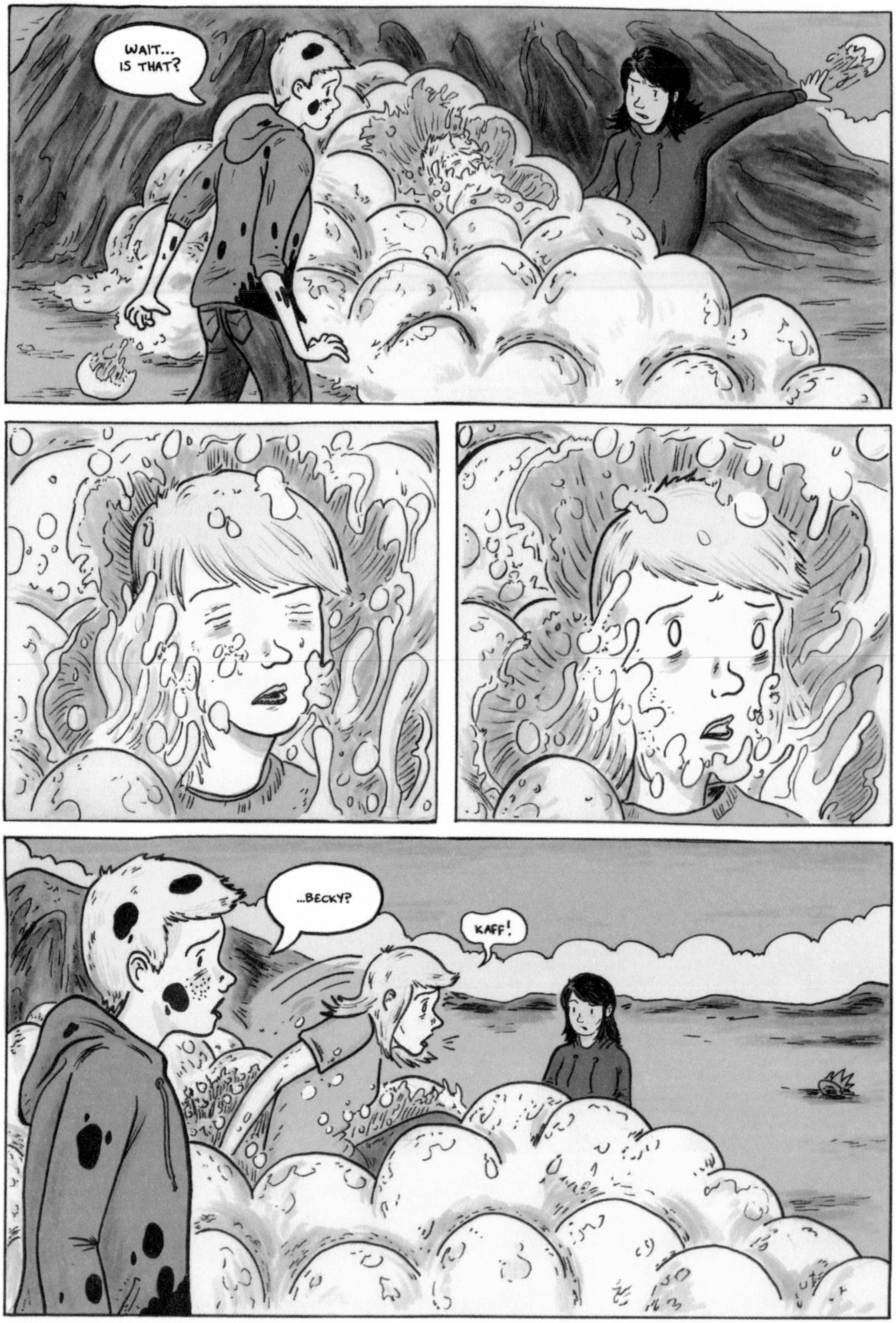
WAIT...
IS THAT?
...BECKY?
KAFF!

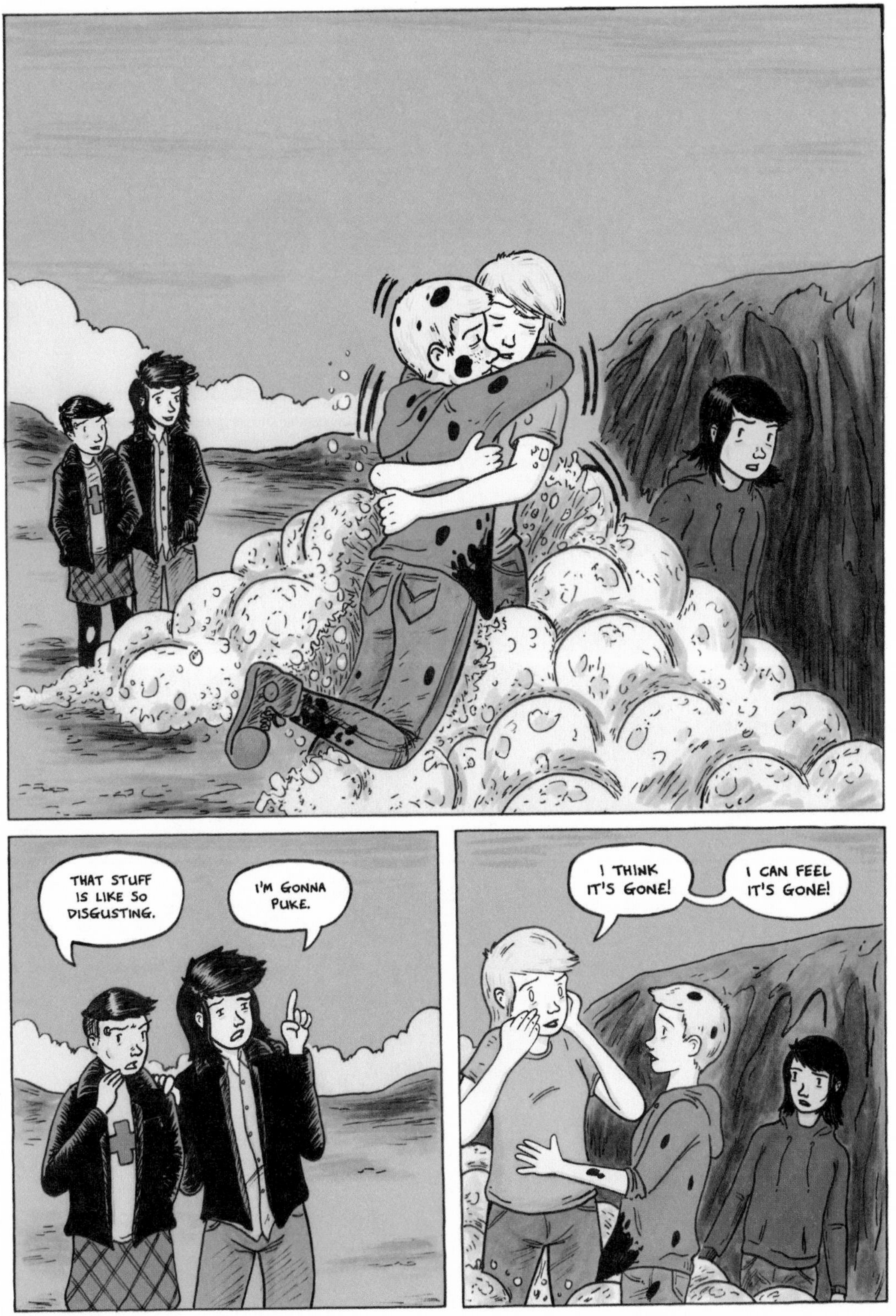
THAT STUFF IS LIKE SO DISGUSTING.
I'M GONNA PUKE.
I THINK IT'S GONE!
I CAN FEEL IT'S GONE!

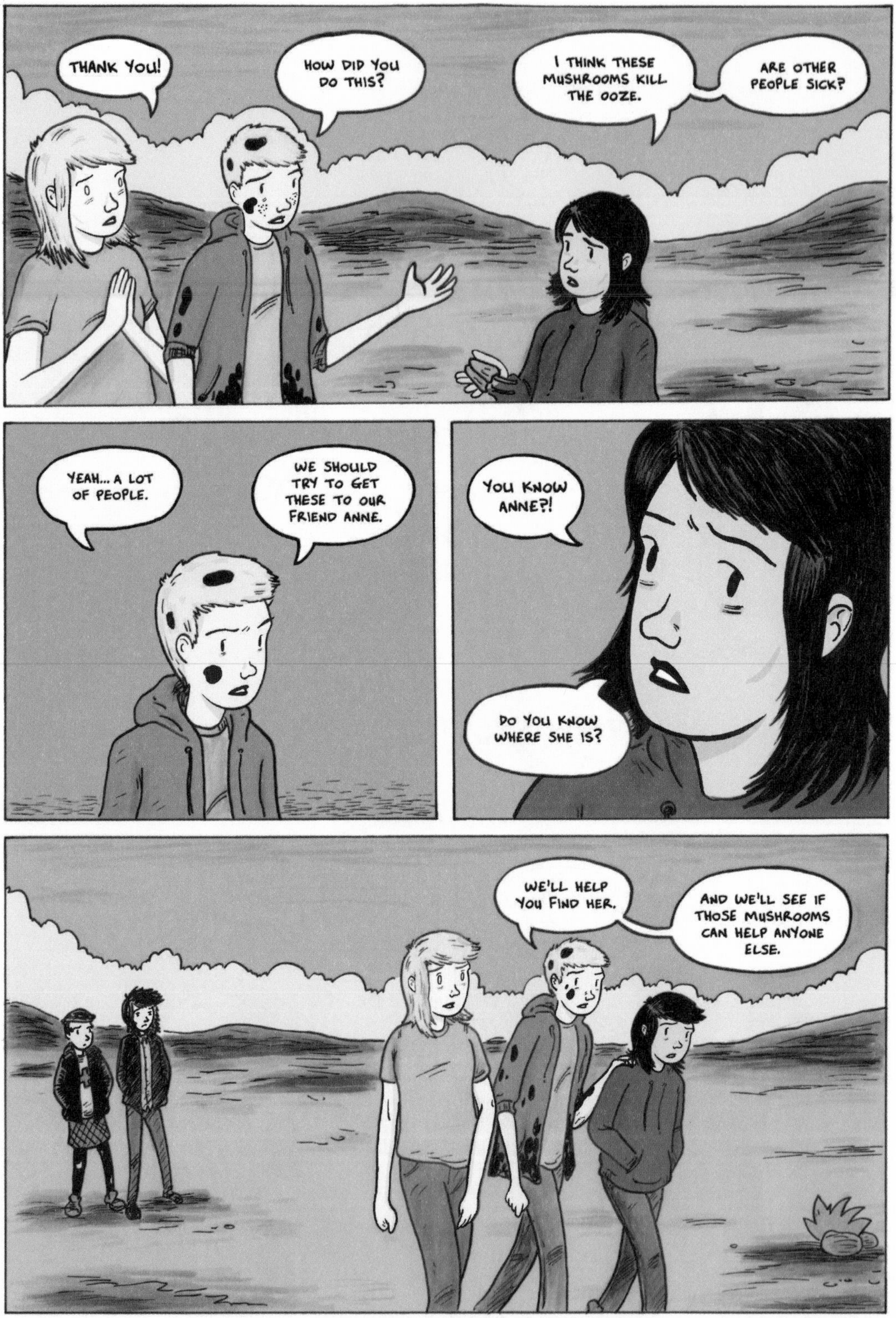
THANK YOU!
HOW DID YOU DO THIS?
I THINK THESE MUSHROOMS KILL THE OOZE.
ARE OTHER PEOPLE SICK?
YEAH... A LOT OF PEOPLE.
WE SHOULD TRY TO GET THESE TO OUR FRIEND ANNE.
YOU KNOW ANNE?!
DO YOU KNOW WHERE SHE IS?
WE'LL HELP YOU FIND HER.
AND WE'LL SEE IF THOSE MUSHROOMS CAN HELP ANYONE ELSE.

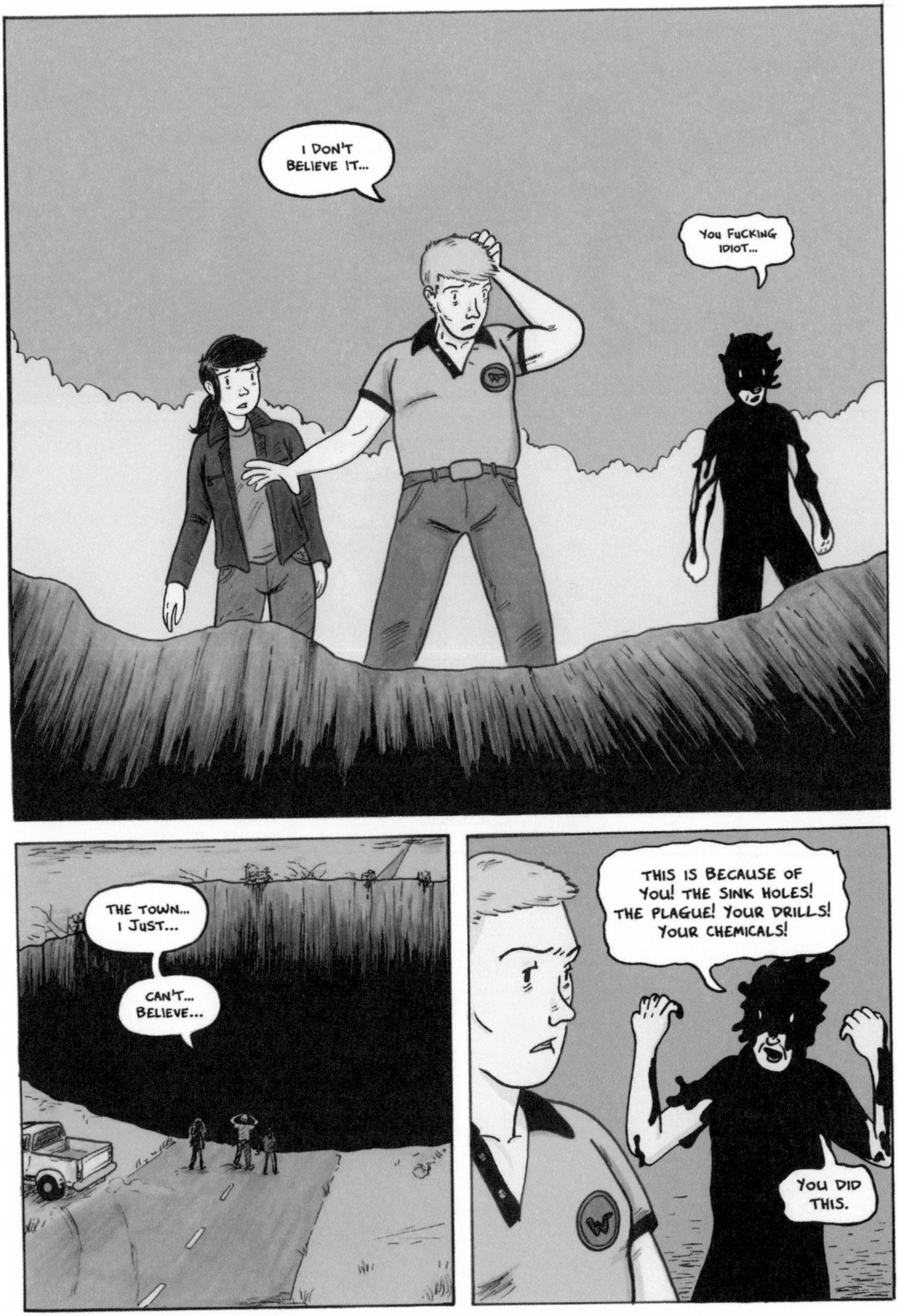
I DON'T BELIEVE IT...
YOU FUCKING IDIOT...
THE TOWN... I JUST...
CAN'T... BELIEVE...
THIS IS BECAUSE OF YOU! THE SINK HOLES! THE PLAGUE! YOUR DRILLS! YOUR CHEMICALS!
YOU DID THIS.

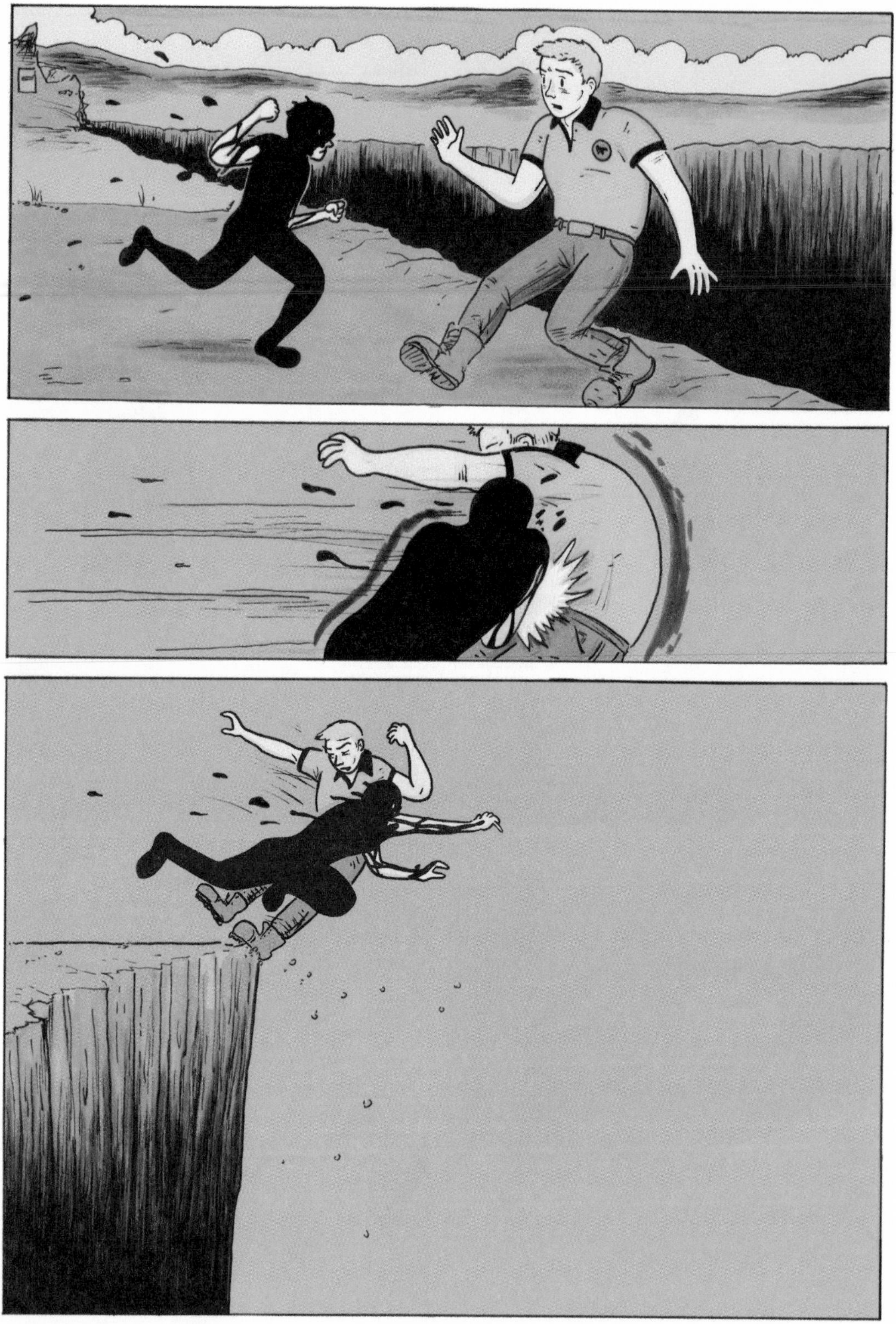

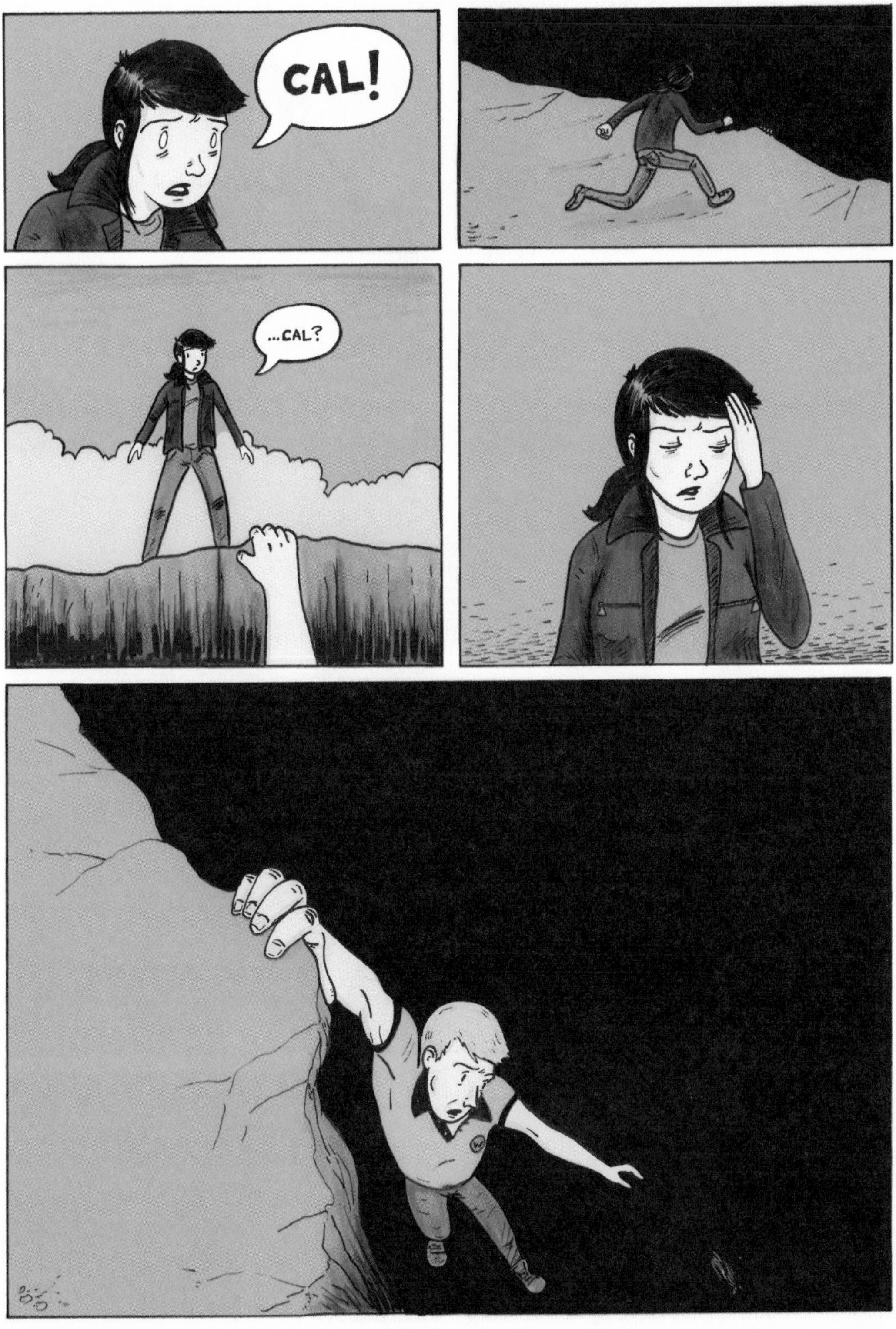
CAL!
...CAL?

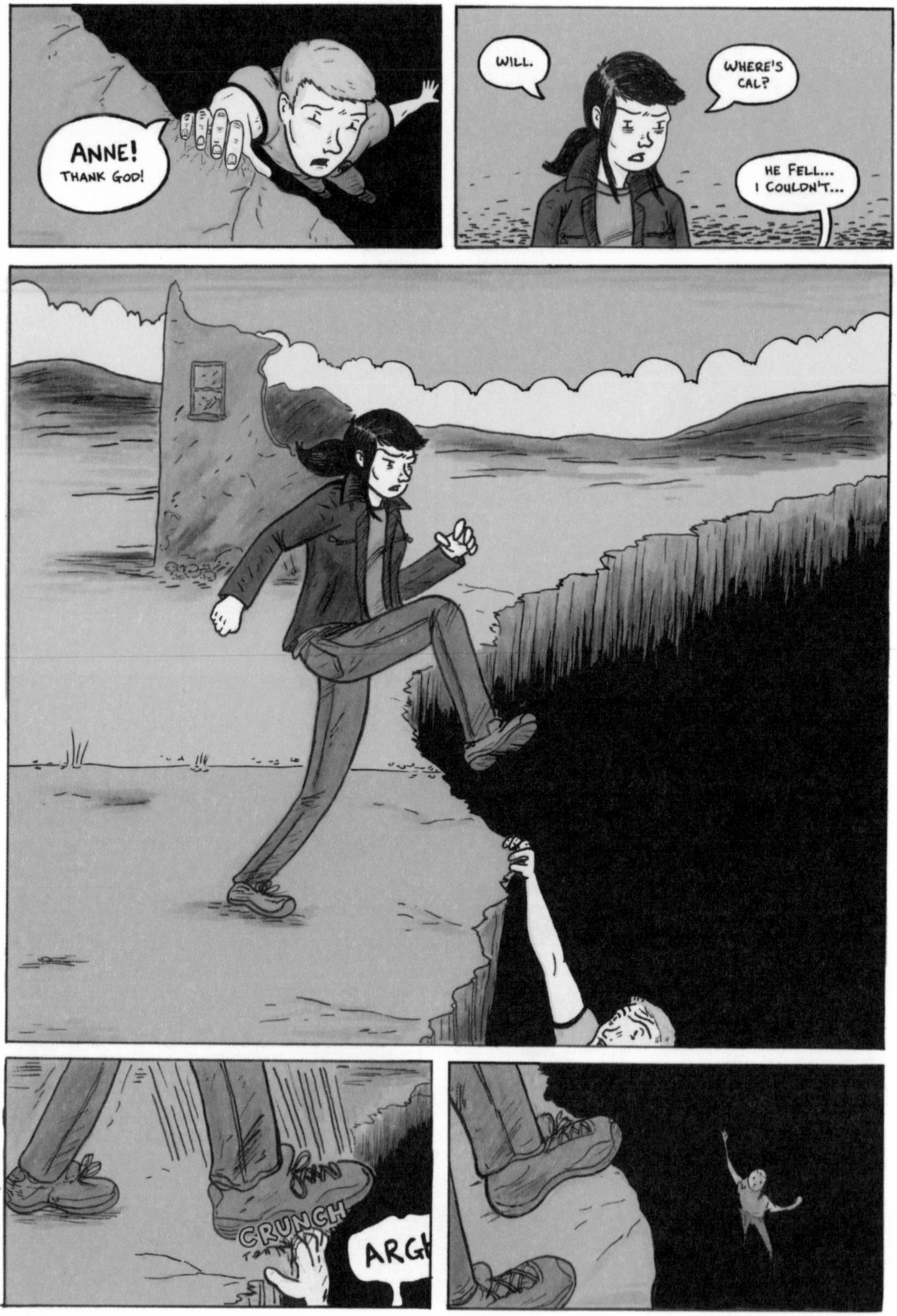
ANNE!
THANK GOD!
WILL.
WHERE'S CAL?
HE FELL... I COULDN'T...
CRUNCH
ARG

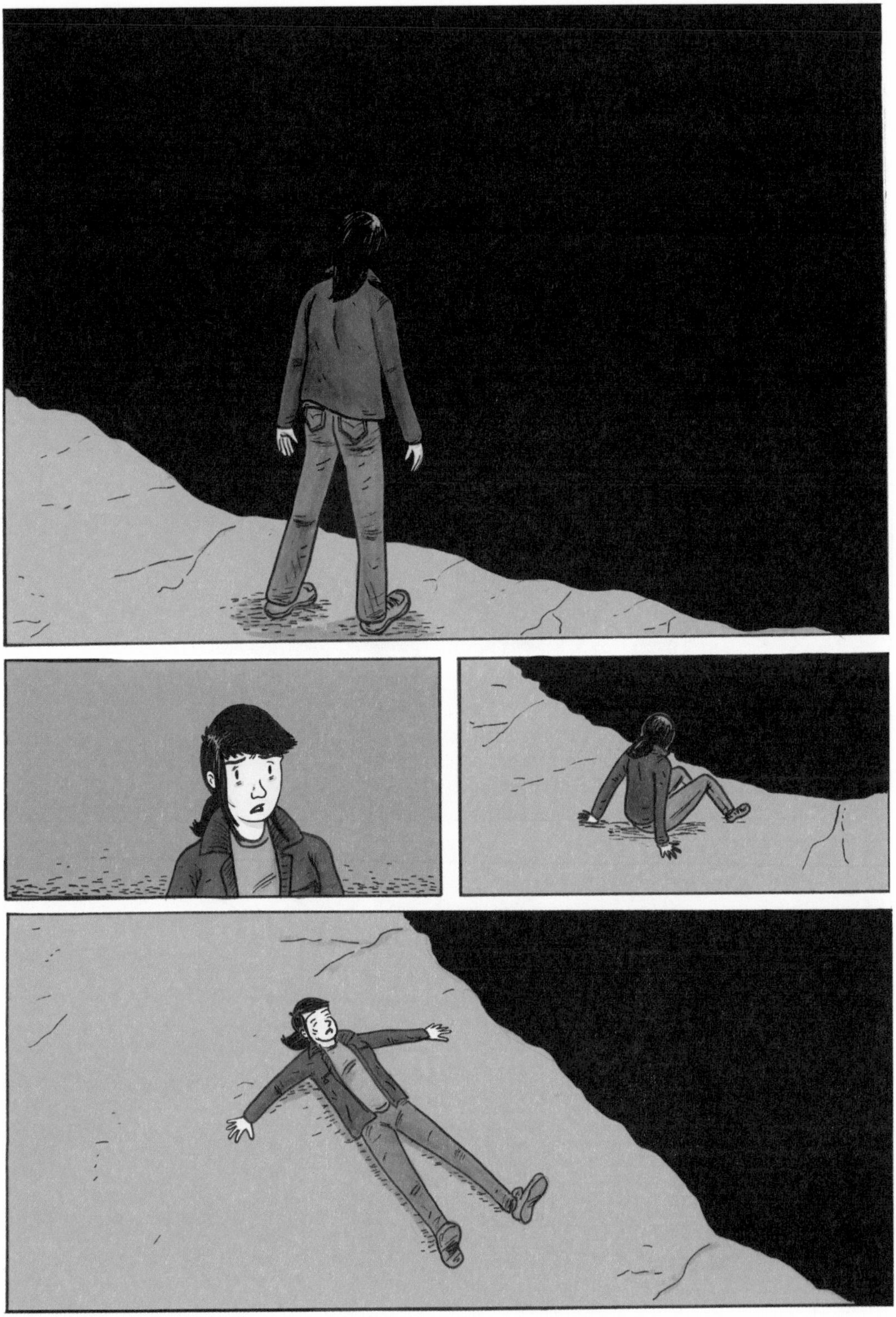

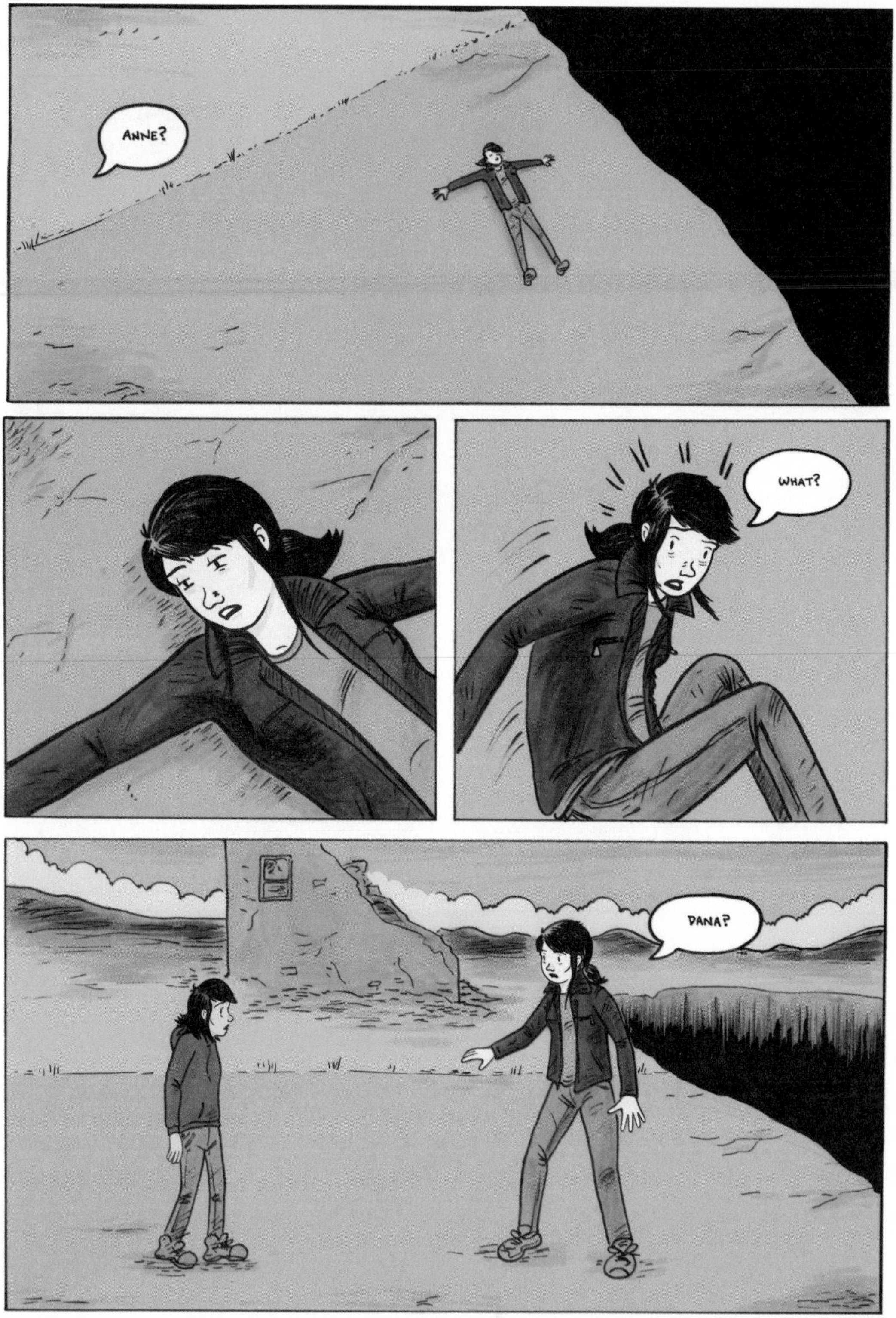
ANNE?
WHAT?
DANA?

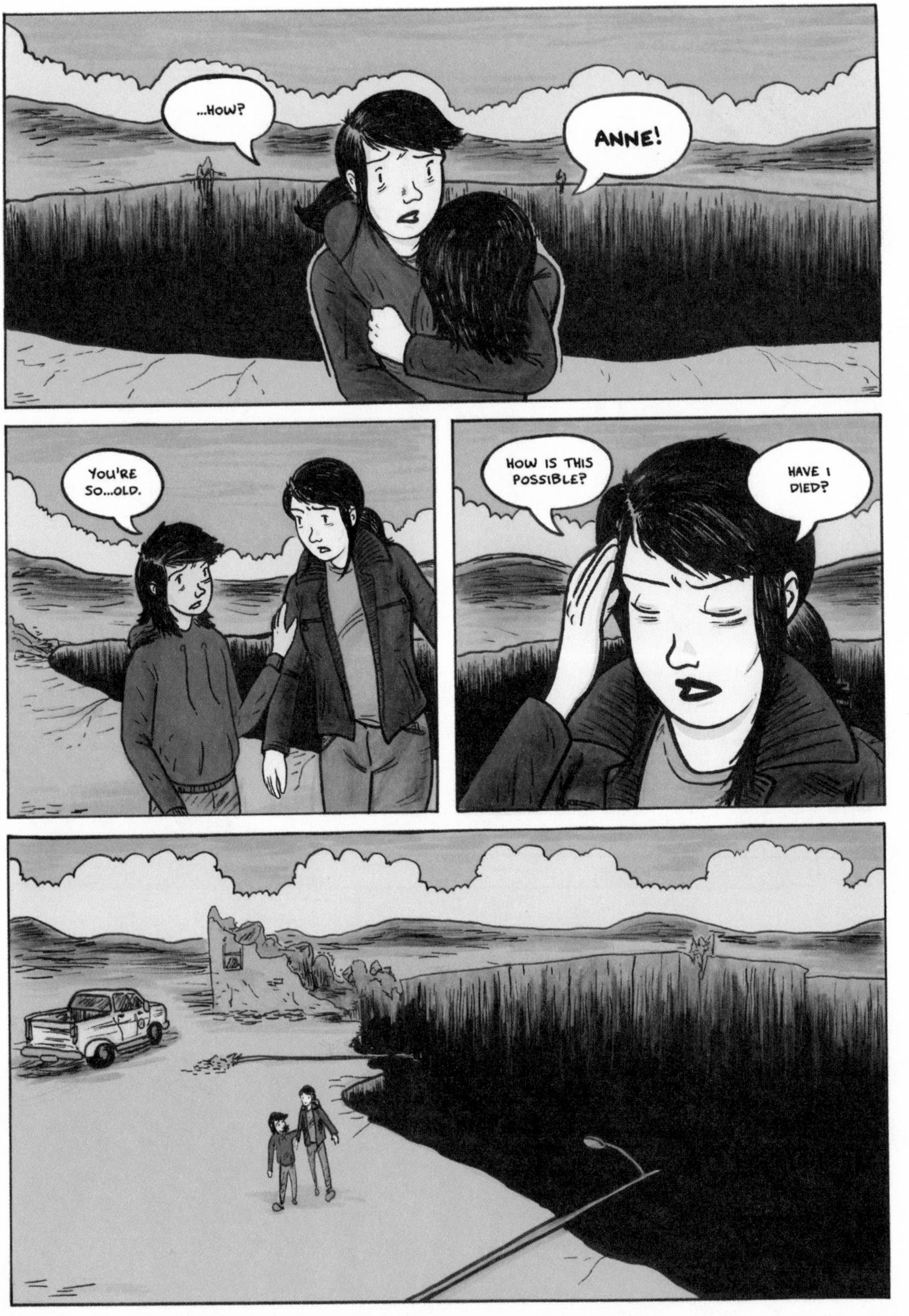
...HOW?
ANNE!
YOU'RE SO...OLD.
HOW IS THIS POSSIBLE?
HAVE I DIED?

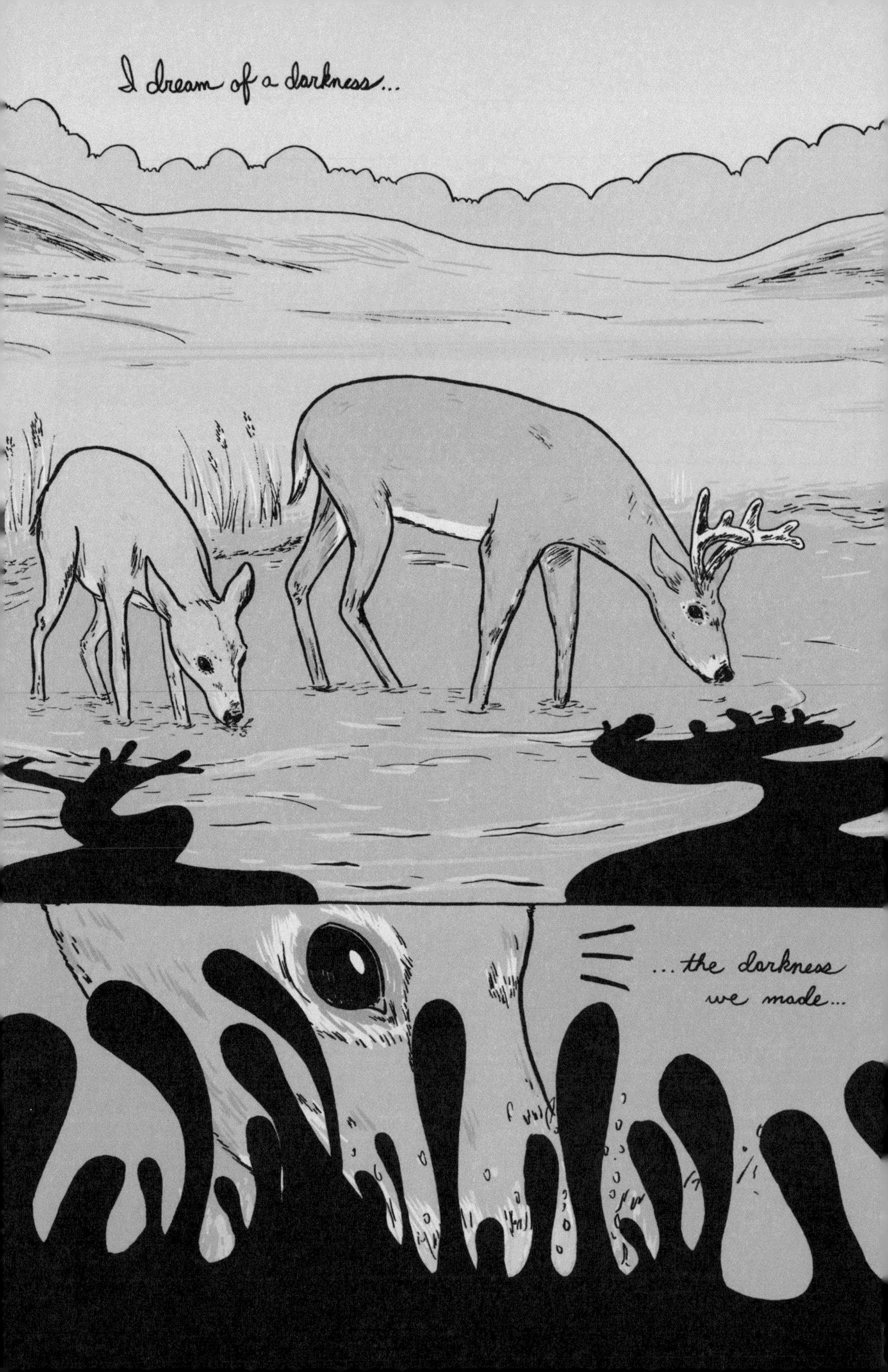
I dream of a darkness...
...the darkness we made...

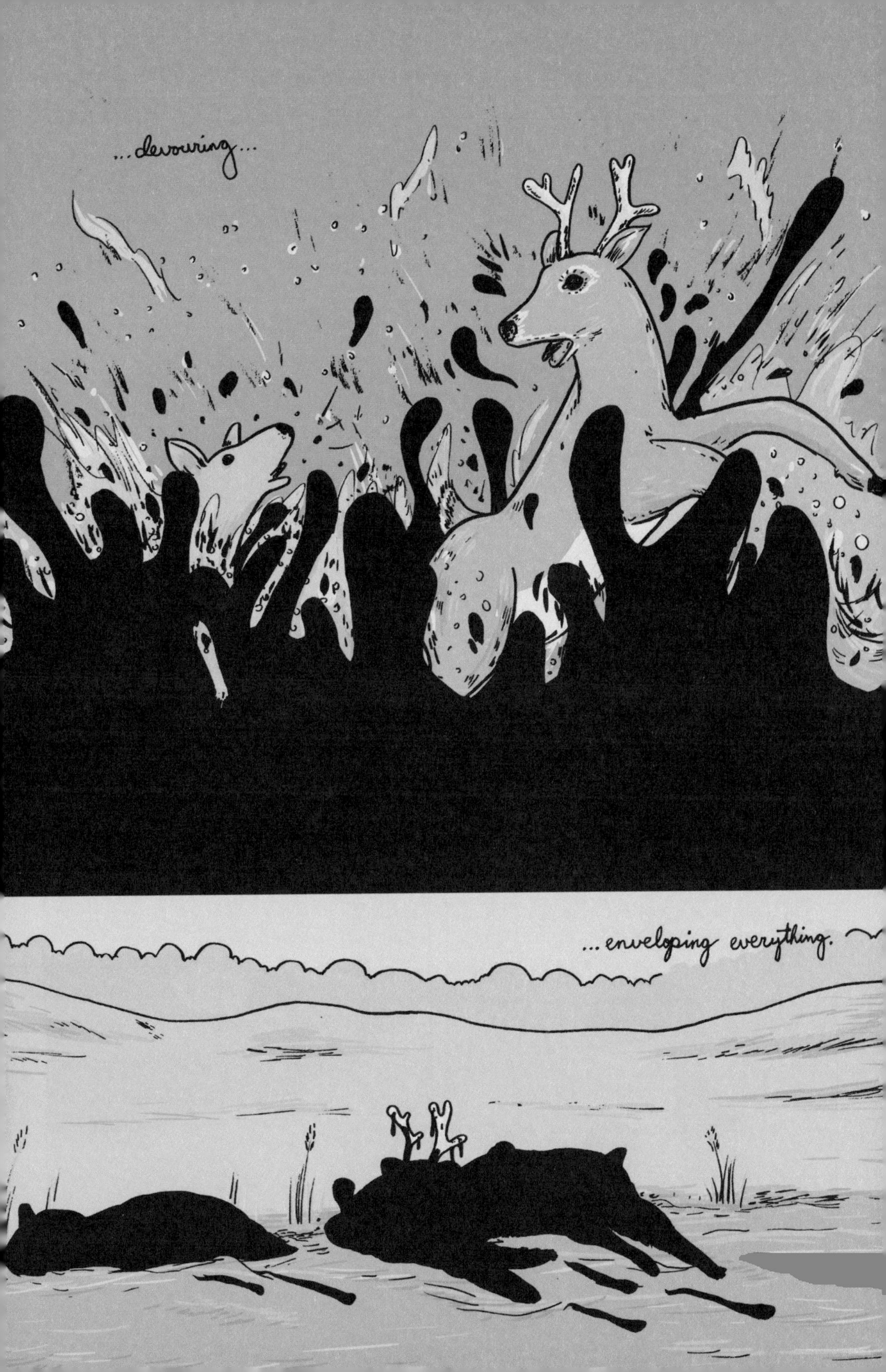
...devouring...
...enveloping everything.

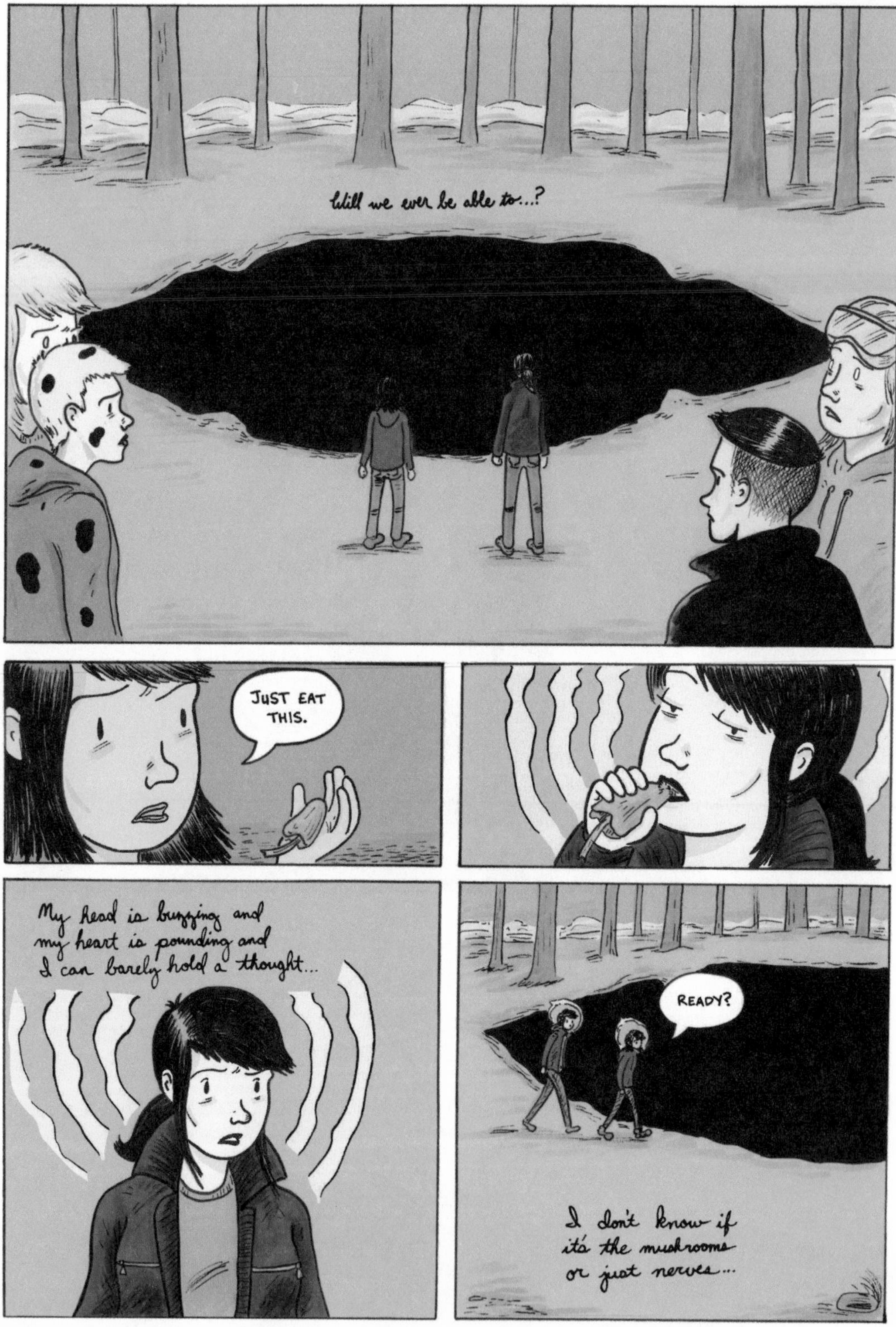
Will we ever be able to...?
JUST EAT THIS.
My head is buzzing and my heart is pounding and I can barely hold a thought...
READY?
I don't know if it's the mushrooms or just nerves...

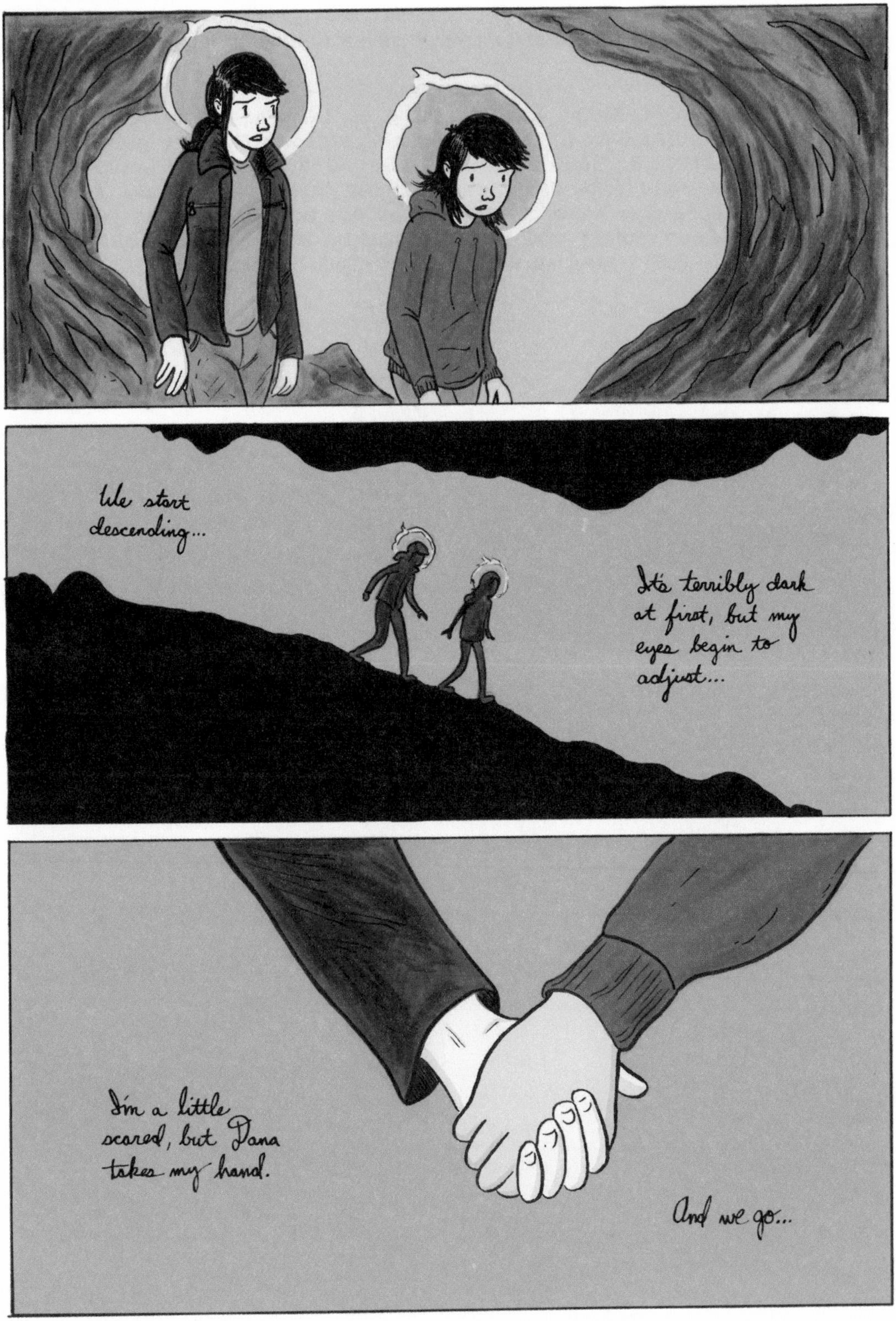
We start descending...
It's terribly dark at first, but my eyes begin to adjust...
I'm a little scared, but Dana takes my hand.
And we go...

THIS BOOK WAS COMPLETED OVER MANY YEARS AND MANY STATE LINES. WITHOUT THE LOVE AND SUPPORT OF THE FOLLOWING GOOD FRIENDS, IT (AND I) LIKELY NEVER WOULD HAVE MADE IT.

MY DEEPEST THANKS TO—
ANDREW A., CHRIS M., KATE R., STEVE G., LEON A., JERMAINE M., ALLISON M., BRENDAN L., DAVE N., NED R., VICTORIA S., MOM, ALEX K., AMANDA A., STEVE B., JESS B., SUNDAY NIGHT WORK CLUB, THE LOUISVILLE CREW, THE NEW YORK CREW, THE VERMONT CREW, THE PA CREW, AND EVERYONE ELSE WHO READ, SUPPORTED, OR PUT UP WITH. SPECIAL THANKS TO MY GOOD, SWEET DOG MAGGIE, WHO HAS BEEN THE VERY BEST PUPPY FAMILIAR I EVER COULD HAVE CONJURED.

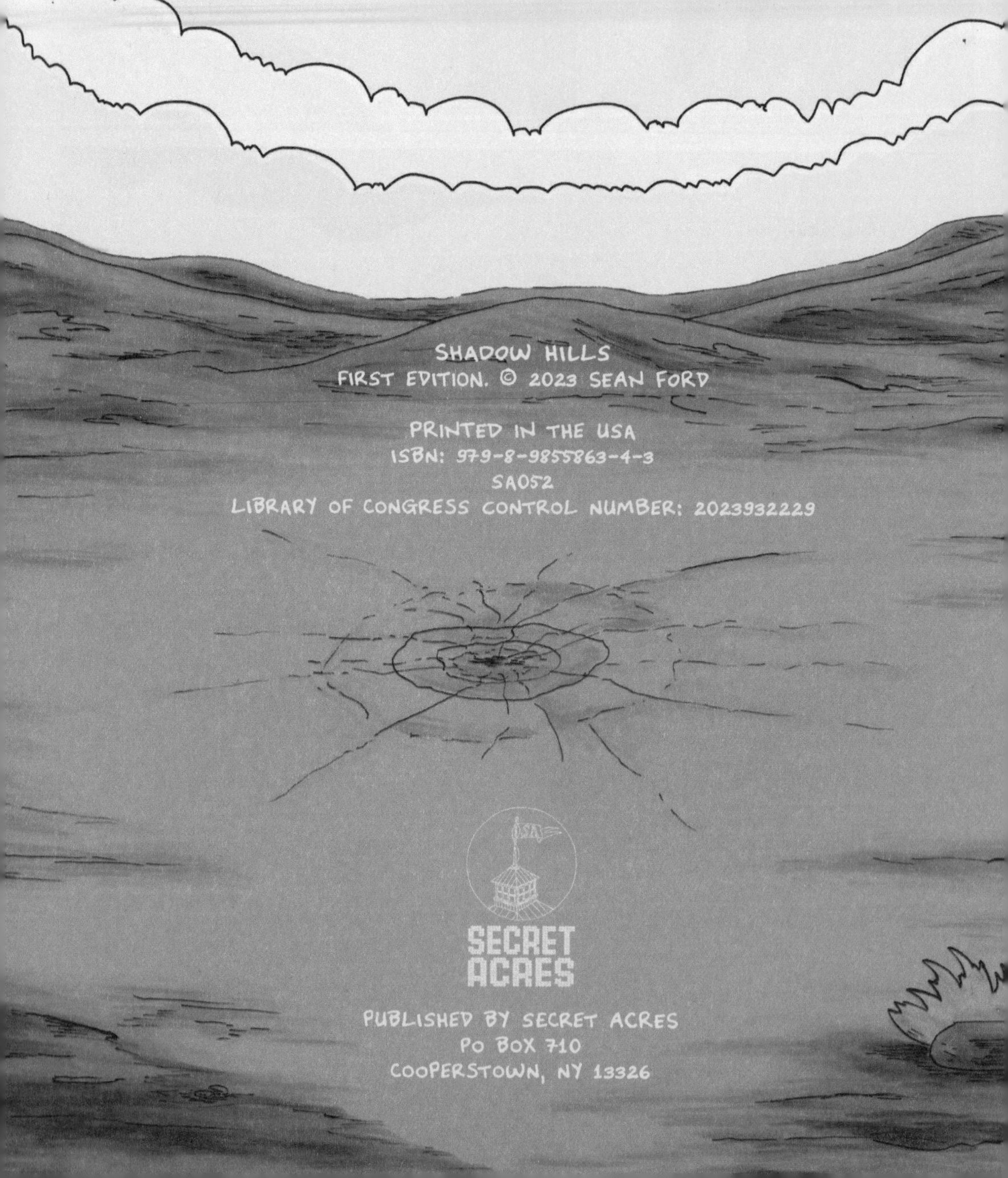

SHADOW HILLS

FIRST EDITION.

PRINTED IN THE USA
ISBN: 979-8-9855863-4-3
SA052
LIBRARY OF CONGRESS CONTROL NUMBER: 2023932229

SECRET ACRES

PUBLISHED BY SECRET ACRES
PO BOX 710
COOPERSTOWN, NY 13326